Writing Fiction

Writing Fiction
A GUIDE TO NARRATIVE CRAFT
Second Edition

Janet Burroway
Florida State University

Scott, Foresman and Company
Glenview, Illinois   London, England

Library of Congress Cataloging-in-Publication Data

Burroway, Janet.
    Writing fiction.

    Bibliography: p.
    Includes index.
    1. Fiction — Technique.   I. Title.
PN3355.B79   1987   808.3   86-15217

89101112131415-KPF-989796959493929190

ISBN 0-673-39246-5

Acknowledgments appear on page vi.

For David Daiches, mentor and friend

ACKNOWLEDGMENTS

Stories

Ray Bradbury. "August 2002: Night Meeting" from *The Martian Chronicles* by Ray Bradbury. Copyright 1950 by Ray Bradbury, ©renewed 1977 by Ray Bradbury. Reprinted by permission of Don Congdon Associates, Inc.

Rosellen Brown. "The Only Way to Make It in New York" from *Street Games* by Rosellen Brown. Copyright © 1972, 1974 by Rosellen Brown. Reprinted by permission of Doubleday & Company, Inc. and Virginia Barber Literary Agency, Inc.

Frederick Busch. "Widow Water." Copyright ©1974 by Frederick Busch. Reprinted from *Hardwater Country* by Frederick Busch by permission of Alfred A. Knopf, Inc. and the author.

Raymond Carver. "Cathedral" from *Cathedral* by Raymond Carver. Copyright ©1981, 1982, 1983 by Raymond Carver. Reprinted by permission of Alfred A. Knopf, Inc. and Collins Harvill Publishers.

John Cheever. "The Bella Lingua." Copyright ©1958 by John Cheever. Reprinted from *The Stories of John Cheever* by permission of Alfred A. Knopf, Inc. and International Creative Management, Inc.

Ralph Ellison, "Battle Royal" from *Invisible Man* by Ralph Ellison. Copyright 1947 by Ralph Ellison. Reprinted by permission of Random House, Inc.

Reginald Gibbons. Letter to Joe Taylor by Reginald Gibbons. Reprinted by permission of the author.

Mary Hood. "How Far She Went" reprinted from *How Far She Went* by Mary Hood, ©1984 by Mary Hood. Reprinted by permission of the University of Georgia Press.

Walter Howerton. "The Persistence of Memory." First appeared in *Great River Review*. Reprinted by permission.

Gabriel Josipovici, "Mobius the Stripper." ©1972 by Gabriel Josipovici. Reprinted by permission of the author and John Johnson, Authors Agents.

Jesse Lee Kercheval, "Underground Women." Published in *Carolina Quarterly* and *London Magazine*. Reprinted by permission of the author.

Jamaica Kincaid. "Girl" from *At the Bottom of the River* by Jamaica Kincaid. Copyright ©1978, 1979, 1981, 1982, 1983 by Jamaica Kincaid. Reprinted by permission of Farrar, Straus and Giroux, Inc. and Pan Books Ltd.

Bobbie Ann Mason. "Shiloh" from *Shiloh and Other Stories* by Bobbie Ann Mason. Copyright ©1982 by Bobbie Ann Mason. Reprinted by permission of Harper & Row, Publishers, Inc., Chatto & Windus, and the author.

Vladimir Nabokov, "Signs and Symbols" from *Nabokov's Dozen* by Vladimir Nabokov. Copyright 1948 by Vladimir Nabokov. Reprinted by permission of Doubleday & Company, Inc. and William Heinemann Limited.

Flannery O'Connor. "Everything That Rises Must Converge" from *Everything That Rises Must Converge* by Flannery O'Connor. Copyright ©1961, 1965 by the Estate of Mary Flannery O'Connor. Reprinted by permission of Farrar, Straus and Giroux, Inc. and Harold Matson Company, Inc.

Grace Paley, "A Man Told Me the Story of His Life" from *Later the Same Day* by Grace Paley. Copyright ©1985 by Grace Paley. Reprinted by permission of Farrar, Straus and Giroux, Inc. and Grace Paley.

James Purdy. "Cutting Edge." Copyright ©1957 by James Purdy. Reprinted by permission of William Morris Agency, Inc. as agents for James Purdy.

Richard Selzer. "The Masked Marvel's Last Toehold" from *Confessions of a Knife* by Richard Selzer. Copyright ©1979 by David Goodman and Janet Selzer, Trustees. Reprinted by permission of Simon & Schuster, Inc.

Joe Taylor. "The Power." First appeared in *TriQuarterly*, a publication of Northwestern University. Reprinted by permission.

Peter Taylor, "The Gift of the Prodigal" from *The Old Forest and Other Stories* by Peter Taylor. Copyright ©1981 by Peter Taylor. Reprinted by permission of Doubleday & Company, Inc., Chatto & Windus, and the author.

E.B. White. "The Second Tree from the Corner" from *The Second Tree from the Corner* by E.B. White. Copyright 1947 by E.B. White. Originally appeared in *The New Yorker* and reprinted by permission of Harper & Row, Publishers, Inc.

(Acknowledgments continued on page 392.)

FOREWORD

There is a myth loose on the land that trying to teach or learn how to write a story is some kind of fraud, like selling shares in the Brooklyn Bridge.

I come to testify that this is false. You can do both. You most certainly can learn how to write fiction and you can teach it, too. The result will most likely be neither fame nor fortune, but rather the best kind of education there is.

My experience conforms to the sow's ear maxim. Intelligence is the essence of a good writer. If you don't have that in some degree there is slim chance of developing expertise at the short story or novel. I believe that the possibilities are equally glum for the scholarly person. The straight-A student who appears to have read everything in the library and wants you to know it finds it too hard to climb down from the lecture platform.

Rather it is the students who are curious about human feelings and behavior, the eternal conflicts of mind and heart, and are forever seeking to satisfy that curiosity, who have the makings of a fiction writer.

But for every one of us, trying in earnest to write fiction is a testing of the principal resources of mind and heart that is bound to turn on some lights in those areas which we never knew we had.

First, our medium is the English language, an instrument of such marvelous complexities that it can portray, like some great cathedral organ, every nuance of human thought and feeling. It is no less than the great mirror of intelligence itself. It follows that, as you develop a facility with our language, you come that much closer to moving mountains and other worthwhile miracles.

Nevertheless, in a good fiction writing class, one that makes everyone feel interested and alive, one talks about the ideas and the people in the story rather than about the language. Whether or not it is a good story depends on whether it is persuasive, rings true, maybe even truer than life itself. When a class is aroused over such issues, everyone is learning what life is really like. If someone were to ask me about the desired goal of education, I would say it is just that.

More specifically, to write persuasive fiction, authors must know human beings, how they look and sound and behave, which is to say have some grasp of psychology, history, philosophy. To know how they speak authors will want an actor's or a linguist's ear for authentic regional and social level voices.

To know what makes a story work writers will want a knowledge of fictional structure that is a match for an architect's or a physicist's. In short, accomplished fiction writers have to acquire, by instinct and training, the knowledge to create a believable world and furnish it with credible people put into credible situations.

Then, the techniques of fiction, understanding the importance of character, conflict, suspense, voice and point of view, is simply the study of human behavior, the very essence of humanism, the be-all of a liberal education. Through it we understand, as best we can, how to live our lives, or perhaps how to make good art out of our three score and ten.

There are plenty of textbooks about writing fiction and they are largely a sorry lot. They smell of chalk dust and are guaranteed to glaze the eye in a matter of minutes.

Janet Burroway has written a textbook that, for an old pro or a curious tenderfoot, is sheer joy to confront. It is honest and practical. It flows with the juice of good humor and good sense. It tells the essentials, the importance of conflict and character and voice, how you must never kiss and tell but rather kiss and show and just as good fiction itself does, goes straight from the idea to the fleshy example.

Any student who has asked the question Janet Burroway proposes in the "Whatever Works" chapter of this book, "Is there a trick which will unlock my words?" will recognize the truth in her reply, which is of course, "No but yes," for finding that trick is no less than the individual search of every writer for his or her own way to the door. We each have to know ourselves and exploit our weaknesses as well as our strengths to find it.

Janet Burroway is a writer of the very first water. Her books include the novels *The Buzzards, Raw Silk,* and *Opening Nights.* Moreover she is a person of great joy and vitality, which is why she is also a wonderful teacher. Writing is feeling. It is joy and sorrow. Janet Burroway vibrates to emotion and she has performed the miracle of getting all that, the life that makes writing a joyous as well as a painful experience, into a book about writing. It is a book that shows you, rather than tells you how to do it.

There is none like it.

JOHN LEGGETT
UNIVERSITY OF IOWA
WRITERS' WORKSHOP

PREFACE TO THE SECOND EDITION

In compiling the Second Edition of *Writing Fiction: A Guide to Narrative Craft*, I have been aided by colleagues in the Associated Writing Programs of America, teachers who have used the First Edition, and especially students who let me know by their questions where I had been unclear or unnecessarily difficult. Though I have not been able to use all their suggestions, I am indebted to all of them for their guidance.

In general I have tried not to change anything for the sake of novelty, nor to fix what ain't broke. But I have added some passages for clarification, included a new chapter (now Chapter 2) on the process of writing and the problems of beginning and revising, and I have tried to focus more clearly on the problem of theme in what is now Chapter 10.

I have replaced about half the stories, generally in the direction of modern realism. Teachers and students alike consistently felt that the most useful stories for the purpose of this text were in that range, and that those which presented major problems of interpretation distracted from the concentration on technique. For that reason I have expunged some quirkiness and experimentalism that I admire—and hope that readers will encounter in other anthologies—and have at the same time tried to choose alternatives that offer variety of both subject matter and style.

I would particularly like to thank these people for their generous help: Jim Hall of Florida International University; George Wolfe of the University of Alabama; Ruth M. Wahlstrom of Heidelberg College; Philip H. Schneider of Wichita State; Robert Farnsworth of Colby College; James Gallagher of the Community College of Allegheny County, Boyce Campus; Joel Lipman of the University of Toledo; Michael Kane of Emerson College; John Gerlach of Cleveland State; June Berkeley of Ohio University; David File of Catholic University; Vanessa Ochs of Colgate University; Harriet Rosenblum of Monroe Community College; Allan Hirsh of Central Connecticut State; Helen Raines of Caspar College; Charles Bersiel of Metropolitan State; Alexis Levitin of SUNY Plattsburgh; Barbara Winder of Western Connecticut State; and Sander Zulauf of the County College of Morris. Finally, I would like to thank Joseph Opiela at Little, Brown and Nancy DeCubellis for their advice and support.

PREFACE TO THE FIRST EDITION

This book is the result of a course in "Narrative Techniques" at Florida State University, gradually developed over a period of nine years. I inherited the course—or at least its title—from the Pulitzer Prize-winning novelist Michael Shaara, who had been superbly successful at it. But he had left no hints on how to teach creative writing. Thus, the book developed because of my initial lack of direction. Although I could react with reasonable competence and confidence to what was already written in workshop, I was overwhelmed by the task of devising lectures and assignments.

On the theoretical side there was the persistence of the academic controversy over whether it is worth teaching "creative writing" at all; whether the ability to write was an innate gift to which teaching was irrelevant and the academic atmosphere destructive.

It seemed to me self-evident that talent can be taught in no subject; neither history nor trigonometry nor music nor physical therapy. But each art and science involves, aside from the divine fire, some rules, techniques, devices, artifices, and contrivances. These can be taught. The truly talented will come to them of his or her own accord, but at a cost of years. And if, in the stingiest assessment, the classroom might offer a beginning writer a few tricks of the trade, there is always also the possibility that form is substance, and that a study of technique is the very thing that lets talent or genius take root.

On the practical side, I had reason to believe that writing can be taught, because I was taught to write. Some of my teachers were encouraging and some were harsh; some ruminated and some dictated technique. One got me an agent; one told me to quit. But every one of them gave me something I could not have got on my own, taught me something I could not have learned alone.

My problem at Florida State, then, was not only how to survive in a teaching situation for which I had no guidelines, but how, somehow, to pay back a little of what I'd been given.

My students clued me in and, over the first three years, taught me what they wanted to know. It became clear that, apart from time, honesty, and an open mind, what they most craved was discipline. Their response to a variety of experimental assignments showed me that they were most enthusiastic about the rigors of simple craft—the consistency of viewpoint, the necessity of crisis action, the value of concrete detail, and so forth.

For that reason, the course and the book that developed follow a traditional division of the art of fiction into elements that will be familiar to those who have studied the short story and the novel as literature. I think this is as it should be (or at least one constructive way it can be); if plot, character, atmosphere, point of view, metaphor, and theme are the elements for which a reader looks, then presumably they are the elements that a writer wants to present.

Each chapter deals with one of these elements, and in addition an early chapter is devoted to the writerly virtue of "showing not telling." I have tried to present each element from the point of view of the writer face-to-face with a blank page, to suggest what the problems are and how they can be solved, quoting illustrations from published authors and student authors, and occasionally inventing a passage myself. Each chapter is followed by two stories that I think have high merit, and by suggestions for discussion that pinpoint the author's technique with regard to the element dealt with in that chapter. I have chosen a variety of stories, some of which are classics, some little known; some simple in structure and theme, some difficult and demanding. Each chapter ends with a series of assignments designed to sharpen skills in dealing with ends of the fictional elements.

In *Writing Fiction* I try to confront and convey as practically as possible what a writer does, and what you can do in order to write better. For that reason I present a number of diagrams, dicta, pigeonholes, and rules—but all these rules are of the sort proved by exception. Henry James said that the only thing we can demand of a novelist *per se* is that he should be interesting. The rules here presented suggest what has been tried and proven interesting in fiction; but the ultimate and only rule is that whatever works, works.

Nevertheless, there is a conviction or prejudice underlying all the advice in these pages, which is that writing is communication. William Sloane, in *The Craft of Writing*, puts it this way: "I believe that literature is for readers and that that is what literature is."

Writing courses got a bad name in America in the forties and fifties for teaching "formula" stories—how to sell to *Post* and *True Confession*. I never knew anyone who taught or took such a course, but the reputation lingers. Today, after Spock, permissiveness, progressive education, and consciousness-raising of many sorts, I perceive the danger for fiction to be the opposite. I rarely meet students who want only to know how to sell. I frequently encounter students who "write only for themselves" or who insist that their outpourings "mean whatever the reader wants them to mean." My reply to this is that it's fine; only leave them in the drawer. If you demand our time for reading, then you must *communicate*. Because the page is a way of getting something from one mind into another, any piece of writing, whether set in type or kept in a notebook, must *mean*.

It's been my experience as both student and teacher that a techniques course or a workshop in which student writing is discussed among teacher and peers can help a beginning writer to *mean*. To begin with, it imposes a deadline, forcing you to produce. It offers an automatic audience, something that even the most successful professional can never be quite certain of finding. Most often, it offers course credit, which is the same thing as getting paid for writing. Above all, it offers a quantity of response. *All* writers, I believe, have some resistance, however faint, to criticism; all are of necessity defensive of their creations. If one person says, "This passage is unclear to me," it's always possible to feel that the critic is stupid or inattentive. But if in the classroom fifteen or twenty critic peers agree that "This passage is unclear," it helps convince us that the responsibility lies with the writer, and the fault with the writing.

A final word: I adopt, and recommend without reservation to teachers and student critics, this attitude toward student writing: that literary standards are absolute, and (except for bad spelling/grammar/punctuation and sloth) forgiveness is also absolute. The quality of the communication is under judgment; the author's character is not.

I'm indebted to so many people for help direct or indirect in the writing of this book that is is difficult to know whom to thank in print. I should single out the Writers' Workshop at the Univeristy of Iowa for time and space to compose half the text; and my sons Tim and Alex Eysselinck for fending off the phone calls while I composed the rest. It is my students who have taught me most, and of these I want to thank especially Patricia Duncan and Bill Beesting. I'm also grateful to my colleagues Jerome Stern, Sheila Taylor, and Elisabeth Muhlenfeld, who share the task of teaching writing at Florida State, and who share their ideas freely and generously. And, finally, my thanks to my reviewers for their helpful suggestions: Edward A. Dornan (Orange Coast College), Max Steele (University of North Carolina-Chapel Hill), and Marilyn Throne (Miami University).

CONTENTS

Writing Fiction

1

A STORY IS A WAR
Story Form and Structure

Conflict, Crisis, and Resolution
Story and Plot
The Short Story and the Novel

What makes you want to write?

It seems likely that the earliest storytellers—in the tent or the harem, around the campfire or on the Viking ship—told stories out of an impulse to tell stories. They made themselves popular by distracting their listeners from a dull or dangerous evening with heroic exploits and a skill at creating suspense: What happened next? And after that? And then what happened?

"Natural storytellers" are still around, and a few of them are very rich. Some are on the best-seller list; more are in television and film. But it's probable that your impulse to write has little to do with the desire or the skill to work out a plot. On the contrary, you want to write because you are sensitive. You have something to say that does not answer the question, What happened next? You share with most—and the best—twentieth-century fiction writers a sense of the injustice, the absurdity, and the beauty of the world; and you want to register your protest, your laughter, and your affirmation.

Yet readers still want to wonder what happened next; and unless you make them wonder, they will not turn the page. You must master plot, because no matter how profound or illuminating your vision of the world may be, you cannot convey it to those who do not read you.

E. M. Forster, in *Aspects of the Novel*, mourns the necessity of storytelling.

> Let us listen to three voices. If you ask one type of man, "What does a novel do?" he will reply placidly: "Well—I don't know—it seems a funny sort of question to ask—a novel's a novel—well, I don't know—I suppose it kind of tells a story, so to speak." He is quite good-tempered and vague, and probably driving a motor bus at the same time and paying no more attention to literature than it merits. Another man, whom I visualize as on a golf-course, will be aggressive and brisk. He will reply: "What does a novel do? Why, tell a story of course, and I've no use for it if it didn't. I like a story. Very bad taste on my part, no doubt, but I like a story. You can take your art, you can take your literature, you can take your music, but give me a good story. And I like a story to be a story, mind, and my wife's the same." And a third man, he says in a sort of drooping regretful voice, "Yes—oh dear yes—the novel tells a story." I respect and admire the first speaker. I detest and fear the second. And the third is myself. Yes—oh dear yes—the novel tells a story. That is the fundamental aspect without which it could not exist. That is the highest factor common to all novels, and I wish that it was not so, that it could be something different—melody, or perception of the truth, not this low atavistic form.

When editors take the trouble to write a rejection letter to a young author (and they do so only when they think the author talented), the gist of the letter most frequently is: "This piece is sensitive (perceptive, vivid, original, brilliant, funny, moving), but it is not a *story*."

How do you know when you have written a story? And if you're not a natural-born wandering minstrel, can you go about learning to write one?

It's interesting that we react with such different attitudes to the words "formula" and "form." A *formula story* is hackwork, the very lowest "atavistic" form of supplying a demand. To write one, you read three dozen copies of *Cosmopolitan* or *Omni*, make a list of what kinds of characters and situations the editors buy, shuffle nearly identical characters around in slightly altered situations, and sit back to wait for the check. Whereas *form* is a term of the highest artistic approbation, even reverence, with overtones of *order, harmony, model, archetype*.

And "story" is a "form" of literature. Like a face, it has necessary features in a necessary harmony. We're aware of the infinite variety of human faces, aware of their unique individuality, which is so powerful that you can recognize a face you know even after twenty years of age and fashion have done their work on it. We're aware that minute alterations in the features can express grief, anger, or joy. If you place side by side two photographs of, say, Brooke Shields and Geronimo, you are instantly aware of the fundamental differences of age, race, sex, class, and century; yet these two faces are more like each other than either is like a foot or a fern, both of which have their own distinctive forms. Every face has two eyes, a nose between them, a mouth below; a forehead, two cheeks, two ears, and a jaw. If a face is missing one of these features, you may say, "I love this face in spite of its lacking a nose," but you must acknowledge the *in spite of*. You can't simply say, "This is a wonderful face."

The same is true of a story. You might say, "I love this piece even though there's no crisis action in it." You can't say, "This is a wonderful story."

Conflict, Crisis, and Resolution

Fortunately, the necessary features of the story form are fewer than those of a face. They are *conflict, crisis,* and *resolution.*

Conflict is the first encountered and the fundamental element of fiction, necessary because in literature, only trouble is interesting.

Only trouble is interesting. This is not so in life. Life offers periods of comfortable communication, peaceful pleasure, and productive work, all of which are extremely interesting to those involved. But such passages about such times by themselves make for dull reading; they can be used as lulls in an otherwise tense situation, as a resolution, even as a hint that something awful is about to happen; they cannot be used as whole plot.

Suppose, for example, you go on a picnic. You find a beautiful deserted meadow with a lake nearby. The weather is splendid and so is the company. The food's delicious, the water's fine, and the insects have taken the day off. Afterward, someone asks you how your picnic was. "Terrific," you reply, "really perfect." No story.

But suppose the next week you go back for a rerun. You set your picnic blanket on an anthill. You all race for the lake to get cold water on the bites, and one of your friends goes too far out on the plastic raft, which deflates. He can't swim and you have to save him. On the way in you gash your foot on a broken bottle. When you get back to the picnic, the ants have taken over the cake, and a possum has demolished the chicken. Just then the sky opens up. When you gather your things to race for the car, you notice an irritated bull has broken through the fence. The others run for it, but because of your bleeding heel the best you can do is hobble. You have two choices: try to outrun him or stand perfectly still and hope he's interested only in a moving target. At this point, you don't know if your friends can be counted on for help, even the nerd whose life you saved. You don't know if it's true that a bull is attracted by the smell of blood. . . .

A year later, assuming you're around to tell about it, you are still saying, "Let me *tell* you what happened last year. . . ." And your listeners are saying, "What a story!"

If this contrast is true of so trivial a subject as a picnic, it is even more so of the great themes of life: birth, love, sex, work, and death. Here is a very interesting love story to *live*: Jan and Jon meet in college. Both are beautiful, intelligent, talented, popular, and well adjusted. They're of the same race, class, religion, and political persuasion. They are sexually compatible. Their parents become fast friends. They marry on graduating, and both get rewarding work in the same city. They have three children, all of whom are healthy, happy, beautiful, intelligent, and popular; the children love and respect their parents to a degree that is the envy of everyone. All the children succeed in work and marriage. Jan and Jon die peacefully, of natural causes, at the same moment, at the age of eighty-two, and are buried in the same grave.

No doubt this love story is very interesting to Jan and Jon, but you can't make a novel of it. The great love stories involve intense passion and a monumental impediment to that passion's fulfillment. So: they love each other passionately, but their parents are sworn enemies (*Romeo and Juliet*). Or: they love each other passionately, but he's black and she's white, and he has an enemy who wants to punish him (*Othello*). Or: they love each other passionately, but she's married (*Anna Karenina*). Or: he loves her passionately, but she falls in love with him only when she has worn out his passion ("Frankly, my dear, I don't give a damn").

In each of these plots, there is both intense desire and great danger to the achievement of that desire; generally speaking, this shape holds good for all plots. It can be called 3-D: *drama* equals *desire* plus *danger*. One common fault of talented young writers is to create a main character who is essentially passive. This is an understandable fault; as a writer you are an observer of human nature and activity, and so you identify easily with a character who observes, reflects, and suffers. But such a character's passivity transmits itself to the page, and the story also becomes passive. Aristotle rather startlingly claimed that a man *is* his desire. It is true that in fiction, in order to engage our attention and sympathy, the central character must *want*, and want intensely.

The thing that the character wants need not be violent or spectacular; it is the intensity of the wanting that counts. She may want, like *The Suicide's Wife* in David Madden's novel, no more than to get her driver's license, but if so she must feel that her identity and her future depend on her getting a driver's license, while a corrupt highway patrolman tries to manipulate her. He may want, like Samuel Beckett's Murphy, only to tie himself to his rocking chair and rock, but if so he will also want a woman who nags him to get up and get a job. She may want, like the heroine of Margaret Atwood's *Bodily Harm*, only to get away from it all for a rest, but if so she must need rest for her survival, while tourists and terrorists involve her in machinations that begin in discomfort and end in mortal danger.

It's important to realize that the great dangers in life and in literature are not necessarily the most spectacular. Another mistake frequently made by young writers is to think that they can best introduce drama into their stories by way of muggers, murderers, crashes, and monsters, the external stock dangers of pulp and TV. In fact, all of us know that the profoundest impediments to our desire most often lie close to home, in our own bodies, personalities, friends, lovers, and families. Fewer people have cause to panic at the approach of a stranger with a gun than at the approach of mama with the curling iron. More passion is destroyed at the breakfast table than in a time warp.

A frequently used critical tool divides possible conflicts into several basic categories: man against man, man against nature, man against society, man against machine, man against God, man against himself. Most stories fall into these categories, and they can provide a useful way of discussing and comparing works. But the employment of categories can be misleading to someone behind the typewriter, insofar as it suggests that literary conflicts take place in these abstract, cosmic dimensions. A writer needs a specific story to tell, and if you sit down to pit "man" against "nature" you will have less of a story than if you pit seventeen-year-old James Tucker of Weehawken, New Jersey, against a two-and-a-half-foot bigmouth bass in the backwoods of Toomsuba, Mississippi. The value of specificity is a point to which we will return (again and again).

Once conflict is sharply established and developed in a story, the conflict must end. There must be a crisis and a resolution. This is not like life either, and although it is so obvious a point, it needs to be insisted on. Order is a major value that literature offers us, and order implies that the subject has been brought to closure. In life this never quite happens. Even the natural "happy endings," marriage and birth, leave domesticity and childbearing to be dealt with; the natural "tragic endings," separation and death, leave trauma and bereavement in their wake. Literature absolves us of these nuisances. Whether or not the lives of the characters end, the story does, and leaves us with a satisfying sense of completion. This is one reason we enjoy crying or feeling terrified or even nauseated by fiction; we know in advance that it's going to be *over*, and by contrast with the continual struggle of living, all that ends, ends well.

What I want to do now is to present several ways—they are all essentially metaphors—of seeing this pattern of *conflict-crisis-resolution* in order to make the shape and its many variations clearer, and particularly to indicate what a crisis action is.

The editor and teacher Mel McKee states flatly that "a story is a war. It is sustained and immediate combat." He offers four imperatives for the writing of this "war" story.

(1) get your fighters fighting, (2) have something—the stake—worth their fighting over, (3) have the fight dive into a series of battles with the last battle in the series the biggest and most dangerous of all, (4) have a walking away from the fight.

The stake over which wars are fought is usually a territory, and it's important that this "territory" in a story be as tangible and specific as Grenada. In James Purdy's short story "Cutting Edge," for example, the war is fought over the territory of a beard, and the fighters get fighting over it in the first paragraph. As with warring nations, the story territory itself can come to represent all sorts of fine abstractions—patriotism, freedom, motherhood, virtue, and God's will— but the soldiers fight yard by yard over a particular piece of grass or sand.

Just as a "police action" may escalate into a holocaust, story form follows its most natural order of "complications" when each battle is bigger than the last. It begins with an open ground skirmish, which does not decide the war. Then one side brings in spies; the other, guerrillas; these actions do not decide the war. So one side brings in the air force; the other answers with antiaircraft. One side takes to missiles, the other answers with rockets. One side has poison gas, and the other has a hand on the nuclear button. Metaphorically, this is what happens in a story. As long as one antagonist can recoup enough power to counterattack, the conflict goes on. But, at some point in the story, one of the antagonists will produce a weapon from which the other cannot recover. *The crisis action is the last battle and occurs when the outcome becomes inevitable*; when, after much doubt, there can no longer be any doubt who wins the particular territory—though there can be much doubt about moral victory. In "Cutting Edge," the war is fought over Bobby's beard, and that war is inevitably finished when he savagely shaves it off. The "walking away from the fight" in this story—its resolution— involves subtle and ambiguous questions of who has really won.

Notice that although a plot involves desire and a danger to that desire, it does not necessarily end happily if the desire is achieved, nor unhappily if it is not. In *Hamlet*, Hamlet's desire is to kill King Claudius, and he is prevented from doing so for most of the play by other characters, intrigues, and his own mental state. When he finally succeeds, it is at the cost of every significant life in the play, including his own. So that although the hero "wins" his particular "territory," the play is a tragedy. In Margaret Atwood's *Bodily Harm*, on the other hand, the heroine ends up in a political prison. Yet her discovery of her own strength and commitment are such that we know that she has achieved salvation.

Novelist Michael Shaara describes a story as a power struggle between equal forces. It is imperative, he argues, that each antagonist have sufficient power to leave the reader in doubt about the outcome. We may be wholly in sympathy with one character, and even reasonably confident that he will triumph. But his antagonist must represent a real and potent danger, and the pattern of the story's complications will be achieved by *shifting the power back and forth from one antagonist to the other.* Finally an action will occur that will shift the power irretrievably in one direction.

It is also important to understand that "power" takes many forms and that some of them have the external appearance of weakness. Anyone who has ever been tied to the demands of an invalid can understand this: sickness can be great strength. Weakness, need, passivity, an ostensible desire not to be any trouble to anybody — all these can be used as manipulative tools to prevent the protagonist from achieving his desire. Martyrdom is immensely powerful, whether we sympathize with it or not; a dying man absorbs all our energies.

Still another way of seeing the shape of the story is in terms of situation-action-situation. The story begins by presenting us with a situation that contains some problem or conflict. The story then recounts an action, and when that action is over we are left with a situation *that is the opposite* of the opening situation. This formula seems oversimplified, but it is very difficult to find a story it does not describe.

The nineteenth-century German critic Gustav Freitag analyzed five-act dramas and came up with a diagram (below) of plot that has come to be known as the Freitag Pyramid. Plot begins, he said, with an exposition,

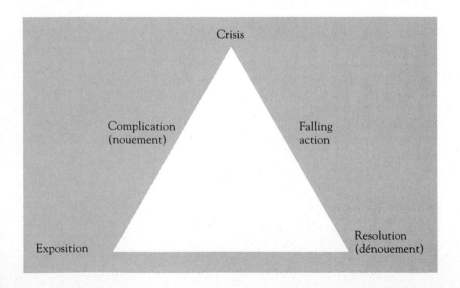

Crisis

Complication
(nouement)

Falling
action

Exposition

Resolution
(dénouement)

followed by complications (or *nouement*, the "knotting up" of the situation) leading to a crisis, which is followed by a "falling action" (or anticlimax), resulting in a resolution (or *dénouement*, "unknotting").

The trouble with this Freitag's useful diagram is that it visually suggests that a crisis comes in the middle of the "pyramid" shape of a plot, whereas even in a five-act drama the crisis is usually saved for the middle of the fifth act; and in modern fiction, particularly the compact short-story form, the falling action is likely to be very brief or nonexistent. Often the crisis action itself implies the resolution, which is not stated but exists as an idea established in the reader's mind.

For our purposes, it is probably more useful to think of story shape as an inverted checkmark. If we take the familiar tale "Cinderella" and look at it in terms of the diagram below, we can see how the various elements reveal themselves even in this simple children's story. At the opening of the tale we're given the basic conflict: Cinderella's mother has died, and her father has married a brutal woman with two waspish daughters. Cinderella is made to do all the dirtiest and most menial work, and she weeps among the cinders. The Stepmother has on her side the strength of ugliness and evil (two very powerful qualities in literature as in life). With her daughters she also has the strength of numbers, and she has parental authority. Cinderella has only beauty and goodness, but (in literature and life) these are also very powerful.

At the beginning of the struggle, the power is very clearly on the Stepmother's side. But the first *event* (action, battle) of the story is that an invitation arrives from the Prince, which explicitly states that *all* the ladies of the land are invited to a ball. Notice that Cinderella's desire is not to triumph over her Stepmother (though she eventually will, much to our satisfaction); such a desire would diminish her goodness. She simply wants to be relieved of her mistreatment. She wants equality, so that the Prince's

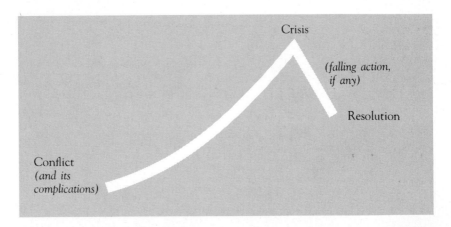

invitation, which specifically gives her a right equal to the Stepmother's and Stepdaughters' rights, shifts the power to her.

The Stepmother takes the power back by blunt force: you may not go; you must get us ready to go. Cinderella does so, and the three leave for the ball.

Then what happens? The Fairy Godmother appears. It is *very* powerful to have magic on your side. The Fairy Godmother offers Cinderella a gown; glass slippers; and a coach, horses, and footmen, giving her more force than she has yet had.

But the magic is not all-potent. It has a qualification that portends bad luck. It will last only until midnight (unlike the Stepmother's authority), and Cinderella must leave the ball before the clock strikes twelve or risk exposure and defeat.

What happens next? She goes to the ball and the Prince falls in love with her—and love is an even more powerful weapon than magic in a literary war. In some versions of the tale, the Stepmother and Stepsisters are made to marvel at the beauty of the Princess they don't recognize, pointing the irony of Cinderella's new power.

And then? The magic quits. The clock strikes twelve, and Cinderella runs down the steps in her rags to her rats and pumpkin, losing a slipper, bereft of her power in every way.

But after that, the Prince sends out a messenger with the glass slipper and a dictum (a dramatic repetition of the original invitation in which all ladies were invited to the ball) that every female in the land is to try on the slipper. Cinderella is given her rights again by royal decree.

What happens then? In most good retellings of the tale, the Stepmother also repeats her assumption of brute authority by hiding Cinderella away, while our expectation of triumph is tantalizingly delayed with grotesque comedy: one sister cuts off a toe, the other a heel, trying to fit into the heroine's rightful slipper.

After that, Cinderella tries on the slipper and it fits. *This is the crisis action.* Magic, love, and royalty join to recognize the heroine's true self; and evil, numbers, and authority are powerless against them. At this point, the power struggle has been decided; the outcome is inevitable. When the slipper fits, no further action can occur that will deprive Cinderella of her desire.

The tale has a brief "falling action" or "walking away from the fight": the Prince sweeps Cinderella up on his white horse and gallops away to their wedding. The story comes to closure with the classic resolution of all comedy: they lived happily ever after. Applied to the diagram, the story's pattern looks like the drawing on page 10.

In the *Poetics*, the first extensive work of extant Western literary criticism, Aristotle referred to the crisis action of a tragedy as a "peripeteia," or reversal of the protagonist's fortunes. Critics and editors agree that a

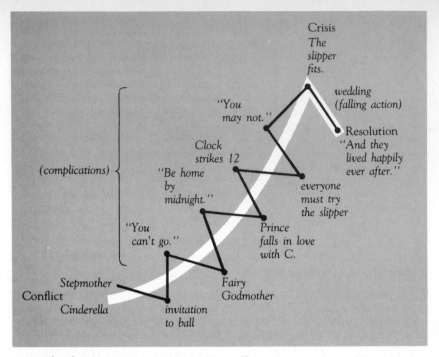

Crisis
The
slipper
fits.

"You
may not."

wedding
(falling action)

Clock
strikes 12

Resolution
"And they
lived happily
ever after."

(complications)

"Be home
by
midnight."

everyone
must try
the slipper

"You
can't go."

Prince
falls in love
with C.

Stepmother

Conflict

Cinderella

Fairy
Godmother

invitation
to ball

reversal of some sort is necessary to all story structure: although the protagonist need not lose power, land, or life, he or she must in some significant way be changed or moved by the action. Aristotle specified that this reversal came about because of "hamartia," which has for centuries been translated as a "tragic flaw" in the protagonist's character, usually assumed to be, or defined as, pride. But more recent critics have defined and translated "hamartia" much more narrowly as a "mistake in identity" whereby the reversal comes about in a "recognition."

It is true that recognition scenes have played a disproportionately large role in the crisis actions of plots both comic and tragic, and that these scenes frequently stretch credibility; it's already been observed that you are unlikely to mistake the face of your mother, son, uncle, or even friend in real life, and yet such mistakes have provided the turning point of many a plot. If, however, the notion of "recognition" is extended to more abstract and subtle realms, it becomes a powerful metaphor for moments of "realization." In other words, the "recognition scene" in literature may stand for that moment in life when we "recognize" that the man we have considered good is evil, the event we have considered insignificant is crucial, the woman we've thought out of touch with reality is a genius, the object we thought desirable is poison. There is in this symbolic way a recognition in "Cinderella." We knew that she was essentially a princess, but until the Prince recognizes her as one, our knowledge must be frustrated.

James Joyce developed a similar idea when he spoke of, and recorded both in his notebooks and in his stories, moments of what he called "epiphany." *Epiphany* as Joyce saw it is a crisis action in the mind, a moment when a person, an event, or a thing is seen in a light so new that it is as if it has never been seen before; at this recognition, the mental landscape of the viewer is permanently changed.

In many of the finest modern short stories and novels, the true territory of conflict is the main character's mind, and so the real crisis action must occur there. Yet it is important to grasp that Joyce chose the word "epiphany" to represent this moment of reversal, and that the word means "*a manifestation of a supernatural being*"; specifically, in Christian doctrine, "the manifestation of Christ to the gentiles." By extension, then, in a short story any mental reversal that takes place in the crisis of a story must be *manifested*; it must be triggered or shown by an action. The slipper must fit. It would not do if the Stepmother just happened to change her mind and give up the struggle; it would not do if the Prince just happened to notice that Cinderella looked like his love. The moment of recognition must be manifested in an action.

This point, that the crisis must be manifested or externalized in an action, is absolutely central, although sometimes difficult to grasp when the conflict of the story takes place in a character's mind.

It is easy to see, for example, how the conflict in a revenge story must end. The common revenge plot, from *Hamlet* to *Beverly Hills Cop*, takes this form: someone important to the hero (father, sister, lover, friend) is killed, and for some reason the authorities who ought to be in charge of justice can't or won't avenge the death. The hero must do so, then, and the crisis action is manifested in the swing of the dagger, the blast of the gun, the swallowing of the poison, whatever.

But suppose the story is about a conflict between two brothers on a fishing trip, and the change that takes place is that the protagonist, believing for most of the action that he holds his older brother in contempt, discovers at the end of the story that they are deeply bound by love and family history. Clearly this change is an epiphany, a mental reversal. A writer insufficiently aware of the nature of crisis action might signal the change in a paragraph that begins "Suddenly Larry remembered their father and realized that Jeff was very much like him." Well, unless that memory and that realization are manifested in an action, the reader is unable to share them, and therefore cannot be moved with the character.

Jeff reached for the old net and neatly bagged the trout, swinging round to offer it with a triumphant, "Got it! We got it, didn't we?" The trout flipped and struggled, filling his nostrils with a smell of weed and water and the fecund mud. Jeff's knuckles were lined with grime. The knuckles and the rich river smell filled him with a memory of their first fishing trip together, the sight of their father's hands on the same scarred net...

and so forth. Here the epiphany, a memory leading to a realization, has been triggered by an action and sensory details that the reader can share; the reader now has a good chance of also being able to share the epiphany.

Purdy's "Cutting Edge," which has the feel of a twentieth-century "slice of life," could be positioned on the diagram with as much certainty as the fairy tale "Cinderella." As has been said, the conflict is over Bobby's beard; he shaves it off. But this crisis action signals a reversal that is internal, subtle, and complex. The story cannot end, "they lived happily ever after" or even "they lived unhappily ever after."

Much great fiction, and the preponderance of serious modern fiction, echoes life in its suggestion that there are no clear or permanent solutions, that the conflicts of character, relationship, and the cosmos cannot be permanently resolved.

Yet the story form demands a resolution. Is there such a thing as a no-resolution resolution? Yes, and it also has a very specific form. Go back to the metaphor that "a story is a war." After the skirmish, after the guerrillas, after the air strike, after the poison gas and the nuclear holocaust, imagine that the two surviving combatants, one on each side, emerge from their fallout shelters. They crawl, then stumble to the fence that marks the border. Each possessively grasps the barbed wire with a bloodied fist. The "resolution" of this battle is that neither side will ever give up and that no one will ever win; *there will never be a resolution*. This is a distinct reversal (the recognition takes place in the reader's mind) of the opening scene, in which it seemed eminently worthwhile to open a ground skirmish. In the statement of the conflict was an inherent possibility that one side or another could win. Inherent in the resolution is a statement that no one can ever win. That is a distinct reversal and a powerful resolution.

Story and Plot

So far, I have used the words "story" and "plot" interchangeably. The equation of the two terms is so common that they are often comfortably understood as synonyms. When an editor says, "This is not a story," the implication is not that it lacks character, theme, setting, or even incident, but that it has no plot.

Yet there is a distinction frequently drawn between the two terms, a distinction simple in itself but that gives rise to manifold subtleties in the craft of narrative and that also represents a vital decision that you as a writer must make: Where does the narrative begin?

The distinction is easily made. A *story* is a series of events recorded in their chronological order. A *plot* is a series of events deliberately arranged so as to reveal their dramatic, thematic, and emotional significance.

Here, for example, is a fairly standard story: A sober, industrious, and rather dull young man meets the woman of his dreams. She is beautiful, brilliant, passionate, and compassionate; more wonderful still, she loves him. They plan to marry, and on the eve of their wedding his friends give him a stag party in the course of which they tease him, ply him with liquor, and drag him off to a whorehouse for a last fling. There he stumbles into a cubicle . . . to find himself facing his bride-to-be. .

Where does this story become interesting? Where does the *plot* begin?

You may start, if you like, with the young man's *Mayflower* ancestry. But if you do, it's going to be a very long story, and we're likely to close the book about the middle of the nineteenth century. You may begin with the first time he meets the extraordinary woman, but again you must cover at least weeks, probably months, in a few pages; and that means you must summarize, skip, and generalize, and you'll have a hard time both maintaining your credibility and holding our attention. Begin at the stag party? Better. If you do so, you will somehow have to let us know all that has gone before, either through dialogue or through the young man's memory, but you have only one evening of action to cover, and we'll get to the conflict quickly. Suppose you begin instead the next morning, when the man wakes with a hangover in bed in a brothel with his bride on his wedding day. Is that, perhaps, the best of all? An immediate conflict that must lead to a quick and striking crisis?

Humphry House, in his commentaries on Aristotle, defines *story* as everything the reader needs to know to make coherent sense of the plot, and *plot* as the particular portion of the story the author chooses to present—the "present tense" of the narrative. The story of *Oedipus Rex*, for example, begins before Oedipus' birth with the oracle predicting that he will murder his father and marry his mother. It includes his birth, his abandonment with hobbled ankles, his childhood with his foster parents, his flight from them, his murder of the stranger at the crossroads, his triumph over the Sphinx, his marriage to Jocasta and his reign in Thebes, his fatherhood, the Theban plague, his discovery of the truth, and his self-blinding and self-banishment. When Sophocles set out to plot a play on this story, he began at dawn on the very last day of it. All the information about Oedipus' life is necessary to understand the plot, but the plot begins with the conflict: How can Oedipus get rid of the plague in Thebes? Because the plot is so arranged, it is the revelation of the past that makes up the action of the play, a process of discovery that gives rise to the significant theme: Who am I? Had Sophocles begun with the oracle before Oedipus' birth, no such theme and no such significance could have been explored.

Forster makes substantially the same distinction between plot and story. A story, he says, is:

> the chopped off length of the tape worm of time . . . a narrative of events arranged in their time sequence. A plot is also a narrative of events, the emphasis falling on causality. "The king died, and then the queen died," is a story. "The king died, and then the queen died of grief," is a plot. The time-sequence is preserved, but the sense of causality overshadows it. Or again: "The queen died, no one knew why, until it was discovered that it was through grief at the death of the king." This is a plot with a mystery in it, a form capable of high development. It suspends the time-sequence, it moves as far away from the story as its limitations will allow. Consider the death of the queen. If it is in a story we say, "and then?" If it is in a plot we ask, "why?"

The human desire to know why is as powerful as the desire to know what happened next, and it is a desire of a higher order. Once we have the facts, we inevitably look for the links between them, and only when we find such links are we satisfied that we "understand." Rote memorization in a science bores almost everyone. Grasp and a sense of discovery begin only when we perceive *why* "a body in motion tends to remain in motion" and what an immense effect this actuality has on the phenomena of our lives.

The same is true of the events of a story. Random incidents neither move nor illuminate; we want to know why one thing leads to another and to feel the inevitability of cause and effect.

Here is a series of uninteresting events chronologically arranged.

Ariadne had a bad dream.
She woke up tired and cross.
She ate breakfast.
She headed for class.
She saw Leroy.
She fell on the steps and broke her ankle.
Leroy offered to take notes for her.
She went to a hospital.

This series of events does not constitute a plot, and if you wish to fashion it into a plot you can do so only by letting us know the meaningful relations among the events. We first assume that Ariadne woke in a temper *because* of her bad dream, and that Leroy offered to take notes for her because she broke her ankle. But why did she fall? Perhaps because she saw Leroy? Does that suggest that her bad dream was about him? Was she, then, thinking about his dream-rejection as she broke her egg irritably on the edge of the frying pan? What is the effect of his offer? Is it a triumph or just another polite form of rejection when, really, he *could* have missed class once to drive her to the x-ray lab? All the emotional and dramatic significance of these ordinary events emerges in the relation of cause to effect, and where such relation can be shown, a possible plot comes into existence.

Ariadne's is a story you might very well choose to tell chronologically: it needs to cover only an hour or two, and that much can be handled in the compressed form of the short story. But such a choice of plot is not inevitable even in this short compass. Might it be more gripping to begin with the wince of pain as she stumbles? Leroy comes to help her up and the yolk yellow of his T-shirt fills her field of vision. In the shock of pain she is immediately back in her dream. . . .

When "nothing happens" in a story, it is because we fail to sense the causal relation between what happens first and what happens next. When something does "happen," it is because the resolution of a short story or a novel describes a change in the character's life, an effect of the events that have gone before. This is why Aristotle insisted with such apparent simplicity on "a beginning, a middle, and an end." A story is capable of many meanings, and it is first of all in the choice of structure, which portion of the story forms the plot, that you offer us the gratifying sense that we "understand."

The Short Story and the Novel

Many editors and writers insist on an essential disjunction between the form of the short story and that of the novel. It is my belief, however, that, like the distinction between story and plot, the distinction between the two forms is very simple, and the many and profound possibilities of difference proceed from that simple source.

A short story is short, and a novel is long.

Because of this, a short story can waste no words. It can deal with only one or a very few consciousnesses. It may recount only one central action and one major change or effect in the life of the central character or characters. It can afford no digression that does not directly affect the action. A short story strives for a single emotional impact, imparts a single understanding, though both impact and understanding may be complex. The virtue of a short story is its density. If it is tight, sharp, economic, well knit, and charged, then it is a good short story because it has exploited a central attribute of the form—that it is short.

All of these qualities are praiseworthy in a novel, but a novel may also be comprehensive, vast, and panoramic. It may have power, not because of its economy, but because of its scope, breadth, and sweep—the virtues of a medium that is long. Therefore, a novel may range through many consciousnesses, cover many years or generations, and travel the world. It may deal with a central line of action and one or several subplots. Many characters may change; many and various effects may constitute our final understanding. Many digressions may be tolerated and will not destroy the balance of the whole as long as they lead, finally, to some nuance of that understanding.

These differences in the possibilities of the novel and short-story forms may directly affect the relationship between story and plot. With the narrative leisure available to a novelist, it may very well be possible to begin with a character's birth, or even ancestry, even though the action culminates in middle or old age.

My own feeling as a writer is that in a novel I may allow myself, and ask the reader to share, an exploration of character, setting, and theme, letting these develop in the course of the narrative. When I am writing a short story, I must reject more, and I must select more rigorously.

One constant principle of artistic effectiveness is that you must discover what a medium cannot do and forget it; and discover what it can do and exploit it. Television is a good medium for domestic drama, but for a battle with a cast of thousands, you need a movie screen twelve feet high. For a woodland scene, watercolor is fine; but for the agony of St. Sebastian, choose oil. If you are writing for radio, the conflict must be expressible in sound; if you are writing a mime, it must be expressible in movement.

This is not to say that one form is superior to another but simply that each is itself and that no medium and no form of that medium can do everything. The greater the limitation in time and space, the greater the necessity for pace, sharpness, and density. For this reason, it is a good idea to learn to write short stories before you attempt the scope of the novel, just as it is good to learn to write a lyric before you attempt an epic or to learn to draw an apple before you paint a god.

Nevertheless, the form of the novel is an expanded story form. It requires a conflict, a crisis, and a resolution, and no technique described in this book is irrelevant to its effectiveness.

Cutting Edge

JAMES PURDY

Mrs. Zeller opposed her son's beard. She was in her house in Florida when she saw him wearing it for the first time. It was as though her mind had come to a full stop. This large full-bearded man entered the room and she remembered always later how ugly he had looked and how frightened she felt seeing him in the house; then the realization it was someone she knew, and finally the terror of recognition.

He had kissed her, which he didn't often do, and she recognized in this his attempt to make her discomfort the more painful. He held the beard to her face for a long time, then he released her as though she had suddenly disgusted him.

"Why did you do it?" she asked. She was, he saw, almost broken by the recognition.

"I didn't dare tell you and come."

"That's of course true," Mrs. Zeller said, "It would have been worse. You'll have to shave it off, of course. Nobody must see you. Your father of course didn't have the courage to warn me, but I knew something was wrong the minute he entered the house ahead of you. I suppose he's upstairs laughing now. But it's not a laughing matter."

Mrs. Zeller's anger turned against her absent husband as though all error began and ended with him. "I suppose he likes it." Her dislike of Mr. Zeller struck her son as staggeringly great at that moment.

He looked at his mother and was surprised to see how young she was. She did not look much older than he did. Perhaps she looked younger now that he had his beard.

"I had no idea a son of mine would do such a thing," she said. "But why a beard, for heaven's sake," she cried, as though he had chosen something permanent and irreparable which would destroy all that they were.

"Is it because you are an artist? No don't answer me," she commanded. "I can't stand to hear any explanation from you . . . ."

"I have always wanted to wear a beard," her son said. "I remember wanting one as a child."

"I don't remember that at all," Mrs. Zeller said.

"I remember it quite well. I was in the summer house near that old broken-down wall and I told Ellen Whitelaw I wanted to have a beard when I grew up."

"Ellen Whitelaw, that big fat stupid thing. I haven't thought of her in years."

Mrs. Zeller was almost as much agitated by the memory of Ellen Whitelaw as by her son's beard.

"You didn't like Ellen Whitelaw," her son told her, trying to remember how they had acted when they were together.

"She was a common and inefficient servant," Mrs. Zeller said, more quietly now, masking her feelings from her son.

"I suppose *he* liked her," the son pretended surprise, the cool cynical tone coming into his voice.

"Oh, your father," Mrs. Zeller said.

"Did he then?" the son asked.

"Didn't he like all of them?" she asked. The beard had changed this much already between them, she talked to him now about his father's character, while the old man stayed up in the bedroom fearing a scene.

"Didn't he always," she repeated, as though appealing to this new hirsute man.

"So," the son said, accepting what he already knew.

"Ellen Whitelaw, for God's sake," Mrs. Zeller said. The name of the servant girl brought back many other faces and rooms which she did not know were in her memory. These faces and rooms served to make the bearded man who stared at her less and less the boy she remembered in the days of Ellen Whitelaw.

"You must shave it off," Mrs. Zeller said.

"What makes you think I would do that?" the boy wondered.

"You heard me. Do you want to drive me out of my mind?"

"But I'm not going to. Or rather it's not going to."

"I will appeal to him, though a lot of good it will do," Mrs. Zeller said. "He ought to do something once in twenty years at least."

"You mean," the son said laughing, "he hasn't done anything in that long."

"Nothing I can really remember," Mrs. Zeller told him.

"It will be interesting to hear you appeal to him," the boy said. "I haven't heard you do that in such a long time."

"I don't think you ever heard me."

"I did, though," he told her. "It was in the days of Ellen Whitelaw again, in fact."

"In *those* days," Mrs. Zeller wondered. "I don't see how that could be."

"Well it was. I can remember that much."

"You couldn't have been more than four years old. How could you remember then?"

"I heard you say to him, *You have to ask her to go.*"

Mrs. Zeller did not say anything. She really could not remember the words, but she supposed that the scene was true and that he actually remembered.

"Please shave off that terrible beard. If you only knew how awful it looks on you. You can't see anything else but it."

"Everyone in New York thought it was particularly fine."

"Particularly fine," she paused over his phrase as though its meaning eluded her.

"It's nauseating," she was firm again in her judgment.

"I'm not going to do away with it," he said, just as firm.

She did not recognize his firmness, but she saw everything changing a little, including perhaps the old man upstairs.

"Are you going to 'appeal' to him?" The son laughed again when he saw she could say no more.

"Don't mock me," the mother said, "I will speak to your father." She pretended decorum. "You can't go anywhere with us, you know."

He looked unmoved.

"I don't want any of my friends to see you. You'll have to stay in the house or go to your own places. You can't go out with us to our places and see our friends. I hope none of the neighbors see you. If they ask who you are, I won't tell them."

"I'll tell them then."

They were not angry, they talked it out like that, while the old man was upstairs.

"Do you suppose he is drinking or asleep?" she said finally.

"I thought he looked good in it, Fern," Mr. Zeller said.

"What about it makes him look good?" she said.

"It fills out his face," Mr. Zeller said, looking at the wallpaper and surprised he had never noticed what a pattern it had before; it showed the sacrifice of some sort of animal by a youth.

He almost asked his wife how she had come to pick out this pattern, but her growing fury checked him.

He saw her mouth and throat moving with unspoken words.

"Where is he now?" Mr. Zeller wondered.

"What does that matter where he is?" she said. "He has to be somewhere while he's home, but he can't go out with us."

"How idiotic," Mr. Zeller said, and he looked at his wife straight in the face for a second.

"Why did you say that?" She tried to quiet herself down.

"The way you go on about nothing, Fern." For a moment a kind of revolt announced itself in his manner, but then his eyes went back to the wallpaper, and she resumed her tone of victor.

"I've told him he must either cut it off or go back to New York."

"Why is it a beard upsets you so?" he wondered, almost to himself.

"It's not the beard so much. It's the way he is now too. And it disfigures him so. I don't recognize him at all now when he wears it."

"So, he's never done anything of his own before," Mr. Zeller protested suddenly.

"Never done anything!" He could feel her anger covering him and glancing off like hot sun onto the wallpaper.

"That's right," he repeated. "He's never done anything. I say let him keep the beard and I'm not going to talk to him about it." His gaze lifted toward her but rested finally only on her hands and skirt.

"This is still my house," she said, "and I have to live in this town."

"When they had the centennial in Collins, everybody wore beards."

"I have to live in this town," she repeated.

"I won't talk to him about it," Mr. Zeller said.

It was as though the voice of Ellen Whitelaw reached her saying, *So that was how you appealed to him.*

She sat on the deck chair on the porch and smoked five cigarettes. The two men were somewhere in the house and she had the feeling now that she only roomed here. She wished more than that the beard was gone that her son had never mentioned Ellen Whitelaw. She found herself thinking only about her. Then she thought that now twenty years later she could not have afforded a servant, not even her.

She supposed the girl was dead. She did not know why, but she was sure she was.

She thought also that she should have mentioned her name to Mr. Zeller. It might have broken him down about the beard, but she supposed not. He had been just as adamant and unfeeling with her about the girl as he was now about her son.

Her son came through the house in front of her without speaking, dressed only in his shorts and, when he had got safely beyond her in the garden, he took off those so that he was completely naked with his back to her, and lay down in the sun.

She held the cigarette in her hand until it began to burn her finger. She felt she should move from the place where he was and yet she did not know where to go inside the house and she did not know what pretext to use for going inside.

In the brilliant sun his body, already tanned, matched his shining black beard.

She wanted to appeal to her husband again and she knew then she could never again. She wanted to call a friend and tell her but she had no friend to whom she could tell this.

The events of the day, like a curtain of extreme bulk, cut her off from her son and husband. She had always ruled the house and them even during the awful Ellen Whitelaw days and now as though they did not even recognize her, they had taken over. She was not even here. Her son could walk naked with a beard in front of her as though she did not exist. She had nothing to fight them with, nothing to make them see with. They ignored her as Mr. Zeller had when he looked at the wallpaper and refused to discuss their son.

"You can grow it back when you're in New York," Mr. Zeller told his son.

He did not say anything about his son lying naked before him in the garden but he felt insulted almost as much as his mother had, yet he needed his son's permission and consent now and perhaps that was why he did not mention the insult of his nakedness.

"I don't know why I have to act like a little boy all the time with you both."

"If you were here alone with me you could do anything you wanted. You know I never asked anything of you...."

When his son did not answer, Mr. Zeller said, "Did I?"

"That was the trouble," the son said.

"What?" the father wondered.

"You never wanted anything from me and you never wanted to give me anything. I didn't matter to you."

"Well, I'm sorry," the father said doggedly.

"Those were the days of Ellen Whitelaw," the son said in tones like the mother.

"For God's sake," the father said and he put a piece of grass between his teeth.

He was a man who kept everything down inside of him, everything had been tied and fastened so long there was no part of him any more that could struggle against the stricture of his life.

There were no words between them for some time; then Mr. Zeller could hear himself bringing the question out: "Did she mention that girl?"

"Who?" The son pretended blankness.

"Our servant."

The son wanted to pretend again blankness but it was too much work. He answered: "No, I mentioned it. To her surprise."

"Don't you see how it is?" the father went on to the present. "She doesn't speak to either of us now and if you're still wearing the beard when you leave it's me she will be punishing six months from now."

"And you want me to save you from your wife."

"Bobby," the father said, using the childhood tone and inflection. "I wish you would put some clothes on too when you're in the garden. With me it doesn't matter, you could do anything. I never asked you anything. But with her..."

"God damn *her*," the boy said.

The father could not protest. He pleaded with his eyes at his son.

The son looked at his father and he could see suddenly also the youth hidden in his father's face. He was young like his mother. They were both young people who had learned nothing from life, were stopped and drifting where they were twenty years before with Ellen Whitelaw. Only *she*, the son thought, must have learned from life, must have gone on to some development in her character, while they had been tied to the shore where she had left them.

"Imagine living with someone for six months and not speaking," the father said as if to himself. "That happened once before, you know, when you were a little boy."

"I don't remember that," the son said, some concession in his voice.

"You were only four," the father told him.

"I believe this is the only thing I ever asked of you," the father said. "Isn't that odd, I can't remember ever asking you anything else. Can you?"

The son looked coldly away at the sky and then answered, contempt and pity struggling together, "No, I can't."

"Thank you, Bobby," the father said.

"Only don't *plead* any more, for Christ's sake." The son turned from him.

"You've only two more days with us, and if you shaved it off and put on just a few clothes, it would help me through the year with her."

He spoke as though it would be his last year.

"Why don't you beat some sense into her?" The son turned to him again.

The father's gaze fell for the first time complete on his son's nakedness.

Bobby had said he would be painting in the storeroom and she could send up a sandwich from time to time, and Mr. and Mrs. Zeller were left downstairs together. She refused to allow her husband to answer the phone.

In the evening Bobby came down dressed carefully and his beard combed immaculately and looking, they both thought, curled.

They talked about things like horse racing, in which they were all somehow passionately interested, but which they now discussed irritably as though it too were a menace to their lives. They talked about the uselessness of art and why people went into it with a detachment that would have made an outsider think that Bobby was as unconnected with it as a jockey or oil magnate. They condemned nearly everything and then the son went upstairs and they saw one another again briefly at bedtime.

The night before he was to leave they heard him up all hours, the water running, and the dropping of things made of metal.

Both parents were afraid to get up and ask him if he was all right. He was like a wealthy relative who had commanded them never to question him or interfere with his movements even if he was dying.

He was waiting for them at breakfast, dressed only in his shorts but he looked more naked than he ever had in the garden because his beard was gone. Over his chin lay savage and profound scratches as though he had removed the hair with a hunting knife and pincers.

Mrs. Zeller held her breast and turned to the coffee and Mr. Zeller said only his son's name and sat down with last night's newspaper.

"What time does your plane go?" Mrs. Zeller said in a dead, muffled voice.

The son began putting a white paste on the scratches of his face and did not answer.

"I believe your mother asked you a question," Mr. Zeller said, pale and shaking.

"Ten-forty," the son replied.

The son and the mother exchanged glances and he could see at once that his sacrifice had been in vain: she would also see the beard there again under the scratches and the gashes he had inflicted on himself, and he would never really be her son again. Even for his father it must be much the same. He had come home as a stranger who despised them and he had shown his nakedness to both of them. All three longed for separation and release.

But Bobby could not control the anger coming up in him, and his rage took an old form. He poured the coffee into his saucer because Mr. Zeller's mother had always done this and it had infuriated Mrs. Zeller because of its low-class implications.

He drank viciously from the saucer, blowing loudly.

Both parents watched him helplessly like insects suddenly swept against the screen.

"It's not too long till Christmas," Mr. Zeller brought out. "We hope you'll come back for the whole vacation."

"We do," Mrs. Zeller said in a voice completely unlike her own.

"So," Bobby began, but the torrent of anger would not let him say the thousand fierce things he had ready.

Instead, he blew savagely from the saucer and spilled some onto the chaste white summer rug below him. Mrs. Zeller did not move.

"I would invite you to New York," Bobby said quietly now, "but of course I will have the beard there and it wouldn't work for you."

"Yes," Mr. Zeller said, incoherent.

"I do hope you don't think I've been. . . ." Mrs. Zeller cried suddenly and they both waited to hear whether she was going to weep or not, but she stopped herself perhaps by the realization that she had no tears and that the feelings which had come over her about Bobby were likewise spent.

"I can't think of any more I can do for you," Bobby said suddenly.

They both stared at each other as though he had actually left and they were alone at last.

"Is there anything more you want me to do?" he said, coldly vicious.

They did not answer.

"I hate and despise what both of you have done to yourselves, but the thought that you would be sitting here in your middle-class crap not speaking to one another is too much even for me. That's why I did it, I guess, and not out of any love. I didn't want you to think that."

He sloshed in the saucer.

"Bobby," Mr. Zeller said.

The son brought out his *What?* with such finished beauty of coolness that he paused to admire his own control and mastery.

"Please, Bobby," Mr. Zeller said.

They could all three of them hear a thousand speeches. The agony of awkwardness was made unendurable by the iciness of the son, and all three paused over this glacial control which had come to him out of art and New York, as though it was the fruit of their lives and the culmination of their twenty years.

Suggestions for Discussion

1. Conflict is introduced in the first sentence: "Mrs. Zeller opposed her son's beard." To what extent is the conflict really about the beard? What, and how much, does the beard come to represent?

2. This story has fewer characters than "Cinderella," but in "Cinderella" the characters line up neatly on two sides of the conflict: Cinderella, Fairy Godmother, and the Prince on the side of *good*; the Stepmother and two Stepsisters on the side of *evil*. In "Cutting Edge" it is not so simple. Identify aspects of the conflict among the three Zellers. Who is in conflict with whom over what?

3. How is a balance of power achieved among the Zellers? What are the strengths of each?

4. There are no overt acts of violence in this story, but some of the actions — sunbathing nude, shaving — take on an atmosphere of violence. Do you agree? How does Purdy achieve this?

5. At the beginning of the story, Mrs. Zeller fails to recognize her son. At the end she realizes that "he would never really be her son again." How is this a reversal or opposite of the opening situation?

6. What are the events of the Zellers' story, as opposed to the plot of "Cutting Edge"? What would be lost if Purdy had begun his narrative with a scene from Bobby's childhood or with the arrival of Ellen Whitelaw?

The Second Tree from the Corner

E. B. WHITE

"Ever have any bizarre thoughts?" asked the doctor.

Mr. Trexler failed to catch the word. "What kind?" he said.

"Bizarre," repeated the doctor, his voice steady. He watched his patient for any slight change of expression, any wince. It seemed to Trexler that the doctor was not only watching him closely but was creeping slowly toward him, like a lizard toward a bug. Trexler shoved his chair back an inch and gathered himself for a reply. He was about to say "Yes" when he realized that if he said yes the next question would be unanswerable. Bizarre thoughts, bizarre thoughts? Ever have any bizarre thoughts? What kind of thoughts *except* bizarre had he had since the age of two?

Trexler felt the time passing, the necessity for an answer. These psychiatrists were busy men, overloaded, not to be kept waiting. The next patient was probably already perched out there in the waiting room, lonely, worried, shifting around on the sofa, his mind stuffed with bizarre thoughts and amorphous fears. Poor bastard, thought Trexler. Out there all alone in that misshapen antechamber, staring at the filing cabinet and wondering whether to tell the doctor about that day on the Madison Avenue bus.

Let's see, bizarre thoughts. Trexler dodged back along the dreadful corridor of the years to see what he could find. He felt the doctor's eyes upon him and knew that time was running out. Don't be so conscientious, he said to himself. If a bizarre thought is indicated here, just reach into the bag and pick anything at all. A man as well supplied with bizarre thoughts as you are should have no difficulty producing one for the record. Trexler darted into the bag, hung for a moment before one of his thoughts, as a hummingbird pauses in the delphinium. No, he said, not that one. He darted to another (the one about the rhesus monkey), paused, considered. No, he said, not that.

Trexler knew he must hurry. He had already used up pretty nearly four seconds since the question had been put. But it was an impossible situation — just one more lousy, impossible situation such as he was always getting himself into. When, he asked himself, are you going to quit maneuvering yourself into a pocket? He made one more effort. This time he stopped at the asylum, only the bars were lucite — fluted, retractable. Not here, he said. Not this one.

He looked straight at the doctor. "No," he said quietly. "I never have any bizarre thoughts."

The doctor sucked in on his pipe, blew a plume of smoke toward the rows of medical books. Trexler's gaze followed the smoke. He managed to make out one of the titles, "The Genito-Urinary System." A bright wave of fear swept cleanly over him, and he winced under the first pain of kidney stones. He remembered when he was a child, the first time he ever entered a doctor's office, sneaking a look at the titles of the books — and the flush of fear, the shirt wet under the arms, the book on t.b., the sudden knowledge that he was in the advanced stages of consumption, the quick vision of the hemorrhage. Trexler sighed wearily. Forty years, he thought, and I still get thrown by the title of a medical book. Forty years and I still can't stay on life's little bucky horse. No wonder I'm sitting here in this dreary joint at the end of this woebegone afternoon, lying about my bizarre thoughts to a doctor who looks, come to think of it, rather tired.

The session dragged on. After about twenty minutes, the doctor rose and knocked his pipe out. Trexler got up, knocked the ashes out of his brain, and waited. The doctor smiled warmly and stuck out his hand. "There's nothing the matter with you — you're just scared. Want to know how I know you're scared?"

"How?" asked Trexler.

"Look at the chair you've been sitting in! See how it has moved back away from my desk? You kept inching away from me while I asked you questions. That means you're scared."

"Does it?" said Trexler, faking a grin. "Yeah, I suppose it does."

They finished shaking hands. Trexler turned and walked out uncertainly along the passage, then into the waiting room and out past the next patient, a ruddy pin-striped man who was seated on the sofa twirling his hat nervously and staring straight ahead at the files. Poor, frightened guy, thought Trexler, he's probably read in the *Times* that one American male out of every two is going to die of heart disease by twelve o'clock next Thursday. It says that in the paper almost every morning. And he's also probably thinking about that day on the Madison Avenue bus.

A week later, Trexler was back in the patient's chair. And for several weeks thereafter he continued to visit the doctor, always toward the end of the afternoon, when the vapors hung thick above the pool of the mind and darkened the whole region of the East Seventies. He felt no better as time went on, and he found it impossible to work. He discovered that the visits were becoming routine and that although the routine was one to which he certainly did not look forward, at least he could accept it with cool resignation, as once, years ago, he had accepted a long spell with a dentist who had settled down to a steady fooling with a couple of dead teeth. The visits, moveover, were now assuming a pattern recognizable to the patient.

Each session would begin with a résumé of symptoms—the dizziness in the streets, the constricting pain in the back of the neck, the apprehensions, the tightness of the scalp, the inability to concentrate, the despondency and the melancholy times, the feeling of pressure and tension, the anger at not being able to work, the anxiety over work not done, the gas on the stomach. Dullest set of neurotic symptoms in the world, Trexler would think, as he obediently trudged back over them for the doctor's benefit. And then, having listened attentively to the recital, the doctor would spring his question: "Have you ever found anything that gives you relief?" And Trexler would answer, "Yes. A drink." And the doctor would nod his head knowingly.

As he became familiar with the pattern Trexler found that he increasingly tended to identify himself with the doctor, transferring himself into the doctor's seat—probably (he thought) some rather slick form of escapism.

At any rate, it was nothing new for Trexler to identify himself with other people. Whenever he got into a cab, he instantly became the driver, saw everything from the hackman's angle (and the reaching over with the right hand, the nudging of the flag, the pushing it down, all the way down along the side of the meter), saw everything—traffic, fare, everything—through the eyes of Anthony Rocco, or Isidore Freedman or Matthew Scott. In a barbershop, Trexler was the barber, his fingers curled around the comb, his hand on the tonic. Perfectly natural, then, that Trexler should soon be occupying the doctor's chair, asking the questions, waiting for the answers. He got quite interested in the doctor, in this way. He liked him, and he found him a not too difficult patient.

It was on the fifth visit, about halfway through, that the doctor turned to Trexler and said, suddenly, "What do you want?" He gave the word "want" special emphasis.

"I d'know," replied Trexler uneasily. "I guess nobody knows the answer to that one."

"Sure they do," replied the doctor.

"Do *you* know what *you* want?" asked Trexler narrowly.

"Certainly," said the doctor. Trexler noticed that at this point the doctor's chair slid slightly backward, away from him. Trexler stifled a small, internal smile. Scared as a rabbit, he said to himself. Look at him scoot!

"What *do* you want?" continued Trexler, pressing his advantage, pressing it hard.

The doctor glided back another inch away from his inquisitor. "I want a wing on the small house I own in Westport. I want more money, and more leisure to do the things I want to do."

Trexler was just about to say, "And what are those things you want to do, Doctor?" when he caught himself. Better not go too far, he mused. Better not lose possession of the ball. And besides, he thought, what the hell goes on here, anyway — me paying fifteen bucks a throw for these séances and then doing the work myself, asking the questions, weighing the answers. So he wants a new wing! There's a fine piece of theatrical gauze for you! A new wing.

Trexler settled down again and resumed the role of patient for the rest of the visit. It ended on a kindly, friendly note. The doctor reassured him that his fears were the cause of his sickness, and that his fears were unsubstantial. They shook hands, smiling.

Trexler walked dizzily through the empty waiting room and the doctor followed along to let him out. It was late; the secretary had shut up shop and gone home. Another day over the dam. "Goodbye," said Trexler. He stepped into the street, turned west toward Madison, and thought of the doctor all alone there, after hours, in that desolate hole—a man who worked longer hours than his secretary. Poor, scared, overworked bastard, thought Trexler. And that new wing!

It was an evening of clearing weather, the Park showing green and desirable in the distance, the last daylight applying a high lacquer to the brick and brownstone walls and giving the street scene a luminous and intoxicating splendor. Trexler meditated, as he walked, on what he wanted. "What do you want?" he heard again. Trexler knew what he wanted, and what, in general, all men wanted; and he was glad, in a way, that it was both inexpressible and unattainable, and that it wasn't a wing. He was satisfied to remember that it was deep, formless, enduring, and impossible of fulfillment, and that it made men sick, and that when you sauntered along Third Avenue and looked through the doorways into the dim saloons, you could sometimes pick out from the unregenerate ranks the ones who had not forgotten, gazing steadily into the bottoms of the glasses on the long chance that they could get another little peek at it. Trexler found himself renewed by the remembrance that what he wanted was at once great and microscopic, and that although it borrowed from the nature of large deeds and of youthful love and of old songs and early intimations, it was not any one of these things, and that it had not been isolated or pinned down, and that a man who attempted to define it in the privacy of a doctor's office would fall flat on his face.

Trexler felt invigorated. Suddenly his sickness seemed health, his dizziness stability. A small tree, rising between him and the light, stood there saturated with the evening, each gilt-edged leaf perfectly drunk with excellence and delicacy. Trexler's spine registered an ever so slight tremor as it picked up this natural disturbance in the lovely scene. "I want the second tree from the corner, just as it stands," he said, answering an imaginary question from an imaginary physician. And he felt a slow pride in realizing that what he wanted none could bestow, and that what he had none could take away. He felt content to be sick, unembarrassed at being afraid; and in the jungle of his fear he glimpsed (as he had so often glimpsed them before) the flashy tail feathers of the bird courage.

Then he thought once again of the doctor, and of his being left there all alone, tired, frightened. (The poor, scared guy, thought Trexler.) Trexler began humming "Moonshine Lullaby," his spirit reacting instantly to the hypodermic of Merman's healthy voice. He crossed Madison, boarded a downtown bus, and rode all the way to Fifty-second Street before he had a thought that could rightly have been called bizarre.

Suggestions for Discussion

1. The story begins with a challenge: "Ever have any bizarre thoughts?" In the course of the story, what bizarre thoughts *does* Trexler have? How bizarre are they?

2. The doctor is clearly in the position of power—a self-confident professional to

whom Trexler has gone for help. What sort of power does Trexler have? Is his habit of identifying with other people a neurotic weakness or a strength?

3. Where does the balance of power begin to shift toward Trexler, and how do you know?

4. What is the crisis action? If Trexler only gets to Fifty-second Street before his bizarre thoughts return, how much of a resolution is the resolution?

5. How much of Trexler's past do you learn in the plot? How would the shape of the short story be affected if White had begun, say, on the day Trexler first decided he needed a psychiatrist?

6. How is the situation at the end of the story the opposite of that at the opening?

WRITING ASSIGNMENTS

1. Write a scene placing two characters in this very fundamental conflict: one wants something the other does not want to give. The something may be anything — money, respect, jewelry, sex, information, a match — but be sure to focus on the one desire.

2. A slightly more complicated variation on the same theme: each of two characters has half of something that is no good without the other half. Neither wants to give up his or her half.

3. Write a short paragraph outlining the conflict between two characters. Then write the crisis scene for this conflict, a scene in which one of the characters "changes his/her mind," that is, realizes something, understands something not understood before, moves from one emotional state to its opposite. Make sure the internal change is shown in, or triggered by, an external action.

4. Write a short story that is a short story in *exactly* one hundred words. Notice that if you're going to manage a conflict, crisis, and resolution in this short compass, you'll have to introduce the conflict immediately.

5. Write a short story of no more than five pages in which the protagonist seems to be weaker than the forces opposing him or her. Give the character one balancing strength. Let him or her triumph.

6. Place a character in conflict with some aspect of nature. The character need not be fighting for survival; the danger may be as small as a mosquito. But balance the forces equally so that the reader is not sure who will "win" until the crisis action happens.

7. Plot an outline (or outline a plot) for a story in which the protagonist does not get what she or he wants — and which nevertheless ends happily.

WHATEVER WORKS
The Writing Process

Get Started
Keep Going
Revise

Get Started

What makes you want *not* to write?

There are a few lucky souls for whom the whole process of writing is easy, for whom the smell of fresh paper is better than air, whose minds chuckle perpetually over their own agility, who forget to eat, and who consider the world at large an intrusion on their good time at the typewriter. But you and I are not among them. Most of us don't like to write at all; we like to have written. We are caught in a guilty paradox in which we grumble over our lack of time and, when we have the time, we sharpen pencils, make phone calls, or clip the hedges. We are in love with words except when we have to face them. Our relationship to writing is uncomfortably like our relationship to dieting, exercise, housework, and charity: we feel better when we have done it, and feel better about ourselves when we have done it, but at any given moment we would rather do something—anything—else.

Of course, all this is overstated, and if there were no pleasure in writing we wouldn't do it. We write for the satisfaction of having wrestled a sentence to the page, the joy of discovering an image, the excitement of having a character come alive; and even the most successful writers will sincerely say that these pleasures—not money, fame, or glamour—are the real rewards of writing. Nevertheless, we forget what such joy and satisfaction feel like when we confront a blank page.

The narrator of Anita Brookner's novel *Look at Me* records a familiar pattern:

> Sometimes it feels like a physical effort simply to sit down at the desk and pull out the notebook. Sometimes I find myself heaving a sigh when I read through what I have already written. Sometimes the effort of putting pen to paper is so great that I literally feel a pain in my head, as if all the furniture of my mind were being rearranged, as if it were being lined up, being got ready for delivery from the storehouse. And yet when I start to write, all this heaviness vanishes, and I feel charged with a kind of electricity, not unpleasant in itself, but leading, inevitably, to greater restlessness.

It helps to know that most writers share this anomalous reluctance, least wanting to do what we most want to do. It also helps to know some of the reasons for that reluctance.

Novelist Richard Koster offers a blanket absolution for what writers tend to think of as "wasting time"—that hour or two of muddled glaring at the page before a word will allow itself to be placed there. In the process of creating a fiction we must divorce ourselves from the real world, he points out. And that is hard. The real world is insistent not only in its distractions but in its brute physical presence. To remove ourselves from that sphere and achieve a state in which our mental world is *more* real requires a disciplined effort of displacement.

We may even sense that it is unnatural or dangerous to live in a world of our own creation. People love to read stories about the dreamer who nobody thinks will come to much, and who turns out to be a genius inventor, scientist, artist, or savior. Part of the reason such stories work is that we like to escape from the way the world really works, including the way it works in us. We all feel the pressure of the practical. The writer may sympathize with the dreamer but forget to sympathize with the dreamer-in-him-or-herself.

There's another impediment to beginning, expressed by a writer character in Lawrence Durrell's *Alexandria Quartet*. Durrell's Pursewarden broods over the illusory significance of what he is about to write, unwilling to begin in case he spoils it. Many of us do this: the idea, whatever it is, seems so luminous, whole, and fragile, that to begin to write about that idea is to commit it to rubble. Knowing in advance that words will never exactly capture what we mean or intend, we must gingerly and gradually work ourselves into a state of accepting what words can do instead. No matter how many times we find out that what words can do is quite all right, we shy again from the next beginning. Against this wasteful impulse I have a motto over my desk, that reads: "Don't Dread; Do." It's a fine motto, and I contemplated it for several weeks before I began writing this chapter.

The mundane daily habits of writers are apparently fascinating. No author offers to answer questions at the end of a public reading without being asked: *Do you write in the morning or at night? Do you write every day? Do you compose on the typewriter?* Sometimes such questions show a hagiographic interest in the workings of genius. More often, I think, they are a plea for practical help: *Is there something I can do to make this job less horrific? Is there a trick that will unlock my words?*

The variety of answers suggests that there is no such magic. Donald Hall will tell you that he spends a dozen hours a day at his desk, moving back and forth between as many projects. Philip Larkin said that he wrote a poem only every eighteen months or so, and never tried to write one that was not a gift. Gail Godwin goes to her workroom every day "because what if the angel came and I wasn't there?" Diane Wakowski thinks that to sit at work against your will is evidence of bourgeois neurosis. Maria Irene Fornes begins her day with a half-hour of loosening-up exercises, finding a comfortable "center of gravity" before she sits down to work. Mary Lee Settle advises that writers who teach *must* work in the morning, before the analytical habits of the classroom take over the brain; George Cuomo replies that he solves this problem by taking an afternoon nap. Dickens could not deal with people when he was working: "The mere consciousness of an engagement will worry a whole day." Sheila Taylor finds her word processor a companionable friend. Hemingway and Thomas Wolfe wrote standing up. Some writers can plop at the kitchen table without clearing the breakfast dishes; some need total seclusion, a beach, a cat, a string quartet.

There is something to be learned from all this, though. It is not an open sesame but a piece of advice older than fairy tales: know thyself. The bottom line is that if you do not at some point write your story down, it will not get written. Having decided that you *will* write it, the question is not *how do you get it done?* but how do *you* get it done? Any discipline or indulgence that actually helps nudge you into position facing the page is acceptable and productive. If jogging after breakfast energizes your mind, then jog before you sit. If you have to pull an all-nighter on a coffee binge, do that. If you have to be chained to your chair, invest in a chain. And if, like me, you are one of the unlucky ones driven by guilt, then welcome your guilt and make sure it drives you toward the desk rather than away. Some schedule, regularity, pattern in your writing day (or night) will always help, but only you can figure out what pattern is for you.

CHOOSING A SUBJECT

Some writers, again, are lucky enough never to be faced with the problem of choosing a subject. The world presents itself to them in terms of conflict, crisis, and resolution: ideas for stories pop into their heads day after day; their only difficulty is choosing among them. In fact, the habit of mind that produces stories *is* a habit and can be cultivated, so that the more and the longer you write, the less likely you are to run out of ideas.

But sooner if not later you may find yourself faced with the desire (or the deadline necessity) to write a story when your mind is a blank. The sour and untrue impulse crosses your thoughts: nothing has ever happened to me. The task you face then is to recognize among all the paraphernalia of your mind a situation, idea, perception, or character that you can turn into a story.

Some teachers and critics advise beginning writers to write only from their personal experience, but I feel that this is a misleading and demeaning rule, producing a lot of dead-grandmother stories and tales of dormitory life. It is certainly true that you must draw on your own experience (including your experience of the shape of sentences). But the trick is to identify what is interesting, unique, original in your experience (including your experience of the shape of sentences), which will therefore surprise and attract the reader.

John Gardner, in *The Art of Fiction*, agrees that "nothing can be more limiting to the imagination" than the advice that you write about what you know. He suggests instead that you "write the kind of story you know and like best."

This is a better idea, because the kind of story you know and like best has also taught you something about the way such stories are told, how they are shaped, what kind of surprise, confict, and change they deal in. Many beginning writers who are not yet avid readers have learned from television more than they realize about structure, the way characters behave and talk, how a joke is arranged, how a lie is revealed, and so forth. The trouble is that if you learn fiction from television, or if the kind of story you know and like best is genre fiction — sci fi, fantasy, romance, mystery — you may have learned about technique without having learned anything about the unique contribution *you* can make to such a story. The result is that you end up writing imitation soap opera or space odyssey, second-rate somebody else instead of first-rate you.

In *Becoming a Writer*, a book that only half-facetiously claims to do what teachers of writing claim cannot be done—to teach genius—Dorothea Brande suggests that the way to begin is not with an idea or a form at all, but with an unlocking of your thoughts at the typewriter. She advises that you rise each day and go directly to your desk (if you have to have coffee, put it in a thermos the night before) and begin writing whatever comes to mind, before you are quite awake, before you have read anything or talked to anyone, before reason has begun to take over from the dream-functioning of your brain. Write for twenty or thirty minutes, then put away what you have written without reading it over. After a week or two of this, pick an additional time during the day that you can salvage a half hour or so to write, and when that time arrives, write, even if you "must climb out over the heads of your friends" to do it. It doesn't matter *what* you write: what does matter is that you develop the habit of beginning to write the moment you sit down to do so. When this habit is developed, Brande says, *then* read your pages over and pick a passage that seems to suggest a simple story. Muse on the idea for a few days, find its shape, fill that shape with people, settings, details from your own experience, observation, and imagination. Take several long walks turning the story over in your mind. Sleep on it—more than once. Finally, pick a definite time when you are going to write the story, and when that time comes, go to the desk and write a complete first draft as rapidly as possible. Then put it away, at least overnight. When you take it out again you will have something to work with, and the business of the reason may begin.

Writing what you know, writing your favorite sort of story, writing, in any case, something—none of these is an *open sesame*, either, but they do hint at the beginning of a beginning. Only if you are intensely interested in your story can you interest the reader. The essential thing is that you write about something you really care about. Identifying that something, however, is not always easy. We are surrounded by received opinion, a constant barrage of information, drama, ideas, and judgments offered us live, printed, and electronic. It is so much easier to know what we *ought* to think and feel than what we actually do. Worthy authorities constantly exhort us to care about worthy causes, only a few of which really touch us, whereas what we care about at any given moment may seem trivial, self-conscious, or self-serving. This, I think, is in large part the value of Brande's first exercise, forcing yourself to write in the intuitively honest period of first light, when the half-sleeping brain is still dealing with its real concerns. Often what seems unworthy is precisely the thing that contains a universal, and by catching it honestly, then stepping back from it, you may achieve the authorial distance that is an essential part of significance. (All you really care about this morning is how you'll look at the dance tonight? This is a trivial obsession that can hit anyone, at any age, anywhere. Write about it as honestly as you can. Now who else might have felt this way? Someone you hate? Someone remote in time from you? Look out: you're on your way to a story.) Sometimes pursuing what you know and feel to its uttermost limits will take you into the realms of fantasy. Sometimes your fantasies will transform themselves into reality.

Eventually you will learn what sort of experience sparks ideas for your sort of story—and you may be astonished at how such experiences accumulate, as if your life were arranging itself to produce material for you. In the meantime, here are a half dozen suggestions for the kind of idea that may be fruitful.

The dilemma, or catch-22. You find yourself facing, or know someone who is facing, or read about someone who is facing, a situation that offers no solution whatsoever. Any action taken would be painful and costly. You have no chance of solving this dilemma in real life, but you're a writer, and it costs nothing to solve it with imaginary people in an imaginary setting, even if the solution is a tragic one. Some writers use newspaper stories to generate this sort of idea. The situation is there in the bland black and white of this morning's news. But who are these people, and how did they come to be in such a mess? Make it up, think it through.

The incongruity. Something comes to your attention that is interesting precisely because you can't figure it out. It doesn't seem to make sense. Someone is breeding pigs in the back yard of a mansion in the most affluent section of town. Who is it? Why is she doing it? Your inventing mind can find the motives and the meanings. An example from my own experience: Once when my phone was out of order I went out very late at night to make a call from a public phone at a supermarket plaza. At something like two in the morning all the stores were closed but the plaza was not empty. There were three women there, one of them with a baby in a stroller. *What were they doing there?* It was several years before I figured out a possible answer, and that answer was a short story.

The connection. You notice a striking similarity in two events, people, places, or periods that are fundamentally unlike. The more you explore the similarity, the more striking it becomes. My novel *The Buzzards* came from such a connection: the daughter of a famous politician was murdered, and I found myself in the position of comforting the dead girl's fiance, at the same time as I was writing lectures on the *Agamemnon* of Aeschylus. Two politicians, two murdered daughters—one in Ancient Greece and one in contemporary America. The connection would not let go of me until I had thought it through and set it down.

The memory. Certain people, places, and events stand out in your memory with an intensity beyond logic. There's no earthly reason you should remember the smell of Aunt K's rouge. It makes no sense that you still flush with shame at the thought of that ball you "borrowed" when you were in fourth grade. But for some reason these things are still vivid in your mind. That vividness can be explored, embellished, given form. Stephen Minot in *Three Genres* wisely advises, though, that if you are going to write from a memory, it should be a memory more than a year old. Otherwise you are likely to be unable to distinguish between what happened and what must happen in the story, or between what is in your mind and what you have conveyed on the page.

The transplant. This is probably writing at its most therapeutic. You find yourself having to deal with a feeling that is either startlingly new to you or else obsessively old. You feel incapable of dealing with it. As a way of distancing yourself from that feeling and gaining some mastery over it, you write about the feeling as precisely as you can, but giving it to an imaginary someone in an imaginary situation. What situation other than your own would produce such a feeling? Who would be caught in that situation? Think it through.

The revenge. An injustice has been done, and you are powerless to do anything about it. But you're not really, because you're a writer. Reproduce the situation with another set of characters, in other circumstances or another setting. Cast the outcome to suit yourself. Punish whomever you choose. Even if the story ends in a similar injustice, you have righted the wrong by enlisting your reader's sympathy on the side of right. (Dante was particularly good at this: he put his enemies in the inferno and his friends in paradise.) Remember too that as human beings we are intensely, sometimes obsessively, interested in our boredom, and you can take revenge against the things that bore you by making them absurd or funny on paper.

Keep Going

A story idea may come from any source at any time. You may not know you have an idea until you spot it in the random jottings of your journal. Once you've identified the idea, the process of thinking it through begins, and doesn't end until you finish (or abandon) the story. Most writing is done between the mind and the hand, not between the hand and the page. It may take a fairly competent typist about three hours to type a twelve-page story. It may take days or months to write it. It follows that, even when you are writing well, most of the time spent writing is not spent putting words on the page. If the story idea grabs hard hold of you, the process of thinking through may be involuntary, a gift. If not, you need to find the inner stillness that will allow you to develop your characters, get to know them, follow their actions in your mind; and it may take an effort of the will to find such stillness.

The metamorphosis of an idea into a story has many aspects, some deliberate and some mysterious. "Inspiration" is a real thing, a gift from the subconscious to the conscious mind. But over and over again, successful writers attest that unless they prepare the conscious mind with the habit of work, the gift does not come. Writing is mind-farming. You have to plow, plant, weed, and hope for growing weather. Why a seed turns into a plant is something you are never going to understand, and the only relevant response to it is gratitude. You may be proud, however, of having plowed.

Many writers besides Dorothea Brande have observed that it is ideal, having turned your story over in your mind, to write the first draft at one sitting, pushing on through the action to the conclusion, no matter how dissatisfied you are with this paragraph, that character, this phrasing, or that incident. There are two advantages to doing this. The first is that you are more likely to produce a coherent draft when you come to the desk in a single frame of mind with a single vision of the whole, than when you write piecemeal, having altered ideas and moods. The second is that fast writing tends to make for fast pace in the story. It is always easier, later, to add and develop than it is to sharpen the pace. If you are the sort of writer who stays on page one for days, shoving commas around and combing the *Thesaurus* for a word with slightly better connotations, then you should probably force yourself to try this method (more than once). A note of caution, though: if you write a draft at one sitting, it will not be the draft you want to show anyone, so schedule the sitting well in advance of whatever deadline you may have.

And the method does not, for a variety of reasons, always work. Obviously it won't work for a novel (though Gabriel Josipovici, the author of "Mobius the Stripper," which is included in this volume, once startled me by observing that the first draft of a novel could be written in a month: "Ten pages a day for thirty days gives you three hundred—and *then* you rewrite it seventeen times").

It may happen—always keeping in mind that a single-sitting draft is the ideal—that as you write, the story takes off of its own accord in some direction totally other than you intended. You thought you knew where you were going and now you don't, and you know that unless you stop for a while and think it through again, you'll go wrong. You may find that although you are doing precisely what you had in mind, it doesn't work, and it needs more imaginative mulching before it will bear fruit. Or you may find, simply, that your stamina gives out, and that though you have done your exercises, been steadfast, loyal, and practiced every writerly virtue known, you're stuck. You have writer's block.

Writer's block is not so popular as it was a few years ago. I suspect people got tired of hearing or even talking about it—sometimes writers can be sensitive even to their own cliches. But it may also be that writers talked so much about the agony of not being able to get on with it, that they began to understand and accept their difficulties. Sometimes the process seems to require working yourself into a muddle and past the muddle to despair; until you have done this it may be impossible suddenly to see what the shape of a thing ought to be. When you're writing this feels terrible. You sit spinning your wheels, digging deeper and deeper into the mental muck. You decide you are going to trash the whole thing and walk away from it—only you can't, and you keep coming back to it like a tongue to an aching tooth. Or you decide you are going to sit there until you bludgeon it into shape—and as long as you sit there it remains recalcitrant. W. H. Auden observed that the hardest part of writing is not knowing whether you are procrastinating or you must wait for the words to come.

I know of no foolproof way of breaking a block, but some of these sometimes work:

1. Put the story away for a minimum of three days, making a solemn appointment with yourself for the day and hour you are going to go back to work on it. Then *really* put it away. Don't peek.

2. Write anything that is not the story. A letter. A grocery list. A bad poem. A journal entry (for therapy only, not as a substitute story) about how hard it is to write and why you are going to give it up entirely.

3. Do something that makes you feel good and involves no words. Play baseball, embroider, iron, feed the ducks, whittle, bake a pie.

4. Do something for your body. Treat it kindly. A hot bath, a bike ride, a haircut, a workout, meditation, or a chocolate sundae—whatever in your mind-set amounts to being kind to yourself. Then be equally kind to the physical body of your writing. Buy a new typewriter ribbon or a felt tip with a wider nib. Straighten the desk. Move it to the window or give it a potted plant.

5. When the hour of reentry arrives, go back to the idea that a one-sitting draft would be ideal. Tell yourself this story isn't going to be wonderful, but it's going to be done. It'll be wonderful some other day.

Revise

William C. Knott, in *The Craft of Fiction*, cogently observes that "anyone can write—and almost everyone you meet these days is writing. However, only the writers know how to rewrite. It is this ability alone that turns the amateur into a pro."

Revising is a process more dreaded than dreadful. The resistance to rewriting is, if anything, greater than the resistance to beginning in the first place. Yet the chances are that once you have committed yourself to a first draft, you'll be unable to leave it in an unfinished and unsatisfying state. You'll be *unhappy* until it's right. Making it right will involve a second commitment, to seeing the story fresh and creating it again with the advantage of this re-vision. In any case you must do it; you must revise. In most cases—not absolutely all, but the overwhelming majority—people who feel good about a first draft are too easily satisfied. Most writers also feel not only committed to what they have put on the page, but defensive on its behalf—wanting, really, only to be told that it is a work of genius, or, failing that, to find out that they got away with it. Therefore, the first exigency of revision is that you learn to hear, absorb, and accept criticism.

Once you have thought your story through, drafted it, and worked on it to the best of your ability, someone else's eyes can help to refresh the vision of your own. Wise professionals rely on the help of an agent or editor at this juncture (although even the wisest still smart at censure); anyone can rely on the reactions of friends, family, or classmates. The trick to making good use of criticism is to be utterly selfish about it. Be greedy for it. Take it all in. Ultimately you are the laborer, the arbiter, *and* the boss in any dispute about your story, so you can afford to consider any problem and any solution.

It used to be popular to speak of "constructive criticism" and "destructive criticism," but these are misleading terms, suggesting that negative criticism is useless and positive suggestions useful. In practice the opposite is usually the case. You're likely to find that the most constructive thing a reader can do is say *I don't believe this, I don't like this, I don't understand this,* pointing to precisely the passages that made you uneasy. This kind of laying-the-finger-on-the-trouble-spot produces an inward groan, but it's also satisfying; you know just where to go to work. Often the most destructive thing a reader can do is offer you a positive suggestion—*Why don't you have him crash the car?*—that is irrelevant to your vision of the story. Be suspicious of praise that is too extravagant, of blame that is too general. If your impulse is to defend the story or yourself, still the impulse. Behave as if bad advice were good advice, and give it serious consideration. You can reject it after you have explored it for anything of use it may offer.

When you feel that you have acquired enough distance from the story to see it anew, go back to work. Make notes of your plans, large and small. Talk to yourself in your journal about what you want to accomplish and where you think you have failed. Let your imagination play with new images or passages of dialogue. Keep a copy of the story as it is so that you can always go back to the original, and then be ruthless with another copy. Eudora Welty advises cutting sections apart and then pinning them back together so that they can be easily re- and re-arranged.

As you plan the revision and as you rewrite, you will know (and your critics will tell you) what problems are unique to your story. There are also general, almost universal, pitfalls that you can avoid if you ask yourself the following questions:

Why should the reader turn from the first page to the second? Is the language fresh? Are the characters alive? Does the first sentence, paragraph, page introduce real tension? If it doesn't, you have probably begun at the wrong place. If you are *unable* to find a way to introduce tension on the first page, you may have to doubt whether you have a story after all.

Is it original? Almost every writer thinks first, in some way or other, of the familiar, the usual, the given. This character is a stereotype, that emotion is too easy, that phrase is a cliché. First-draft laziness is inevitable, but it is also a way of being dishonest. A good writer will comb the work for clichés and labor to find the exact, the honest, and the fresh.

Is it clear? Although ambiguity and mystery provide some of our most profound pleasures in literature, beginning writers are often unable to distinguish between mystery and muddle, ambiguity and sloppiness. You may want your character to be rich with contradiction, but we still want to know whether that character is male or female, black or white, old or young. We need to be oriented on the simplest level of reality before we can share your imaginative world. Where are we? When are we? Who are they? How do things look? What time of day or night is it? What's the weather? What's happening?

Is it self-conscious? Probably the most famous piece of advice to the rewriter is William Faulkner's "kill all your darlings." When you are carried away with the purple of your prose, the music of your alliteration, the hilarity of your wit, the profundity of your insights, then the chances are that you are having a better time writing than the reader will have reading. No reader will forgive you, and no reader should. Just tell the story. The style will follow of itself if you just tell the story.

Where is it too long? Most of us and even the best of us write too long. We are so anxious to explain every nuance, cover every possible aspect of character, action, and setting that we forget the necessity of stringent selection. In fiction, and especially in the short story, we want sharpness, economy, and vivid, telling detail. More than necessary is too much. I have been helped in my own tendency to tell all by a friend who went through a copy of one of my novels, drawing a line through the last sentence of about every third paragraph. Then in the margin he wrote, again and again, "Hit it, baby, and get out." That's good advice for anyone.

Where is it undeveloped? In any first, second, or third draft of a manuscript, there are likely to be necessary passages sketched, skipped, or skeletal. Having put your manuscript away for a few days, try to read it as if you have never seen it before. What information is missing? What actions are incomplete, motives obscure, images inexact? Where does the action occur too abruptly, so that it loses its emotional force?

Where is it too general? Originality, economy, and clarity can all be achieved through the judicious use of significant detail. Learn to spot general, vague, and fuzzy terms. Be suspicious of yourself anytime you see nouns like *someone* and *everything*, adjectives like *huge* and *handsome*, adverbs like *very* and *really*. Seek instead a particular thing, a particular size, an exact degree. This principle is so important to good writing that much of the following chapter is devoted to particularity and detail.

Although the dread of "starting over" is a real and understandable one, the chances are that the rewards of revising will startlingly outweigh the pains. Sometimes a character who is dead on the page will come to life through the addition of a few sentences or significant details. Sometimes a turgid or tedious paragraph can become sharp with a few judicious cuts. Sometimes dropping page one and putting page seven where page three used to be can provide the skeleton of an otherwise limp story. And sometimes, often, perhaps always, the difference between an amateur rough–cut and a publishable story is in the struggle at the rewriting stage.

There follow two versions of "The Power," by Joe Taylor, which illustrate the final revision process of a published story. The two versions are far from an example of a "first rough" and a final. On the contrary, what appears on the left (even-numbered pages) is a much-revised version of the story that the author considered finished enough to send to *Triquarterly* magazine. On the right (odd-numbered pages) the story appears as it was published in *Triquarterly*, after consultation between author and editor, and still further revision.

The most useful way to observe the changes (and the fairest to the story) is to read the final (boxed) version, which appears on the right page, all the way through; then read the letter from *Triquarterly* editor Reginald Gibbons. Finally, go back and compare the final with the earlier version; the changed words and passages have been underlined. Observe where and how the author has been able to incorporate the editor's advice and where additional revisions were made. Note that in the final version spaces have been left to indicate cuts from the earlier version. The blank spaces do not appear in the published version. Decide where you think the story has been improved in clarity, drama, pace, sharpness, and so forth.

The Power

JOE TAYLOR

"The Father God is a time God and He say my time come soon."

Medea didn't want to answer Momma Jack, so she looked to the woman's hands as they clutched the iron skillet. Except for their shivering, the tiny hands would have been lost on the blackened iron. Medea heard Momma Jack's hard breathing.

Momma Jack didn't have to say what she did, because Medea had been born with a veil over her face and could see the future. In a vision only two nights before she had seen Momma Jack stretching her arms out for Jesus. And a bright light hurried in, making Momma Jack's old slave dress crumble to the ground in a pile of brown dust. Momma Jack's naked skin shone so black an hot that it woke Medea. For the rest of the night, she had listened, making sure that she could hear Momma Jack breathing on the other side of the room—heavy, like she was now.

"Don't leave me die here. Take me to where my mother come. Where my poppa come. Where Jesus sit and wait for me with a white robe in His hand."

Momma Jack's arm jumped from the skillet and grabbed Medea. The tiny nails bit like a dog's rabid burning jaw, and Medea thought that maybe it was the hand of Jesus calling her too. She looked into Momma Jack's eyes. A black-cloaked horseman rode through them.

"Momma Jack, you ain't going nowheres." Her eyes followed the old woman's dull brown dress to the ground.

"Don't lie to me, child. You got the power, but I don't need the power to know what I know. Take me to the water and soon. My spirit can't abide to have its final rest in this land of white sin."

Late that night, when even the crickets were afraid to talk, Medea knelt beside her mattress. Her long yellow hands worked one another in the black air until they began to jerk and hit her face. Her head beat back and forth, whipping her hair about her shoulders and eyes. She fell backwards, hugging herself, and stared at the heavy roof beams until she could see through the darkness.

All the niggers walked in a long line two by two. They was going to the big waters. And when the sun showed on them, it wasn't hot no more. Then a white come up on a horse, shaking his hand at the niggers and the sun, yelling with his mouth as open as a door. But Brother Wilson lifted his arms and a storm come up and the earth moved. And the white was gone.

The Power

JOE TAYLOR

"The Father God is a time God and He say my time come soon."

Medea didn't want to answer Momma Jack, so she looked to the woman's hands as they clutched the iron skillet. Except for their shivering so, the tiny hands would have been lost on the blackened iron.

Medea didn't want to answer because she had been born with a veil over her face and could see the future. In a vision only two nights before she had seen Momma Jack stretching her arms out for Jesus. And a bright light had hurried in, making Momma Jack's old slave dress crumble to the ground in a pile of brown dust. Momma Jack's naked skin had shown so black and hot that it woke Medea. For the rest of the night she had listened, making sure she could hear Momma Jack's hard breathing on the other side of the dark room.

"Soon, child. Don't leave me die here. Take me to where my mother come. Where my poppa come. Where Jesus sit and wait for me with a white robe in His hand." Momma Jack's own hand jumped from the black skillet and grabbed Medea.

The tiny nails bit like a dog's rabid jaw, and Medea thought that maybe it was Jesus calling her now, too. She looked into Momma Jack's eyes. A black-cloaked horseman rode through them.

"Momma Jack, you ain't going nowheres." She looked down along the old woman's dull brown dress to the ground.

"Don't lie to me, child. You got the power, but I don't need the power to know what I know. Take me to the water and soon. My spirit can't abide to have its final rest in this land of white sin."

Late that night, when even the crickets were afraid to talk, Medea knelt beside her mattress. Her long yellow hands worked one another in the black air until they began to jerk and hit her face. Her head beat back and forth, whipping her hair about her shoulders and eyes. She fell backwards, hugging herself, and stared at the heavy roof beams until she could see through the darkness.

All the niggers walked in a long line two by two. They was going to the big waters. And when the sun showed on them, it wasn't hot no more. Then a white come up on a horse, shaking his hand at the niggers and the sun, yelling with his mouth as open as a door. But Brother Wilson lifted his arms and a storm come up and the earth moved. And the white was gone.

Medea crawled to her mattress. A bug scratched over her leg and she angrily kicked it away. *Why wasn't there nothing of what to do about Momma Jack?* She sweat in a turning sleep until a cardinal chitted that it was time to fix the Loomises' breakfast.

"It's coming one hot day," she told the bird's voice as she pulled her dress over her head. Already her lips were wet. She walked past the door and covered her eyes from the daylight.

"No need on waking me. My work ain't with the whites no more."

"Miss Wilma say—"

"You heard me, girl!"

Medea nodded and walked outside. She saw the cardinal sitting on one of the dogwoods separating the quarters from the house.

"It's coming one hot day, Mr. Cardinal," she repeated. Then she began to pray for Momma Jack. She prayed in the kitchen when she put new wood on the embers. She prayed on the worn path outside when she went to get the eggs. The two-toothed boy used to fetch eggs for her and Momma Jack, but he left for the North with his momma after his daddy joined the army. The young master said they all three were killed in a swamp. *What swamp around here? Momma Jack asked that night. None Swamp, that's what.* Medea stopped in the cellar on her way back and lifted a slab of bacon off the line.

And when she went back inside, she rolled biscuits and prayed some more for Momma Jack. Master's preacher said that when the niggers die, they get fresh white sack cloth and go up to heaven to wait on their masters some more. Jesus wouldn't let that happen, though.

"Medea, where's Momma Jack? She didn't come to wake us."

Medea turned to see Miss Wilma. She always noticed her hands before anything else, for Miss Wilma's hands talked more than her mouth. They were still today.

"She sick, Miss Wilma."

"Well, couldn't you have stopped up?"

"Yes, Miss Wilma, but I was going to let you sleep."

"You forgot, you mean . . . how sick is she? You think I should send for Doctor Head?"

"No, Miss Wilma. She be all right."

"Well don't let her start root-curing herself. Tell her I'll come by tomorrow if she doesn't get better. And give her some tea and honey to sweat it out."

"Yes, Miss Wilma."

Their eyes met briefly. Miss Wilma stood gripping the bannister looking down at Medea. It was like the time four months ago they had stared at one another—both of them waking in the early morning when the light had barely managed to slip in the windows. Medea had awakened with a vision. She saw Master Loomis sitting on a big white horse with his big

A bug scratched over her leg and Medea angrily kicked it away. *Why wasn't there nothing of what to do about Momma Jack?* She crawled to her mattress and sweated in a turning sleep until a cardinal chitted that it was time to fix the Loomises' breakfast.

"It's coming one hot day," she told the bird's voice as she pulled her dress over her head. Already her lips were wet. She walked past the door and covered her eyes from the sunrise.

"No need on waking me. My work ain't with whites no more," Momma Jack said.

"Miss Wilma say—"

"You heard me, girl!"

Medea nodded and walked outside. She saw the cardinal sitting on one of the dogwoods separating the quarters from the house.

"It's coming one hot day, Mr. Cardinal," she repeated. Then she began to pray for Momma Jack. She prayed in the kitchen when she put new wood on the embers. She prayed on the worn path outside when she went to get eggs. The two-toothed boy used to fetch them for her and Momma Jack, but he had left for the North with his momma after his daddy joined the army. The young master said they all three were killed in a swamp. *What swamp around here? Momma Jack asked that night. None Swamp, that's what.* Medea stopped in the cellar and lifted a slab of bacon off the line.

And when she went back to the big house, she rolled biscuits and prayed some more for Momma Jack. Master's preacher said that when the niggers die, they get fresh brown sackcloth and go up to heaven to wait on their masters like old. Jesus wouldn't let that happen, though.

"Medea, where's Momma Jack? She didn't come to wake us."

Medea turned to see Miss Wilma. She always noticed her hands before anything else, for Miss Wilma's hands talked more than her mouth. They were still today.

"She sick, Miss Wilma."

"Well, couldn't you have stopped up?"

"Yes, Miss Wilma, but I was going to let you sleep."

"You forgot, you mean ... How sick is she? Lord, I have enough troubles. You think I should send for Doctor Head?"

"No, Miss Wilma. She be all right."

Their eyes met briefly. Miss Wilma stood gripping the bannister looking down at Medea. It was like the time four months ago they had stared at one another—both of them awake in the early morning when the light had barely managed to slip in the windows. Medea had awakened with a vision. She saw Master Loomis sitting on a big white horse with his big wide hat. Then the horse fell like a dropped rag doll and the hat floated down like a great leaf to cover the horse and Master Loomis. His left <u>hand jerked</u> out from under the hat's brim and reached for Medea's face, but the fingers began to smolder <u>and glow with hell-flame</u> before they could touch her. So Medea went to the house and quietly walked through it, shaking her dress at a mouse in the hall. Then her and Miss Wilma met just <u>like they were now,</u> except that Miss Wilma <u>looked</u> once at Medea, <u>then turned and walked up the stairs,</u> holding her hands to her eyes.

<u>It was just like that now.</u> Sometimes it seemed that all Miss Wilma had to do was look at Medea.

"Maybe I'll go see Momma Jack today. You put in some extra biscuit— no, you make some extra pancake batter for her."

"Yes, Miss." Medea saw Miss Wilma's hand <u>tremble slightly</u> when she turned.

Miss Becky's pancakes. It was the only thing the white child would eat come late. Miss Wilma was right—she did have enough trouble without an old sick nigger. Medea lifted her head. So they would leave tonight. She told herself she knew they were going all along. She pushed the biscuit into the oven. Hadn't that been what the dream last night had meant? Now that she thought about it, she remembered seeing Momma Jack walking too. <u>And she herself must have stood beside the woman, going to the water.</u>

<u>Daniel said</u> the good water was to the North. And the army was to the West. And <u>he put</u> his hands on her back like he never had before and slid them down her spine and <u>over her loins, then</u> she stopped them. *Not with you going away to get shot. Is that what you see?* He held back from her body and widened his eyes. She looked at his still lips. *I don't see nothing this time. A nigger woman can only think about the past and now.* But you got the power. You think ahead. *I can think to nine months ahead, and know what I shouldn't think now, with you going off like some white man.* She held onto his arms, feeling her cool skin <u>spring</u> against his heavy veins. He said he had to fight to set him and her free. He said he would send word. He said he would come back. <u>She looked</u> away into a dark corner.

Medea reached for the flour <u>she had just</u> put away and <u>loped out three cups.</u> So they would go to the North where Daniel said, because he was a smart man in most things. She breathed the smell of biscuit baking. If Lord Jesus could make <u>biscuit and honey,</u> He could lead Momma Jack and her to the water like two padding dogs. She thought of Daniel's big feet and cracked completely through an egg, leaving half of it to spill over the side of the bowl.

That evening, when Medea went to the quarters, Momma Jack was still in bed. In the twilight, Medea could only see one tiny bump under the cover.

wide hat. Then the horse fell like a dropped rag doll and the hat floated down like a great leaf to cover the horse and Master Loomis. His left hand had jerked out from under the hat's brim and reached for Medea's face, but the fingers began to smolder before they could touch her. So Medea went to the house and quietly walked through it, shaking her dress at a mouse in the hall. Then her and Miss Wilma met just like now, except that Miss Wilma had looked once at Medea, and turned and run up the stairs, holding her hands to her eyes—sometimes it seemed that all Miss Wilma had to do was look at Medea.

"Maybe I'll go see Momma Jack today. You put in some extra biscuit—no, you make some extra pancake batter for her."

"Yes, Miss." Medea saw Miss Wilma's hand shake when she turned.

Miss Becky's pancakes. It was the only thing the white child would eat come late. Miss Wilma was right—she did have enough trouble without an old sick nigger. Medea lifted her head. So they would leave tonight. She told herself she knew they were going all along. She pushed the biscuit into the oven. Hadn't that been what the dream last night had meant? Now that she thought about it, she remembered seeing Momma Jack walking too.

Daniel once said the good water was to the north. And the army was to the west. And he had put his hands on her like he never had before and slid them down her spine and over her backside until she stopped them. *Not with you going away to get shot. Is that what you see?* He held back from her body and widened his eyes. She looked at his still lips. *I don't see nothing this time. A nigger woman can only think about the past and now.* But you got the power. You think ahead. *I can think to nine months ahead, and know what I shouldn't think now, with you going away like some white man.* She had held onto his arms, feeling her cool skin against his heavy veins. He said he had to fight to set him and her free. He said he would send word. He said he would come back. She had looked away into a dark corner.

Medea reached for the flour she just put away and measured three cups for pancakes. So they would go to the North where Daniel said, because he was a smart man in most things. She breathed the smell of biscuit baking. If Lord Jesus could make honey and biscuit, He could lead Momma Jack and her to the water like two padding dogs. She thought of Daniel's big feet and cracked completely through an egg, leaving half of it to spill over the side of the bowl.

That evening, when Medea went to the quarters, Momma Jack was still in bed. In the twilight, Medea could only see one tiny bump under the cover.

"I am resting for my journey to Jesus."

Medea pulled a thin slab of dried beef from under her dress and grinned: "Young Master said you might need this."

"I am resting for my journey to Jesus."

Medea dropped the beef on the table and went to the older woman. She reached for her cheek, but Momma Jack's hand grabbed hers, leaving it wet with fever.

"Take me, Jesus!"

"Tonight, we go tonight."

Momma Jack focused on Medea's face, then relaxed her grip. She stood and walked Medea to a corner of the room which was littered with the belongings of the three house niggers who had already left. She pointed a finger to a molding patchwork and Medea looked under it. There were two knotted and rolled sheets.

"Miss Wilma come today." Momma Jack leaned to unknot one of the sheets. Inside it were biscuits, a jar of molasses, and two torn pages from the Bible. Momma Jack had owned these last ever since Medea could remember. Momma Jack pointed to the biscuits and looked up to Medea.

"She know," Medea said.

"She don't need niggers no more. She need the help of the Lord."

Medea nodded and went for the meat on the table. Re-tying the granny knot of her sheet after putting the meat in, she looked to see the old woman standing with a pair of sheep's shears pointing at her hair.

"What for?" Medea pressed against her hair with both hands.

"To keep the white man's eyes in his own yard, yellow girl."

They sat away from the door, staring through a chink in the wall, waiting for the last lantern to go out in the house. Medea held her near-bare head while Momma Jack hummed.

* * *

"Which way you footwalking, child? That's South." Momma Jack grabbed Medea's chin and pointed towards the dark sky. "You see that twinkling? You look and see good. It's a dipper full of milk and honey. Now you follow those two stars. See the bright star at the end? That's the Lord's promise to the nigger. That's North."

They started walking again.

"There's only one star brighter than that star. You be finding that star soon enough without an old woman's help." Momma Jack laughed.

Medea was quiet, though she wanted to know what star Momma Jack was talking about. But no one just asked Momma Jack a question like they asked Medea to see the future. The night air slipped under her arms and she wondered if Daniel made it to Lexington.

"You sure that dark boy Daniel hitched his pants to the army and not to you?"

"I am resting for my journey to Jesus."

Medea pulled a thin slab of dried beef from under her dress and grinned. "Young Master said you might need this."

"I am resting for my journey to Jesus."

Medea dropped the beef on the table and went to the older woman. She reached for her cheek, but Momma Jack's hand grabbed hers, leaving it wet with fever.

"Take me, Jesus!"

"Tonight, we go tonight."

Momma Jack focused on Medea's face, then relaxed her grip. She stood and walked to a corner of the room which was littered with the belongings of the three house niggers who had already left. She pointed a finger to the molding patchwork and Medea looked under it. There were two knotted and rolled sheets.

"Miss Wilma come today." Momma Jack undid one of the sheets. Inside it were biscuits, a jar of molasses, and two torn pages from the Bible. Momma Jack had owned these last ever since Medea could remember. Momma Jack pointed to the biscuits.

"She know," Medea said.

"She don't need niggers no more. She need the help of the Lord."

Medea nodded and went for the meat on the table. Re-tying her sheet after putting the meat in, she turned to see the old woman standing with a pair of sheep's shears.

"What for?" Medea pressed against her hair with both hands.

"To keep the white man's eyes in his own yard, yellow girl."

They sat away from the door, staring through a chink in the wall, waiting for the last lantern to go out in the house. Medea held her near-bare head while Momma Jack hummed.

* * *

"Which way you foot-walking, child? That's South." Momma Jack grabbed Medea's chin and lifted it towards the sky. "You see that twinkling? You look good and see. It's a dipper full of milk and honey. Now you follow those two stars. See the bright star at the end? That's the Lord's promise to the nigger. That's North."

They started walking again.

"There's only one star brighter than that star. You be finding it soon enough without an old woman's help." Momma Jack laughed.

Medea was quiet, though she wanted to know what star Momma Jack was talking about. But no one just asked Momma Jack a question like they asked Medea to see the future. The night air slipped under her arms and she wondered if Daniel had made it to Lexington.

"You sure that dark boy Daniel hitched his pants to the army and not you?"

"Momma Jack, I'm no fool."

"That's because you listen to Momma Jack. But we all be fools. Some just more lucky. Especially so with men."

Medea looked to the old woman walking next to her in the shapeless dark. She wanted to touch her, but she was afraid. So she walked, one foot in front of the other, shaking a long stick to scare away snakes.

Momma Jack's brains worked all the time. It wasn't like her own power. The night Daniel had left she ate three cloves of garlic and burned a tiny blue candle to see if she could bring on the power. But it never worked that way, and she only felt sick.

Momma Jack told her it was good that the power only worked like it did because that meant it was life power, not death power. It was only death power that a person could use all the time. Death power was blood with the Devil. Sometimes Medea thought she might like to talk with the Devil, just to see. But whenever she thought this, she would sing a song to Jesus.

Momma Jack stopped and leaned against a tree. Medea heard her sack fall to the ground. Then Momma Jack reached to touch the stick Medea was carrying.

"A worrisome person can't trust in the Lord enough. You young, so you be more worrisome. But you think of the Lord when you fret and things will be good."

Medea started to pick up the knapsack and twist it about hers, but Momma Jack held her back.

"You tell me my future now."

"Momma Jack, I can't do it that way."

"You tell me if Jesus will carry me all the way to the water."

Medea dropped the stick and satchel to the ground and rubbed her hands together. She looked up into the leaves of the tree they were under and saw walnuts readying to fall. A star twinkled now and then among them as she swayed her head back and forth. She at last stopped in a shiver.

"Momma Jack, I prayed to Jesus, but I just can't see. You told me yourself that it don't work like that."

"Did you pray to Jesus?"

"Yes, but I didn't see."

"Did you pray to Jesus?"

"Momma Jack, I just told you so."

"Then we will go as far as He wants. There is more than one kind of power, do you know that?"

"Yes'm."

"No you don't."

"Momma Jack, I'm no fool."

"That's because you listen to Momma Jack. But we all be fools. Some just more lucky. Especially so with men."

Medea looked to the old woman walking next to her in the shapeless dark. She wanted to touch her, but was afraid. So she walked, one foot in front of the other, shaking a long stick to scare away snakes.

Momma Jack's brains worked all the time. It wasn't like her own power. The night Daniel had left she ate three cloves of garlic and burned a tiny blue candle to see if she could bring on the power. But she only felt sick.

Momma Jack told her that it was good that the power only worked like it did because that meant that it was life power, not death power. It was only death power that a person could use all the time. Death power was blood with the Devil. Sometimes Medea thought she might like to talk with the Devil, just to see. But whenever she thought this, she would sing a song to Jesus.

Momma Jack stopped and leaned against a tree. Medea heard her sheet fall to the ground. Momma Jack reached to touch the stick Medea was carrying.

"A worrisome person can't trust in the Lord enough. You young, so you be more worrisome. But you think of the Lord when you fret and things will be good."

Medea started to pick up the sheet and twist it about her own, but Momma Jack held her back.

"You tell me my future now."

"Momma Jack, I can't do it that way."

"You tell me if Jesus will carry me all the way to the water."

Medea put the knotted sheet and her stick on the ground and rubbed her hands together. She looked into the leaves of the tree they were under and saw walnuts readying to fall. A star twinkled now and then among them as she swayed her head back and forth. She at last stopped in a shiver.

"Momma Jack, I prayed to Jesus, but I just can't see. You told me yourself that it don't work like that."

"Did you pray to Jesus?"

"Yes, but I didn't see."

"Did you pray to Jesus?"

"Momma Jack, I just told you so."

"Then we will go as far as He wants. There is more than one kind of power, do you know that?"

"Yes'm."

"No you don't."

* * *

They had finally stopped by a creek because Momma Jack had said that heaven would sound like that every night. Medea awoke mid-morning with the sun's light in her eyes. She kept her hands over them as long as she could before she had to scratch the chigger bites from the night before. She hoped heaven would just have the creek's sounds.

Between scratching, she noticed the old woman's hands tightly gripping each shoulder despite the heat. It would come soon, one or two days at the most, and she would be alone. Maybe she could carry Momma Jack the rest of the way since she was so skinny.

And after that—*stupid nigger, don't think of to come.* Medea pulled at the weeds and broken twigs with her toes, rocking herself backwards and forwards. She closed her eyes and let her head sway with the motion.

But nothing would come. Nothing about herself, Momma Jack, or Daniel. Not even about the Loomises. She stopped rocking. She didn't need the power to know what Miss Wilma was doing now. Two more niggers gone, she is saying—Momma Jack and the yellow witch girl. And young Master John is saying he will hop on a mare and give them niggers what. But Miss Wilma just twists her hands and says it's two less mouths to feed and two less reasons for the Yankees to come snooping around with their *Habeas Corpus.* Medea giggled and twisted her hands hard like Miss Wilma did everytime she said those words. She imagined Miss Wilma's eyes looking straight at young Master John: You tend to your sisters and your work.

Medea thought of Miss Becky. All the niggers said she was the dumbest white girl they had ever seen—propping herself on that watertower like it was taking her to Sweet Jesus Land. They said she proves what's going to happen to all whites. Then they asked Medea to see in a vision.

All the graveyards rattle, both white and nigger. And the white graves with their big stones get cracked by lightning and thunder-holes, then thrown into the mud. The little nigger graves with their wood crosses grow roses of all colors which bring birds and honeybees. That the first step, the Lord says.

Medea remembered all the old and the very young listening to her in the woods around a fire no bigger than her foot. They all nodded as she spoke, and their heads and hands showed as happy together as she had ever seen. It was like they were already in heaven. So she told the second step, where the Lord Jesus come down with a thousand angels all carrying a jar of honey in their left hand and a jar of perfume in their right. And they put the honey in all the niggers' wounds and tears and whipmarks, and poured the perfume over their black faces.

When she said this, some of the old people had already begun to cry and call for Jesus.

* * *

They had finally stopped by a creek because Momma Jack had said that heaven would sound like that every night. Medea awoke mid-morning with the sun's light in her eyes. She kept her hands over them as long as she could before she had to scratch the chigger bites from the night before. She hoped heaven would just have the creek's sounds.

Between scratchings, she noticed the old woman's hands tightly gripping each shoulder despite the heat. It would come soon, one or two days at the most. Maybe she could carry Momma Jack the rest of the way since she was so skinny. And after that—*stupid nigger, don't think of to come.* Medea pulled at the weeds and broken twigs with her toes, rocking herself backwards and forwards. She closed her eyes and let her head sway with the motion.

But nothing would come. Nothing about herself, Momma Jack, or Daniel. Not even about the Loomises. She stopped rocking. She didn't need the power to know what Miss Wilma was doing now. Two more niggers gone, she is saying—Momma Jack and the yellow witch girl. And young Master John is saying he will hop on a mare and give them niggers what. But Miss Wilma just twists her hands and says it's two less mouths to feed and two less reasons for the Yankees to come snooping around with their *habeas corpus.* Medea giggled and twisted her hands hard like Miss Wilma did every time she said those words. She imagined Miss Wilma's eyes looking straight at young Master John: "You tend to your sisters and your work."

Medea thought of Miss Becky. All the niggers said she was the dumbest white girl they had ever seen—propping herself in that hayloft like it was taking her to Sweet Jesus Land. They said she proves what's going to happen to all whites. Then they asked Medea to see in a vision.

All the graveyards rattle, both white and nigger. And the white graves with their big stones get cracked by lightning and thunder-holes, then thrown in the mud. The little nigger graves with their wood crosses grow roses of all colors which bring birds and honeybees. That the first step, the Lord says.

Medea remembered all the old and the very young listening to her in the woods around a fire no bigger than her foot. They all nodded as she spoke, and their heads and hands showed as happy together as she had ever seen. It was like they were already in heaven. So she told the second step, where the Lord Jesus come down with a thousand angels all carrying a jar of honey in their left hand and a jar of perfume in their right. And they put the honey in all the niggers' wounds and tears and whip marks, and poured perfume over their black faces.

When she said this, some of the old people had already begun to cry and call for Jesus.

Medea heard a noise off aways. She tried to see through the thick bushes she lay under, but couldn't. She listened. The noise wasn't getting any nearer; it just stayed. She looked to Momma Jack with her hands folded about her. The noise stayed the same. Medea crawled off under the brush, quietly pushing one dangling vine away at a time.

"Mr. Snake, stay in your hole."

Medea crawled until the noise got louder. It was men talking. She looked through the dark and light green tangle until she could see a horse's leg and blue trousers standing by it. The men's voices drifted along the creek and curled up to where she lie.

"One'll get you five not a one will dance with you."

"They see this stripe and they'll be fighting for my hand."

"More than like their daddies'll be fightin' to draw a bead on those Union buttons."

Medea heard the laughter. Suddenly, the horse shifted against the leg of the man holding it.

"Here, you calm down now. You smell a rebel?"

The men stopped laughing. Medea looked over her shoulder but there was nothing there except more vines. She wondered if she should go up to the soldiers and say that her nigger husband was in the army. Where was he, they would say. Where's the proof you're married, they would say. Or, if they didn't they would take her off to the North and what would Momma Jack do about her water then? Or they might even give them back to the Loomises for the reward young Master John would put in the papers.

Medea quickly twitched her nose. She bent it first to the ground, then up into the air. A smell came from there that bit into her throat and stomach. She quickly began to crawl away, for it was the smell of death.

Halfway back to Momma Jack she heard shots, then felt the heavy hooves of horses on the ground beneath her. All of it seemed to come from every direction, so she lay as still as she could until it was quiet and a breeze lifted a dead leaf against her nose.

She got back to Momma Jack. The old woman lay still and curled into herself. Medea crawled even faster, then saw Momma Jack's hand reach into the dirt and twitch at a fly. Then the old woman rolled on her side and pulled at her sack.

So Medea knew what the smell had meant. She prayed for the soldiers, for the young boy going to the dance. She prayed until the sun shoved over the middle of the sky. Then she pressed on Momma Jack's thin shoulders and offered her some jerky and biscuit. Momma Jack shook her head no.

"The Lord says you got to eat if you want to get to Him. Don't you spite the Lord."

The two women quietly ate.

Medea heard a sudden noise. She tried to see through the thick bushes she lay under, but couldn't. She listened. The noise wasn't getting any nearer; it just stayed. She looked to Momma Jack with her hands folded about her, then crawled off under the brush, quietly pushing one dangling vine away at a time.

"Mr. Snake, stay in your hole."

Medea crawled until the noise got louder. It was men talking. She looked through the green leafy tangle until she could see a horse's leg and a pair of blue trousers. The men's voices drifted along the creek and curled up to where she lay.

"One'll get you five not a one will dance with you."

"They see this stripe and they'll be fighting for my hand."

"More than like their daddies'll be fightin' to draw a bead on those Union buttons."

Medea heard the laughter. Suddenly, the horse shifted against the blue trousers.

"Here, you calm down now. You smell a rebel?"

The men stopped laughing. Medea looked over her shoulder, but there was nothing there except more vines. She wondered if she should go up to the soldiers and say that her nigger husband was in the army. Where was he, they would say. Where's the proof you're married, they would say. Or, if they didn't, they would take her off to the North and what would Momma Jack do about her water then? Or they might even give them back to the Loomises for the reward young Master John would put in the papers.

Medea twitched her nose. She bent it first to the ground, then up into the air. A smell came from there that bit into her throat and stomach. She quickly began to crawl away, for it was the smell of death.

Halfway back to Momma Jack she heard shots, then felt the heavy hooves of horses on the ground beneath her. Noise came from every direction, so she lay as still as she could until a quiet breeze finally lifted a dead leaf against her nose.

She got in sight of Momma Jack. The old woman was curled into herself. Medea crawled even faster, then saw Momma Jack's hand reach into the dirt to shake off a fly.

Medea sat beside Momma Jack and prayed for the soldiers, for the young boy going to the dance. She prayed as the sun scooted down from mid-sky. And all the time she kept her nose nervously in the air. At sunset, she pressed Momma Jack's thin shoulder and offered her some jerky and biscuit. Momma Jack shook her head no.

"The Lord says you got to eat if you want to get to Him. Don't you spite the Lord."

* * *

"What did you do while this old woman slept most day?"

Medea looked to the small grey cloud stuck underneath the moon like a pillow for its head: "I heard Union soldiers talk."

"Did they say anything?"

"No."

"How come you didn't talk with them? Ask for food?"

"They rode off too quick." Medea breathed out heavily, reminded of the morning's smell.

"Was you going to ask them?"

"No."

"Good."

They walked on. Every time Medea looked over to Momma Jack, her head was hanging low to the ground like it was weighed with the dark. Finally, Momma Jack glanced up and spoke:

"There was a barnyard chicken once. It was a sweet white and its feathers never got associated with the dirt like all the other chickens. The roosters all stretched their necks and lifted their spurs whenever they saw this chicken approaching by. Though you might think some of the other chickens was righteous jealous, they never was, 'cause the cream white never cackled loud or spread its feathers up in the women chickens' face.

"Then once a fox come. This fox had the longest red fur that lifted in the wind and blew honeysuckle smell all around. The fox had two old bloodhounds draw it around in a wagon while it sat back and licked its snout and fur. 'Go faster,' it would say. Or, 'Go slower.' And the bloodhounds did just that.

"This particular day it yelled 'Stop!' and the dogs did. It had driven by the chicken coop with its nose in the air to avoid the smell, but by chance had seen the cream white feathers walking about.

"'Come here, chicken,' it commanded.

"The chicken did this because all the farm animals went like the fox said.

"'Would you like to ride with me and go to the big house over the hill? We will have a fine dinner and you won't eat old chicken scratch no more. And my two bloodhounds will pull us in the moonlight to listen to the fiddles play at the other fine houses. Just step up.' And the fox put out his paw and pointed his snout directly at the cream white. She jumped in and rode with her neck held high showing its milk white feathers. So high she never saw the fox's teeth.

"When they got home, the fox called for his cook and pointed to the cream white. 'Stupid chicken,' he said, 'did you think I would let a pile of feathers ride with my fine fur?'"

Medea looked from Momma Jack to the moon, then to the ground in front of her.

With a frown, Momma Jack reached for some biscuit. After several small, mad bits, she looked up. "What did you do while this old woman slept most day?"

"I heard Union soldiers talk."

"Did they say anything?"

"No."

"How come you didn't talk with them? Ask for food?"

"They rode off too quick." Medea breathed out heavily, reminded of the morning's smell. She looked to a small gray cloud stuck underneath the rising moon like a pillow.

"Was you going to ask them?"

"No."

"Good."

They finished eating and started to walk. Every time Medea looked over to Momma Jack, her head was hanging low to the ground like it was weighed with the dark.

"Those soldiers . . ." Momma Jack started.

"Yes'm?"

"You do the same when I'm gone."

"Do you understand who the chicken is?"

"Yes'm."

"No you don't—not yet. But you remember when I'm gone."

"Momma Jack, you ain't—"

"Don't try to take heaven from me, witch girl."

* * *

In the late morning, Medea shaded her eyes and watched Momma Jack until her neck muscles hurt. Her breath seemed to drift about in a heavy, hot cloud. Move, a voice said. She reached for Momma Jack's face, stopping just short to let her fingers slide along the woman's sleeve instead. Momma Jack needed sleep.

She turned and thought of mashed potatoes and red-eye gravy. And eggs. And four biscuits underneath a cupful of thick honey mixed with butter. Medea reached for her satchel and snatched her hand back to shake off two ants. More crawled out of the sheet, so she had to shake the remaining biscuit and jerky off. She hung the sack as high as she dare on a bush, afraid it would attract attention. It barely bent the branch; if the river was as far away as Momma Jack said, she couldn't afford to be eating every time she got the least hungry.

But she could hunt for more food. Medea looked up through the branches and needles of the pines for the sun. *You keep him smiling on your right of the morning and burning on your left of evening, if anything happens to Momma Jack. And you pray to the Lord who put him there.* Medea stood above Momma Jack, who was sweating in a tight curl. She prayed that Jesus would leave her a little longer since she was so little and quiet. Just a while longer . . . .

From the top of a small rise she spotted a paw-paw tree. She ran and climbed it, managing to knock down a skirtful of fruit moving from one branch to another. Looking to her work below, she felt dizzy and grabbed a branch with both hands. A paw-paw hung near her and knocked against her head. She thanked the Lord and ate. Rubbing her tongue on the roof of her mouth, she let one of the big seeds shoot out to stick on a branch near her hand. A black ant crawled up to it and stopped, twisting his head whiskers in every direction. We all put here to work some foolishness, Medea thought.

In the distance behind, where they had already travelled, she saw smoke rise over the pine tops. They must have passed near a cabin in the night. That would be the dogs they heard. Momma Jack had said they should walk faster.

"They ain't barking at us. We too far off," Medea protested.

"Barking dogs mean no good one way or another. If your little child arms be too tired, give me your sack."

"Momma Jack, you ain't—"

"Don't try to take heaven from me, witch girl."

* * *

Late the next morning, Medea shaded her eyes and watched Momma Jack until her neck muscles hurt. Move, a voice said. She reached for Momma Jack's face, stopping just short. Momma Jack needed sleep.

But she could go hunt for more food. Medea looked up through the branches and needles of the pines for the sun. *You keep him smiling on your right of the morning and burning on your left of evening, if anything happens to Momma Jack. And you pray to the Lord who put him there.* Medea stood above Momma Jack, who was sweating. She prayed that Jesus would leave her a little longer since she was so tiny and quiet. . . .

From the top of a small rise she spotted a pawpaw tree. She ran and climbed it, managing to knock down a skirtful of fruit by moving from one branch to another. Looking to her work below, she felt dizzy and grabbed a branch with both hands. A pawpaw hanging near knocked against her head. She thanked the Lord and ate.

In the distance behind, where they had already traveled, she saw smoke rise over the pine tops. They must have passed near a cabin in the night. That would be the dogs they heard. Momma Jack had said they should walk faster.

"They ain't barking at us. We too far off," Medea protested.

"Barking dogs mean no good one way or another. If your little child arms be too tired, give me your sack."

The smoke drifted off and Medea smiled. Her, twice as big as Momma Jack, and the old woman still talking about her 'child arms.' Momma Jack had cared for her more than anyone alive—even Daniel, because Momma Jack didn't go off to <u>fight a war.</u> Momma Jack said she was the one who pulled Medea from her mother and took the sac from around her head. *Your eyes wasn't like other baby eyes. They was open before they was closed. And they looked around the room before you cried out, like they was inspecting and approving. That's why you had that veil over your face. You don't believe, you ask Aunt Phoebe. She was there, too.*

Medea twisted to climb down the tree, but stopped tight, her hand digging <u>into a knot.</u> Between pear-shaped leaves she could see the river.

"Momma Jack!" She hurried <u>down the tree,</u> letting <u>the paw-paw</u> roll against the trunk with a scratching rattle. On the ground, both her feet stopped tight.

Momma Jack be going to the river to die.

"Momma Jack!" Medea pulled hard at her dress and <u>she turned</u> to look for the river. But from the ground it couldn't be seen—only more trees and tangly bushes. Medea walked back to the tree and held onto its bark; she still couldn't see the water, even on tiptoes. *Momma Jack might never see it.* They could walk around forever. <u>They could eat apples and nuts and paw-paws and sleep in the pine needles forever. She stooped for the paw-paw she had dropped, then hugged the tree.</u>

Her and Momma Jack was walking, one arm over the other, in a bright field of corn. And each time the yellow-green tassels would tickle across Medea's eyes, Momma Jack would point and laugh. And her <u>thin black hands</u> would twist a husk off with a snap and shake it in Medea's face, which was laughing too. And when they stopped laughing, Momma Jack would tell a story <u>so they could</u> laugh again.

Medea opened her eyes. *The Father God is a time God and He say my time come soon.* What say did she have <u>against the Lord?</u> What say did she have to keep <u>another</u> believer down here in this land of sin? The Devil had just come through her as surely as he had through the pharaoh's magic men. She was evil and full of sin. That was the only power she had, and it showed through her yellow skin. Medea <u>bit softly</u> into the <u>grey bark</u> of the paw-paw tree.

"Momma Jack, Momma Jack."

Momma Jack was all afire. She was walking on the waters with her hands reaching up to the sky when a rip tore that blue down its middle and light flowed out like a river <u>in flood.</u> The light was so bright that Medea had to cover her eyes. But she could still see Momma Jack. Then Momma Jack sunk under the waters, and faces and hands all began to wave <u>to Medea.</u> The waters bubbled, and Momma Jack's fingers came up, weaving like they was reaching. Two angels held them and pulled Momma Jack until she was a glowing star high above.

The smoke drifted off and Medea smiled. Her, twice as big as Momma Jack, and the old woman still talking about her "child arms." Momma Jack had cared for her more than anyone alive—even Daniel, because Momma Jack didn't go off to fight some war. Momma Jack said she was the one who pulled Medea from her mother and took the sac from around her head. *Your eyes wasn't like other baby eyes. They was open before they was closed. And they looked around the room before you cried out, like they was inspecting and approving. That's why you had that veil over your face. You don't believe, you ask Aunt Phoebe. She was there, too.*

Medea twisted to climb down the tree, but stopped tight, her hand digging into a gummy knot. Between pear-shaped leaves she could see the river.

"Momma Jack!" She hurried down, letting the half-eaten pawpaw roll against the trunk with a scratching rattle. On the ground, both her feet stopped tight.

Momma Jack be going to the river to die.

"Momma Jack!" Medea pulled hard at her dress and turned to look for the river. But from the ground it couldn't be seen—only more trees and tangly bushes. Medea walked back to the tree and held onto its bark; she still couldn't see the water, even on tiptoes. *Tiny Momma Jack might never see it.* They could walk around forever. Medea hugged the tree.

Her and Momma Jack was walking, one arm over the other, in a bright field of corn. And each time the yellow-green tassels would tickle across Medea's eyes, Momma Jack would point and laugh. And her thin hands would twist a husk off with a snap and shake it in Medea's face, which was laughing too. And when they stopped laughing, Momma Jack would tell a story and they would laugh again.

Medea opened her eyes. *The Father God is a time God and He say my time come soon.* What say did she have to keep a believer down here in this land of sin? The Devil had just come through her as surely as he had through the pharaoh's magic men. She was evil and full of pride. That was the only power she had, and it showed through her yellow skin. Medea softly bit into the bark of the pawpaw tree.

"Momma Jack, Momma Jack."

Momma Jack was all afire. She was walking on the waters with her hands reaching up to the sky when a rip tore that blue down its middle and light flowed out like a river in spring flood. The light was so bright that Medea had to cover her eyes. But she could still see Momma Jack. Then Momma Jack sunk under the waters, and faces and hands all began to wave at Medea. The waters bubbled, and Momma Jack's fingers came up, weaving like they was reaching. Two angels held them and pulled Momma Jack until she was a glowing star high above.

Medea ran back to where they had slept <u>the morning.</u>

"Momma. Momma, the river is ahead. The river."

Her left eye opened, then <u>a right.</u>

"What you <u>be talking?"</u>

"The river. I saw it from a paw-paw tree."

"You be doing best to stay with your visions. We ain't near far enough yet."

"But I saw it. And I saw a vision, too." Medea <u>tightened her body,</u> sorry she had spoke.

"You see this old body going to heaven?" The woman jumped <u>and</u> grabbed Medea, <u>pulling at her face.</u> "Tell me, you see that?"

<u>Medea shook her head yes.</u>

"Praise God Jesus! I will shine like <u>the sun!"</u>

<u>Momma Jack tiptoed</u> to kiss Medea's cheeks, then held them between her hands. As the hands pushed up, Medea tried to smile.

"Let us go see this river of yours, child."

They passed the tree where Medea had first seen the river. Momma Jack stopped and pointed to the paw-paws on the ground, but Medea <u>shook her head and</u> kept her arms by her side.

"And what are you going to do when Momma Jack is taken into this river of yours?"

Medea shook her head.

"God is a time God. He put us on earth with the white man so we could see the bad ways. When He sees that we know enough of the bad ways, He take us up to heaven for the good. Not before we see, though. Judas, he went before. Do you want to be like him?" Momma Jack pointed again to the fruit, and Medea slipped them into her sheet.

"Now which way is this river of yours?"

Medea swept her arm and they began to walk.

When they reached the water, Momma Jack laughed. "You give me one of <u>those paw-paws you picked.</u> I need my strength to walk a lot farther than this piddling pretend creek. What kind of boat you think come up and down this? My momma and daddy come on a boat with a sail, not on two bumped logs."

Medea rushed Momma Jack and grabbed her in a hug, rubbing her nose in her hair and kissing her brow and temples.

"You'd better stop that. This trickle of water won't kill me, but you will yet."

Medea kept hold of Momma Jack's elbows and danced around her in a laugh.

"You stop now, before you have me <u>seeing visions."</u>

"Nigger wenches!"

They nearly fell. Medea smelled the air and her stomach went sick. She

Medea ran back to where they had slept that morning.

"Momma! Momma! The river is ahead. The river."

Her left eye opened, then her right.

"What you talking?"

"The river. I saw it from a pawpaw tree."

"You be doing best to stay with your visions. We ain't near far enough yet."

"But I saw it. And I saw a vision, too." Medea tightened, sorry she had spoke.

"You see this old body going to heaven?" The woman jumped and grabbed Medea. "Tell me, you see that?"

Medea nodded yes.

"Praise God Jesus! I will shine like the sun!" Momma Jack tiptoed to kiss Medea's cheeks, then held them between her hands. As the hands pushed up, Medea tried to smile.

"Let us go see this river of yours, child."

They passed the tree where Medea had first seen the river. Momma Jack stopped and pointed to the pawpaws on the ground, but Medea kept her arms by her side.

"And what are you going to do when Momma Jack is taken into this river of yours?"

Medea shook her head.

"God is a time God. He put us on earth with the white man so we could see the bad ways. When He sees that we know enough of the bad ways, He take us up to heaven for the good. Not before we see, though. Judas, he went before. Do you want to be like him?" Momma Jack pointed again to the fruit, and Medea slipped them into her sheet.

"Now which way is this river of yours?"

Medea swept her arm and they began to walk.

When they reached the water, Momma Jack laughed. "You give me one of those pawpaws. I need my strength to walk a lot farther than this piddling pretend creek. What kind of boat you think come up and down this? My momma and daddy come on a boat with a sail, not on two bumped logs."

Medea rushed Momma Jack and grabbed her in a hug, rubbing her nose in her hair and kissing her brow and temples.

"You better stop that. This trickle of water won't kill me, but you will yet."

Medea kept hold of Momma Jack's elbows and danced around her in a laugh.

"You stop now, before you have me seeing visions," Momma Jack said. "Nigger wenches!"

They nearly fell. Medea smelled the air and her stomach went sick. She turned to see a white man on a horse, his arms crossed in front of him.

"You two getting ready to take a social swim?"

"No sir, we just come for a drink."

"Come from where?"

"Master's, sir."

"Master's well run dry? Master who?"

Medea looked to the hooves of the white man's horse as they clumsily moved about, and she pulled her toes in.

"Master Wilson."

"That right, old woman?"

"Yes sir."

"Lived here my whole life. Know everybody. Don't know no Wilson's. Now where you two nigger wenches going? Be quick!" The Man walked his horse forward a step and Medea crossed her feet.

"My momma, sir, she be sick. We going across the river to the doctor."

"Onliest doctor is southwest in Cynthiana. Maybe you're going to a city doctor in Cincinnati, though."

"No sir. We're going to a root doctor. White doctor won't take care of Momma. She got shivers what all the niggers been dying of. Some white's too. Fourteen in six weeks."

The white man backed his horse off two steps. Medea looked up for a moment. He watched her hard and she wanted to cover all her body and arms, but she didn't move. Then he looked to Momma Jack as she coughed and spit on the ground, calling to the Lord to save her from the cold.

"Hell, why don't you all goddamn go to Ohio?" He pulled something from his saddle, and Medea thought he was going to shoot them. Instead, he threw a sack to the ground.

"Give what's left of that to Lincoln."

They watched the man ride off, then Momma Jack stooped to the ground to look in the sack.

"Hardtack."

They could still see him hugging the shore of the river, riding fast.

"White man hates himself when the Lord moves him to do good."

They crossed the river and moved as fast as they could that day in case the man changed his mind. They were forced to stop when they neared some open fields bearing only dried-out corn stalks.

"The Lord provides for all things. He knows when an old nigger is getting tired."

* * *

The moon passed to full that night.

"You know what that young Loomis was thinking?"

"I know he never thinks nothing good. He worse than his dead daddy."

"I seen him looking at you like a dog smelling passed ground."

Medea breathed in as deeply as she could.

turned to see a white man on a horse, his arms crossed meanly.

"You two getting ready to take a social swim?"

"No sir, we just come for a drink."

"Come from where?"

"Master's, sir."

"Master's well run dry? Master who?"

Medea looked to the hooves of the white man's horse as they clumsily moved about, and she pulled her toes in.

"Master Wilson."

"That right, old woman?"

"Yes sir."

"Lived here my whole life. Know everybody. Don't know no Wilsons. Now where you two nigger wenches going? Be quick!" The man walked his horse forward and Medea crossed her feet.

"My momma, sir, she be sick. We going across the river to the doctor."

"Onliest doctor is southwest in Cynthiana. Maybe you're going to a Northern doctor in Cincinnati, though."

"No sir. We're going to a root doctor. White doctor won't take care of Momma. She got the shivers what all the niggers been dying of. Some whites, too. Fourteen in six weeks."

The white man backed his horse off two steps. Medea looked up for a moment. He watched her hard and she wanted to cover her body and arms, but she didn't move. Then he looked to Momma Jack as she coughed and spit on the ground, calling to the Lord to save her from the shivers.

"Hell, why don't you all goddamn go to Ohio?" He pulled something from his saddle, and Medea thought he was going to shoot them. Instead, he threw a sack to the ground.

"Give what's left of that to Lincoln."

They watched the man ride off, then Momma Jack stooped to look in the sack. "Hardtack," she said.

They could still see him hugging the shore of the river, riding fast.

"White man hates himself when the Lord moves him to do good."

* * *

The moon passed to full that night.

"You know what that young Loomis was thinking?"

"I know he never thinks nothing good. He worse than his dead daddy."

"I seen him looking at you like a dog smelling passed ground."

Medea breathed in as deeply as she could.

Momma Jack didn't say <u>anything, and they just</u> kept walking.

"You won't be going back there when Momma Jack goes to heaven? You won't be going back looking for that dark boy Daniel?"

"He made his choice." Medea watched the moist leaves shining <u>on the moonlit ground.</u>

"Plenty of others will want a different choice. You bide your time for a good man with a strong head to match his arms."

A cloud passed over the moon. Medea watched Momma Jack staring at the great circle that was <u>left afterwards.</u>

"In two days, rain. It was like this when your mother died from having too many too fast." Momma Jack hadn't taken her eyes from the circle <u>around the moon.</u> "Do you know why you have the power?"

"Because I was born with a veil over my head."

"That's your white blood talking. What you say is right, but more than that is right. You was born with the power because the Lord knows how weak flesh is. He took your momma from the niggers, so he gave them you. You will help plenty of flesh on this earth if you find the rest of the power."

"What other power is there, Momma Jack?" Medea tried to follow the woman's gaze into the sky.

"When the Lord made the sun, He said, 'You can fly across this narrow line I scratch out everyday, no matter how hot or tired <u>you might be.</u> Or, you can stay underneath in the big ice celler where it is cool. If you work to fly across the line, you will be the brightest star in heaven and your sweat will water all the plants and flowers on this earth I'm showing you. And <u>their faces</u> will lift up to thank you come each morning. If you stay where <u>it is cool,</u> it will be dark and <u>the bugs will</u> keep you company.'"

Momma Jack looked down to the ground and shifted her sack.

"You see where that sun is <u>everyday—the same place as his sister."</u> <u>Momma Jack lifted Medea's face, but it dropped again.</u>

* * *

A day later, they both could smell the river. One walked with her head to the ground; the other with her nose in the air, breathing short and fast. Medea <u>shivered on feeling the hot thin shoulder brush against her own</u> <u>with their steps. She watched</u> her left foot move out, trying to keep pace with Momma Jack's right one. <u>For the first time,</u> she noticed that Momma Jack was missing two toenails.

"Momma, what happened to your <u>foot?"</u> The <u>quick</u> breaths stayed the same, and only the heat from Momma Jack's jostling shoulder answered. Medea asked her question again; it was the first time she had ever dared this. But the breath and the heat answered the same. Medea felt ashamed and watched the pine needles thinning to river rock and sand with each step.

Momma Jack didn't say anything for a minute, and they just kept on walking.

"You won't be going back there when Momma Jack goes to heaven? You won't be going back looking for that dark boy Daniel?"

"He made his choice." Medea watched the moist leaves shining in the moonlight.

"Plenty of others will want a different choice. You bide your time for a good man with a strong head to match his arms."

A cloud passed over the moon. Medea watched Momma Jack staring at the great circle that was left behind.

"In two days, rain. It was like this when your mother died from having too many too fast." Momma Jack hadn't taken her eyes from the circle. "Do you know why you have the power?"

"Because I was born with a veil over my head."

"That's your white blood talking. What you say is right, but more than that is right. You was born with the power because the Lord knows how weak flesh is. He took your momma from the niggers, so he gave them you. You will help plenty of flesh on this earth if you find the rest of the power."

"What other power is there, Momma Jack?" Medea tried to follow the woman's gaze into the sky.

"When the Lord made the sun, He said, 'You can fly across this narrow line I scratch out everyday, no matter how hot or tired <u>you might be.</u> Or, you can stay underneath in the big ice celler where it is cool. If you work to fly across the line, you will be the brightest star in heaven and your sweat will water all the plants and flowers on this earth I'm showing you. And <u>their faces</u> will lift up to thank you come each morning. If you stay where <u>it is cool,</u> it will be dark and the <u>bugs will</u> keep you company.'"

Momma Jack looked down to the ground and shifted her sack.

"You see where that sun is <u>everyday—the same place as his sister."</u> <u>Momma Jack lifted Medea's face, but it dropped again.</u>

A day later, they both could smell the river. One walked with her head to the ground, the other with her nose in the air, breathing short and fast. Medea watched her own left foot move out, trying to keep pace with Momma Jack's right. She noticed that Momma Jack was missing two toenails.

"Momma, what happened to your foot?"

The quick breaths stayed the same, and only the heat from Momma Jack's jostling shoulder answered. Medea asked her question again; it was the first time she had ever dared this. But the breath and the heat answered the same. Medea felt ashamed and watched the pine needles thinning to river rock and sand with each step.

The wet morning air crawled into Medea's body like it was a tub soaking a washcloth. She felt her breasts scratch against the cloth of her dress, then felt a drop of sweat drain between them onto her stomach. Soon, the dress was flattened against her. Dust was beginning to cake around Momma Jack's foot, in between the two toes missing the nails.

Medea held her left hand to her eyes. "When we get to the river, I bet we can cross and go to Ohio. Union people there will help us."

A pine needle had become stuck in Momma Jack's toes and Medea stooped to pick it out, but was stopped short as Momma Jack's hand gripped her arm and pulled her along.

"Show all the children heaven like you showed me, preacher woman. Do you hear?"

"Yes'm."

"Do you hear?"

"Yes'm."

"I know you do, child."

The feet stopped and Medea felt her elbow being dropped. She stared to the ground, then felt Momma Jack shiver and grab her arm all the tighter. Momma Jack's other hand pointed to what lay in front of them. Medea followed it to see the Ohio River lazily carrying a broken plank along its shining sheet of water.

Momma Jack fell against Medea and she could feel the old woman's hot skin even through her own dress. Momma Jack's mouth stayed open, grabbing for air.

"The water will save you, Momma. The water will cool you."

Momma Jack's mouth kept working, but nothing would come out. Medea dropped her satchel.

"The water, it will save you. It is cool."

They stumbled forward, Medea screaming as she stepped on a broken rock, but they reached the water. There, Medea cradled Momma Jack in her arms, "The cool water, Momma, how cool." Momma Jack's arm tore at her dress and throat in a wild thrash, then floated up with the current. It seemed to Medea that she heard a child's giggle. Then both of Momma Jack's arms began to float in the current, slapping against Medea's head each time she shifted off her stinging foot. Momma Jack's mouth slipped sideways into the water.

"No, Jesus!" Medea shuffled backwards, then slipped. She scooted along the bottom, frantically holding Momma Jack. At last she stopped, safe near the shore.

But both of Momma Jack's hands reached back into the current and her head bent down. Medea blew at a fly that landed on Momma Jack's neck and shook the woman. The thin arms slapped the water once, then straightened again to follow the current.

Medea rocked her Momma Jack.

"When we get to the river, I bet we can cross and go to Ohio. Union people there will help us."

A pine needle stuck between Momma Jack's bleeding toes and Medea stooped to pick it out, but Momma Jack gripped her arm and pulled her along.

"Show all the children heaven like you showed me, preacher woman. Do you hear?"

"Yes'm."

"Do you hear?"

"Yes'm."

"I know you do, child."

The hand dropped from Medea's elbow to point at what lay in front of them. Medea kept her eyes hard to the ground.

"Preacher woman!"

Medea looked up to see a broken plank being lazily carried by a shining sheet of water. Suddenly, Momma Jack's mouth jerked open for air and she fell against Medea. The old woman's skin burned hot even through their two dresses.

"The water will save you, Momma. The water will cool you."

Momma Jack's mouth kept working but nothing would come out or go in. Medea dropped her sheet.

"The water will save you. The water."

They stumbled forward, Medea screaming as she stepped on a broken rock. At the bank, she cradled Momma Jack and waded in.

"The water."

Momma Jack's arm tore with a single thrash, then floated up with the current. It seemed to Medea that she heard a child's giggle as Momma Jack's mouth slipped sideways into the river.

"No, Jesus!" Medea shuffled frantically backwards. At last she stopped near the shore.

But the two arms reached back into the current and the head bent down. A fly landed, and Medea shook it off the woman. The thin arms slapped the water once, then straightened again to obediently follow the river's flow.

Medea rocked her Momma Jack.

A man was walking over the water towards them, all on fire and glowing brighter than the river. His right hand held out a white robe <u>for Momma Jack; his left reached and</u> Medea could feel Momma Jack reaching, <u>too.</u> The man came closer until their hands touched, and the smell of honeysuckle floated along the river's water and angels splashed perfume up in Medea's face. Medea saw her own mother waving at her with another white robe in her hand. "Come," her mother's mouth said, "Come <u>now</u> with me and Momma Jack into the arms of sweet Paradise."

"Devil work!"

Medea kissed Momma Jack's gaping mouth and let her go. She watched as the brown dress floated alongside <u>the old woman's limp</u> hands. When Momma Jack had drifted nearly to the middle of the river, a log bumped her, <u>then somehow sucked her under.</u>

Medea waded to the shore and looked across the water to Ohio, letting the river's cool breeze dry her face. Hundreds of hands and eyes <u>awaited her.</u> She lifted two torn pages of the Word and the hands and eyes glowed happier than they had ever been. <u>"Life is a river,"</u> she sang out, <u>"that washes out our sins."</u> The faces hummed and nodded, for she had the power.

A man was walking over the water towards them, all on fire and glowing brighter than the river. His right hand held out a white robe; Medea could feel Momma Jack reaching for it. The man came closer until their hands touched, and the smell of honeysuckle floated along the river's water and angels splashed perfume up in Medea's face. Medea saw her own mother waving at her with another white robe in her hand. "Come," her mother's voice said. "Come with me and Momma Jack into the arms of sweet Paradise."

"Devil work!"

Medea kissed Momma Jack's gaping mouth and let her go. She watched as the brown dress floated alongside the limp hands. When Momma Jack had drifted nearly to the middle of the river, a log bumped her, then both disappeared.

Medea waded to the shore and looked across the water to Ohio, letting the river's cool breeze dry her face. Hundreds of hands and eyes were watching her. She lifted two torn pages of the Word and the hands and eyes glowed happier than they had ever been. "The Father God is a time God," she told them, "and He see our time is soon." The faces hummed and nodded, for she had the power.

17 Feb. 1982

Joe Taylor
342 Pennell Circle #2
Tallahassee, Florida 32304

Dear Joe Taylor,

Your story languished here for quite a while before it got to my desk; partly that was because I became editor on Sept. 1, and since then things have been very hectic, and it was a while before I began to catch up with old business. Partly it was simply ineptitude, because we really *don't* hang onto mss. that long, and I want to apologize first of all for the delay.

I like the story quite a bit. I have some questions, though, that I want to put to you, before I can talk to you about publishing it in TQ.

I have gone through it with a blue pencil marking a number of little things. For example, on p. 46, the reason I question the sentence beginning "Then her and Miss Wilma" is that it's not always clear from what vantage point the sentences are uttered. If it's Medea's mind at work, such a sentence seems fine. But I then doubt that Medea sees a hand "tremble" — wouldn't it "shake" for her? This slight (very slight) wobbling of tone of voice is one little thing. Other changes I suggest are just to keep it clear where the story is standing now and again, or who is speaking.

Would Medea use the word "loins"? I think not. Something earthier is needed there (p. 46). Likewise, "feeling her cool skin spring against his arms" — "spring" sounds too poetic, out of voice for her. Sometimes it just seems to be the wrong word; "granny knot" is a kind of boyscout technical term, isn't it, for the wrong kind of square knot. Is that word in Medea's mind? Likewise "knapsack" seems wrong, and "satchel." We're looking at a tied up sheet, aren't we?

What's the "watertower" that Becky props herself on (p. 52)?

(I don't always make such minute comments on stories, but this one seemed close to being very good indeed, and I wanted to give you my reactions. They continue:)

I'm not sure Momma Jack's fable adds much at all to the story. And in general I think the story's too long, so you might think about cutting the fable. In itself, it doesn't have a lot of power, I think, and so it is a temporary slackening, not a heightening, of the narrative (pp. 56-58).

Also, while Momma Jack is telling her story, it seems to be afternoon of the morning when Medea heard the Union soldiers. When the next section starts on p. 58, it is "late morning"—of the next day? If so, that needs clarifying, so the time sense isn't confusing and distracting to the reader. I think I would cut from "In the late morning" to "some foolishness, Medea thought." These paragraphs don't add anything I can see to the characterization, and feel, as narrative, rather slow. There's no forward progress in them, just description. But when it picks up "In the distance behind . . ." I feel the pace pick up again. Then you'd have to straighten out details like "to climb down the tree" (p. 60) so they would make sense without the part you've cut out.

You do want Medea to see the water, so I suppose cutting out that part entirely won't do; but that passage does need to be a lot shorter. Consider also cutting the lines marked in blue on p. 64, which don't add much, and move at a different, rather explanatory pace, whereas ending with Momma Jack's comment on whites seems very strong, to me.

Cut paragraph marked on p. 68? ("The wet morning air . . . missing the nails.")

I wonder if you could come back, at the very end, to "God is a time God," or something stronger than "Life is a river." I know you can't put much more than the appropriate platitude in her mouth, however powerful it is in *this* circumstance; but that particular one seems lacking in the historical weight that makes your story something more than costume drama or historical document. An objection of another reader here was that the whole basis of the story was improbable or rather pointless superstition; but I have argued that what makes the story good is that it places this religious faith in the historical circumstance that validated it as a true power, the power needed to get up and run north, out of the hands of the slaveholders; "How accept a story that is concerned with bogus belief?" my rationalist reader wondered. And I answered, it is not about belief, entirely, but about walking to freedom, driven by a certainty that was not available in another way, to those two women. And anyway, I'm too much a believer in a dozen different gods not to take at least some of the religious weight of the story seriously in its own right. I think the scene when Medea smells the death of the Union soldiers is wonderful; and indeed, I marked a later phrase for cutting out, because it only added an explanatory hint about this. I thought the first time through the story that their walk to the river was repetitive in its episodes. I think shortening the pawpaw scene will solve that — that's the only part that really drags. But any other compressing you can do will help it a lot, I think. If it were about 24 pp (still a long story) it would be better, move faster, provoke a more intense response. The ending troubles me the most, and I have already said why. I think it's necessary for you to make sure that the reader *cannot* look down on Medea and Momma Jack as if they were exhibits of the outlandish. I think you invest them with considerable dignity, and if you go through the story again, you might, I think, consider what tiny details might be altered to reinforce this without hammering at it.

I have made a photocopy of the story, so that I could send this copy back to you with my marks.

Would you consider making these small revisions? I don't usually line-edit a story at this stage, but after it's accepted. However, I wanted to give you this response immediately. If you could shorten it slightly, and perhaps put a little more surprise into the ending, though I don't wish you to falsify in any way what it is you wish to do in that last page — if you could do that, I would be extremely pleased to get the story back from you, and I would like to publish it in TriQuarterly, probably in the fall 1982 issue.

Payment would be $15 per printed page, on publication, and TQ would purchase first North American serial rights to the story, would reserve the right to republish it at any time in its own publication(s), and wishes to be acknowledged in any future publication in which the story appears as its first publisher. I can repeat all these details when I accept the story formally, after I see your revisions.

I hope you won't be offended by my insistence with all these details of revision. I only wish to make the story as strong as possible. I am a meddling editor because I'm not an editor at all, but a poet. And I've only been editor of this magazine for a little while.

Please accept my apologies again for the delayed response; please do let me know if you wish to work on the story some, and how you react to my suggestions. I hope in the meantime it has not been accepted elsewhere, because I would like TQ to have a chance at it.

Would you also tell me something about yourself? I don't know your other work, mentioned in your cover letter. Do you know my friend Hunt Hawkins, who teaches in the English dept. at FSU?

Best wishes.

Sincerely,
Reginald Gibbons
Editor
TriQuarterly

Suggestions for Discussion

1. A few of the changes in the final version of "The Power" are simply corrections of typos or grammatical errors—even a careful professional author can occasionally err. But many involve a thoughtful altering of a single word or phrase. Identify a few of these. Which contribute to clarity? Characterization? Atmosphere? Other?

2. Compare the changes of tense on pages 46-47. How is the final version clearer?

3. Compare the versions of Miss Wilma's dialogue on pages 44-45. How do the changes alter and/or clarify her character?

4. Throughout, in the final version the author has cut the satchel that Medea carries in the earlier draft. Why?

5. Do you agree with the editor that Momma Jack's fable pages 56-58 "doesn't have a lot of power," and represents a "temporary slackening, not a heightening"? Was the author well-advised to cut it?

6. How has the author seamed the story so that the excision of the fable doesn't interrupt the flow?

7. Identify other cuts. Which help the speed and flow of the story? Has anything been lost? What has been gained?

8. Identify the conflict, crisis, and resolution of "The Power." Describe how, and how radically, the resolution has been changed by the rewriting of the final paragraph.

9. If you were the editor, are there other changes you would ask the author to make?

RETROSPECT

Imagine for the moment that you are the editor of a magazine that is going to publish "The Cutting Edge" and "The Second Tree from the Corner." Are there any suggestions for changes that you would make to either author? What, and why?

WRITING ASSIGNMENTS

1. If you did assignment 4 in chapter 1 (the 100-word short story), rewrite your story making it at least three times as long, so that the development enriches the action and the characters.

2. If you did any other assignment from chapter 1, rewrite your piece improving it in any way you can, but also cutting its original length by at least one quarter.

3. A class project: Spend about a half-hour in class writing a scene that involves a conflict between two characters. Make a copy of what you write. Take one copy home and rewrite it. Send the other copy home with another class member for him or her to make critical comments and suggestions. Compare your impulses with those of your reader. On the following day, *forgive* your reader. On the day after that, rewrite the passage once more, incorporating any of the reader's suggestions that prove useful.

4. Identify the kernel of a short story from your experience of one of the following:

> first memory
> a dream
> parents
> loss
> unfounded fear
> your body
> yesterday

Write a page about your chosen subject. Outline the plot of a short story based on what you have written. Write the first page of the story. Rewrite it.

3

SEEING IS BELIEVING
Showing and Telling

Significant Detail
The Active Voice
Prose Rhythm
Mechanics

The purpose of all the arts, including literature, is to quell boredom. People recognize that it feels good to feel and that not to feel is unhealthy. "I don't feel anything" can be said in fear, defiance, or complaint. It is not a boast. The final absence of feeling is death.

But feeling is also dangerous, and it can be deadly. Both the body and psyche numb themselves in the presence of pain too strong to bear. People often (healthily and unhealthily) avoid good feelings — intimacy, power, speed, drunkenness, possession — having learned that feelings have consequences and that powerful feelings have powerful consequences.

Literature offers feelings for which we do not have to pay. It allows us to love, condemn, condone, hope, dread, hate, without any of the risks those feelings ordinarily involve. Fiction must contain ideas, which give significance to characters and events. If the ideas are shallow or untrue, the fiction will be correspondingly shallow or untrue. But the ideas must be experienced through or with the characters; they must be *felt* or the fiction will fail also.

Much nonfiction writing, including literary criticism, also wants to persuade us to feel one way rather than another, and some—polemics, propaganda—exhort us to feel strongly. But nonfiction works largely by means of reason and reasoning in order to appeal to and produce emotion. Fiction tries to reproduce the emotional impact of experience. And this is a more difficult task, because written words are symbols representing sounds, and the sounds themselves are symbols representing things, actions, qualities, spatial relationships, and so on. Written words are thus at two removes from experience. Unlike the images of film and drama, which directly strike the eye and ear, they are transmitted first to the mind, where they must be translated into images.

In order to move your reader, the standard advice runs, "show, don't tell." This dictum can be confusing, considering that all a writer has to work with is words. What it means is that your job as a fiction writer is to focus attention, not on the words, which are inert, nor on the thoughts these words produce, but through these to felt experience, where the vitality of understanding lies. There are techniques for accomplishing this—for making narrative vivid, moving, and resonant—which can be partly learned and can always be strengthened.

Significant Detail

In *The Elements of Style*, William Strunk, Jr., writes:

> If those who have studied the art of writing are in accord on any one point, it is on this: the surest way to arouse and hold the attention of the reader is by being specific, definite and concrete. The greatest writers . . . are effective largely because they deal in particulars and report the details that matter.

Specific, definite, concrete, particular details—these are the life of fiction. Details (as every good liar knows) are the stuff of persuasiveness. Mary is sure that Ed forgot to go pay the gas bill last Tuesday, but Ed says, "I know I went, because this old guy in a knit vest was in front of me in the line, and went on and on about his twin granddaughters"—and it is hard to refute a knit vest and twins even if the furnace doesn't work. John Gardner in *The Art of Fiction* speaks of details as "proofs," rather like those in a geometric theorem or a statistical argument. The novelist, he says, "gives us such details about the streets, stores, weather, politics, and concerns of Cleveland (or wherever the setting is) and such details about the looks, gestures, and experiences of his characters that we cannot help believing that the story he tells us is true."

A detail is "definite" and "concrete" when it appeals to the senses. It should be seen, heard, smelled, tasted, or touched. The most superficial survey of any bookshelf of published fiction will turn up dozens of examples of this principle. Here is a fairly obvious one.

It was a narrow room, with a rather high ceiling, and crowded from floor to ceiling with goodies. There were rows and rows of hams and sausages of all shapes and colors—white, yellow, red and black; fat and lean and round and long—rows of canned preserves, cocoa and tea, bright translucent glass bottles of honey, marmalade and jam. . . .

I stood enchanted, straining my ears and breathing in the delightful atmosphere and the mixed fragrance of chocolate and smoked fish and earthy truffles. . . . I spoke into the silence, saying: "Good day" in quite a loud voice; I can still remember how my strained, unnatural tones died away in the stillness. No one answered. And my mouth literally began to water like a spring. One quick, noiseless step and I was beside one of the laden tables. I made one rapturous grab into the nearest glass urn, filled as it chanced with chocolate creams, slipped a fistful into my coat pocket, then reached the door, and in the next second was safely round the corner.

THOMAS MANN, *Confessions of Felix Krull, Confidence Man*

The shape of this passage is a tour through the five senses. Mann lets us see: *narrow room, high ceiling, hams, sausages, preserves, cocoa, tea, glass bottles, honey, marmalade, jam.* He lets us smell: *fragrance of chocolate, smoked fish, earthy truffles.* He lets us hear: *"Good day," unnatural tones, stillness.* He lets us taste: *mouth, water like a spring.* He lets us touch: *grab, chocolate creams, slipped, fistful into my coat pocket.* The writing is alive because we do in fact live through our sense perceptions, and Mann takes us past words and through thought to let us perceive the scene in this way.

In the process, a number of ideas *not* stated reverberate off the sense images, so that we are also aware of a number of generalizations the author might have made but does not need to make: we will make them ourselves. Mann could have had his character "tell" us: *I was quite poor, and I was not used to seeing such a profusion of food, so that although I was very afraid there might be someone in the room and that I might be caught stealing, I couldn't resist taking the risk.*

This version would be very flat, and none of it is necessary. The character's relative poverty is inherent in the tumble of images of sight and smell; if he were used to such displays, his eyes and nose would not dart about as they do. His fear is inherent in the "strained unnatural tones" and their dying away in the stillness. His desire is in his watering mouth, his fear in the furtive speed of "quick" and "grab" and "slipped."

The points to be made here are two, and they are both important. The first is that the writer must deal in sense detail. The second is that these must be the details "that matter." As a writer of fiction you are at constant pains, not simply to say what you mean, but to mean more than you say. Much of what you mean will be an abstraction or a judgment. But if you write in abstractions or judgments, you are writing an essay, whereas if you let us use our senses and do our own generalizing and interpreting, we will be involved as participants in a real way. Much of the pleasure of reading comes from the egotistical sense that we are clever enough to understand. When the author explains to us or interprets for us, we suspect that he or she doesn't think us bright enough to do it for ourselves.

A detail is *concrete* if it appeals to one of the five senses; it is *significant* if it also conveys an idea or a judgment or both. *The window sill was green* is concrete, because we can see it. *The window sill was shedding flakes of fungus-green paint* is concrete and also conveys the idea that the paint is old, suggests the judgment that the color is ugly. The second version can also be seen more vividly.

Here is a passage from a young writer, which fails through lack of appeal to the senses.

> Debbie was a very stubborn and completely independent person, and was always doing things her way despite her parents' efforts to get her to conform. Her father was an executive in a dress manufacturing company, and was able to afford his family all the luxuries and comforts of life. But Debbie was completely indifferent to her family's affluence.

This passage contains a number of judgments we might or might not share with the author, and she has not convinced us that we do. What constitutes stubbornness? Independence? Indifference? Affluence? Further, since the judgments are supported by generalizations, we have no sense of the individuality of the characters, which alone would bring them to life on the page. What things was she always doing? What efforts did her parents make to get her to conform? What level of executive? What dress manufacturing company? What luxuries and comforts?

> Debbie would wear a tank top to a tea party if she pleased, with fluorescent earrings and ankle-strap sandals.
> "Oh, sweetheart." Mrs. Chiddister would stand in the doorway wringing her hands. "It's not *nice*."
> "Not who?" Debbie would say, and add a fringed belt.

Mr. Chiddister was Artistic Director of the Boston branch of Cardin, and had a high respect for what he called "elegant textures," which ranged from handwoven tweed to gold filigree, and which he willingly offered his daughter. Debbie preferred her laminated wrist bangles.

We have not passed a final judgment on the merits of these characters, but we know a good deal more about them, and we have drawn certain interim conclusions that are our own and not forced on us by the author. Debbie is independent of her parents' values, rather careless of their feelings, energetic, and possibly a tart. Mrs. Chiddister is quite ineffectual. Mr. Chiddister is a snob, though perhaps Debbie's taste is so bad we'll end up on his side.

But maybe that isn't at all what the author had in mind: the point is that we weren't allowed to know what the author did have in mind. Perhaps it was more like this version.

One day Debbie brought home a copy of *Ulysses*. Mrs. Strum called it "filth" and threw it across the sunporch. Debbie knelt on the parquet and retrieved her bookmark, which she replaced. "No, it's not," she said.

"You're not so old I can't take a strap to you!" Mr. Strum reminded her.

Mr. Strum was controlling stockholder of Readywear Conglomerates, and was proud of treating his family, not only on his salary, but on his expense account. The summer before he had justified their company on a trip to Belgium, where they toured the American Cemetery and the torture chambers of Ghent Castle. Entirely ungrateful, Debbie had spent the rest of the trip curled up in the hotel with a shabby copy of some poet.

Now we have a much clearer understanding of "stubbornness," "independence," "indifference," and "affluence," both their natures and the value we are to place on them. This time our judgment is heavily weighted in Debbie's favor — partly because people who read books have a sentimental sympathy with people who read books — but also because we hear hysteria in "filth" and "take a strap to you," whereas Debbie's resistance is quiet and strong. Mr. Strum's attitude toward his expense account suggests that he's corrupt, and his choice of "luxuries" is morbid. The passage does contain two overt judgments, the first being that Debbie was "entirely ungrateful." Notice that by the time we get to this, we're aware that the judgment is Mr. Strum's and that Debbie has little enough to be grateful for. We understand not only what the author says but that she means the opposite of what she says, and we feel doubly clever to get it; that is the pleasure of irony. Likewise, the judgment that the poet's book is "shabby" shows Mr. Strum's crass materialism toward what *we* know to be the finer things. At the very end of the passage, we are denied a detail that we might very well be given: *what* poet did Debbie curl up with? Again, by this time we understand that we are being given Mr. Strum's view of the situation and that it's Mr. Strum (not Debbie, not the author, and certainly not us) who wouldn't notice the difference between John Keats and Stanley Kunitz.

It may be objected that both rewrites of the passage are longer than the original. Doesn't "adding" so much detail make for long writing? The answer is yes and no. *No* because in the rewrites we know so much more about the values, activities, life-styles, attitudes, and personalities of the characters that it would take many times the length of the original to "tell" it all in generalizations. *Yes* in the sense that detail requires words, and if you are to realize your characters through detail, then you must be careful to select the details that convey the characteristics essential to our understanding. You can't convey a whole person, nor a whole action, nor everything there is to be conveyed about a single moment of a single day. You must select the significant.

No amount of concrete detail will move us unless it also implicitly suggests meaning and value. Following is a passage that fails, not through lack of appeal to the senses, but through lack of significance.

> Terry Landon, a handsome young man of twenty-two, was six foot four and broad shouldered. He had medium-length thick blond hair and a natural tan, which set off the blue of his intense and friendly long-lashed eyes.

Here we have a good deal of sense information, but we still know very little about Terry. There are so many broad-shouldered twenty-two-year-olds in the world, so many blonds, and so on. No value rises out of the images themselves, and the author is forced to provide judgments, from which we mainly understand that the author wants us to like Terry: Why else would he be handsome, natural, intense, *and* friendly? We refuse to like him, just as we would refuse to like him in life until we knew some individual or intimate thing that would set him apart from all the other blond blue-eyed twenty-two-year-olds in the world—until we felt we knew him, in fact. This sort of cataloguing of characteristics suggest an all-points bulletin: *male Caucasian, medium height, blond hair, last seen wearing gray raincoat.* Such a description may help the police locate a suspect in a crowd, but the assumption is that the identity of the person is not known. As an author, you want us to know the character individually and immediately. Often it is not necessary to give any APB information to achieve this objective.

> "Oh, I say, chaps." Benedict Pendleton was bouncing on his heels and pinching at the bridge of his nose. "Can I come along?"

We do not know the color of Pendleton's hair, his height, the brand of the shoes in question, or the shape of his nose. But we hear that he's anxious and we see that he's awkward; we conclude that the "chaps" probably don't want him along.

Such APB details can render an action as well as a character without rendering it meaningful.

Danny carried the high-heeled terrycloth slippers, the heels hooked over the edge of his hands, across the blue-flecked linoleum to Jane, who was frying eggs and hickory-smoked bacon in a cast-iron skillet at the stove. He put the right slipper on the formica top, took the spatula out of her hand, and handed her the left slipper. "Aren't your feet cold?" he asked.

This is better writing than the passages about Debbie and Terry. We have been allowed to see and hear and, perhaps, to smell the bacon. But we are impatient with the details because they leave us very much in doubt about the relationship between Danny and Jane, and it is this emotional value that interests us most. Is he concerned for her comfort or annoyed at her carelessness? Affectionate or stentorian? What importance is there, if any, in the color of the linoleum, the way he carries the slippers? Does his taking the spatula out of her hand signify high-handed male chauvinism, gentle intimacy, amusement? By what details could we understand these things?

The fact is that all our ideas and judgments are formed through our sense perceptions, and daily, moment by moment, we receive information that is not merely sensuous in this way. Four people at a cocktail party may *do* nothing but stand and nibble canapes and may *talk* nothing but politics and the latest films. But you feel perfectly certain that X is furious at Y, who is flirting with Z, who is wounding Q, who is trying to comfort X. You have only your senses to observe with. How do you reach these conclusions? By what gestures, glances, tones, touches, choices of words?

It may be that this constant emphasis on judgment makes the author, and the reader, seem opinionated or self-righteous. "I want to present my characters objectively/neutrally. I'm not making any value judgments. I want the reader to make up his own mind." This can be a legitimate position, and the whole school of the *nouveau roman* strives, in fiction, to be wholly objective and to eschew the judgmental. But this is a highly sophisticated experimental form, and it entails a difficulty and a danger. The difficulty is that human beings *are* constantly judging: *How was the film? He seemed friendly. What a boring class! Do you like it here? What did you think of them? That's kind of you. Which do you want? I'm not convinced. She's very thin. That's fascinating. I'm so clumsy. You're gorgeous tonight. Life is crazy, isn't it?*

The danger is that when we are not passing such judgments, it's because we aren't much interested. We are "indifferent." Although you may not want to sanctify or damn your characters, you do want us to care about them, and if you refuse to direct our judgment, you may be inviting our indifference. Usually, when you "don't want us to judge," you mean that you want our feelings to be mixed, paradoxical, complex. *She's horribly irritating, but it's not her fault.*

He's sexy, but there's something cold about it underneath. If this is what you mean, then you must direct our judgment in both or several directions, not in none.

Significant detail is necessary to the living quality of fiction even when we are not dealing with major characters or specific points in time. Joseph Conrad defined the writer's task as "a single-minded attempt to render the highest kind of justice to the visible universe." Flannery O'Connor, in a letter to a young author (Ben Griffith), advised, "You have to let the things in the story do the talking. . . . The first thing is to see the people every minute. . . . You have got to learn to paint with words. . . . Ford Madox Ford said you couldn't have somebody sell a newspaper in a story unless you said what he looked like" (from *The Habit of Being*).

In the following paragraph from Virginia Woolf's *Mrs. Dalloway*, we are introduced, through the protagonist's consciousness, to an anonymous crowd and four other characters, none of whom we ever see again.

> The crush was terrific for the time of day. Lords, Ascot, Hurlingham, what was it? she wondered, for the street was blocked. The British middle classes sitting sideways on the tops of omnibuses with parcels and umbrellas, yes, even furs on a day like this, were, she thought, more ridiculous, more unlike anything there has ever been than one could conceive; and the Queen herself held up; the Queen herself unable to pass. Clarissa was suspended on one side of Brook Street; Sir John Buckhurst, the old Judge on the other, with the car between them (Sir John had laid down the law for years and liked a well-dressed woman) when the chauffeur, leaning ever so slightly, said or showed something to the policeman, who saluted and raised his arm and jerked his head and moved the omnibus to the side and the car passed through.

The whole range of British class and class consciousness is conveyed in this brief passage through the use of significant detail. Clarissa's wry attitude toward the British middle classes is given credence by the fussiness of "parcels and umbrellas" and the pretension of "furs on a day like this." The judge's aristocratic hauteur is carried in the clichés he would use, "laid down the law" and "liked a well-dressed woman." That the Queen's chauffeur is described as leaning "ever so slightly" shows his consciousness of his own position's superiority to that of the policeman who "saluted" him but then exercises his own brand of authority as he "jerked his head" to order the traffic about. Only the Queen is characterized by no detail of object or action, and that she is not emphasizes her royal remoteness: "the Queen herself . . . the Queen herself."

Even a character who doesn't exist except as a type or function will come to life if presented through significant detail, as in this example from *The Right Stuff* by Tom Wolfe.

The matter mustn't be bungled!—that's the idea. No, a man should bring the news when the time comes, a man with some official or moral authority, a clergyman or a comrade of the newly deceased. Furthermore, he should bring the bad news in person. He should turn up at the front door and ring the bell and be standing there like a pillar of coolness and competence, bearing the bad news on ice, like a fish.

For a character who is just "a man," we have a remarkably clear image of this personage! Notice how Wolfe moves us from generalization toward sharpness of image, gradually bringing the nonexistent character into focus. First he has only a gender; then a certain abstract quality, "authority"; then a distinct role, "a clergyman or a comrade." Then he appears "in person" at the front door, then acts, ringing the doorbell. Finally, his quality is presented to us in the sharp focus of similes that also suggest his deadly message: *pillar, ice, fish.*

The point is not that an author must never express an idea, quality, or judgment. In the foregoing passages from Mann, Woolf, and Wolfe, each author uses several generalizations: *I stood enchanted, delightful atmosphere; the crush was terrific, more unlike anything there has ever been than one could conceive; the matter mustn't be bungled; coolness and competence.* The point is that in order to carry the felt weight of fiction, these abstractions must be realized through an appeal to the senses. It is in the details that they live.

Exciting discoveries in brain research, particularly the work done in brain evolution by Dr. Paul MacLean at the University of Washington, suggest that there may be a biological justification for the old literary rule "show, don't tell." Scientists conclude that the brain has evolved in three layers, from reptile to mammal to primate, each layer adapting to its successor but not being entirely replaced by it. Human beings therefore have a "triune brain," each layer operating with separate purposes and in different ways.

The reptile brain, or *R-complex*, operates ritualistically and repetitiously, always in the service of preservation of the individual or the species. At least twenty-eight separate functions for this brain have been identified, having to do with choosing the nest, preparing the nest, defending the nest, choosing a mate, displaying for the mate, and so forth.

The mammalian brain, or *limbic system*, apparently developed in such a way as to give mammals a greater range of choice in reacting to situations that threatened the individual or the species. This brain takes in information through the five senses, and then produces a wide variety of sense responses within the body.

The primate brain, or *neocortex*, also takes in information through the five senses, but it has a much more complex system of categorization, comparison, and connection, does not produce bodily responses, and is not particularly concerned with preservation. The human brain can therefore store and compare information in such a way as to remember, conclude, and predict. The capacity for empathy and altruism are made possible by these workings, since the human brain can compare without constantly referring itself to its own interest.

Here is an example of how the limbic system and the neocortex would react to the same situation: You break an egg on the edge of the skillet; the egg stinks and spreads. Your human brain takes this information in through the senses of sight and smell, and then rapidly concludes, remembers, and predicts: "That egg is rotten. That's the third time I've bought rotten eggs from Pearson's Market; I won't buy them there again. This afternoon I'll be able to get back there between class and supper, and I'm sure the clerk will give me my money back because he was so embarrassed about that bad chicken last month, poor guy." Meanwhile, the same information of sight and smell is being taken in by the mammalian brain, which reacts physically: your stomach surges, a spasm grips the back of your throat, your tongue jerks forward, and you gasp, "Gyaagh!" This may be a particularly literal example of a "gut reaction," but the slang contains a scientific truth: The physical reaction of the body to sense information *is what emotion is*.

Clearly, language and literature belong primarily to the human brain with its computerlike possibilities of comparison and symbolic meaning. Yet if as a fiction writer you deal in abstraction and comparison only, if you name qualities rather than provide sense images, you will not penetrate to the layer of the brain where emotion lies. If, however, you provide concrete details that appeal to the senses, both the human and the mammalian brain will be electrically excited, and your reader will both think *and* feel.

The Active Voice

If your prose is to be vigorous as well as vivid, if your characters are to be people who do rather than people to whom things are done, if your descriptions are to "come to life," you must make use of the active voice.

The active voice occurs when the subject of a sentence performs the action described by the verb of that sentence: *She spilled the milk.* When the passive voice is used, the object of the active verb becomes the subject of the passive verb: *The milk was spilled by her.* The passive voice is more indirect than the active; the subject is acted upon rather than acting, and the effect is to weaken the prose and to distance the reader from the action.

The passive voice does have an important place in fiction, precisely because it expresses a sense that the character is being acted upon. If a prison guard is kicking the hero, then *I was slammed into the wall; I was struck blindingly from behind and forced to the floor* appropriately carries the sense of his helplessness.

In general, you should seek the active voice in all prose and use the passive only when the actor is unknown or insignificant or you want to achieve special stylistic effects like the one above.

But there is one other common grammatical construction that is *effectively passive* in fiction and can distance the reader from a sense of immediate experience. All the verbs that we learn in school to call *linking verbs* are effectively passive because they invite complements that tend to be generalized or judgmental: *Her hair was beautiful. He was very happy. The room seemed expensively furnished. They became morose.* Let her hair bounce, tumble, cascade, or swing; we'll see better. Let him laugh, leap, cry, or hug a tree; we'll experience his joy.

Compare the passage about Debbie in the middle of page 80 with the rewrite in the middle of page 81. In the generalized original we have *was stubborn, was doing things, was executive, was able, was indifferent.* Apart from the compound verb *was doing*, all these are linking verbs. In the rewrite the characters *brought, called, threw, knelt, retrieved, replaced, said, reminded, justified, toured, spent,* and *curled up.* What energetic people! The rewrite contains two linking verbs: Mr. Strum *was stockholder* and *was proud*, and these properly represent static states, a position and an attitude.

One beneficial side effect of active verbs is that they tend to call forth significant details. If you say "she was shocked," you are telling us; but if you are to show us that she was shocked through an action, you are likely to have to search for an image as well. "She clenched the arm of the chair so hard that her knuckles whitened." *Clenched* and *whitened* actively suggest shock, and at the same time we see her knuckles on the arm of the chair.

To be is the most common of the linking verbs and also the most overused, but all the linking verbs invite generalization and distance. *To feel, to seem, to look, to appear, to experience, to express, to show, to demonstrate, to convey, to display* — all these suggest in fiction that the character is being acted upon or observed by someone rather than doing something. *She felt happy/sad/amused/mortified* does not convince us. We want to see her and to infer her emotion for ourselves. *He very clearly conveyed his displeasure.* It isn't clear to us. How did he convey it? To whom?

Most linking verbs have active as well as effectively passive forms, and it is important to distinguish them. *She felt sad* is effectively passive, but *she felt his forehead* is an action. If *the magician appeared*, he is acting; but if *he appeared annoyed*, then the verb is a linking verb and the only action implied is that of the observer who perceives this.

Linking verbs, like the passive voice, can appropriately convey a sense of passivity or helplessness when that is the desired effect. Notice that in the passage by Mann quoted earlier in this chapter, where Felix Krull is momentarily stunned by the sight of the food before him, the linking verbs are used: *It was a narrow room, there were rows and rows*, while all the colors and shapes buffet his senses. Only as he gradually recovers can he *stand, breathe, speak,* and eventually *grab*.

In the following excerpt from Lawrence Durrell's *Justine*, Melissa is trapped into a ride she doesn't want, and we feel her passivity with her while the car and the headlights take all the power.

> Melissa was afraid now.... She was aghast at what she had done.... There was no way of refusing the invitation. She dressed in her shabby best and carrying her fatigue like a heavy pack followed Selim to the great car which stood in deep shadow. She was helped in beside Nessim. They moved off slowly into the dense crepuscular evening of an Alexandria which, in her panic, she no longer recognized. They scouted a sea turned to sapphire and turned inland, folding up the slum, toward Mareotis and the bituminous slag-heaps of Mex where the pressure of the headlights now peeled off layer after layer of the darkness.

Was afraid, was aghast, was no way, was helped in—all imply Melissa's impotence. The active verbs that apply specifically to her either express weakness (*she followed*) or are negated (*no longer recognized*); the most active thing she can manage is to dress. In contrast, the "great car" *stands,* and it is inside, and under the power of, the car, that they *move off, scout, turn,* and *fold up;* it is the headlights that *peel off.*

I don't mean to suggest either that Durrell is deliberately using a linking verb here, the passive or the active voice there, or that as an author you should analyze your grammar as you go along. Most word choice is instinctive, and instinct is often the best guide. I do mean to suggest that you should be aware of the vigor and variety of available verbs and that if a passage lacks energy it may be because your instinct has let you down. How often *are* things or are they acted *upon,* when they could more forcefully *do?*

A note of caution about active verbs: make sparing use of what John Ruskin called the "pathetic fallacy"—the attributing of human emotions to natural and man-made objects. Even a description of a static scene can be invigorated if the houses *stand,* the streets *wander,* and the trees *bend.* But if the houses *frown,* the streets *stagger drunkenly,* and the trees *weep,* we will feel more strain than energy in the writing.

Prose Rhythm

Novelists and short-story writers are not under the same obligation as poets to reinforce sense with sound. In prose, on the whole the rhythm is all right if it isn't clearly wrong. But it can be wrong if, for example, the cadence contradicts the meaning; on the other hand, rhythm can greatly enhance the meaning if it is sensitively used.

> The river moved slowly. It seemed sluggish. The surface lay flat. Birds circled lazily overhead. Jon's boat slipped forward.

In this extreme example, the short, clipped sentences and their parallel structures—subject, verb, adverb—work against the sense of slow flowing movement. The rhythm could be effective if the character whose eyes we're using is not appreciating or sharing the calm; otherwise it needs recasting.

> The surface lay flat on the sluggish, slow-moving river, and the birds circled lazily overhead as Jon's boat slipped forward.

There is nothing very striking about the rhythm of this version, but at least it moves forward without obstructing the flow of the river.

> The first impression I had as I stopped in the doorway of the immense City Room was of extreme rush and bustle, with the reporters moving rapidly back and forth in the long aisles in order to shove their copy at each other, or making frantic gestures as they shouted into their many telephones.

This long and leisurely sentence cannot possibly provide a sense of rush and bustle. The phrases need to move as fast as the reporters; the verbiage must be pared down because it slows them down.

> I stopped in the doorway. The City Room was immense, reporters rushing down the aisles, shoving copy at each other, bustling back again, flinging gestures, shouting into telephones.

The poet Rolfe Humphries remarked that "*Very* is the least *very* word in the language." It is frequently true that adverbs expressing emphasis or suddenness—*extremely, rapidly, suddenly, phenomenally, quickly, immediately, instantly, definitely, terribly, awfully*—slow the sentence down so as to dilute the force of the intended meaning. "'It's a very nice day,'" said Humphries, "is not as nice a day as 'It's a day!'" Likewise, "They stopped very abruptly" is not as abrupt as "They stopped."

The rhythm of an action can be imitated by the rhythm of a sentence in a rich variety of ways. In the example above, simplifying the clauses helped create a sense of rush. James Joyce, in the short story "The Dead," structures a long sentence with a number of prepositional phrases so that it carries us headlong.

Lily, the caretaker's daughter, was literally run off her feet. Hardly had she brought one gentleman into the little pantry behind the office on the ground floor and helped him off with his overcoat than the wheezy hall-door bell clanged and she had to scamper along the bare hallway to let in another guest.

Lily's haste is largely created by beginning the sentence, "Hardly had she brought...," so that we anticipate the clause that will finish the meaning, "than the bell clanged...." Our anticipation forces us to scamper like Lily through the intervening actions.

Not only action but also character can be revealed and reinforced by sensitive use of rhythm. In Tillie Olsen's "Tell Me a Riddle," half a dozen grown children of a couple who have been married for forty-seven years ask each other what, after all this time, could be tearing their parents apart. The narrative answers:

> Something tangible enough.
> Arthritic hands, and such work as he got, occasional. Poverty all his life, and there was little breath left for running. He could not, could not turn away from this desire: to have the troubling of responsibility, the fretting with money, over and done with; to be free, to be *care*free where success was not measured by accumulation, and there was use for the vitality still in him.

The old man's anguished irritability is conveyed by syncopation, the syntax wrenched, clauses and qualifiers erupting out of what would be their natural place in the sentence, just as they would erupt in the man's mind. Repetition conveys his frustration: "He could not, could not..." and "to be free, to be *care*free...."

Just as action and character can find an echo in prose rhythm, so it is possible to help us experience a character's emotions and attitudes through control of the starts and stops of prose tempo. In the following passage from *Persuasion*, Jane Austen combines generalizations, passive verbs, and a staccato speech pattern to produce a kind of breathless blindness in the heroine:

> ...a thousand feelings rushed on Anne, of which this was the most consoling, that it would soon be over. And it was soon over. In two minutes after Charles's preparation, the others appeared; they were in the drawing room. Her eye half met Captain Wentworth's, a bow, a courtesy passed; she heard his voice; he talked to Mary, said all that was right, said something to the Miss Musgroves, enough to mark an easy footing; the room seemed full, full of persons and voices, but a few minutes ended it.

Sometimes a contrast in rhythm can help reinforce a contrast in characters, actions, attitudes, and emotions. In this passage from Frederick Busch's short story "Company," a woman whose movements are relatively confined watches her husband move, stop, and move again.

> Every day did not start with Vince awake that early, dressing in the dark, moving with whispery sounds down the stairs and through the kitchen, out into the autumn morning while groundfog lay on the milkweed burst open and on the stumps of harvested corn. But enough of them did.
> I went to the bedroom window to watch him hunt in a business suit.
> He moved with his feet in the slowly stirring fog, moving slowly himself with the rifle held across his body and his shoulders stiff. Then he stopped in a frozen watch for woodchucks. His stillness made the fog look faster as it blew across our field behind the barn. Vince stood. He waited for something to shoot. I went back to bed and lay between our covers again. I heard the bolt click. I heard the unemphatic shot, and then the second one, and after a while his feet on the porch, and soon the rush of water, the rattle of the pots on top of the stove, and later his feet again, and the car starting up as he left for work an hour before he had to.

The long opening sentence is arranged in a series of short phrases to move Vince forward. By contrast, "But enough of them did" comes abruptly, its abruptness as well as the sense of the words suggesting the woman's alienation. When Vince starts off again more slowly, the repetition of "moved . . . slowly stirring . . . moving slowly" slows down the sentence to match his strides. "Vince stood" again stills him, but the author also needs to convey that Vince stands for a long time, waiting, so we have the repetitions, "he stopped . . . His stillness . . . Vince stood. He waited. . . ." As his activity speeds up again, the tempo of the prose speeds up with another series of short phrases, of which only the last is drawn out with a dependent clause, "as he left for work an hour before he had to," so that we feel the retreat of the car in the distance. Notice that Busch chooses the phrase "the rush of water," not the flow or splash of water, as the sentence and Vince begin to rush. Here meaning reinforces a tempo that in turn reinforces meaning.

Mechanics

Significant detail, the active voice, and prose rhythm are techniques for achieving the sensuous in fiction, means of taking the reader past the words and the thought to feeling and experience. None is much use if the reader's eye is wrenched back to the surface; for that reason a word or two ought to be said here about the mechanics of the written language.

Spelling, grammar, and punctuation are a kind of magic; their purpose is to be invisible. If the sleight of hand works, we will not notice a comma or a quotation mark but will translate each instantly into a pause or an awareness of voice; we will not focus on the individual letters of a word but extract its sense whole. When the mechanics are incorrectly used, the trick is revealed and the magic fails; the reader's focus is shifted from the story to its surface. The reader is irritated at the author, and of all the emotions he was willing to experience, irritation at the author is not one.

There is no intrinsic virtue in standardized mechanics, and you can depart from them whenever you produce an effect that adequately compensates for the attention called to the surface. But only then. Unlike the techniques of narrative, the rules of spelling, grammar, and punctuation can be coldly learned anywhere in the English-speaking world — and they should be learned by anyone who aspires to write. Poor mechanics read instant amateurism to an editor. Perhaps a demonstrated genius can get away with sloppy mechanics, but in that case some other person must be hired to fill in. Since ghostwriters and editors are likely to be paid more per hour for their work than the author, this would constitute a heavy drain on the available resources of those who publish fiction.

Everything That Rises Must Converge

FLANNERY O'CONNOR

Her Doctor had told Julian's mother that she must lose twenty pounds on account of her blood pressure, so on Wednesday nights Julian had to take her downtown on the bus for a reducing class at the Y. The reducing class was designed for working girls over fifty, who weighed from 165 to 200 pounds. His mother was one of the slimmer ones, but she said ladies did not tell their age or weight. She would not ride the buses by herself at night since they had been integrated, and because the reducing class was one of her few pleasures, necessary for her health, and *free*, she said Julian could at least put himself out to take her, considering all she did for him. Julian did not like to consider all she did for him, but every Wednesday night he braced himself and took her.

She was almost ready to go, standing before the hall mirror, putting on her hat, while he, his hands behind him, appeared pinned to the door frame, waiting like Saint Sebastian for the arrows to begin piercing him. The hat was new and had cost her seven dollars and a half. She kept saying, "Maybe I shouldn't have paid that for it. No, I shouldn't have. I'll take it off and return it tomorrow. I shouldn't have bought it."

Julian raised his eyes to heaven. "Yes, you should have bought it," he said. "Put it on and let's go." It was a hideous hat. A purple velvet flap came down on one side of it and stood up on the other; the rest of it was green and looked like a cushion with the stuffing out. He decided it was less comical than jaunty and pathetic. Everything that gave her pleasure was small and depressed him.

She lifted the hat one more time and set it down slowly on top of her head. Two wings of gray hair protruded on either side of her florid face, but her eyes, sky-blue, were as innocent and untouched by experience as they must have been when she was ten. Were it not that she was a widow who had struggled fiercely to feed and clothe and put him through school and who was supporting him still, "until he got on his feet," she might have been a little girl that he had to take to town.

"It's all right, it's all right," he said. "Let's go." He opened the door himself and started down the walk to get her going. The sky was a dying violet and the houses stood out darkly against it, bulbous liver-colored monstrosities of a uniform ugliness though no two were alike. Since this had been a fashionable neighborhood forty years ago, his mother persisted in thinking they did well to have an apartment in it. Each house had a narrow collar of dirt around it in which sat, usually, a grubby child. Julian walked with his hands in his pockets, his head down and thrust forward and his eyes glazed with the determination to make himself completely numb during the time he would be sacrificed to her pleasure.

The door closed and he turned to find the dumpy figure, surmounted by the atrocious hat, coming toward him. "Well," she said, "you only live once and paying a little more for it, I at least won't meet myself coming and going."

"Some day I'll start making money," Julian said gloomily—he knew he never would—"and you can have one of those jokes whenever you take the fit." But first they would move. He visualized a place where the nearest neighbors would be three miles away on either side.

"I think you're doing fine," she said, drawing on her gloves. "You've only been out of school a year. Rome wasn't built in a day."

She was one of the few members of the Y reducing class who arrived in hat and gloves and who had a son who had been to college. "It takes time," she said, "and the world is in such a mess. This hat looked better on me than any of the others, though when she brought it out I said, 'Take that thing back. I wouldn't have it on my head,' and she said, 'Now wait till you see it on,' and when she put it on me I said, 'We-ull,' and she said, 'If you ask me, that hat does something for you and you do something for the hat, and besides,' she said, 'with that hat, you won't meet yourself coming and going.'"

Julian thought he could have stood his lot better if she had been selfish, if she had been an old hag who drank and screamed at him. He walked along, saturated in depression, as if in the midst of his martyrdom he had lost his faith. Catching sight of his long, hopeless, irritated face, she stopped suddenly with a grief-stricken look, and pulled back on his arm. "Wait on me," she said. "I'm going back to the house and take this thing off and tomorrow I'm going to return it. I was out of my head. I can pay the gas bill with that seven-fifty."

He caught her arm in a vicious grip. "You are not going to take it back," he said. "I like it."

"Well," she said, "I don't think I ought. . . ."

"Shut up and enjoy it," he muttered, more depressed than ever.

"With the world in the mess it's in," she said, "it's a wonder we can enjoy anything. I tell you, the bottom rail is on the top."

Julian sighed.

"Of course," she said, "if you know who you are, you can go anywhere." She said this every time he took her to the reducing class. "Most of them in it are not our kind of people," she said, "but I can be gracious to anybody. I know who I am."

"They don't give a damn for your graciousness," Julian said savagely. "Knowing who you are is good for one generation only. You haven't the foggiest idea where you stand now or who you are."

She stopped and allowed her eyes to flash at him. "I most certainly do know who I am," she said, "and if you don't know who you are, I'm ashamed of you."

"Oh hell," Julian said.

"Your great-grandfather was a former governor of this state," she said. "Your grandfather was a prosperous landowner. Your grandmother was a Godhigh."

"Will you look around you," he said tensely, "and see where you are now?" and he swept his arm jerkily out to indicate the neighborhood, which the growing darkness at least made less dingy.

"You remain what you are," she said. "Your great-grandfather had a plantation and two hundred slaves."

"There are no more slaves," he said irritably.

"They were better off when they were," she said. He groaned to see that she was off on that topic. She rolled onto it every few days like a train on an open track. He knew every stop, every junction, every swamp along the way, and knew the exact point at which her conclusion would roll majestically into the station: "It's ridiculous. It's simply not realistic. They should rise, yes, but on their own side of the fence."

"Let's skip it," Julian said.

"The ones I feel sorry for," she said, "are the ones that are half white. They're tragic."

"Will you skip it?"

"Suppose we were half white. We would certainly have mixed feelings."

"I have mixed feelings now," he groaned.

"Well let's talk about something pleasant," she said. "I remember going to Grandpa's when I was a little girl. Then the house had double stairways that went up to what was really the second floor—all the cooking was done on the first. I used to like to stay down in the kitchen on account of the way the walls smelled. I would sit with my nose pressed against the plaster and take deep breaths. Actually the place belonged to the Godhighs but your grandfather Chestny paid the mortgage and saved it for them. They were in reduced circumstances," she said, "but reduced or not, they never forgot who they were."

"Doubtless that decayed mansion reminded them," Julian muttered. He never spoke of it without contempt or thought of it without longing. He had seen it once when he was a child before it had been sold. The double stairways had rotted and been torn down. Negroes were living in it. But it remained in his mind as his mother had known it. It appeared in his dreams regularly. He would stand on the wide porch, listening to the rustle of oak leaves, then wander through the high-ceilinged hall into the parlor that opened onto it and gaze at the worn rugs and faded draperies. It occurred to him that it was he, not she, who could have appreciated it. He preferred its threadbare elegance to anything he could name and it was because of it that all the neighborhoods they had lived in had been a torment to him—whereas she had hardly known the difference. She called her insensitivity "being adjustable."

"And I remember the old darky who was my nurse, Caroline. There was no better person in the world. I've always had a great respect for my colored friends," she said. "I'd do anything in the world for them and they'd. . . ."

"Will you for God's sake get off that subject?" Julian said. When he got on a bus by himself, he made it a point to sit down beside a Negro, in reparation as it were for his mother's sins.

"You're mighty touchy tonight," she said. "Do you feel all right?"

"Yes I feel all right," he said. "Now lay off."

She pursed her lips. "Well, you certainly are in a vile humor," she observed. "I just won't speak to you at all."

They had reached the bus stop. There was no bus in sight and Julian, his hands still jammed in his pockets and his head thrust forward, scowled down the empty street. The frustration of having to wait on the bus as well as ride on it began to creep up his neck like a hot hand. The presence of his mother was borne in upon him as she gave a pained sigh. He looked at her bleakly. She was holding herself very erect under the preposterous hat, wearing it like a banner of her imaginary dignity. There was in him an evil urge to break her spirit. He suddenly unloosened his tie and pulled it off and put it in his pocket.

She stiffened. "Why must you look like *that* when you take me to town?" she said. "Why must you deliberately embarrass me?"

"If you'll never learn where you are," he said, "you can at least learn where I am."

"You look like a—thug," she said.

"Then I must be one," he murmured.

"I'll just go home," she said. "I will not bother you. If you can't do a little thing like that for me . . ."

Rolling his eyes upward, he put his tie back on. "Restored to my class," he muttered. He thrust his face toward her and hissed. "True culture is in the mind, the *mind*," he said, and tapped his head, "the mind."

"It's in the heart," she said, "and in how you do things and how you do things is because of who you *are*."

"Nobody in the damn bus cares who you are."

"I care who I am," she said icily.

The lighted bus appeared on top of the next hill and as it approached, they moved out into the street to meet it. He put his hand under her elbow and hoisted her up on the creaking step. She entered with a little smile, as if she were going into a drawing room where everyone had been waiting for her. While he put in the tokens, she sat down on one of the broad front seats for three which faced the aisle. A thin woman with protruding teeth and long yellow hair was sitting on the end of it. His mother moved up beside her and left room for Julian beside herself. He sat down and looked at the floor across the aisle where a pair of thin feet in red and white canvas sandals were planted.

His mother immediately began a general conversation meant to attract anyone who felt like talking. "Can it get any hotter?" she said and removed from her purse a folding fan, black with a Japanese scene on it, which she began to flutter before her.

"I reckon it might could," the woman with the protruding teeth said, "but I know for a fact my apartment couldn't get no hotter."

"It must get the afternoon sun," his mother said. She sat forward and looked up and down the bus. It was half filled. Everybody was white. "I see we have the bus to ourselves," she said. Julian cringed.

"For a change," said the woman across the aisle, the owner of the red and white canvas sandals. "I come on one the other day and they were thick as fleas—up front and all through."

"The world is in a mess everywhere," his mother said. "I don't know how we've let it get in this fix."

"What gets my goat is all those boys from good families stealing automobile tires," the woman with the protruding teeth said. "I told my boy, I said you may not be rich but you been raised right and if I ever catch you in any such mess, they can send you on to the reformatory. Be exactly where you belong."

"Training tells," his mother said. "Is your boy in high school?"

"Ninth grade," the woman said.

"My son just finished college last year. He wants to write but he's selling typewriters until he gets started," his mother said.

The woman leaned forward and peered at Julian. He threw her such a malevolent look that she subsided against the seat. On the floor across the aisle there was an abandoned newspaper. He got up and got it and opened it out in front of him. His mother discreetly continued the conversation in a lower tone but the woman across the aisle said in a loud voice, "Well that's nice. Selling typewriters is close to writing. He can go right from one to the other."

"I tell him," his mother said, "that Rome wasn't built in a day."

Behind the newspaper Julian was withdrawing into the inner compartment of his mind where he spent most of his time. This was a kind of mental bubble in which he established himself when he could not bear to be a part of what was going on around him. From it he could see out and judge but in it he was safe from any kind of penetration from without. It was the only place where he felt free of the general idiocy of his fellows. His mother had never entered it but from it he could see her with absolute clarity.

The old lady was clever enough and he thought that if she had started from any of the right premises, more might have been expected of her. She lived according to the laws of her own fantasy world, outside of which he had never seen her set foot. The law of it was to sacrifice herself for him after she had first created the necessity to do so by making a mess of things. If he had permitted her sacrifices, it was only because her lack of foresight had made them necessary. All of her life had been a struggle to act like a Chestny without the Chestny goods, and to give him everything she thought a Chestny ought to have; but since, said she, it was fun to struggle, why complain? And when you had won, as she had won, what fun to look back on the hard times! He could not forgive her that she had enjoyed the struggle and that she thought *she* had won.

What she meant when she said she had won was that she had brought him up successfully and had sent him to college and that he had turned out so well—good looking (her teeth had gone unfilled so that his could be straightened), intelligent (he realized he was too intelligent to be a success), and with a future ahead of him (there was of course no future ahead of him). She excused his gloominess on the grounds that he was still growing up and his radical ideas on his lack of practical experience. She said he didn't yet know a thing about "life," that he hadn't even entered the real world—when already he was as disenchanted with it as a man of fifty.

The further irony of all this was that in spite of her, he had turned out so well. In spite of going to only a third-rate college, he had, on his own initiative, come out with a first-rate education; in spite of growing up dominated by a small mind, he had ended up with a large one; in spite of all her foolish views, he was free of prejudice and unafraid to face facts. Most miraculous of all, instead of being blinded by love for her as she was for him, he had cut himself emotionally free of her and could see her with complete objectivity. He was not dominated by his mother.

The bus stopped with a sudden jerk and shook him from his meditation. A woman from the back lurched forward with little steps and barely escaped falling in his newspaper as she righted herself. She got off and a large Negro got on. Julian kept his paper lowered to watch. It gave him a certain satisfaction to see injustice in daily operation. It confirmed his view that with a few exceptions there was no one worth knowing within a radius of three hundred miles. The Negro was well dressed and carried a brief-case. He looked around and then sat down on the other end of the seat where the woman with the red and white canvas sandals was sitting. He immediately unfolded a newspaper and obscured himself behind it. Julian's mother's elbow at once prodded insistently into his ribs. "Now you see why I won't ride on these buses by myself," she whispered.

The woman with the red and white canvas sandals had risen at the same time the Negro sat down and had gone further back in the bus and taken the seat of the woman who had got off. His mother leaned forward and cast her an approving look.

Julian rose, crossed the aisle, and sat down in the place of the woman with the canvas sandals. From this position, he looked serenely across at his mother. Her face had turned an angry red. He stared at her, making his eyes the eyes of a stranger. He felt his tension suddenly lift as if he had openly declared war on her.

He would have liked to get in conversation with the Negro and to talk with him about art or politics or any subject that would be above the comprehension of those around them, but the man remained entrenched behind his paper. He was either ignoring the change of seating or had never noticed it. There was no way for Julian to convey his sympathy.

His mother kept her eyes fixed reproachfully on his face. The woman with the protruding teeth was looking at him avidly as if he were a type of monster new to her.

"Do you have a light?" he asked the Negro.

Without looking away from his paper, the man reached in his pocket and handed him a packet of matches.

"Thanks," Julian said. For a moment he held the matches foolishly. A NO SMOKING sign looked down upon him from over the door. This alone would not have deterred him; he had no cigarettes. He had quit smoking some months before because he could not afford it. "Sorry," he muttered and handed back the matches. The Negro lowered the paper and gave him an annoyed look. He took the matches and raised the paper again.

His mother continued to gaze at him but she did not take advantage of his momentary discomfort. Her eyes retained their battered look. Her face seemed to be unnaturally red, as if her blood pressure had risen. Julian allowed no glimmer of sympathy to show on his face. Having got the advantage, he wanted desperately to keep it and carry it through. He would have liked to teach her a lesson that would last her a while, but there seemed no way to continue the point. The Negro refused to come out from behind his paper.

Julian folded his arms and looked stolidly before him, facing her but as if he did not see her, as if he had ceased to recognize her existence. He visualized a scene in which, the bus having reached their stop, he would remain in his seat and when she said, "Aren't you going to get off?" he would look at her as at a stranger who had rashly addressed him. The corner they got off on was usually deserted, but it was well lighted and it would not hurt her to walk by herself the four blocks to the Y. He decided to wait until the time came and then decide whether or not he would let her get off by herself. He would have to be at the Y at ten to bring her back, but he could leave her wondering if he was going to show up. There was no reason for her to think she could always depend on him.

He retired again into the high-ceilinged room sparsely settled with large pieces of antique furniture. His soul expanded momentarily but then he became aware of his mother across from him and the vision shriveled. He studied her coldly. Her feet in little pumps dangled like a child's and did not quite reach the floor. She was training on him an exaggerated look of reproach. He felt completely detached from her. At that moment he could with pleasure have slapped her as he would have slapped a particularly obnoxious child in his charge.

He began to imagine various unlikely ways by which he could teach her a lesson. He might make friends with some distinguished Negro professor or lawyer and bring him home to spend the evening. He would be entirely justified but her blood pressure would rise to 300. He could not push her to the extent of making her have a stroke, and moreover, he had never been successful at making any Negro friends. He had tried to strike up an acquaintance on the bus with some of the better types, with ones that looked like professors or ministers or lawyers. One morning he had sat down next to a distinguished-looking dark brown man who had answered his questions with a sonorous solemnity but who had turned out to be an undertaker. Another day he had sat down beside a cigar-smoking Negro with a diamond ring on his finger, but after a few stilted pleasantries, the Negro had rung the buzzer and risen, slipping two lottery tickets into Julian's hand as he climbed over him to leave.

He imagined his mother lying desperately ill and his being able to secure only a Negro doctor for her. He toyed with that idea for a few minutes and then dropped it for a momentary vision of himself participating as a sympathizer in a sit-in demonstration. This was possible but he did not linger with it. Instead, he approached the ultimate horror. He brought home a beautiful suspiciously Negroid woman. Prepare yourself, he said. There is nothing you can do about it. This is the woman I've chosen. She's intelligent, dignified, even good, and she's suffered and she hasn't thought it *fun*. Now persecute us, go ahead and persecute us. Drive her out of here, but remember, you're driving me too. His eyes were narrowed and through the indignation he had generated, he saw his mother across the aisle, purple-faced, shrunken to the dwarf-like proportions of her moral nature, sitting like a mummy beneath the ridiculous banner of her hat.

He was tilted out of his fantasy again as the bus stopped. The door opened with a sucking hiss and out of the dark a large, gaily dressed, sullen-looking colored woman got on with a little boy. The child, who might have been four, had on a short plaid suit and a Tyrolean hat with a blue feather in it. Julian hoped that he would sit down beside him and that the woman would push in beside his mother. He could think of no better arrangement.

As she waited for her tokens, the woman was surveying the seating possibilities—he hoped with the idea of sitting where she was least wanted. There was something familiar-looking about her but Julian could not place what it was. She was a giant of a woman. Her face was set not only to meet opposition but to seek it out. The downward tilt of her large lower lip was like a warning sign: DON'T TAMPER WITH ME. Her bulging figure was encased in a green crepe dress and her feet overflowed in red shoes. She had on a hideous hat. A purple velvet flap came down on one side of it and stood up on the other; the rest of it was green and looked like a cushion with the stuffing out. She carried a mammoth red pocketbook that bulged throughout as if it were stuffed with rocks.

To Julian's disappointment, the little boy climbed up on the empty seat beside his mother. His mother lumped all children, black and white, into the common category, "cute," and she thought little Negroes were on the whole cuter than little white children. She smiled at the little boy as he climbed on the seat.

Meanwhile the woman was bearing down upon the empty seat beside

Julian. To his annoyance, she squeezed herself into it. He saw his mother's face change as the woman settled herself next to him and he realized with satisfaction that this was more objectionable to her than it was to him. Her face seemed almost gray and there was a look of dull recognition in her eyes, as if suddenly she had sickened at some awful confrontation. Julian saw that it was because she and the woman had, in a sense, swapped sons. Though his mother would not realize the symbolic significance of this, she would feel it. His amusement showed plainly on his face.

The woman next to him muttered something unintelligible to herself. He was conscious of a kind of bristling next to him, a muted growling like that of an angry cat. He could not see anything but the red pocketbook upright on the bulging green thighs. He visualized the woman as she had stood waiting for her tokens — the ponderous figure, rising from the red shoes upward over the solid hips, the mammoth bosom, the haughty face, to the green and purple hat.

His eyes widened.

The vision of the two hats, identical, broke upon him with the radiance of a brilliant sunrise. His face was suddenly lit with joy. He could not believe that Fate had thrust upon his mother such a lesson. He gave a loud chuckle so that she would look at him and see that he saw. She turned her eyes on him slowly. The blue in them seemed to have turned a bruised purple. For a moment he had an uncomfortable sense of her innocence, but it lasted only a second before principle rescued him. Justice entitled him to laugh. His grin hardened until it said to her as plainly as if he were saying aloud: Your punishment exactly fits your pettiness. This should teach you a permanent lesson.

Her eyes shifted to the woman. She seemed unable to bear looking at him and to find the woman preferable. He became conscious again of the bristling presence at his side. The woman was rumbling like a volcano about to become active. His mother's mouth began to twitch slightly at one corner. With a sinking heart, he saw incipient signs of recovery on her face and realized that this was going to strike her suddenly as funny and was going to be no lesson at all. She kept her eyes on the woman and an amused smile came over her face as if the woman were a monkey that had stolen her hat. The little Negro was looking up at her with large fascinated eyes. He had been trying to attract her attention for some time.

"Carver!" the woman said suddenly. "Come heah!"

When he saw that the spotlight was on him at last, Carver drew his feet up and turned himself toward Julian's mother and giggled.

"Carver!" the woman said. "You heah me? Come heah!"

Carver slid down from the seat but remained squatting with his back against the base of it, his head turned slyly around toward Julian's mother, who was smiling at him. The woman reached a hand across the aisle and snatched him to her. He righted himself and hung backwards on her knees, grinning at Julian's mother. "Isn't he cute?" Julian's mother said to the woman with the protruding teeth.

"I reckon he is," the woman said without conviction.

The Negress yanked him upright but he eased out of her grip and shot across the aisle and scrambled, giggling wildly, onto the seat beside his love.

"I think he likes me," Julian's mother said, and smiled at the woman. It was the smile she used when she was being particularly gracious to an inferior. Julian saw everything lost. The lesson had rolled off her like rain on a roof.

The woman stood up and yanked the little boy off the seat as if she were snatching him from contagion. Julian could feel the rage in her at having no weapon like his mother's smile. She gave the child a sharp slap across his leg. He howled once and then thrust his head into her stomach and kicked his feet against her shins. "Be-have," she said vehemently.

The bus stopped and the Negro who had been reading the newspaper got off. The woman moved over and set the little boy down with a thump between herself and Julian. She held him firmly by the knee. In a moment he put his hands in front of his face and peeped at Julian's mother through his fingers.

"I see yoooooooo!" she said and put her hand in front of her face and peeped at him.

The woman slapped his hand down. "Quit yo' foolishness," she said, "before I knock the living Jesus out of you!"

Julian was thankful that the next stop was theirs. He reached up and pulled the cord. The woman reached up and pulled it at the same time. Oh my God, he thought. He had the terrible intuition that when they got off the bus together, his mother would open her purse and give the little boy a nickel. The gesture would be as natural to her as breathing. The bus stopped and the woman got up and lunged to the front, dragging the child, who wished to stay on, after her. Julian and his mother got up and followed. As they neared the door, Julian tried to relieve her of her pocketbook.

"No," she murmured. "I want to give the little boy a nickel."

"No!" Julian hissed. "No!"

She smiled down at the child and opened her bag. The bus door opened and the woman picked him up by the arm and descended with him, hanging at her hip. Once in the street she set him down and shook him.

Julian's mother had to close her purse while she got down the bus step but as soon as her feet were on the ground, she opened it again and began to rummage inside. "I can't find but a penny," she whispered, "but it looks like a new one."

"Don't do it!" Julian said fiercely between his teeth. There was a streetlight on the corner and she hurried to get under it so she could better see into her pocketbook. The woman was heading off rapidly down the street with the child still hanging backward on her hand.

"Oh little boy!" Julian's mother called and took a few quick steps and caught up with them just beyond the lamp-post. "Here's a bright new penny for you," and she held out the coin, which shone bronze in the dim light.

The huge woman turned and for a moment stood, her shoulders lifted and her face frozen with frustrated rage, and stared at Julian's mother. Then all at once she seemed to explode like a piece of machinery that had been given one ounce of pressure too much. Julian saw the black fist swing out with the red pocketbook. He shut his eyes and cringed as he heard the woman shout, "He don't take nobody's pennies!" When he opened his eyes, the woman was disappearing down the street with the little boy staring wide-eyed over her shoulder. Julian's mother was sitting on the sidewalk.

"I told you not to do that," Julian said angrily. "I told you not to do that!"

He stood over her for a minute, gritting his teeth. Her legs were stretched out in front of her and her hat was on her lap. He squatted down and looked her in the face. It was totally expressionless. "You got exactly what you deserved," he said. "Now get up."

He picked up her pocketbook and put what had fallen out back in it. He picked the hat up off her lap. The penny caught his eye on the sidewalk and he picked that up and let it drop before her eyes into the purse. Then he stood up and leaned over and held his hands out to pull her up. She remained immobile. He sighed. Rising above them on either side were black apartment buildings, marked with irregular rectangles of light. At the end of the block a man came out of a door and walked off in the opposite direction. "All right," he said, "suppose somebody happens by and wants to know why you're sitting on the sidewalk?"

She took the hand and, breathing hard, pulled heavily up on it and then stood for a moment, swaying slightly as if the spots of light in the darkness were circling around her. Her eyes, shadowed and confused, finally settled on his face. He did not try to conceal his irritation. "I hope this teaches you a lesson," he said. She leaned forward and her eyes raked his face. She seemed trying to determine his identity. Then, as if she found nothing familiar about him, she started off with a headlong movement in the wrong direction.

"Aren't you going on to the Y?" he asked.

"Home," she muttered.

"Well, are we walking?"

For answer she kept going. Julian followed along, his hands behind him. He saw no reason to let the lesson she had had go without backing it up with an explanation of its meaning. She might as well be made to understand what had happened to her. "Don't think that was just an uppity Negro woman," he said. "That was the whole colored race which will no longer take your condescending pennies. That was your black double. She can wear the same hat as you, and to be sure, " he added gratuitously (because he thought it was funny), "it looked better on her than it did on you. What all this means," he said, "is that the old world is gone. The old manners are obsolete and your graciousness is not worth a damn." He thought bitterly of the house that had been lost for him. "You aren't who you think you are," he said.

She continued to plow ahead, paying no attention to him. Her hair had come undone on one side. She dropped her pocketbook and took no notice. He stooped and picked it up and handed it to her but she did not take it.

"You needn't act as if the world had come to an end," he said, "because it hasn't. From now on you've got to live in a new world and face a few realities for a change. Buck up," he said, "it won't kill you."

She was breathing fast.

"Let's wait on the bus," he said.

"Home," she said thickly.

"I hate to see you behave like this," he said. "Just like a child. I should be able to expect more of you." He decided to stop where he was and make her stop and wait for a bus. "I'm not going any farther," he said, stopping. "We're going on the bus."

She continued to go on as if she had not heard him. He took a few steps and caught her arm and stopped her. He looked into her face and caught his breath. He was looking into a face he had never seen before. "Tell Grandpa to come get me," she said.

He stared, stricken.

"Tell Caroline to come get me," she said.

Stunned, he let her go and she lurched forward again, walking as if one leg were shorter than the other. A tide of darkness seemed to be sweeping her from him. "Mother!" he cried. "Darling, sweetheart, wait!" Crumpling, she fell to the pavement. He dashed forward and fell at her side, crying, "Mamma, Mamma!" He turned her over. Her face was fiercely distorted. One eye, large and staring, moved slightly to the left as if it had become unmoored. The other remained fixed on him, raked his face again, found nothing and closed.

"Wait here, wait here!" he cried and jumped up and began to run for help toward a cluster of lights he saw in the distance ahead of him. "Help, help!" he shouted, but his voice was thin, scarcely a thread of sound. The lights drifted farther away the faster he ran and his feet moved numbly as if they carried him nowhere. The tide of darkness seemed to sweep him back to her, postponing from moment to moment his entry into the world of guilt and sorrow.

1. This story contains a conflict about "color," black and white. In what way does O'Connor use details of bright color — red, green, purple, yellow—to bring this conflict into focus? How do these colors further the plot?

2. The third paragraph of the story details the fatal hat. Whose are the judgments in this paragraph, the author's or Julian's? How do you know? Try substituting passive verbs for active in the description of the hat. What is the effect?

3. Contrast the images of the Godhigh house as the mother remembers it on page 95 with both Julian's memory of it in the next paragraph and his fantasies about it. How much information do these three sets of details convey about the house, the way the world has changed, the conflict between Julian and his mother, the contrasts and similarities in their characters? How does O'Connor direct your sympathies and judgments in these two paragraphs?

4. The paragraph beginning, "The lighted bus appeared on top of the next hill" (page 96), is arranged in sentences with parallel structures: subject, verb, object. Why? What is the emotional impact of this monotonous rhythm?

5. Analyze the arrival of the black woman in the green-and-purple hat for the active and passive voice (page 100). The paragraph beginning, "He was tilted out of his fantasy," uses mainly active verbs, whereas the next paragraph uses mainly linking verbs. Why?

6. On page 103, the paragraph beginning, "He stood over her for a minute," and the following two paragraphs report, in a relatively external way, what happens in a scene highly charged with emotion. What are the generalizations and judgments not "told" in this passage but conveyed through detail and action?

7. Identify all the "story" elements of "Everything That Rises Must Converge" that are not part of the "plot." Why must the plot begin where it does? Why is it nevertheless necessary to reveal elements of the past in the course of the action?

Widow Water

FREDERICK BUSCH

What to know about pain is how little we do to deserve it, how simple it is to give, how hard to lose. I'm a plumber. I dig for what's wrong. I should know. And what I think of now as I remember pain is the fat young man and his child, their staggering house, the basement filled with death and dark water, the small perfect boy on the stone cellar steps who wept, the widow's coffee gone cold.

They called on Friday to complain that the pump in their basement wouldn't work. Theirs is shallow-well country, a couple of miles from the college, a place near the fast wide river that once ran the mill that all the houses of the town depended on. The railroad came, the town grew, the large white clapboard houses spread. By the time their seedlings were in the middle growth, the mill had failed, the houses had run to blisters of rotted wood on the siding and to gaps in the black and green roofs. The old ones were nearly all dead and the railroad came twice a day, from Utica to Binghamton, to Utica from Binghamton, carrying sometimes some freight, sometimes a car of men who maintain d the nearly useless track. And the new people came, took their children for walks on the river to the stone foundations of the mill. They looked at the water and went home. People now don't know the water as they should. I'm a plumber, I should know.

I told him I couldn't come on a Friday afternoon in April, when the rains were opening seams and seals and cellars all through the county. Bella was making coffee for us while I took the call, and I snapped my fingers for her to turn around. She did, all broad—not fat, though—and full of colors—red in her face, yellow in her hair going gray, the gold in her tooth, her eyes blue as pottery—and I pointed at the phone. She mouthed a mimic "Today, today, today," and I nodded, and she nodded back and poured the almost boiling water out into the instant coffee, which dissolved.

He said, "So you see, sir, we can use your help."

I said, "Yessir, sounds like a problem."

"No water, and we've got a boy who isn't toilet-trained. It gets kind of messy."

"I imagine."

"So do you think you could . . ."

"Yessir?"

"Come kind of soon?"

"Oh, I'll come kind of soon. It just won't be today."

"You're sure you couldn't . . ."

"Yessir."

"Come today?"

"Yessir."

"Yes sir, what?"

"Yessir, I'm sure I can't come."

Bella rapped on the table with her big knuckles to tell me to come and sit. I nodded, pointed at the telephone, waited for him to try once more. He was from the college—he would try once more.

He said, "But no water—for how long? The weekend? All week?"

I heard a woman whisper in the background with the harshness of a wife making peace, and then he said, "Uh—I mean, do you know when you can come?"

I said, "When're you up?"

"Excuse me?"

"When do you wake up?"

"We'll be up. Just tell me when."

I said, "I'll be there tomorrow morning, early, if that's all right."

"I mean, how early?"

"You get up, Mr. Samuels, and you have yourself a comfortable breakfast, and I'll be there for a cup of your coffee."

He hung on the line, waiting for more. I gave him nothing more, and he said, "Thanks. I mean, we'll see you tomorrow, then. Thank you."

"Thank *you* for calling, Mr. Samuels, and I'll see you soon."

He said, "Not soon enough," and chuckled and didn't mean the laugh.

I chuckled back and meant it, because coffee was waiting, and Bella, and a quiet hour before I went back out to clear a lonely lady's pipe in a fifty-foot well. I said, "Good-bye, Mr. Samuels."

He said, "Yes," which meant he was listening to his whispering wife, not me, and then he said, "Yes, good-bye, thank you very much, see you soon."

I blew on my coffee and Bella turned the radio off—she'd been listening to it low to hear if she'd won the fur coat someone in Oneida was giving away—and we sat and ate bran muffins with her blueberry jam and talked about nothing much; we said most of it by sitting and eating too much together after so many years of coffee and preserves.

After a while she said, "A professor with a problem."

"His pump won't turn off. Somebody sold him a good big Gould brand-new when he moved in last summer, and now it won't turn off and he's mad as hell."

"Well, I can understand that. They hear that motor banging away and think it's going to explode and burn their house down. They're city people, I suppose."

"Aren't they ever. I know the house. McGregory's old place near the Keeper farm. It needs work."

"Which they wouldn't know how to do."

"Or be able to afford," I said. "He's a young one and a new professor. He wouldn't earn much more than the boys on Buildings and Grounds. I'll bill him—he won't have the money in the house or at the bank, probably—and we'll wait a couple of months."

Bella said, "We can wait."

"We will."

"What did you tell him to do?"

"I told him to unplug the pump."

"He wasn't satisfied."

"I guess I wouldn't be."

"Abe," she said, "what's it like to be young as that?"

I said, "Unhappy."

She said, "But happy, too."

"A little of that."

She bent her gray and gold head over the brown mug of dark brown coffee and picked at the richness of a moist muffin. She said, still looking down, "It's hard."

I said, "It gets easier."

She looked up and nodded, grinned her golden tooth at me, said, "Doesn't it?"

Then I spent the afternoon driving to New Hartford to the ice-cream plant for twenty-five pounds of sliced dry ice. I had them cut the ice into ten-inch-long slivers about three-quarters of an inch around, wrapped the ice in heavy brown paper, and drove it back to Brookfield and the widow's jammed drill point. It's all hard-water country here, and the crimped-pipe points they drive down for wells get sealed with calcium scales if you wait enough years, and the pressure falls, the people call, they worry about having to drill new wells and how much it will cost and when they can flush the toilets again. They worry how long they'll have to wait.

I went in the cellar door without telling her I was there, disconnected the elbow joint, went back out for the ice, and when I had carried the second bundle in, she was standing by her silent well in the damp of her basement, surrounded by furniture draped in plastic sheets, firewood stacked, cardboard boxes of web-crusted Mason jars, the growing heaps of whatever in her life she couldn't use.

She was small and white and dressed in sweaters and a thin green housecoat. She said, "Whatever do you mean to do?" Her hands were folded across her little chest, and she rubbed her gnarled throat. "Is my well dead?"

"No, ma'am. I'd like you to go upstairs while I do my small miracle here. Because I'd like you not to worry. Won't you go upstairs?"

She said, "I live alone —"

I said, "You don't have to worry."

"I don't know what to do about—this kind of thing. It gets more and more of a problem—this—all this." She waved her hand at what she lived in and then hung her hands at her sides.

I said, "You go on up and watch the television. I'm going to fix it up. I'll do a little fixing here and come back tonight and hook her up again, and you be ready to make me my after-dinner coffee when I come back. You'll have water enough to do it with."

"Just go back upstairs?" she said.

"You go on up while I make it good. And I don't want you worrying."

"All right, then," she said, "I'll go back up. I get awfully upset now. When these—things. These—I don't know what to do anymore." She looked at me like something that was new. Then she said, "I knew your father, I think. Was he big like you?"

"You know it," I said. "Bigger. Didn't he court you one time?"

"I think everybody must have courted me one time."

"You were frisky," I said.

"Not like now," she said. Her lips were white on her white face, the flesh looked like flower petals. Pinch them and they crumble, wet dust.

"Don't you feel so good now?"

"I mean kids now."

"Oh?"

"They have a different notion of frisky now."

"Yes they do." I said. "I guess they do."

"But I don't feel so good," she said. "This. Things like this. I wish they wouldn't happen. Now. I'm very old."

I said, "It keeps on coming, doesn't it?"

"I can hear it come. When the well stopped, I thought it was a sign. When you get like me, you can hear it come."

I said, "Now listen: You go up. You wrap a blanket around you and talk on the telephone or watch the TV. Because I guarantee. You knew my father. You knew my father's word. Take mine. I guarantee."

"Well, if you're guaranteeing."

I said, "That's my girl." She was past politeness so she didn't smile or come back out of herself to say good-bye. She walked to the stairs and when she started to shuffle and haul the long way up, I turned away to the well pipe, calling, "You make sure and have my coffee ready tonight. You wait and make my after-dinner coffee, hear? There'll be water for it." I waited until she went up, and it was something of a wait. She was too tired for stairs. I thought to tell Bella that it looked like the widow hadn't long.

But when she was gone, I worked. I put my ear to the pipe and heard the sounds of hollowness, the emptiness under the earth that's not quite silence—like the whisper you hear in the long-distance wires of the telephone before the relays connect. Then I opened the brown paper packages and started forcing the lengths of dry ice down into the pipe. I carried and shoved, drove the ice first with my fingers and then with a piece of copper tube, and I filled the well pipe until nothing more would go. My fingers were red, and the smoke from dry ice misted up until I stood in an underground fog. When nothing more would fit, I capped the pipe, kicked the rest of the ice down into the sump—it steamed as if she lived above a fire, as if always her house were smoldering—and I went out, drove home.

I went by the hill roads, and near Excell's farm I turned the motor off, drifted down the dirt road in neutral, watching. The deer had come down from the high hills and they were moving carefully through the fields of last year's corn stumps, grazing like cattle at dusk, too many to count. When the truck stopped I heard the rustle as they pulled the tough silk. Then I started the motor—they jumped, stiffened, watched me for a while, went back to eating: A man could come and kill them, they had so little fear—and I drove home to Bella and a tight house, long dinner, silence for most of the meal, then talk about the children while I washed the dishes and she put them away.

And then I drove back to the house that was dark except for one lighted window. The light was yellow and not strong. I turned the engine off and coasted in. I went downstairs on the tips of my toes because, I told myself, there was a sense of silence there, and I hoped she was having some rest. I uncapped the well pipe and gases blew back, a stink of the deepest cold, and then there was a sound of climbing, of filling up, and water banged to her house again. I put the funnel and hose on the mouth of the pipe and filled my jeep can, then capped the check valve, closed the pipe that delivered the water upstairs, poured water from the jeep can through the funnel to prime the pump, switched it on, watched the pressure needle climb to thirty-eight pounds, opened the faucet to the upstairs pipes, and heard it gush.

I hurried to get the jeep can and hose and funnel and tools to the truck, and I had closed the cellar door and driven off before she made the porch to call me. I wanted to get back to Bella and tell her what a man she was married to—who could know so well the truths of ice and make a dead well live.

Saturday morning the pickup trucks were going to the dump, and the men would leave off trash and hard fill, stand at tailgates, spitting, talking, complaining, shooting at rats or nothing, firing off, picking for scrap, and I drove to see the professor and his catastrophe.

His house was tilted. It needed jacks. The asbestos siding was probably all that kept the snow out. His drainpipes were broken, and I could see the damp spots where water wasn't carried off but spilled to the roof of his small porch to eat its way in and gradually soften the house for bad winter leaks. The lawn at the side of his drive was rutted and soft, needed gravel. The barn he used for a garage would have to be coated with creosote or it would rot and fall. A child's bright toys lay in his yard like litter. The cornfield behind his house went off to soft meadow and low hills, and everything was clean and growing behind where they lived; for the view they had, they might as well have owned the countryside. What they didn't own was their house.

He met me at the back steps, all puffy and breasted in his T-shirt, face in the midst of a curly black beard, dirty glasses over his eyes like a mask. He shook my hand as if I were his surgeon. He asked me to have coffee, and I told him I wouldn't now. A little boy came out, and he was beautiful: blond hair and sweetly shaped head, bright brown eyes, as red from weather as his father was pale, a sturdy body with a rounded stomach you would want to cup your hand on as if it were a breast, and teeth as white as bone. He stood behind his father and circled an arm around his father's heavy thigh, put his forehead in his father's buttocks, and then peeped out at me. He said, "Is this the fixing man? Will he fix our pump?"

Samuels put his hand behind him and squeezed the boy's head. He said, "This is the plumber, Mac." He raised his eyebrows at me and smiled, and I liked the way he loved the boy and knew how the boy embarrassed him too.

I kneeled down and said, "Hey, Mac."

The boy hid his face in his father's behind.

I said, "Mac, do you play in that sandbox over there?"

His face came out and he said, very politely, "Would you like to play with me?"

I said, "I have to look at your pump, Mac."

He nodded. He was serious now. He said, "Daddy broke it last night, and we can't fix it again."

I carried my tool pack to the cellar door—the galvanized sheeting on top of it was coming loose, several nails had gone, the weather was getting behind it and would eat the wood away—and I opened it up and started down the stone steps to the inside cellar door. They came behind me, then Samuels went ahead of me, turning on lights, scuffing through the mud and puddles on his concrete floor. The pump was on the wall to the left as I came in. The converted coal furnace in front of me leaked oil where the oilfeed came in. Stone foundation cracking that was two hundred years old, vent windows shut when they should have been opened to stop the dry rot, beams with the adze scars in them powdering almost as we watched: that was his cellar—and packing cartons and scraps of wood, broken chairs, a table with no legs. There was a stink of something bad.

I looked at the pump, breathed out, then I looked at Mac. He breathed out too. He sounded like me. I grinned at him and he grinned back.

"We're the workers," he said. "Okay? You and me will be the workers. But Daddy can't fix anymore. Mommy said so."

Samuels said, "We'll leave him now, Mac."

I said, "How old is he?"

Mac said, "Six years old."

Samuels said, "Three. Almost three and a half."

"And lots of boy," I said.

Mac said, "I'm a worker."

Samuels said, "All right, Mac."

Mac said, "Can't I stay here? Daddy? I'm a *worker*."

Samuels said, "Would we be in the way? I'd like to learn a little about this thing if I can."

Mac shook his head and smiled at me. He said, "What are we going to do with our Daddy?"

Samuels said, "Okay, buddy."

Mac raised his brows and shrugged his little arms.

Samuels said, "Out, Mac. Into the yard. Play in the sandbox for a while." He said, "Okay? I'll call you when we need some help."

"Sure!" Mac said.

He walked up the steps, arms slanted out to balance himself, little thighs pushing up on the steps. From outside, where we couldn't see him anymore, the boy called, "Bye and I love you," and ran away.

Samuels held his arms folded across his chest, covering his fleshy breasts. He uncrossed his arms to push his glasses up on his face when they slipped from the bridge of his flat nose. He said, "The water here—I tried to use the instruction book last night, after I talked to you. I guess I shouldn't have done that, huh?"

"Depends on what you did, Mr. Samuels." I unrolled the tool pack, got ready to work.

"I figured it wouldn't turn off on account of an air block in the pipes. The instructions mentioned that."

"Oh."

"So I unplugged the pump as you told me to, and then I drained all the water out—that's how the floor got so wet. Then it all ran into that hole over there."

"The sump."

"Oh, *that's* what a sump is. Then that motor like an outboard engine with the pipe—"

"The sump pump. The water collects in the hole and pushes the float up and the motor cuts in and pumps the water out the side of the house—over there, behind your hot-water heater."

"Oh."

"Except your sump pump isn't plugged in."

"Oh. I wondered. And I was fooling with the motor and this black ball fell off into the water."

"The float. So it wouldn't turn itself *off* if you did keep it plugged in.

Don't you worry, Mr. Samuels, we'll pump her out later. Did you do anything else to the well pump?"

He pushed his glasses up and recrossed his arms. "I didn't know what else to do. I couldn't make it start again. We didn't have any water all night. There wasn't any pressure on the gauge."

"No. You have to prime it."

"Prime it?"

"I'll show you, Mr. Samuels. First, you better let me look. Right?"

"Sorry. Sorry. Do you mind if I stay here, though?" He smiled. He blushed under his whiskers. "I really have to learn something about how— this whole thing." He waved his arms around him and then covered up.

I said, "You can stay, sure. Stay."

I started to work a wrench on the heavy casing bolts, and when I'd got the motor apart from the casing, water began to run to the floor from the discharge pipe over the galvanized tank.

He said, "Should I . . ."

"Excuse me?"

"There's water coming down. Should I do anything about it?"

I said, "No, thank you. No. You just watch, thank you."

After a while the trickle slowed, and I pulled the halves apart. I took the rubber diaphragm off, put the flashlight on the motor, poked with a screwdriver, found nothing. I expected nothing. It had to be in the jet. I put the light on that and looked in and saw it, nodded, waited for him to ask.

He said, "You found it?"

"Yessir. The jet's blocked. That's what it sounded like when you called. Wouldn't let the pressure build up, so the gauge wouldn't know when to stop. It's set at forty pounds, and the block wouldn't let it up past—oh, twenty-eight or thirty, I'd say. Am I right?"

"Uh, I don't know. I don't know *anything* about these things."

I said, "When this needle hits forty, it's what you should be getting. Forty pounds of pressure per square inch. If you'd read the gauge you'd have seen it to be about thirty, I calculate. That would've told you the whole thing."

"I thought the gauge was broken."

"They generally don't break. Generally, these things work. Usually it's something simpler than machines when you can't get water up."

He pushed his glasses and covered up, said, "God, what I don't know."

I said, "It's hard to live in a house, isn't it? But you'll learn."

"Jesus, I hope so. I don't know. I hope so. We never lived in a house before."

"What'd you live in? Apartment houses?"

"Yeah—where you call the janitor downstairs and he comes up while you're at work and you never see him. Like magic. It's just all better by the time you get home."

"Well, we'll get this better for you."

He frowned and nodded very seriously. "I'll bet you will," he said. It was a gift he gave me, a bribe.

I said, "So why don't you go on up and ask the missus for about three inches of aluminum foil. Would you do that? And a coat hanger, if you don't mind."

"Coat hanger?"

"Yessir. If you don't mind."

He walked across the floor to the wooden steps that went upstairs above the furnace; he tried to hide the sway and bounce of his body in the way that he walked, the boy coming down the outside concrete steps as the father went up the inside ones. "Do you need any help?" the boy said.

I said, "Mac, you old helper. Hello."

"Do you need any help?"

"I had a boy like you."

"A little bit big, like me?"

"Little bit big. Except now he's almost a daddy too."

He said, "Is he *your* daddy now?"

I said, "Not yet."

"Not yet?"

"Not for a while."

"Oh. Well, then what happened to him?"

"He just got big. He grew up."

"Does he go to the college?"

"He's bigger than that, even."

Mac smiled and showed his hand, fingers held together. "*That* big? So big?"

"Bigger," I said.

Mac said, "That's a big boy you have."

Samuels handed me the foil and coat hanger. I rolled the foil around a cigar until it was a cylinder, and I stuck it in the well side of the nozzle. I opened the hanger and straightened her out.

Mac said, "What's he doing, Daddy?"

Samuels said, "I don't know. I don't know, Mac. Why don't you go outside? I don't know."

I said, "Mr. Samuels, I wonder if you would hold that foil firmly in there and cup your hand under it while I give her a shove."

He held. Mac watched him. I pushed at the other side of the jet, felt it, pushed again, and it rolled down the aluminum foil to his palm: a flat wet pebble half the size of the nail on his little finger. He said, "That's it? That's all it is? This is what ruined my life for two days?"

I said, "That's all it ever takes, Mr. Samuels. It came up with the water—you have to have gravel where there's water—and it lodged in the jet, kept the pressure from building up. If it happens again, I'll put a screen in at the check valve. May never happen again. If it does, we'll know what to do, won't we?"

Samuels said, "I wonder when I'll ever know what to do around here."

I said, "You'll learn."

I fastened the halves of the pump together, then went out for my jeep can, still half full from the widow's house. I came back in and I unscrewed the pipe plug at the top of the pump and poured the water in, put the plug back on, connected the pump to the switch.

Mac jumped, then stood still, holding to his father's leg.

The pump chirred, caught on the water from the widow's well, drew, and we all watched the pressure climb to forty, heard the motor cut out, heard the water climb in the copper pipes to the rest of the house as I opened the valve.

I was putting away tools when I heard Samuels say, "Now keep away from there!" I heard the *whack* of his hand on Mac's flesh, and heard the weeping start, in the back of the boy's throat, and then the wail. Samuels said, "That's *filthy* in there—Christ knows what you've dragged up. And I *told* you not to mess with things you don't know anything about. Dammit!"

Mac wailed louder. I watched his face clench and grow red, ugly. He put his left sleeve in his mouth and chewed on it, backed away to the stone steps, fumbled with his feet and stepped backwards up one step. "But *Dad*-dy," he said. "But *Dad*-dy." Then he stood on the steps and chewed his sleeve and cried.

Samuels said, "God, look at that."

I said, "There's that smell you've been smelling, Mr. Samuels. Mouse. He must've fallen into the sump and starved to death and rotted there. That's what you've been smelling."

"God. Mac—go up and wash your hands. Mac! Go upstairs and wash your hands. I mean *now!*"

The small brown lump of paws and tail and teeth, its stomach swollen, the rest looking almost dissolved, lay in its puddle on the floor beside the sump. The stink of its death was everywhere. The pump cut in and built the pressure up again. Mac stood on the cellar steps and cried. His father pushed his glasses up and looked at the corpse of the rotted mouse and hugged his arms around himself and looked at his son. I walked past Samuels, turned away from the weeping boy, and pushed up at the lever that the float, if he had left it there, would have released on the sump pump. Nothing happened, and I stayed where I was, waiting, until I remembered to plug the sump pump in. I pushed the lever again, its motor started, the filthy reeking water dropped, the wide black rubber pipe it passed through on the ceiling swung like something alive as all that dying passed along it and out.

I picked the mouse up by its tail after the pump had stopped and Samuels, waiting for my approval, watching my face, had pulled out the plug. I carried my tools under my arm and the jeep can in my hand. I nodded to Samuels and he was going to speak, then didn't, just nodded back. I walked past Mac on the steps, not crying anymore, but wet-faced and stunned. I bent down as I passed him. I whispered, "What shall we do with your Daddy?" and went on, not smiling.

I walked to the truck in their unkempt drive that went to the barn that would fall. I carried the corpse. I thought to get home to Bella and say how sorry I was for the sorrow I'd made and couldn't take back. I spun the dripping mouse by its tail and flung it beyond the barn into Keeper's field of corn stumps. It rose and sank from the air and was gone. I had primed the earth. It didn't need the prime.

Suggestions for Discussion

1. "Widow Water" begins with a pronouncement containing three generalizations. How are these generalizations justified or earned by the details that complete the paragraph?

2. Identify the active and linking verbs in the second paragraph. Try substituting the passive voice for the active—what happens to the vigor of the passage?

3. In the scene between the plumber-narrator and his wife Bella, what and how much do you learn about the relationship between them? What sorts of abstraction or judgment are conveyed through concrete detail?

4. Throughout the story the plumber details the problems of wells, pipes, and hard-water country, and also his solutions for the problems. Presumably the purpose of these details is not to teach us plumbing maintenance. What purpose do they serve?

5. Focus on the rhythm of the widow's speech on pages 108-109. How does this rhythm help to characterize her?

6. On pages 110-111 Professor Samuels's house is described in a series of concrete details. To what extent do these details also characterize the professor himself?

7. The paragraph beginning with "The small brown lump" on pages 115-116 contains eight sentences. Except for the first, all of these begin with the parallel structure subject-verb. What is the *emotional* effect of this rhythm? How does the use of active verbs help to reveal the narrator's emotion?

RETROSPECT

1. Identify the active and linking verbs in the three opening paragraphs of "Cutting Edge." Do they help to imply active and passive states in the characters?

2. Consider the rhythm of the paragraph beginning, "The doctor sucked in on his pipe," on page 25 of "The Second Tree from the Corner." How does the rhythm contribute to Trexler's emotional shifts?

3. In "The Second Tree from the Corner," whatever it was that happened on the Madison Avenue bus is mentioned three times, but White never tells us what it was. Why is this detail denied us? What effect does the author achieve by the omission?

WRITING ASSIGNMENTS

1. Take the passage "Danny carried the...slippers" on page 83, and rewrite it twice. Keep the basic action the same; you may alter the details in any way. In one rewrite, let us feel that the relationship is in deep trouble. In the other, let it charm us.

2. Paint a self-portrait in words. Prop a mirror in front of you and describe, in the most focused sight details you can manage, twenty or thirty things that you see. Then try to distance yourself from your portrait and choose the two or three details that most vividly and concisely convey the image you want to present. What attitude do you want the reader to have? Should we find you funny, intense, pitiable, vain, dedicated? Add a detail of sound, touch, smell, or taste that will help convey the image.

3. Make a list of four qualities that describe a character real or imagined. Then place that character in a scene and write the scene so that the qualities are conveyed through significant detail. Use no generalizations and no judgments. No word on your list will appear in the scene.

4. Write a description of a rural landscape, a city street, or a room. Use only active verbs to describe inanimate as well as animate things. Avoid the pathetic fallacy.

5. Write about a boring situation. Convince us that the situation is boring and that your characters are bored or boring or both. Fascinate us. Or

make us laugh. Use no generalizations, no judgments, and no verbs in the passive voice.

6. Write about one of the following and suggest the rhythm of the subject in your prose: a machine, a vehicle, a piece of music, sex, something that goes in a circle, an avalanche.

7. Write about a character who begins at a standstill; works up to great speed (in a vehicle or on foot, pursued or pursuing, competing in a sport—or let the rush be purely emotional); and comes to a halt again, either gradually or abruptly. Let the prose rhythm reflect the changes.

BOOK PEOPLE
Kinds of Character

Individual, Typical, and Universal Characters
Round and Flat Characters
The Aristotelian Hero

Human character is in the foreground of all fiction, however the humanity might be disguised. Anthropomorphism may be a scientific sin, but it is a literary necessity. Bugs Bunny isn't a rabbit; he's a plucky youth in ears. Peter Rabbit is a mischievous boy. Brer Rabbit is a sassy rebel. The romantic heroes of *Watership Down* are out of the Arthurian tradition, not out of the hutch. And that doesn't cover fictional *rabbits*.

Henri Bergson, in his essay "On Laughter," observes:

> ... the comic does not exist outside the pale of what is strictly human. A landscape may be beautiful, charming or sublime, or insignificant and ugly; it will never be laughable.

Bergson is right, but it is just as true that only the human is tragic. We may describe a landscape as "tragic" because nature has been devastated by industry, but the tragedy lies in the cupidity of those who wrought the havoc, in the dreariness, poverty, or disease of those who must live there. A conservationist or ecologist (or a novelist) may care passionately about nature and dislike people because of it; then we say he or she "identifies" with nature (a wholly human capacity) or "respects the natural unity" (of which humanity is a part) or wants to keep the earth "habitable" (for whom?) or "values nature for its own sake" (using standards of value that nature does not share). By all available evidence, the universe is indifferent to the destruction of trees, property, peoples, and planets. Only people care.

If this is so, then your fiction can be only as successful as the characters who move it and move within it. Whether they are "drawn from life" or are "pure fantasy" — and all fictional characters lie somewhere between the two — we must find them interesting, we must find them believable, and we must care about what happens to them.

Individual, Typical, and Universal Characters

Characters, we're told, should be *individual, typical,* and *universal.* I don't think this truism is very helpful to a practicing writer. For example, I don't think you can *set out to be* "universal" in your writing.

It is true, I believe, that if literature has any social justification or use it is that readers can identify the common humanity in, and can therefore identify with, characters vastly different from themselves in century, geography, gender, culture, and beliefs; and that this enhances the scope of the reader's sympathy. It is also true that if the fiction does not have this universal quality — if a middle-class American male author creates as protagonist a middle-class American male with whom only middle-class American male readers can sympathize — then the fiction is thin and small. William Sloane voices the "frightening" demand of the reader in his book *The Craft of Writing:* "Tell me about me. I want to be more alive. Give me *me.*" But unfortunately the capacity for universality, like talent, is a trick of the genes or a miracle of the soul, and if you aim for the universal, you're likely to achieve the pompous.

If you're determined to create a "typical" character, you're likely to produce a caricature, because people are typical only in the generalized qualities that lump them together. *Typical* is the most provincial adjective in a writer's vocabulary, signaling that you're writing only for those who share your assumptions. A "typical schoolgirl" in Dar es Salaam is a very different "type" from one in San Francisco. Furthermore, every person is typical of many things successively or simultaneously. She may be in turn a "typical" schoolgirl, bride, divorcee, and feminist. He may be at one and the same time a "typical" New Yorker, math professor, doting father, and adulterer. It is in the confrontation and convolution of types that much of our individuality is produced.

If an author sets out deliberately to produce types rather than individuals, then that author invariably wants to condemn or ridicule those types. Joyce Carol Oates illustrates the technique in "How I Contemplated the World from the Detroit House of Correction and Began My Life Over Again."

Sioux Drive

George, Clyde G. 240 Sioux. A manufacturer's representative; children, a dog, a wife. Georgian with the usual columns. You think of the White House, then of Thomas Jefferson, then your mind goes blank on the white pillars and you think of nothing.

Typicality invites judgment. We can identify only with characters who come alive to us through their individuality.

It may clarify the distinctions among the universal, the typical, and the individual if you imagine this scene: The child chases a ball into the street. The tires screech, the bumper thuds, the blood geysers into the air, the pulp of the small body lies inert on the asphalt. How would a bystander react? (It is universal?) How would a passing doctor react? (Is it typical?) How would Dr. Henry Lowes, just coming from the maternity ward of his own hospital, where his wife has had her fourth miscarriage, react? (Is it individual?) Each question narrows the range of convincing reaction, and as a writer you want to convince in each range. If you succeed in the third, you are likely to have succeeded in the other two.

Except where you want us to find your characters ridiculous or heinous or both, then, the rule of thumb is to aim for the individual (which means the specific, concrete, definite, and particular). The typical will take care of itself. The universal can't be forced.

Round and Flat Characters

We're also told that characters should be *round* rather than *flat*. A flat character is one who has only one distinctive characteristic, exists only to exhibit that characteristic, and is incapable of varying from that characteristic. A round character is many faceted and is capable of change. Several critics have, however, persuasively defended flat characters. Eric Bentley suggests in *The Life of the Drama* that if a messenger's function in a play is to deliver his message, it would be very tedious to stop and learn about his psychology. The same is true in fiction; the Queen's chauffeur in the passage from *Mrs. Dalloway* (see chapter 3) exists for no purpose but leaning "ever so slightly," and we do not want to hear about his children or his hernia. Nevertheless, onstage even a flat character has a face and a costume, and in fiction detail can give even a flat character a few angles and contours. The servant classes in the novels of Henry James are notoriously absent as individuals because they exist only in their functions (*that excellent creature had already assembled the baggage*, etc.), whereas Charles Dickens, who peoples his novels with dozens of flat characters, brings even these alive in detail.

> And Mrs. Miff, the wheezy little pew opener—a mighty dry old lady, sparely dressed, with not an inch of fullness anywhere about her—is also here.
>
> *Dombey and Son*

To borrow a notion from George Orwell's *Animal Farm*, all good characters are created round, but some are created rounder than others.

But the central characters in your story or novel need to be not merely round, but spherical. They should contain enough conflict and contradiction so that we can recognize them as belonging to the contradictory human race; and they should be, as we are or hope we are, capable of change.

The Aristotelian Hero

Aristotle, in the *Poetics*, listed four requirements of a successful hero—he should be "*good, appropriate, like,* and *consistent*"—and although literature has changed a great deal in the twenty-three intervening centuries, I believe that these four qualities remain necessary attributes of a fully three-dimensional character; and I believe that they throw light on the critical notions of universal, typical, individual, flat, and round.

GOOD

"There will be an element of character," Aristotle says, "if . . . what a person says or does reveals a certain moral purpose; and a good element of character, if the purpose so revealed is good." It might seem that the antiheroes, brutes, hoods, whores, perverts, and bums who people modern literature do very little in the way of "revealing good moral purpose." The history of Western literature shows a movement downward and inward: downward through society from royalty to gentry to the middle classes to the lower classes to the dropouts; inward from heroic action to social drama to individual consciousness to the subconscious to the unconscious. What has remained consistent is that, for the time spent in an author's world, we understand and identify with the protagonist or protagonists, we "see their point of view," and the fiction succeeds largely because we are willing to grant them a goodness that we would not grant them in life. Aristotle goes on to explain that "such goodness is possible in every type of personage, even in a woman or a slave, though the one is perhaps an inferior, and the other a wholly worthless being"—and the sentence strikes us as both offensive and funny. But in Aristotle's society, women and slaves were legally designated inferior and worthless, and what Aristotle is saying is precisely what Ken Kesey acknowledges when he picks the inmates of an "Institute of Psychology" as his heroes: that the external status granted by society is not an accurate measure of "good moral purpose."

> This new redheaded admission, McMurphy, knows right away he's not a Chronic... The Acutes look spooked and uneasy when he laughs, the way kids look in a schoolroom when one ornery kid is raising too much hell. . . .
> . . . "Which one of you claims to be the craziest? Which one is the biggest looney? Who runs these card games? It's my first day, and what I like to do *is* make a good impression straight off on the right man if he can prove to me he *is* the right man. Who's the bull goose looney here?"
> *One Flew Over the Cuckoo's Nest*

If you met McMurphy in real life, you'd probably say he was "crazy" and you'd hope he would be locked up. If you encountered the Neanderthals of William Golding's *The Inheritors* on your evening walk, you'd run. If you were forced to live with the visionaries of Doris Lessing's *Four-Gated City* or the prisoners of Jean Genêt's *Our Lady of the Flowers*, you would live in skepticism and fear. But while you read you expand your mental scope by identifying with, temporarily "becoming," a character who convinces you that the inmates of the asylum are saner than the staff, that the apemen are more human than *Homo sapiens*, that mental breakdown is mental breakthrough, that perversion is purer than the sexual code by which you live. For the drama audiences of fourth-century B.C. Athens, it was easier to see human nobility embodied in the heroic external actions of those designated by class as noble. It is largely because literature has moved inward, within the mind, that it is possible to move downward in social status—

even to women and slaves!—and maintain this sympathy. In his own mind everyone is fundamentally justified, however conscious he is of his flaws—indeed, the more conscious of his flaws, the better he is. As readers we are allowed to borrow a mind. Fiction, as critic Laurence Gonzales said of rock music, "lets you wander around in someone else's hell for a while and see how similar it is to your own."

You won't, of course, want us to identify with all of your people all of the time. In the *Poetics*, Aristotle was describing the tragic hero, and he also described tragedy as presenting people as "better than they are" and comedy as presenting them as "worse than they are." Bergson points out that we can't find a character comic if we identify too closely with him or her; comedy requires that we maintain an intelligent and somewhat callous distance.

It nevertheless holds true that there is "an element of character" only when "a certain moral purpose is revealed" and that you achieve identification with your characters when you reveal that purpose as good. Since as a writer you want to move us, you will almost inevitably want us to identify with at least your central character. Sometimes this identification can be achieved by contrasting the "good purpose" of the central character with the more questionable moral elements of characters around her or him. Notice that in the following passage from Willa Cather, which presents a character both more familiar and more morally ambiguous than mad McMurphy, the protagonist is surrounded by moral attitudes left vague, cliché, and "typical" although he himself is carefully detailed.

> It was Paul's afternoon to appear before the faculty of the Pittsburgh High School to account for his various misdemeanors. He had been suspended a week ago, and his father had called at the Principal's office and confessed his perplexity about his son. Paul entered the faculty room suave and smiling. His clothes were a trifle outgrown, and the tan velvet on the collar of his open overcoat was frayed and worn; but for all that there was something of the dandy about him, and he wore an opal pin in his neatly knotted black four-in-hand, and a red carnation in his buttonhole. This latter adornment the faculty somehow felt was not properly significant of the contrite spirit befitting a boy under the ban of suspension.
>
> *Paul's Case*

As readers we immediately identify with the miscreant. Indeed, I am both a parent and a faculty member, but in the space of this paragraph Willa Cather makes me Paul. I'm instinctively unwilling to identify with a father who abandons his son to the principal's office, equally unwilling to identify with a faculty that thinks in terms of "properly significant" and "contrite spirit." The shabby bravery of Paul's attire is "good" in a way that these other attitudes are not. And when, in the next paragraph, Cather tells me that Paul's eyes "were remarkable for a certain hysterical brilliancy, and he continually used them in a conscious, theatrical sort of way, peculiarly offensive in a boy," I am certain to view remarkable eyes, their brilliance and theatricality, even their hysteria, as the direct opposite of offensive.

APPROPRIATE

Aristotle offends again when he explains what he means by "appropriate." "The character before us may be, say, manly; but it is not appropriate in a female character to be manly." Again, he offends because our ideas of *female* and *manly* have changed, not because we have outgrown a sense of what is appropriate. We are dealing here again with the idea of the "typical," which includes all the biological and environmental influences that form us. A Baptist Texan behaves differently from an Italian nun; a rural schoolboy behaves differently from a professor emeritus at Harvard. If you are to succeed in creating an individual character, particular and alive, you will also inevitably know what is appropriate to that sort of person and will let us know as much as we need to know to feel the appropriateness of the behavior.

We need to know soon, for instance, preferably in the first paragraph, the character's gender, age, and race or nationality. We need to know something of his or her class, period, and region. A profession (or the clear lack of it) and a marital status help, too. Almost any reader can identify with almost any character; what no reader can identify with is confusion. When some or several of the fundamentals of type are withheld from us — when we don't know whether we're dealing with a man or a woman, an adult or a child — the process of identifying cannot begin, and the story is slow to move us.

None of the information need come as information; it can be implied by appearance, tone, action, or detail. But we need it in order to know "what to expect" of a character; that is, what is appropriate. In the passage from "Paul's Case," we are told that the protagonist is a male high school student. "High school" and "principal" make him American (if we heard of the *préfet* of a *lycée* we'd know we were in France), and the details of his attempt at dandyism suggest the first half of the twentieth century and also that Paul is not as high in the middle class as he would like to be. By concentrating on what is "not appropriate" to Paul's station, Cather implies a good deal about what that station is. And of course we're delighted when a character "acts against type" — when the old lady talks tough, the Count belches, or the cop cuddles a stray. Still, the behavior has to be within the range of the character's possibilities. The notion of "against type" itself suggests how severely we judge an action as appropriate or not.

In the next example William Melvin Kelley pitches his protagonist straight into the conflict. Only the character's gender is given us directly, but by the end of the story's opening paragraph, we know a lot about his life and type.

> To find this Cooley, the Black baby's father, he knew he would have to contact Opal Simmons. After dressing, he began to search for her address and number. Tam, very organized for a woman, saved everything. Among the envelopes containing the sports-clothes receipts, a letter from her dressmaker asking for payment, old airline tickets, the nursery school bill, the canceled checks and deposit slips, he finally found Opal's address.
>
> *Passing*

We know from the apparently "irrelevant" collection of bills that the protagonist is middle class, married, a father, affluent, and perhaps (that letter from the dressmaker) living at the edge of his income. Because he specifies a "Black baby," we know that he is white. We also know something about his attitudes toward both blacks ("this Cooley") and women ("very organized for a woman"). With an absolute minimum of exposition, letting us share the search for the address, Kelley has drawn clear boundaries of what we may expect from a character whose name we don't yet know.

Similarly, at the opening of *The Bear,* William Faulkner gives us as information only the age and gender of the protagonist. Then, launching into the boy's mental image of the bear, he gives us as if incidentally the rural but upper-class, sporting atmosphere in which the boy lives, with its sense of inheritance, legend, and awe.

> He was ten. But it had already begun, long before that day when at last he wrote his age in two figures and he saw for the first time the camp where his father and Major de Spain and old General Compson and the others spent two weeks each November and two weeks again each June. He had already inherited then, without ever having seen it, the tremendous bear with one trap-ruined foot which, in an area almost a hundred miles deep, had earned itself a name, a definite designation like a living man.

Students of writing are sometimes daunted by the need to give so much information immediately. Once again, the trick is to find telling details that will convey the information indirectly, while our attention remains on the desire or emotion of the character. Nobody wants to read a story that begins:

> She was a twenty-eight-year-old suburban American woman, relatively affluent, who was extremely distressed when her husband Peter left her.

But most of that, and much more besides, could be contained in a few details:

> After Peter left with the VCR, the microwave and the key to the garage, she went down to the kitchen and ate three jars of peanut butter without tasting a single spoonful.

I don't mean to imply that it is necessarily easy to signal the essentials of type immediately. It would be truer to say that it is necessary and hard. The opening paragraph of a story is its second strongest statement (the final paragraph is the strongest) and sets the tone for all that follows. If the right words don't come to you as a gift, you may have to sit sifting and discarding the inadequate ones for a long time before you achieve both clarity and interest.

LIKE

There is a critical controversy over what Aristotle meant by "likeness," but I think the two interpretations cast light on the necessities of character. The first is that by "like" Aristotle meant "natural"—that we should find the character credibly human, that his or her actions and reactions should ring true. The sense here is akin to the idea of "universal," without the symphonic overtones. Of course the range of credible human actions is vast, and again the trick is to convince us that *this* person would do this; if you do, we're unlikely to complain that *a* person wouldn't. But if your readers and critics say, "I don't believe anybody would act this way," prick up your ears, swallow your answer, believe it, and go back to work.

The second interpretation of "like" comes from Aristotle's comparison of the writer and the portrait painter. Each, he says, attempts to capture the best possible "likeness" of the model. In literature this would seem to mean that, if the writer is depicting Ulysses or Achilles, he should be true to the historical characteristics of the hero. This is a limiting notion, but as the characters of your fiction live only on the page, you need be true only to them. And the characters of your fiction do live only on the page. It can't be too strongly stressed that a person who exists in the form of words exists only in that form. "But that's the way it happened" is never a justification for an action that lacks credibility. "But that's the way she is" will never convince us that the character is true to life. If we update Aristotle's painting analogy, the important question is: is the camera in focus? If the image is sharp, it will be a better likeness than if it's blurred.

Here are three examples of quickly drawn, tightly focused characters. Notice in each how attention to particular detail also indicates the typical and convinces us of human "likeness."

With no map sense, I took a trip by myself to San Francisco Chinatown and got lost in the Big City. Wandering in a place very different from our own brown and gray Chinatown, I suddenly heard my own real aunt calling my name. She was my youngest aunt, my modern aunt just come from Hong Kong. We screamed at each other the way our villagers do, hugged, held hands. "Have you had your rice yet?" we shouted. "I have. I have had my rice." "Me too. I've eaten too," letting the whole strange street know we had eaten.

MAXINE HONG KINGSTON, *China Men*

M. Willy was not huge, he was bulbous. The powerful skull, the slightly protuberant eyes, the nose, which was short and had no visible bridge, the drooping cheeks—every one of his features approximated to the curve. His mouth, under the heavy gray-gold moustaches that he dyed for a long while, was narrow, dainty and agreeable looking, and had something faintly English about its smile. As for his dimpled chin, which was small, weak, you might even say fragile, it seemed the best thing to hide it. Which M. Willy did, at first with a sort of glorified imperial, then with a short beard. It has been said that he bore a marked resemblance to Edward VII. To do justice to a less flattering but no less august truth, I would say that, in fact, the likeness was to Queen Victoria.

COLETTE, *Earthly Paradise*

Headeye, he was following me. I knowed he was following me. But I just kept goin, like I wasn't payin him no mind. Headeye, he never fish much, but I guess he knowed the river as good as anybody. But he aint know where the fishin was good. Thas why I knowed he was followin me. So I figured I better fake him out. I aint want nobody with a mojo bone followin me. . . . Headeye, he o.k., cept when he get some kinda notion in that big head of his. Then he act crazy. Trying to show off his age. He older'n me, but he little for his age. Some people say readin too many books will stunt your growth. Well, on Headeye everythin is stunted cept his eyes and his head.

HENRY DUMAS, *Ark of Bones*

As a writer you may have the lucky, facile sort of imagination to which characters spring full-blown, complete with gestures, histories, and passions. Or it may be that you haven't and that you need to explore in order to exploit, to draw your characters out gradually, get to know them, and coax them into being. That can be lucky, too.

For either kind of writer, but especially the latter, keeping a journal is an invaluable help. A journal lets you coax and explore without committing yourself to anything or anyone. It allows you to know everything about your character whether you use it or not. You must know everything, because in order to have the density of fiction, your characterization must present the iceberg tip that implies the underwater bulk of heredity, environment, experience, and human nature. Before you put a character in a story, know how well that character sleeps. Know what the character eats for lunch and how much it matters, what he or she buys and how the bills get paid, how he or she spends what we call working hours. Know how your character would prefer to spend evenings and weekends and why such plans get thwarted. Know what memories the character has of pets and parents, cities, snow, or school. You may use none of this information in the brief segment of your character's life that is your plot, but knowing it may teach you how your bookperson taps a pencil or twists a lock of hair, and when and why. When you know these things, you will have taken a step past invention toward the moment of imagination in which you become your character, live in his or her skin, and produce an action that, for the reader, rings universally true.

A major advantage of keeping a journal regularly is that it will put you in the habit of observing in words, finding a phrase to catch whatever has caught your eye. Whatever invites your attention or sympathy, your anger or curiosity may be the beginning of invention. *Whoever* catches your attention may be the beginning of a character. If the library assistant annoys you or the loner at the corner of the bar intrigues you, make a few notes. Start with what you observe, the obvious traits of type—age, gender, color, class. Try to capture a gesture or the messages that features and clothing send. Invent a reason for that harshness or that loneliness; invent a past. Then try taking the character out of context and setting him or her in another. Get your character in trouble, and you may be on your way to a short story.

It is interesting and relevant that actors schooled in what is called the "Stanislavski Method" write biographies of the characters they must play. Adherents of "The Method" believe that in the process of inventing a dramatic character's past the actor will find points of emotional contact with that role and so know how to make the motives and actions prescribed by the script natural and genuine. As a writer you can also use "The Method," imagining much that you will not bring specifically to "the script" but that will enrich your sense of that character until you know with absolute certainty how he or she will move, act, react, and speak.

CONSISTENT

Aristotle says that an author should make characters "consistent and the same throughout"—that is, again, that their actions should be plausible in light of what we know about them—for "even if inconsistency should be part of the man . . . he should still be consistently inconsistent." It is with this last injunction that we leave the area of plausibility and acknowledge the complexity of character. "Consistently inconsistent" does not mean that a character should be continually behaving unnaturally or acting against type. On the contrary, Aristotle here acknowledges the continuing conflict *within* character that is the source of most human trouble and most literature.

Conflict is at the core of character as it is of plot. If plot begins with trouble, then character begins with a person in trouble; and trouble most dramatically occurs because we all have traits, tendencies, and desires that are at war, not simply with the world and other people, but with other of our own traits, tendencies, and desires. All of us probably know a woman of the strong, striding, independent sort, attractive only to men who like a strong and striding woman. And when she falls in love? She becomes a clinging sentimentalist. All of us know a father who is generous, patient, and dependable. And when the children cross the line? He smashes crockery and wields a strap. All of us are gentle, violent; logical, schmaltzy; tough, squeamish; lusty, prudish; sloppy, meticulous; energetic, apathetic; manic, depressive. Perhaps you don't fit that particular list of contradictions, but you are sufficiently in conflict with yourself that as an author you have characters enough in your own psyche to people the work of a lifetime if you will identify, heighten, and dramatize these consistent inconsistencies.

If you think of the great characters of literature, you can see how consistent inconsistency brings each to a crucial dilemma. Hamlet is a strong and decisive man, who procrastinates. Dorothea Brooke of *Middlemarch* is an idealistic and intellectual young woman, a total fool in matters of the heart. Ernest Hemingway's Francis Macomber wants to test his manhood against a lion and cannot face the test. Here, in a moment of crisis from *Mom Kills Self and Kids*, Alan Saperstein reveals with great economy the consistent inconsistency of his protagonist, a man who hadn't much time for his family until their absence makes clear how dependent he has been on them.

> When I arrived home from work I found my wife had killed our two sons and taken her own life.
> I uncovered a blast of foul, black steam from the pot on the stove and said, "Hi, hon, what's for dinner?" But she did not laugh. She did not bounce to her feet and pirouette into the kitchen to greet me. My little one didn't race into my legs and ask what I brought him. The seven-year-old didn't automatically beg me to play a game knowing my answer would be a tired, "Maybe later."

It is, of course, impossible to know to what degree Shakespeare, Eliot, Hemingway, or Saperstein used consistent inconsistencies of which they were aware in themselves to build and dramatize their characters. An author works not only from his or her own personality but also from observation and imagination, and I fully believe that you are working at full stretch only when all three are involved. The question of autobiography is a complicated one, and as writer you frequently won't know yourself how much you have experienced, how much you have observed, and how much you have invented. Actress Mildred Dunnock once observed that "Drama is possible because people can feel what they haven't experienced"; if this is true of audiences and readers, I see no reason the capacity should be denied to writers. A vast proportion of our experience is mental, and it is safe to say that all your writing is autobiographical in the sense that it must have passed through your mind.

It *is* important to avoid writing from other writing, including film and television; it is primarily in the creation of character that we recognize stale stuff. It can be excellent training to imitate the *style* of any writer from Milton to Mailer (consider it training, not publishable work). Any *plot*, as Shakespeare illustrated nicely, can be furnished with new meaning if it is refurbished with new people. But unless the characters are newly thought through and mentally experienced by the author, they are stock characters; like livestock, they are hard to tell apart.

Here are a couple of suggestions for making character fresh and forceful in your mind before you start writing. If the character is based on you or on someone you know, drastically alter the model in some external way: change blond to dark or thin to thick; imagine the character as the opposite gender or radically alter the setting in which the character must act. Part of the trouble with writing directly from experience is that you know too much about it—what "they" did, how you felt. Under such circumstances it's hard to know whether everything in your mind is getting onto the page. An external alteration forces you to re-see, and so to see more clearly, and so to convey more clearly what you see.

On the other hand, if the character is created primarily out of your observation or invention and is unlike yourself, try to find an *internal* area that you have in common with the character. If you are a blond slender young woman and the character is a fat balding man, do you nevertheless have in common a love of French *haute cuisine*? Are you haunted by the same sort of dream? Do you share a fear of public performance or a susceptibility to fine weather?

I can illustrate these techniques only from my own writing, because I am the only author whose self I can identify with any certainty in fictional characters. In writing a recent novel, I wanted to open with a scene in which the heroine buries a dog in her backyard. I had recently buried a dog in my backyard. I wanted to capture the look and feel of red Georgia earth at sunrise, the tangle of roots, and the smell of decay. But I knew that I was likely to make the experience too much my own, too little my character's. I set about to make her not-me. I have long dark hair, an ordinary figure, and I tend to live in Levi's. I made Shaara Soole:

> ... big boned, lanky, melon-breasted, her best feature was a head of rusty barbed-wire hair that she tried to control with a wardrobe of scarves and headband things. Like most costume designers, she dressed with more originality than taste, usually on the Oriental or Polynesian side, sometimes with voluminous loops of thong and matte metal over an ordinary shirt. This was somewhat eccentric in Hubbard, Georgia, but Shaara may have been oblivious to her eccentricity, being so concerned to keep her essential foolishness in check.

Having thus separated Shaara from myself, I was able to bury the dog with her arms and through her eyes rather than my own. On the other hand, a few pages later I was faced with the problem of introducing her ex-husband, Boyd Soole. I had voluminous notes on this character, and I knew that he was almost totally unlike me. A man, to begin with, and a huge man, a theater director with a natural air of power and authority and very little interest in domestic affairs. I sat at my desk for several days, unable to make him move convincingly. My desk oppressed me, and I felt trapped and uncomfortable, my work thwarted, it seemed, by the very chair and typewriter. Then it occurred to me that Boyd was *also* sitting at a desk trying to work.

> The dresser at the Travelodge was some four inches too narrow and three inches too low. If he set his feet on the floor his knees would sit free of the drawer but would be awkwardly constricted left and right. If he crossed his legs, he could hook his right foot comfortably otuside the left of the kneehole but would bruise his thigh at the drawer. If he shifted back he was placed at an awkward distance from his script. And in this position he could not work.

This passage did not instantly allow me to live inside Boyd Soole's skin, nor did it solve all my problems with his characterization. But it did let me get on with the story, and it gave me a flash of sympathy for him that later grew much more profound than I had foreseen.

Often, identifying what you have in common with the feelings of your character will also clarify what is important about him or her to the story—why, in fact, you chose to write about such a person at all. Even if the character is presented as a villain, you have something in common, and I don't mean something forgivable. If he or she is intolerably vain, watch your own private gestures in front of the mirror and borrow them. If he or she is cruel, remember how you enjoyed hooking the worm.

There is no absolute requirement that a writer need behave honestly in life; there is absolutely no such requirement. Great writers have been public hams, domestic dictators, emotional con artists, and Nazis. What is required for fine writing is honesty on the page—not how the character *should* react at the funeral, the surprise party, in bed, but how she or he *does*. In order to develop such honesty of observation on the page, you must begin with a willing honesty of observation (though mercifully not of behavior) in yourself.

Girl

JAMAICA KINCAID

Wash the white clothes on Monday and put them on the stone heap; wash the color clothes on Tuesday and put them on the clothesline to dry; don't walk barehead in the hot sun; cook pumpkin fritters in very hot sweet oil; soak your little cloths right after you take them off; when buying cotton to make yourself a nice blouse, be sure that it doesn't have gum on it, because that way it won't hold up well after a wash; soak salt fish overnight before you cook it; is it true that you sing benna in Sunday school?; always eat your food in such a way that it won't turn someone else's stomach; on Sundays try to walk like a lady and not like the slut you are so bent on becoming; don't sing benna in Sunday school; you mustn't speak to wharf-rat boys, not even to give directions; don't eat fruits on the street—flies will follow you; *but I don't sing benna on Sundays at all and never in Sunday school*; this is how to sew on a button; this is how to make a buttonhole for the button you have just sewed on; this is how to hem a dress when you see the hem coming down and so to prevent yourself from looking like the slut I know you are so bent on becoming; this is how you iron your father's khaki shirt so that it doesn't have a crease; this is how you iron your father's khaki pants so that they don't have a crease; this is how you grow okra—far from the house, because okra tree harbors red ants; when you are growing dasheen, make sure it gets plenty of water or else it makes your throat itch when you are eating it; this is how you sweep a corner; this is how you sweep a whole house; this is how you sweep a yard; this is how you smile to someone you don't like too much; this is how you smile to someone you don't like at all; this is how you smile to someone you like completely; this is how you set a table for tea; this is how you set a table for dinner; this is how you set a table for dinner with an important guest; this is how you set a table for lunch; this is how you set a table for breakfast; this is how to behave in the presence of men who don't know you very well, and this way they won't recognize immediately the slut I have warned you against becoming; be sure to wash every day, even if it is with your own spit; don't squat down to play marbles—you are not a boy, you know; don't pick people's flowers—you might catch something; don't throw stones at blackbirds, because it might not be a blackbird at all; this is how to make a bread pudding; this is how to make doukona; this is how to make pepper pot; this is how to make a good medicine for a cold; this is how to make a good medicine to throw away a child before it even becomes a child; this is how to catch a fish; this is how to throw back a fish you don't like, and that way something bad won't fall on you; this is how to bully a man; this is how a man bullies you; this is how to love a man, and if this doesn't work there are other ways, and if they don't work don't feel too bad about giving up; this is how to spit up in the air if you feel like it, and this is how to move quick so that it doesn't fall on you; this is how to make ends meet; always squeeze bread to make sure it's fresh; *but what if the baker won't let me feel the bread?*; you mean to say that after all you are really going to be the kind of woman who the baker won't let near the bread?

Suggestions for Discussion

1. This very short story is written in the form of a single ongoing sentence. How does it nevertheless have the form of a story? What are the conflict, crisis, and resolution?

2. How, without any description as such, does Kincaid manage to make you see the characters?

3. What details signal the essentials of type in the girl and her mother— age, gender, race, nationality, class (period, profession, marital status)?

4. How would you describe the "universals" of character that are achieved in "Girl"?

5. What "flat" characters are included? To what extent are they characterized?

6. The story contains several details that, if you live in the continental United States, are likely to be obscure to you: *benna, dasheen, doukona*. It's also possible that you can't exactly see pumpkin fritters, wharf-rat boys, an okra tree, a pepper pot. How much does it matter? How much do sound, tone, and approximate meaning add to your understanding?

7. The story is full of moral admonitions and certainly in Aristotle's terms "reveals a moral purpose." Is the moral purpose of the speaker identical to the moral purpose of the story? Who in the story is "good"? In what way? Where does your sympathy lie? Why?

8. Even in this short compass, Kincaid manages to create the character of the daughter in such a way that we see her consistent inconsistency. Identify it.

The Persistence of Memory

WALTER HOWERTON

Sometimes I wish I could have gone to Vietnam and been a killer in a green suit and jungle boots with a nickname like Halftrack or Iron Mike or Shake-and-Bake or Crazy Davy written in crude letters on the back of my steel helmet. Sometimes I would like to have known the intimate skill of field stripping an M-16 in the dark or the sensual seconds between the tossing of an armed hand grenade and its blast. I would like to have known the shudder of a chopper, the slosh of rice paddies, the rattle of small arms fire, the crump of mortars, the scream of artillery, the roar of supporting jets. I would like to recall the sweet taste of the earth at the bottom of a foxhole, the acrid smell of burned powder, the tingle of Agent Orange, the glow of phosphorus, the joy of C-ration peaches. I would like to remember the fear of pungi stakes and tripwires and Bouncing Bettys. Sometimes I wish I knew what I-Corps was like, or the Mekong Delta, Chu Lai, Hué, or Saigon; I would like to have walked down The Street Without Joy. Sometimes I wish I could have marked time with a felt-tipped pen on the sides of my helmet; I would have counted the days in clusters with a slash for every fifth day and as the days passed and the count grew the replacements would have envied me my time. And, as the count neared 365, I would have known that I had changed, that I was no longer the Green Grunt who had made the first mark, that I was almost a veteran. I would know that only a raw recruit could envy those marks as the simple passing of time and I would shake my head. As a veteran, I would be able to look at the marks on my helmet and understand them as more than time; they would measure distance, too. If I were a veteran, I would know that those marks were mileposts measuring the distance between The War and The World. If I were a veteran, I would understand space and time; I would understand the distance between The War and The World. I would join a veterans' organization.

My father is a veteran; he is a member of a veterans' organization; it is not the kind of organization I could belong to if I had gone to Vietnam and come home 365 days later. There is no space between my father's war and his world. They call it a World War and he believes them; my father and his friends believe that they have cut the world down to size and put their mark on it. It is a narrow war and my father and the other members of his organization celebrate it in a room the size of a mobile home which they have named after a local hero, someone who died in action and won medals for it. They sit and talk about it over cold beers and their slender meeting room is wide enough to hold anything they have to say. They speak proprietorially; it is a proprietary war. They made it and it is theirs. It is as long and narrow as a smalltown shoestore and they tend it with the pride of shopkeepers. If I asked my father how far it was from the war to the world, he would shake his head and look at me like I was a raw recruit. But in his war he never marked the days on the side of his helmet; he and his friends speak fondly of The Duration; the war I could have gone to would have been wider than a shoestore. The day I registered for the draft, my father took me to drink beer with the veterans. He bought me a beer and put his hand on my shoulder. My boy here just signed up for the draft, he said. He squeezed my shoulder. It won't be long now. The mailman will drop that letter in the box. Greetings. That's what the letter says. Greetings. Am I right? The veterans nodded. Any day now, my father said and his hand stayed on my shoulder. It won't be long now. Somebody ordered another round. The veterans talked about the letter, the draft, basic training. They agreed that if they were younger they would be the first to go to Vietnam or wherever. They couldn't agree about how to say Vietnam, but they all agreed that I was a lucky boy. What are you going to try for? one of them said. Infantry, just like his dad, my father said. How about paratroops? someone else said. I was a paratrooper. Women just love a paratrooper. He nudged me with his elbow. My father laughed and squeezed my shoulder again. I think I'm going to try for a deferment, I said. My father lifted his hand off my shoulder and the World War and the war and the world all slipped.

Sometimes I wish I could have flown into Vietnam, banking sharply over the dense green jungle, could have disembarked in the dusty heat in my dress greens and swapped them for jungle fatigues, could have packed away my shiny stateside shoes and laced up my jungle boots, could have put on my helmet and my flak jacket and gone to a base camp, could have lived in a hootch and been a part of a perimeter, could have had a sapper in black pajamas breach the wire where I was waiting, could have looked him in the eye and shot him dead even as he lobbed his grenade among us, could have thrown myself onto the grenade and become a piece of architecture my father could understand, something long and narrow made of cement blocks with brick veneer, something with my name over the door and a flagpole out front, something with my medals in a glass case alongside my uniform, my boots, my helmet, my photograph, the flag that had draped my coffin, something that looked like a store, something he could call his own. My father has never had his own store; he has always managed stores for other people. There have been large stores and small stores, but not one of them has been my father's store, though he has always spoken of them in a proprietary way. There have been toy stores and shoe stores, drugstores and grocery stores, but my father has always called them The Store, making them sound pure and mysterious and beyond the grasp of adjectives; he has always spoken of putting up stock, taking inventory, building displays, reading the register tapes with managerial propriety, though he has never been a proper manager. There has always been a lien against his authority. He has been a manager trainee, an assistant manager, a relief manager, a produce manager; he has never been able to make himself into something as pure and simple as The Store; there has always been a compromising adjective. I have to get back to the store, he said to the veterans when he had taken his hand from my shoulder. We're taking inventory. The store, the war, I said. It's all the same to you.

My father has been places I have never been. He has been to Italy, North Africa, Pennsylvania, South Texas; they are the places he passed through while becoming a veteran. He has been shot at by people who couldn't speak English. He could never understand why I would want to pass up a similar opportunity. There were mornings when we would sit over our bacon and eggs and he would tell me the places he had been, but he could never tell me what they looked like or how they smelled or what the people were like except that they all carried guns and none of them could speak English. If I were to travel to Italy or North Africa, I would expect them to smell like bacon and eggs. There were other mornings when he talked about being afraid, but he could never tell me what it felt like. Everyone is afraid, he said; it's natural. When I try to picture what it was like for my father to be afraid, it smells like bacon and eggs. Later, there were mornings when my father would tell me that only sissies tried to get out of going. I could have gone to college if the World War hadn't come along, he said, but I wouldn't have asked for a deferment even if I'd had the chance. Only sissies wanted deferments, he said. And a sissy is always a sissy. Remember that. It's something you can never get away from. People will always remember. My father named some. So they smell like bacon and eggs? I asked. My father tried to sell me the Army, coax me, shame me; I played with what he said and how he said it. It became our breakfast ritual, never spontaneous enough to become a fight. We wrapped ourselves in the smell of bacon and eggs and protected each other like strangers or enemies, each observing the defenses of the other, fearing spontaneous combustion.

Sometimes I wish I could have been a part of a perfect ambush on the Ho Chi Minh trail, could have blacked my face and worn leaves on my helmet, could have lain without moving while they walked among us, could have triggered the Claymore from the darkness and watched the tracers burn across the night, could have illuminated the enemy with a parachute flare and eliminated them with short bursts from my M-16 on full-automatic, could have counted the bodies at dawn and marched back to base camp tired but not too tired to be ferried down to Saigon on a chopper, to brag a little in the bars, to find a beautiful and petite bar girl who spoke only enough English to quote a price; I would have paid for the whole night. (Dear Dad, just a quick note before we go out on patrol again. Did you ever do a night ambush? We just did. Charlie walked right into it and we cut him to pieces. It was just like in the training films. Remember how beautiful you said tracers were at night? You were right! And you were right about something else, too. It's natural to be afraid. They tell us it's healthy. When you're afraid, it feels even better to get the job done right. We did such a good job that they gave us a few days of R and R in Saigon. What a filthy place. People live in the street and beg Americans for food and money. They don't speak much English. Do you think it's easier to do things to people who don't speak English? Anyway, we drank beer and did all of the stuff soldiers do on leave. More later, Dad. Right now it's time to see if Charlie is dumb enough to walk into another trap. Your son.) I have never written my father a letter; I have never been to a place from which I could have written to him in a language he could understand. I have never been to Southern Italy or North Africa; I have never been to South Texas or Pennsylvania. I have avoided the places my father has been and limited my travels to places he has never seen. I keep the details from him. We talk in lists and the places we have been burn like tracers between us when we name them. At least they seem to, but I have never seen tracers burn. I have never been in an ambush; I have never been to Vietnam.

I once got as close to Vietnam as California, but by then the war was over. I never had to flee to Canada, but I have vacationed in British Columbia. Still, I have been closer than that to Saigon and Toronto without leaving home. In 1963-64, I carried my draft card in my pocket (as required by law and to buy beer for my underaged friends); being I-A was being closer to Saigon than I understood then. Understanding came later. I did not set out to oppose the war; I set out to avoid the draft; fighting against the war came much later. By 1968, we were calling draft cards tickets to Saigon and my ticket had been issued and expedited. I-A again. Near Saigon again, but even nearer to Toronto. My father doesn't know how close I have been to Toronto; he only knows how far I stayed from Saigon.

My father is a handsome man when he is alone. I have always liked to peek at him around doorframes when he is sitting reading the paper, spy on him from behind the shrubbery while he mows the lawn, watch him from the window while he washes the car, stand outside in the dark and study him while he sits at his desk and smokes his pipe. Perhaps that is why I chose to stop so late, to stand in the dark, to look through the window, to tap so lightly on the door. I am leaving in the morning, I said. I am leaving on the bus. I came by to tell you. I already have my ticket. He did not ask me where I was going, how long I was planning to stay, when I was coming back. At the hospital they said I would probably be better off if I moved away, I said. They said I had probably wanted to run away as a child. They said I was frightened of the idea of running away. Now I am an adult, I said. I don't have to run away. I am old enough to make my own decisions and I have decided to go away. I wanted to tell you, I said. As I talked, my father remained as handsome as if I were not in the room. In fear and confusion I quoted my old political science professor to him. He said it's the wrong damn war at the wrong damn time, I said. College, my father said, hospitals. He walked to his desk and shuffled his papers. Do you understand? I said. My father doesn't write letters; he does not even write thank you notes. He does not write sentences. My father makes lists. He uses three-by-five notepads, the kind with red glue down one edge. He has lists of names, places, things to do, things to buy, lists for the auto mechanic, for his employees at the store, lists for the maid. They are taped to the refrigerator, to his shaving mirror; lists of phone numbers are taped to the wall, a list of the birds he has seen at his feeder is taped to the kitchen window; he used to tape lists to my door. His desk is cluttered with them; the old ones and the new ones shuffle together; he never crosses off the items he has bought or the things he has done, never checks up on the auto mechanic or the maid. He took a list from his desk, folded it in half and handed it to me. When you are on the bus to wherever you are going, he said. You have fooled a lot of people, he said. Someday you'll wish you had a home to come to. His hair is curly, his forehead broad, his eyes gray, his nose straight, his lips firm and fine, his chin definite, his lists neatly printed in square letters. MY SON: *1) College. 2) Marriage. 3) Fatherhood. 4) Deferment. 5) Divorce. 6) Insanity.* He is a remarkably handsome man.

Sometimes I wish I could have gone to basic training and had my hair cropped, received a uniform that would not fit, slept in a long, narrow barracks room when sleep was allowed, had a bunk (or a rack or a sack) and a locker, done calisthenics before dawn, double-timed to breakfast, stood in chow lines, cleaned floors with a toothbrush, learned close-order drill, crawled through muddy infiltration courses, run through obstacle courses, heard bugles blow, cleaned my weapon, made my bed tightly enough for a quarter to bounce on it, pulled K.P., learned about entrenching tools and shelter halves, been yelled at by my sergeant about things I did not know how to do. Suck it in! Double-time! Left! Left! Left! Right! Left! Run! March! Forward march! To the rear, march! Attention! Shoulder arms! Port arms! Eyes right! Halt! Parade rest! At ease! Fire! Squeeze 'em off! Fire! Fire! It would only have lasted eight weeks and when it was over I would have had a leave, would have worn my dress greens, would have caught a bus home. I would have saluted my father at the station and brought home gifts for my brothers, jackets and caps which said I DID IT AT FORT JACKSON, S.C. I would have talked about sergeants and Nam and having to report. I would have waited for orders to be cut and come through. When I boarded another bus and found a window seat, I would have saluted my father again. I would have returned past the sentries to sergeants who never make mistakes. I would have done things by the numbers.

When I was born, my father did not want me to have his name, but that is the name I got. Later, when I didn't want it either, he laughed and said it hadn't been his idea. When I asked him what he had wanted to name me, he said he couldn't remember. When I told him I wanted to be called Spike or Rusty or Buster, he laughed again and said they sounded like the names off of baseball cards and that if I wanted a name like that I would have to make the team. Besides, he said, look at Mickey Mantle; he doesn't need one of those names. I was too fat, too slow, afraid of the ball. I never made the team. Still later, my father told me that I thought I was too good for my name and not long after that he told me my name was too good for me. The name we share is long, cold, formal; we share nearly half the alphabet, but there are no lively diminutives hiding among all those letters. I once knew a judge whose name was Santiago, but those of us who knew him well called him Jimmy. Our name is not like that; our name allows no special familiarity in the private celebrations of the office or the dinner table. When I was a child, relatives attached "Big" to my father's name and "Little" to mine so that we would know to speak when spoken to. Those practical adjectives still linger on the lips of aged grandmothers, aging aunts and uncles, seldom seen cousins, those to whom we are related by blood and marriage. We wear them like harnesses and drag our names behind us through Christmas dinners and family reunions with the dumb patience of draft animals. Perhaps my father and I can survive the carnage of accumulated holidays to shake hands over the smooth silver lid of the last of their coffins, speak each other's name unmodified, and go our separate ways. Perhaps we are waiting for that to happen, or, perhaps, we are simply sitting in our separate rooms, each waiting for the other to die. Ours is not the sort of name to which sympathy affixes itself; it is the kind of name which might appropriately accrue the prefixes and suffixes of authority and accomplishment and be cited, hated or admired in its rigid entirety. After My Lai it was as easy to blame it on Lt. William Calley as it was to hate Gen. William Westmoreland or President Lyndon Baines Johnson or Richard Milhous Nixon; the letters of their names and titles bind together into hateful units. My father and I are bound together by an impenetrably cohesive alphabet, neither of us able to carry away enough letters to make a name for himself. It was harder to hate Lt. Calley when they called him Rusty.

Sometimes I wish I could have been ordered to Vietnam, ordered to stand at attention, to stand at ease, ordered to hurry and then ordered to wait, ordered to eat, to sleep, to march, to dig, to walk point on patrol, to try to kill or die, could have had sergeants scream at me that there are three ways to do anything, The *wrong* way! The *right* way! And the *Army* way!, and answered, Yes, Sergeant. Louder! Yes, Sergeant! LOUDER! YES, SERGEANT!, could have had someone tell me what to wear and how to wear it, what to carry and how to carry it, what to say and how to say it, who to kill and how to do it, could have had sergeants who said it all in the same, flat, correct scream. You make your rack like this! You shine your shoes like this! You wear your flak jacket like this! You hold your weapon like this! You fire your rounds like this! You use your bayonet like this! You torch your hootches like this! You grease your gooks like this! I would have been under orders or awaiting orders; I would have been assigned to duty or awaiting reassignment; I would have known that even if I did not know someone knew and that orders were being cut to let me know, too. Shortly after I did not go to Vietnam, my father made a mistake and ordered too much of something, or not enough of something for The Store; he was fired. I called him long-distance from a phone booth where I had gotten off the bus. Welcome to the ranks of the gainfully unemployed, I said. Speak for yourself, he said. I have contacts; people know me; they know my work. Have you filed for unemployment? I asked. I've never had any trouble getting a job, he said. I've always had a job. Even when I was a boy I had a paper route. Two paper routes, he said. There's always room for a man who's willing to do his job, he said. If we had been sitting over bacon and eggs, I would have asked him what he thought of Lt. Calley doing his job. Instead, I asked, Why did you get fired? My fault, he said. I made a mistake. They said something and I heard them say something else. They were right; I was wrong, he said. No sour grapes here. Don't you worry about that. I made a mistake and I'm paying for it. Something will turn up. Why did you call? he said. To welcome you to the ranks of the unemployed, I said. I know why you called, he said. Why? I asked. Misery loves company, he said. When I asked him about Lt. Calley, he hung up. I waited for the operator to tell me how to pay for the call; as I waited, I read the instructions printed on the front of the phone. My father would have read the instructions first; he would have had the correct change; he would not have had to run to the service station across the street for more quarters. My father always does things by the numbers, the rules, the directions, the instructions. He does not make mistakes and if he does it is because the directions were unclear. I once received a beautiful model car for Christmas, a 1954 Cadillac Coupe de Ville with chrome bumpers and rubber tires. I spread it out on the kitchen table; I opened the glue with a pin; I began to glue. Have you read the directions? my father said. No, I said. Then you are doing it wrong, he said. He pulled apart the pieces I had already glued. He sat down with the directions. I left the table. The next morning, the Cadillac was back in its box, all of the pieces in their proper compartments. I have to write the company, he said. The directions aren't clear. The company never answered to his satisfaction. The Cadillac is still in its box. My father does not build Cadillacs without directions and I do not read directions. I am sure he has a list of his mistakes and my mistakes; that is the kind of man he is; I am just as sure that the Cadillac doesn't appear on either one of them.

My father measures his life in mistakes. The biggest mistake I ever made was not staying in the Army after the war, he has always said and I am sure it is number one on his list. I am sure that the list says MISTAKES in large block letters across the top and that right under that, in letters almost as large, it says, 1) Army. He makes them and lists them; he looks at the list and shakes his head. He loves to keep score, to take inventory, to count things one by one, to subtotal and then total; he loves the gadgetry of addition and subtraction, large adding machines, pocket calculators, cash registers, stopwatches, metronomes; he has devised his own elaborate method for keeping track of baseball games; he knows when teams have been mathematically eliminated from the pennant races. He knows all the rules that govern baseball, basketball, football; he hates designated hitters, three-point baskets, shot clocks and player strikes; he loves the four-corners offense in college basketball because it stays within the old rules. If he were in better health, he might be a referee, an umpire, but things happened inside him in North Africa, got worse in Sicily, and finally broke him down after Salerno. He blames himself for it. The Army got him patched up and sent him home as soon as it could; the war wasn't even over. He still gets a small disability check; he didn't get a purple heart. He still thinks leaving the Army was the biggest mistake he ever made, something he did to himself, something he did to the Army, something that ruined his life. He still thinks he had a choice, that he did the wrong thing, that there was a right thing to do and he didn't do it. My father says that he studies his mistakes; I suspect he just watches them accumulate.

My father has always tried to do the right thing; he has followed the directions, read the labels, requested more information, awaited further instructions, filled in the blanks, played by the rules, avoided overeating, overheating, freezing temperatures, changed his oil, rotated his tires, not changed horses in mid-stream, not counted his chickens before they hatched, eaten an apple a day, looked before leaping, never played with fire, walked softly and carried a big stick, shaken well before using, kept out of the reach of children, stored in a cool, dry place, put in a well-marked container, been obedient, cheerful, thrifty, brave, clean, reverent, done unto others, stopped, looked and listened, honored his father and mother, closed cover before striking, avoided entangling alignments, been wary of the military-industrial complex, asked not what his country could do for him, squeezed tubes from the bottom, put up or shut up, lived and let live, paid the piper, had regular check-ups, read manufacturers' warranties, read the fine print, followed suggested maintenance schedules, kept his feet on the ground, his eyes open, and his house in order. His isolation is complete. There will always be wars and rumors of wars, he says. He speaks from the soft middle ground between his father and his son, neither of whom know anything about wars at all. His father worked as a welder in a railroad yard during World War I; his son worked at excuses and reasons for staying out of the Vietnam War; he alone did not make excuses. And after he had gone to war and come home again, after he had packed his uniform away, after he had told his father how he would do it again if he had to, while he was still thin, weak and shuffling, his father had asked him what it was really like over there, overseas? And he had said, There is no way you can understand it. His father pressed him, begging for details. I did what had to be done, he said. What did you do? Things, he said. Things to win the war. I did my duty. You wouldn't understand. You were a welder when you had the chance to make the world safe for democracy. Something happened to him over there, my grandfather said; he was different when he came home. He has never told me anything that happened either, I said. He has only told me what he has told you. He said it wasn't like the movies. He has told me the names of the ships he was on, the battles he fought in, the countries he was in, the name of the rifle he used. He gave me his name, rank and serial number. It was a big war, he said. A big war. You are not even willing to go to a little war. My grandfather and I have never asked for a body count; we aren't interested in inventories. We would like for my father to tell us a good story; we know how it's done; we have read the literature; we know titles and authors, know about action in the Pacific, the cold at The Bulge, the glowing machine gun barrels at Guadalcanal. We would not care if he lied to us as long as he would take us with him to North Africa and Italy. I didn't grow up hating war; I only hated my father's version of it. My father's war is stillborn, all figures and facts, dates, names and numbers. We want to know why leaving the Army is the biggest mistake he ever made. War is hell, my father says, but there is no fire in his voice. He thinks we cannot understand his story, but what we cannot understand is the way he has chosen to tell it. I helped break the Axis, he said, but you are not even willing to keep the dominoes from tumbling across Asia. It's the wrong damn war, I said. There will always be wars, he said. I don't want to be a prisoner of war, I said. But sometimes I wish I could have gone to Vietnam so I could tell him the story. My father lives in artless isolation, clinging like an immigrant to his native tongue.

My father didn't raise me to be a soldier. There is graphic proof. They are my favorite pictures in the family album. They are photographs of me, but they say very little about me; they are not a record of how I was or who I was; rather, they are a record of what my father used to be. They are pictures of my father at play, my father full of hope, speculating on the diverse possibilities of the future. They do not document birthdays, holidays, bicycles or picnics; they document nothing but my father's eye. They are staged photographs, their borders filled with costumes, props, imagination. In one, I am a carpenter; in another, I am a baseball player; in a third, I wear the jacket and cap from my father's old band uniform and hold his instrument to my lips; in the fourth, I am wearing my father's high-topped rubber boots and hoeing in the garden; finally, I am sitting in my highchair wearing nothing but a diaper and a pencil behind my ear; there is a typewriter on the tray in front of me. There are no toys in the pictures. The hammers and saws, levels and squares, the bat, the ball and glove, the saxophone, the shovel and hoe, the typewriter and pencil are all real. The shoes, the hats, the uniforms are all adult sizes, rolled, tucked and baggy. They are all his. There is patience and care in each picture; the costumes fit as well as possible; I hold the tools of the trade properly, naturally; in each of them I work confidently and contentedly. I reflect my father's pleasure and confidence. When I look at them now I see my father as an artist I have never known. There are many more pictures of me in the album, me with Christmas trees and birthday cakes, me with relatives, me going to school, me playing with my friends, me as a Cub Scout and then a Boy Scout, me in school plays, me winning honorable mention in the science fair, going to the prom, graduating from high school, getting married, me and my bicycle, my dog, my child. They are all flat, standard, documenting acquisitions and accomplishments; many of them show a decided unwillingness on the part of the subject and a growing unwillingness on the part of the photographer. The distance between the subject and the camera grows; backgrounds begin to dominate and, finally, there is nothing but scenery, pictures of the sea and the mountains, vacant farmhouses and empty fields, famous birthplaces and monuments. Then, there are empty pages. My father's camera is in his bottom desk drawer, hidden under a clutter of photographs which have no sequence and nesting among the many rolls of undeveloped film. He does not know what is on them and he says that he no longer cares. Once, I looked at the album with him, laughing and remembering. You were a Boy Scout, he said. You played in the band. You sang in the choir. You had bicycles and scooters, Lincoln logs and Erector sets. You went on vacations to historical places. You had things I never had. I never raised you to be what you are, he said. But he did. He never photographed me in his Army uniform.

My father did not teach me to be a fighter, a ballplayer, a gardener, or a typist; instead, he taught me the alphabet. It must have been with the same patience that he used in taking those photographs, but I don't remember learning it. I only remember reciting it with him in my darkened bedroom, preserving its unity as if the omission of a single letter would destroy sleep. He would recite it to me; we would say it together; I would recite it to him. If I make a mistake, he would make me begin again, emphasizing the bonds that held A to B and B to C, emphasizing the inevitable progress from A to Z. On the nights when I didn't get it right, he would leave me to my nightmares saying, Practice, practice, practice; on the nights when I preserved order without error, he would tuck the blanket under my chin and I would sleep soundly. My father liked cigars, the cheap ones that come five to a package. He rarely smoked them, lighting them only as a brief formality, letting them go out, then chewing the cold stub. His breath when he breathed the alphabet or kissed my cheek smelled of chewed cigars and his skin had the slightest odor of sweet, cheap cigar smoke. My alphabet has always smelled like that. When I had learned how to say it night after night without having to start over, he began to teach me how the letters looked. He cut letters from magazines and newspapers, cartons and labels; each morning there would be a few of them beside my breakfast. Find me an A, he would say, and I would search through the pile until I found it. We would smile together. The piles grew larger and when I could find all of the letters, he taught me how to arrange them on the table in front of me. He glued the alphabet to a piece of colored paper and kissed me on the cheek. You did it, he said, handing me the paper. It's yours, he said. Alphabetical order. He put it on the wall of my room. I did that, I said. Then he taught me how to take the alphabet apart and make words. When I spelled a word correctly, he would glue it onto a sheet of colored paper. The walls of my room filled with words on red paper, blue paper, yellow or green paper, one word to a page, all neatly glued and artfully arranged, each word preserved in the isolated integrity of its own alphabet. I became the repository for my father's alphabetical hopes, just as I had been for his photographic hopes. But when I learned to read sentences, my father lost interest. It was as if the bonds which held the letters together was sufficient and that the introduction of grammar some-how corrupted the purity of the language he wanted me to learn. I began to read myself away from him; accomplishing enough in a short time to begin reading war stories; I looked for him in them, but he was never there. I asked him why I couldn't find him in the stories. War isn't like it is in books, he said. It just wasn't like that. What was it like? I asked. Not like that, he said. That's all. I read about war in Europe, war in the Pacific, the air war, the ground war, the sea war. I knew the names of the tanks, airplanes and ships. I memorized the war in Italy and North Africa. I gave heroes my father's face and my father's cigar smell. I read about machine guns and foxholes, D-Day, Pearl Harbor, VE Day, VJ Day. My father was everywhere, then he was nowhere. I outgrew war stories. Do you think you will ever outgrow war stories? I asked him. Do you ever think you will grow up? I said. The war has been over for more than twenty years, I said. Twenty years. In your books, he said. In your books it's been over for twenty years.

In Vietnam we would have carried our lucky charms. I would have had one, too, something small to keep death away, something hard or magic to deflect incoming enemy rounds harmlessly into the dark green jungle or painfully into the sweating green bodies of my companions—a rabbit's foot or four-leaf clover, a picture to kiss, a lucky marble to finger in my pocket, a pair of socks that never got washed and were always worn on patrol, a crucifix on a chain, a locket in my pocket with a lock of my true love's hair, a Bible to stop a slug, a prayer on a plastic-coated card, a poem, a silver dollar, a gris-gris to wear on a leather thong around my neck—something to save me by mystery or physics from the activities of steel. In Vietnam we would have been men of steel—steel helmets, steel-soled boots, flak jackets—but what we couldn't cover with steel we would have covered with luck. My father carried a picture of my mother at Anzio; I have little faith in photography. I would have had a simple leather pouch hanging from a leather thong. I would have carried the alphabet in it. The letters would have been small, dry, light, the letters that go into alphabet soup. As we prepared to march into the jungle, I would have shaken a few of them into my hand. I would have spelled the safest word I could find and popped it into my mouth. I would have sucked on the word until it softened, swallowed it, digested it. What wasn't covered by steel would have been covered by language. I would have swallowed my alphabet in small ho-meopathic doses and as my tour of duty neared its end I would have become immune to the activities of steel. And on the last patrol I would have eaten the safest word, smiling as it became soft and gummy in my mouth, grinning as it became sweeter to the taste, as carbohydrate became simple sugar. I would have survived the last patrol; I would have left the war for the world; there would have been a large sign in front of the house.

It would have said WELCOME HOME. Home sweet home. Later, I would have gone to see my father at The Store and he would have called his friends; we would all have gone to the veterans' hall. We would have spoken a language which no one else could understand and it would have made all our wars seem the same.

Home is hard to swallow. It never turns sweet on my tongue; I don't have the juices to digest it. My father swallowed it whole. Sometimes it is as if he has swallowed his entire vocabulary whole; he speaks in unmasticated chunks. Home. The Store. The War. Song titles. Broken lyrics. Proverbs. Old sayings. Clichés. He speaks them without relish, says things without savoring them. When he leaves for The Store, he says, Keep the home fires burning. When he calls from The Store, he asks, How are things on the home front? He describes his work at The Store as Being in the trenches or Bringing home the bacon. And when he comes home at night, he says, There's no place like home, or, Home sweet home, or, Home from the hill, or, Home is where the heart is. He follows home teams; he shops at locally owned businesses. He believes in homework. If they wanted you to do it in study hall, he says, they wouldn't call it *home* work. Sometimes, it's hard not to laugh, but laughter is always a mistake. He is not a laughing man; home, The Store, The War are not laughing matters. But I laughed. When he said, I've been in the trenches bringing home the bacon, I laughed. I laughed for all of the times I had wanted to laugh before. Stop! he said, but I couldn't stop. It's not funny, he said. I kept laughing. A man has to provide a home for his family, he said. I've worked like a slave so you can have a home. I went to war so you can have a home. I've always tried to make a good home for you. As long as you are in my home, he said, you will do what I say! Stop! he said. You've had it too easy. Life in the trenches is tough. By the time I was your age, I had been to war. By the time I was your age, I was in for the duration. Not me, I said; I'm not in for the duration. Someday, he said, you will wish you had a place to call home. I laughed. I am taller than my father and I am heavier. When he raised his hand to hit me, I grabbed his wrist. I held him away from me; he didn't struggle. Instead, he inhaled. It was a deep breath. I waited for him to speak. He didn't. He held the breath and swallowed. He swallowed home, The Store, The War. I felt the strength leave his arm and relaxed my grip. I searched his face for signs of age. Anger, confusion, fear twitched his cheeks and twisted his mouth. But he did not grow old; instead, he looked younger and I was frightened. It was the face a German infantryman might have aimed at on the beach at Anzio or in the hills near Salerno. It was not a veteran's face; it was a recruit's face. It was a foreign and familiar face. His eyes sparkled and died. If he had spoken, it would have been a language I could not have understood. My father leans on words; he gives them weight rather than meaning. I have never known the meaning of home, but I know how much it weighs.

In Vietnam, I would have learned the code of war. I am sure Rusty Calley knows the code of war. If we had been boys together, we would have played Army; we would have worn our surplus packs and carried leftover canteens on our web belts; we would have shouldered our stick guns and called them by the names we had learned from our fathers—M-1, Tommy-gun, B.A.R., or bazooka; we would have lobbed pine cone hand grenades and called them pineapples or potato mashers; we would have dug our foxholes and called our mothers' garden trowels entrenching tools; we would have brandished bayonets made of discarded table knives. We would have drawn straws to determine who got to be the GIs and who got to be the Krauts or the Japs. The oldest and strongest would have been our officers; the youngest and weakest would have been their men. We would have taken long drinks from our canteens and drawn maps on the ground with our bayonets. We would have dug in. We would have hunted and killed each other through the long summer afternoons; there would have been rules about the dead and the wounded. We would have taken each other prisoner and there would have been rules about taking prisoners. Boys who play army are fanatics about rules. Sometimes they are written in block letters on sheets of notebook paper; sometimes they are committed to memory. But they are always there—rules, codes, conventions governing the quick and the dead. But in the heat of our battles we always did what we had to do. No one wanted to be among the dead or the wounded, no one wanted to be a prisoner of war. Sometimes our games would have ended in angry arguments between the living and the dead over the rules of the game. In Vietnam there would have been no arguments between the living and the dead. Rusty would have been my lieutenant and I would have been one of his men. We would have hunted and killed through the hot afternoons. We would have stood together over the shallow ditch near My Lai 4. Those in the ditch would have cried out; perhaps, they would have cited the rules of the game. Rusty and I would have looked at each other and shrugged because we could not understand a word they were saying. The code of war is a conspiracy of language; Rusty and I would have understood each other; we would not have understood those who cried in the ditch. We would have understood that we did not want to be among the dead and the wounded, that we did not want to be prisoners of war; we would have understood that we did not understand those in the ditch. We would have done what we had to do. The code of war has nothing to do with the rules of the game; the code of war is a conspiracy of language. Walking away from My Lai, we would have practiced the code.

We would have learned to encase elaborate explanations in dense mono-syllables; we would have smothered fear and rage in thick silence; we would have translated the screams of the dying into a language that only we could understand. When people asked us about it, our answers would have been enshrouded in the code of war. They would never really have understood. My father and I don't speak the same language, but Rusty Calley spoke a language that my father could understand. They're going to crucify that poor kid, my father said. They're going to crucify him for doing his job. But he killed innocent people, I said. Noncombatants. He killed noncombatants in a ditch. War is hell, my father said. It is something Rusty and I might have said, leaving My Lai.

I have tried to break the code of war. I have read all of the books, seen all of the movies, memorized maps, studied photographs. I have tried to make friends with veterans. I eat in restaurants owned by Vietnamese refugees. On the nights when I am most desperate, I eat big meals in places with names like *Saigon* or *The Mekong* or *Chu Lai Charlie's*, then I go to rap sessions with the Vietnam vets. I sit in their circle and pass myself off as one of them. I talk to them about the places on my maps and tell them stories from the books I've read. I talk about coming into Danang, about R and R in Saigon, about napalm and air strikes, about Khé Sanh and Tet and Hué, about the Mekong Delta and life in I-Corps. I have told them about my wounds and medals and about the buddies I have lost; I have flown dustoffs for them in my helicopter; I have been a medic passing out M and Ms to the hopelessly wounded; I have been a private and a sergeant and an officer. Usually, they listen politely, sympathetically, as I weave a surface of war, then, someone else begins to talk. I try to remember what they say, but they have seen and done things, they have heard things for which there seem to be no words. When they lapse into silence, I speak up. I try to keep things going. I mention Agent Orange and they nod. They hate Vietnamese food. One night, in a storefront vets center, I told them about the ambush. I told them how carefully it was planned, how we camouflaged ourselves, blacked our faces, waited. We watched the night where the trail was supposed to be. I told them how I liked night ambushes because it was easier not to see. But the sky began to get lighter. Still, nothing happened. We relaxed and thought about getting back to our hootches. Then, while we were still thinking about home, the VC came down the trail. It's not supposed to happen like this, I said. But it happened anyway. They came. We triggered our Claymores and squeezed off our rounds in short bursts. I told them about the VC who looked me in the face. I told them about his face. It was a recruit's face, I said, a foreign and familiar face. It was a hard face to kill. He took a deep breath as if he were about to speak to me. He raised his hand. His eyes sparkled and died. He swallowed. When I had finished my story, there was silence. Then, the veterans gathered around me, put their hands on me and their arms over me. I wish my father had been there.

If home is where the heart is, I am lost. I have been places my father has never seen, but home is always another place, another time. I am nearly twenty years away from home, nearly twenty years away from the times and the places where I belonged. I am that far from the rhetoric and the music and the Pentagon; I am that far from the Days of Rage in Chicago; I am that far from being drafted; I am that far from Vietnam. I am as far from all of that as my father was from the beach at Anzio when he made a list of my life. Sometimes, I look at the list he gave me, look at the block letters, look at my life as he saw it. MY SON: 1) College. 2) Marriage. 3) Fatherhood. 4) Deferment. 5) Divorce. 6) Insanity. He waited for me on the beach, but I never came. They were the best years of my life.

I did no more to end the war in Vietnam than my father did to drive the Germans out of Italy. Rusty Calley did more to end the war than I did. There was a space between what he said he did at My Lai and the photographic evidence; it was a space as large as the one between the pictures my father took of me as a child dressed up like a man and the man I have become. It is the space in which the code of war begins to be broken. It is the space in which wars end.

My father and I are not home together. He went to his war and I did not go to mine. He marched across Africa and Italy; I marched across Washington and Chicago. Each of us has been places that the other has never seen. Biological necessity makes us claim each new day for our own; we crow our differences across the years that separate us. I have read the history of the war he went to and of the war I did not go to. But history is only a perch from which to crow. There is a space around history, a space between what is seen and what is said. It is the space between history and memory. It is a place where veterans live together, a place where our chronological longings find embraces. It is a place where time is deflated and hangs limply in the leafless trees. It is a broad expanse. It is the beach at Anzio; it is Pennsylvania Avenue. My father waits for me on the beach; I wander along the avenue in search of him. Chronology put him here ahead of me, but I am catching up. Perhaps we will meet by chance and if I had gone to Vietnam I would know what to say. Perhaps we will not meet by chance. Perhaps it is enough that we are here alone together, beyond words, biding our time, keeping our distance with the best years of our lives.

Suggestions for Discussion

1. "The Persistence of Memory" is poetic in structure, in that it is arranged in sections with the alternating refrain lines, "Sometimes I wish . . . " and "My father . . . " Is it also structured as a story? The subject is war, but what is the war of the story; how do the battles of it escalate? Is there a crisis action?

2. The opening section introduces a portrait of a Vietnam veteran, which the narrator is not. To what extent does this fantasy portrait characterize the narrator as he is?

3. Howerton uses many clichés of the "typical" veterans of both the Vietnam War and the Second World War. To what extent does this typicality make us pass judgment on war, soldiering, the father, the son?

4. Identify several nonmilitary images of the father that suggest typicality. How in the accumulation and convolution of these images does an individual character emerge?

5. "My father is a handsome man when he is alone" (page 138). The implication is clearly that he is less handsome when not alone. How do the details help to specify what the narrator means by this?

6. The father concerns himself with lists, instructions, photographs, the alphabet. How do these concerns provide a contrast with the son? How do they provide a link?

7. One theme of "The Persistence of Memory" is the inability of both father and son to tell their stories to each other. ". . . He could never tell me what they looked like or how they smelled . . . " "I have never been to a place from which I could have written him in a language he could understand." How does the denial of detail itself become an element of characterization?

8. Identify the consistent inconsistency of the narrator.

9. The girl of "Girl" and the narrator of "The Persistence of Memory" are different in race, gender, age, nationality, class—virtually every fundamental of type. Nevertheless, they reveal striking similarities in their relationship to a same-sex parent and what we have come to call the generation gap. What universals does a comparison reveal?

RETROSPECT

1. To what extent is Trexler in "The Second Tree from the Corner" a typical character, and how does his typicality force us to judge him? Where and how does his individuality invite us to identify with him?

2. What is Julian's consistent inconsistency in "Everything That Rises Must Converge"? Is he "good"?

3. Show how the character types of both the plumber and the professor in Frederick Busch's "Widow Water" are revealed through their individual characteristics.

WRITING ASSIGNMENTS

1. Keep a journal daily for two weeks. Each day, write a paragraph about a character drawn from memory, observation, or invention. Each day, also go back and add to a former characterization. Focus on details: Try to invent a past, motives, memories, and situations for the characters that interest you most.

2. At the end of the two weeks, assess yourself and decide what habit of journal keeping you can develop and stick to. A page a day? A paragraph a day? Three pages a week? Then do it. Your journal need not, of course, record only ideas for characters. Probably at least once a day you have a thought worth wording, and sometimes it's better to write one sentence a day than to let the habit slide. Like exercise and piano practice, a journal is most useful when it's kept up regularly and frequently. If you pick an hour during which you write each day, no matter how much or little, you may find yourself looking forward to, and saving things up for, that time.

3. There follows a list of familiar "types," each of them comic or unsympathetic to the degree that they have become cliché. Write a short character sketch of one or two of them, but individualizing the character through particular details that will make us sympathize and/or identify with him or her.

an absent-minded professor
a lazy laborer
a rock band groupie
an aging film star
a domineering wife
her timid husband
a tyrannical boss
a staggering drunk

4. In the sociological science of "garbology," human habits are assessed by studying what people throw away. Write a character sketch by describing the contents of a wastebasket or garbage can.

5. For an exercise (only), try writing a character sketch without any of the elements of type. We shouldn't be able to tell the age, race, gender, nationality, or class of your character. Can you do it? Is it satisfying?

6. Briefly describe a character who is as unlike yourself as you can imagine. Then get inside this character's head; give him or her one mental habit, desire, fear, love, or longing that you have. Make us see the character as "good."

7. Pick two contrasting or contradictory qualities of your own personality (consistent inconsistencies). Create a character that embodies each, and set them in conflict with each other. Since you are not writing about yourself but aiming at heightening and dramatizing these qualities, make each character radically different from yourself in at least one fundamental aspect of type: age, race, gender, nationality, or class.

THE FLESH MADE WORD
Methods of Character Presentation

The Indirect Method: Authorial Interpretation
The Direct Methods
Character: A Summary

Exploring everything there is to know about your character, identifying a pattern of consistent inconsistency, externally altering a character drawn from life, or finding an internal point of contact with an alien character— all are part of the mental process that can enrich your characterization before you begin your story.

In the writing itself, there are five basic *methods of presentation,* and employing a variety of these methods can help you to draw a full character. If you produce a conflict among the methods, this can also help you create a three-dimensional character.

The Indirect Method: Authorial Interpretation

The indirect method of presenting a character is *authorial interpretation*— "telling" us the character's background, motives, values, virtues, and the like. The advantages of the indirect method are enormous, for its use leaves you free to move in time and space; to know anything you choose to know whether the character knows it or not; and, godlike, to tell us what we are to feel. The indirect method allows you to convey a great deal of information in a short time.

> The most excellent Marquis of Lumbria lived with his two daughters, Caroline, the elder, and Luisa; and his second wife, Doña Vicenta, a woman with a dull brain, who, when she was not sleeping, was complaining of everything, especially the noise. . . .
>
> The Marquis of Lumbria had no male children, and this was the most painful thorn in his existence. Shortly after having become a widower, he had married Doña Vicenta, his present wife, in order to have a son, but she proved sterile.
>
> The Marquis' life was as monotonous and as quotidian, as unchanging and regular, as the murmur of the river below the cliff or as the liturgic services in the cathedral.
>
> MIGUEL DE UNAMUNO, *The Marquis of Lumbria*

The disadvantages of this indirect method are outlined in chapter 3. Indeed, in the passage above, it may well be part of Unamuno's purpose to convey the "monotonous and quotidian" quality of the Marquis' life by this summarized and distanced rehearsal of facts, motives, and judgments. Nearly every author will use the indirect method occasionally, and you may find it useful when you want to cover the exposition quickly. Occasionally you may convince us that you are so much more knowledgeable about a character than we can be, and so much more subtle at analyzing him or her, that we will accept your explanations. *Very* occasionally an author will get away with explaining the characters as much as, or more than, they are presented. Henry James is such an author; he is not an author I would advise anyone to imitate.

> Mrs. Touchett was certainly a person of many oddities, of which her behavior on returning to her husband's house after many months was a noticeable specimen. She had her own way of doing all that she did, and this is the simplest description of a character which, although it was by no means without benevolence, rarely succeeded in giving an impression of softness. Mrs. Touchett might do a great deal of good, but she never pleased.
>
> *Portrait of a Lady*

The very clear presence of the author in this passage, commenting, guiding our reactions, is the hallmark of James's prose, and (although it is by no means without benevolence) the technique is a difficult one to sustain. Direct presentation of the characters is much more likely to please the modern reader.

The Direct Methods

There are four methods of direct presentation: *appearance, speech, action,* and *thought*. A character may also be presented through the opinions of other characters, which may be considered a second indirect method. When this method is employed, however, the second character must give his or her opinions in speech, action, or thought. In the process, the character is inevitably also characterized. Whether we accept the opinion depends on what we think of that character as he or she is thus directly characterized. In this scene from Jane Austen's *Mansfield Park*, for example, the busybody Mrs. Norris gives her opinion of the heroine.

> ". . . there is something about Fanny, I have often observed it before, — she likes to go her own way to work; she does not like to be dictated to; she takes her own independent walk whenever she can; she certainly has a little spirit of secrecy, and independence, and nonsense, about her, which I would advise her to get the better of."
>
> As a general reflection on Fanny, Sir Thomas thought nothing could be more unjust, though he had been so lately expressing the same sentiments himself, and he tried to turn the conversation, tried repeatedly before he could succeed.

Here Mrs. Norris's opinion is directly presented in her speech, Sir Thomas's in his thoughts, each of them being characterized in the process; it is left to the reader to decide (without much difficulty) whose view of Fanny is the more reliable.

APPEARANCE

Of the four methods of direct presentation, appearance is especially important because our eyes are our most highly developed means of perception, and we receive more non-sensuous information by sight than by any other sense. Beauty is only skin deep, but people are embodied, and whatever beauty there is in them must somehow surface in order for us to perceive it—and whatever ugliness, too. Such surfacing involves speech and action as well as appearance, but it is appearance that prompts our first reaction to people, and everything they wear and own bodies forth some aspect of their inner selves.

Writers are sometimes inclined to neglect or even deny this. The choice of writing as a profession or avocation usually contains an implicit rejection of materialism (an English degree won't get you a job; your folks wish you'd major in business; starving in a gloomy basement is a likely option), and writers are concerned to see beyond mere appearances.

In fact, much of the tension and conflict in character does proceed from the truth that appearance is not reality. But in order to know this, we must see the appearance, and it is often in the contradiction between appearances that the truth comes out. Features, shape, style, clothing, objects can make statements of internal values that are political, religious, social, intellectual, and essential. The woman in the Ultrasuede jacket with the cigarette holder is making a different statement from the one in the holey sweatshirt with the palmed joint. Even a person who has forsaken our materialistic society altogether, sworn off supermarkets, and gone to the country to grow organic potatoes has a special relationship with his or her hoe. However indifferent we may be to our looks, that indifference is the result of experiences with our bodies. A twenty-two-year-old Apollo who has been handsome since he was six is a very different person from the man who spent his childhood cocooned in fat and burst the chrysalis at age sixteen.

Following are four very brief portraits of women, in which each is mainly characterized by such trivialities as fabric, hairdo, and cosmetics. It would nevertheless be impossible to mistake the essential nature of any one of them for that of any of the others.

Mrs. Withers, the dietician, marched in through the back door, drew up, and scanned the room. She wore her usual Betty Grable hairdo and open-toed pumps, and her shoulders had an aura of shoulder pads even in a sleeveless dress.

MARGARET ATWOOD, *The Edible Woman*

My grandmother had on not just one skirt, but four, one over the other. It should not be supposed that she wore one skirt and three petticoats; no, she wore four skirts; one supported the next, and she wore the lot of them in accordance with a definite system, that is, the order of the skirts was changed from day to day. . . . The one that was closest to her yesterday clearly disclosed its pattern today, or rather its lack of pattern: all my grandmother Anna Bronski's skirts favored the same potato color. It must have been becoming to her.

GÜNTER GRASS, *The Tin Drum*

How beautiful Helen is, how elegant, how timeless: how she charms Esther Songford and how she flirts with Edwin, laying a scarlet fingernail on his dusty lapel, mesmerizing.

She comes in a chauffered car. She is all cream and roses. Her stockings are purest silk; her underskirt, just briefly showing, is lined with lace.

FAY WELDON, *Female Friends*

As soon as I entered the room, a pungent odor of phosphorus told me she'd taken rat poison. She lay groaning between the quilts. The tatami by the bed was splashed with blood, her waved hair was matted like rope waste, and a bandage tied round her throat showed up unnaturally white. . . . The painted mouth in her waxen face created a ghastly effect, as though her lips were a gash open to the ears.

MASUJI IBUSE, "Tajinko Village"

In the next example, John Irving combines the indirect method with a direct presentation of appearance. Although this passage covers a period of time, gives us Jenny's opinion and her mother's, and passes a judgment, the characterization focuses on a vivid physical image of Jenny.

> Jenny was twenty-two. She had dropped out of college almost as soon as she'd begun, but she had finished her nursing-school program at the head of her class and she enjoyed being a nurse. She was an athletic-looking young woman who always had high color in her cheeks; she had dark, glossy hair and what her mother called a mannish way of walking (she swung her arms), and her rump and hips were so slender and hard that, from behind, she resembled a young boy. In Jenny's opinion, her breasts were too large; she thought the ostentation of her bust made her look "cheap and easy."
> In fact she was nothing of the kind. . . .

The World According to Garp

Sense impressions other than sight are also a part of the way a character "appears." A limp handshake or a soft cheek; an odor of Chanel, oregano, or decay—if we are allowed to taste, smell, or touch a character through the narrative, then these sense impressions characterize the way looks do.

The sound and associations of a character's name, too, can give a clue to personality: the affluent Mr. Chiddister in chapter 3 is automatically a more elegant sort than the affluent Mr. Strum; Huck Finn must have a different life from that of the Marquis of Lumbria. Although names with a blatant meaning—Joseph Surface, Billy Pilgrim, Martha Quest—tend to stylize a character and should be used sparingly if at all, ordinary names can hint at traits you mean to heighten, and it is worth combing any list of names, including the telephone book, to find suggestive sounds. My own telephone book yields, at a glance this morning, Linda Holladay, Marvin Entzminger, and Melba Peebles, any one of which might set me to speculating on a character.

Sound also characterizes as a part of "appearance" insofar as sound represents timbre, tenor, or quality or noise and speech, the characterizing reediness or gruffness of a voice, the lift of laughter or stiffness of delivery.

SPEECH

Speech, however, characterizes in a way that is different from appearance, because speech represents an effort, mainly voluntary, to externalize the internal and to manifest not merely taste or preference but also deliberated thought. Like fiction itself, human dialogue attempts to marry logic to emotion.

We have many means of communicating that are direct expressions of emotion: laughing, leering, shaking hands, screaming, shouting, shooting, making love. We have many means of communicating that are symbolic and emotionless: mathematical equations, maps, checkbooks, credit cards, and chemical formulas. Between body language and pure math lies language, in which judgments and feelings take the form of structured logic: in vows, laws, news, notes, essays, letters, and talk; and the greatest of these is talk.

Because speech has this dual nature, the place of dialogue in fiction is especially important. Its purpose is never merely to convey information. Dialogue may do that, but it must also simultaneously characterize, advance the action or develop the conflict, set the scene, foreshadow, or remind. William Sloane, in *The Craft of Writing*, says:

> There is . . . a tentative rule that pertains to all fiction dialogue. It must do more than one thing at a time or it is too inert for the purposes of fiction. This may sound harsh, but I consider it an essential discipline.

In considering Sloane's "tentative rule," I place the emphasis on *rule*. With dialogue as with significant detail, when you write you are constantly at pains to mean more than you say. If a significant detail must both call up a sense image and *mean*, then the character's words, which presumably mean something, should simultaneously suggest image, personality, or emotion. Even rote exchanges can call up images. A character who says, "It is indeed a pleasure to meet you," carries his back at a different angle, dresses differently, from a character who says, "Hey, man, what it is?"

In the three very brief speeches that follow are three fictional men, sharply differentiated from each other, not only by what they say, but by how they say it. How much do you know about each? How does each look?

"I had a female cousin one time—a Rockefeller, as it happened —" said the Senator, "and she confessed to me that she spent the fifteenth, sixteenth and seventeenth years of her life saying nothing but, 'No, thank you.' Which is all very well for a girl of that age and station. But it would have been a damned unattractive trait in a *male* Rockefeller."

KURT VONNEGUT, *God Bless You, Mr. Rosewater*

"Hey, that's nice, Grandma," says Phantom as he motions me to come in the circle with him. "I'll tell you what. You can have a contest too. Sure. I got a special one for you. A sweater contest. You get all the grannies out on the porch some night when you could catch a death a chill, and see which one can wear the most sweaters. I got an aunt who can wear fourteen. You top that?"

ROBERT WARD, Shedding Skin

The Knight looked surprised at the question. "What does it matter where my body happens to be?" he said. "My mind goes on working all the same. In fact, the more head downward I am, the more I keep inventing new things.

"Now the cleverest thing of the sort that I ever did," he went on after a pause, "was inventing a new pudding during the meat course."

LEWIS CARROLL, Through the Looking-Glass

Use your journal to experiment with speech patterns that will characterize. Some people speak in telegraphically short sentences missing various parts of speech. Some speak in convoluted eloquence or rhythms tedious with qualifying phrases. Some rush headlong without a pause for breath until they're breathless; others are measured or terse or begrudge even forming a sentence. Listen to the patterns of speech you hear and try to catch difference of character through syntax — the arrangement of words within a sentence. Then put two or more of these characters in a scene and see how much their differing voices can have to do with conflict.

Here is an exchange among three members of a Chinese-American family in which the subject of the talk is political but in which much more than politics is conveyed.

In fact, he hardly ever stopped talking, and we kids watched the spit foam at the corners of his mouth. . . . It was more like a lecture than a conversation. . . .

"Actually these aren't dreams or plans," Uncle Bun said. "I'm making predictions about ineluctabilities. This Beautiful Nation, this Gold Mountain, this America will end as we know it. There will be one nation, and it will be a world nation. A united planet. Not just Russian Communism. Not just Chinese Communism. World Communism."

He said, "When we don't need to break our bodies earning our daily living any more, and we have time to think, we'll write poems, sing songs, develop religions, invent customs, build statues, plant gardens and make a perfect world." He paused to contemplate the wonders.

"Isn't that great?" I said after he left.

"Don't get brainwashed," said my mother. "He's going to get in trouble for talking like that."

MAXINE HONG KINGSTON, China Men

Uncle Bun is richly characterized by his idealistic eloquence, but so are the narrator and her mother in their brief reactions. The contrast between Uncle Bun's "predictions about ineluctabilities" and the narrator's "Isn't that great?" makes her both a teenager and Americanized, whereas the mother's hostile practicality comes out in her blunt imperative.

This passage also illustrates an essential element of conflict in dialogue: tension and drama are heightened when characters are constantly (in one form or another) saying no to each other. Here the mother is saying a distinct no to both Uncle Bun and her daughter. In the following exchange from Ernest Hemingway's *The Old Man and the Sea*, the old man feels only love for his young protégé, and their conversation is a pledge of affection. Nevertheless, it is the old man's steady denial that lends the scene tension.

"Can I go out and get sardines for you tomorrow?"

"No. Go and play baseball. I can still row and Rogelio will throw the net."

"I would like to go. If I cannot fish with you, I would like to serve in some way."

"You brought me a beer," the old man said. "You are already a man."

"How old was I when you first took me in a boat?"

"Five and you were nearly killed when I brought the fish in too green and he nearly tore the boat to pieces. Can you remember?"

"I can remember the tail slapping and banging and the thwart breaking and the noise of the clubbing. I can remember you throwing me into the bow where the wet coiled lines were and feeling the whole boat shiver and the noise of you clubbing him like chopping a tree down and the sweet blood smell all over me."

"Can you really remember that or did I just tell it to you?"

"I remember everything from when we first went together."

The old man looked at him with his sunburned, confident loving eyes.

"If you were my boy I'd take you out and gamble," he said. "But you are your father's and your mother's and you are in a lucky boat."

Neither of these characters is consciously eloquent, and the dialogue is extremely simple. But look how much more it does than "one thing at a time"! It provides exposition on the beginning of the relationship; and it conveys the mutual affection of the two and the conflict within the old man between his love for the boy and his loyalty to the parents. It conveys the boy's eagerness to persuade and carries him into the emotion he had as a small child while the fish was clubbed. The dialogue represents a constant shift of power back and forth between the boy and the old man, as the boy, whatever else he is saying, continues to say *please*; and the old man, whatever else he is saying, continues to say *no*.

It's interesting that the same law of plausibility operates in dialogue as in narrative. We will tend to believe a character who speaks in concrete details and to be skeptical of one who generalizes or who delivers judgments unsupported by example. Uncle Bun is eloquent and attractive, but he hardly convinces us he has the formula for a perfect world. When the boy in the Hemingway passage protests, "I remember everything," however, we believe him because of the vivid details in his memory of the fish. If one character says, "It's perfectly clear from all his actions that he adores me and would do anything for me," and another says, "I had my hands all covered with the clay slick, and he just reached over to lift a lock of hair out of my eyes and tuck it behind my ear" — which character do you believe is the more loved?

Often the most forceful dialogue can be achieved by *not* having the characters say what they mean. People in extreme emotional states — whether of fear, pain, anger, or love — are at their least articulate. There is more narrative tension in a love scene where the lovers make anxious small talk, terrified of revealing their feelings, than in one where they hop into bed. A character who is able to say "I hate you!" hates less than one who bottles the fury and pretends to submit, unwilling to expose the truth. Dialogue often fails if it is too eloquent; the characters debate ideas with great accuracy or are able to define their feelings precisely and honestly. But often the purpose of human exchange is to conceal as well as to reveal; to impress, hurt, protect, seduce, or reject.

The scene that follows is complex. It is from Joan Didion's novel *A Book of Common Prayer*. The dialogue involves six characters and centers on a seventh, who is absent. The absent *norteamericana* is an object of intense interest to some of these characters, of complete indifference to others. Their conversation is mainly at cross-purposes; and, in the rich mix of insinuation, inattention, prodding, threat, and non sequitur, all of them are saying no to the others, either by refusing to come out with what they mean or by refusing to respond to what has been said.

> "Charlotte Douglas is ill," I said after Christmas lunch in the courtyard at Victor and Bianca's.
>
> No one had spoken for twenty minutes. I had timed it. I had counted the minutes while I watched two mating flies try to extricate themselves from a melting chocolate shaving on the untouched Bûche de Noël. The children had already been trundled off quarreling to distribute nut cups to veterans, Gerardo had already made his filial call from St. Moritz. Elena had already been photographed in her Red Cross uniform and had changed back into magenta crêpe de chine pajamas. Isabel had drunk enough champagne to begin crying softly. Antonio had grown irritable enough with Isabel's mournful hiccups to borrow a pistol from the guard at the gate and take aim at a lizard in the creche behind Bianca's fountain. Antonio was always handling guns, or smashing plates. As a gesture toward the spirit of Christmas he had refrained from smashing any plates at lunch, but the effort seemed to have exhausted his capacity for congeniality. Had Antonio been born in other circumstances he would have been put away early as a sociopath.
>
> Bianca remained oblivious.

Bianca remained immersed in the floor plan for an apartment she wanted Victor to take for her in the Residencia Vista del Palacio. Bianca had never been apprised of the fact that Victor already had an apartment in the Residencia Vista del Palacio. For five of these twenty minutes it had seemed to me up in the air whether Antonio was about to shoot up Bianca's creche or tell Bianca about the Residencia Vista del Palacio.

"I said *la norteamericana* is sick."

"Send her to Dr. Schiff," Antonio muttered. Dr. Schiff was Isabel's doctor in Arizona. "Let the great healer tell *la norteamericana* who's making her sick."

Victor only gazed at the sky. I did not know whether Victor had seen Charlotte Douglas since the night he took her from the Embassy to the Residencia but I did know that a Ministry courier had delivered twenty-four white roses to the Caribe on Christmas Eve.

"So is Jackie Onassis sick," Elena said. Elena was leafing fretfully through a back issue of *Paris-Match*. "Or she was in September."

"So am I sick," Isabel said. "I need complete quiet."

"I should think that's what you have," Elena said.

"Not like Arizona." Isabel said. "I should have stayed through December, Dr. Schiff begged me. The air. The solitude. The long walks, the simple meals. Yoghurt at sunset. You can't imagine the sunsets."

"Sounds very lively," Elena said without looking up. "I wonder if Gerardo knows Jackie Onassis."

"If that's the *norteamericana* Grace is talking about I think she had every right to marry the Greek," Bianca said. "Not that I would ever care to live in Athens. I wonder about the view from the Residencia."

"Grace was talking about a different *norteamericana*, Bianca." Victor leaned back and clipped a cigar. "Of no interest to you. Or Grace."

"This *norteamericana* is of interest only to Victor." Antonio seemed to be having trouble drawing a bead on the lizard. "But she could tell you about the view from the Residencia. She's an expert on the view from the Residencia. Victor should introduce you to her."

"I don't meet strangers," Bianca said. "As you know. I take no interest. Look here, the plan for the eleventh floor. If we lived up that high we'd have clear air. No fevers."

"Almost like Arizona," Elena said, "I wonder if Gerardo knows Jacqueline de Ribes."

"Arizona," Isabel said. "I wonder what Dr. Schiff is doing today."

Antonio fired twice at the lizard.

The lizard darted away.

Two porcelain wise men shattered.

"Eating yoghurt in the sunset I presume," Elena said.

"Dr. Schiff doesn't believe in guns," Isabel said.

"What do you mean exactly, Isabel, '*Dr. Schiff doesn't believe in guns*'?" Antonio thrust the pistol into Isabel's line of sight. "*Does Dr. Schiff not believe in the 'existence' of guns? Look at it. Touch it. It's there. What does Dr. Schiff mean exactly?*"

Isabel closed her eyes.

Elena closed the copy of *Paris-Match*.

Imagine how the tension of this scene would disappear if the narrator asked Victor just exactly what his relationship was with Charlotte Douglas, if Antonio spilled everything he knew to Bianca, if Elena told Isabel she was a self-centered idiot, and if Antonio then shot them all. The dialogue reveals character and danger precisely because it does not reveal the relevant information and refuses to divulge the undercurrent of emotion.

Examine your dialogue to see if it does more than one thing at time. Do the sound and syntax characterize by region, education, attitude? Do the choice of words and their syntax reveal that he or she is stiff, outgoing, stifling anger, ignorant of the facts, perceptive, bigoted, afraid? Is the conflict advanced by no-dialogue? Is the drama heightened by the characters' inability or unwillingness to tell the whole truth?

Once you are comfortable with the voice of your character, it is well to acknowledge that everyone has many voices and that what that character says will be, within his or her verbal range, determined by the character *to whom* it is said. All of us have one sort of speech for the vicar and another for the man who pumps the gas. Huck Finn, whose voice is idiosyncratically his own, says "Yes, sir," to the Judge, and "Maybe I am, maybe I ain't," to his degenerate dad.

Dialect is a tempting, and can be an excellent, means of characterizing, but it is difficult to do well and easy to overdo. Dialect should always be achieved by word choice and syntax, and misspellings kept to a minimum. They distract and slow the reader, and worse, they tend to make the character seem stupid rather than regional. There is no point in spelling phonetically any word as it is ordinarily pronounced: almost all of us say things like "fur" for *for*, "uv" for *of*, "wuz" for *was*, "an" for *and*, "sez" for *says*. Nearly everyone drops the *g* in words ending in *ing*, at least now and then. When you misspell these words in dialogue, you indicate that the speaker is ignorant enough to spell them that way when he or she writes. Even if you want to indicate ignorance, you may alienate the reader by the means you choose to do so.

These "rules" for dialect have changed in the past fifty years or so, for largely political reasons. Nineteenth-century authors felt free to misspell the dialogue of foreigners, the lower classes, and racial, regional, and ethnic groups. This literary habit persisted into the first decades of the present century. But the world is considerably smaller now, and its consciousness has been raised. Dialect, after all, is entirely relative, and an author who seems unaware of this may sound like a bigot. The word *bath* pronounced by an Englishman may sound like *bahth* to an American, and pronounced by an American may sound like *banth* to an Englishman, but both know how the word is spelled and resent the implied mockery. Liverpudlians have been knighted; the White House has been inhabited by a Texan, a Georgian, and a Californian; and we resent the implication that regionality is ignorance. Ignorance itself is a charged issue. If you misspell a foreign accent or black English, the reader is likely to have a political rather than a literary reaction. A line of dialogue that runs, "Doan rush me nun, Ah be gwine," reads as caricature, whereas, "Don't rush me none, I be going" makes legitimate use of black English syntax and lets us concentrate on the meaning and emotion.

In dialect or standard English, the bottom-line rule is that dialogue must be speakable; conversely, if it isn't speakable, it isn't dialogue.

> "Certainly I had had a fright I wouldn't soon forget," Reese would say later, "and as I slipped into bed fully dressed except for my shoes, which I flung God-knows-where, I wondered why I had subjected myself to a danger only a fool would fail to foresee for the dubious pleasure of spending one evening in the company of a somewhat less than brilliant coed."

Nobody would say this because it can't be said. It is not only convoluted beyond reason; it stumbles over its alliteration, *only a fool would fail to foresee for,* and takes more breath than the human lungs can hold. Read your dialogue aloud and make sure it is comfortable to the mouth, the breath, and the ear. If not, then it won't ring true as talk.

Identifying dialogue sometimes presents more of a problem than it needs to. The purpose of a *dialogue tag* is to make clear who is speaking, and it usually needs to do nothing else. *Said* is quite adequate to the purpose. People also *ask* and *reply* and occasionally *add, recall, remember,* or *remind.* But sometimes an unsure writer will strain for emphatic synonyms: *she gasped, he whined, they chorused, John snarled, Mary spat.* This is unnecessary and obtrusive, because although unintentional repetition usually makes for awkward style, the word *said* is as invisible as punctuation. When reading we're scarcely aware of it, whereas we are forced to be aware of *she wailed.* If it's clear who is speaking without any dialogue tag at all, don't use one. Usually an identification at the beginning of a dialogue passage and an occasional reminder are sufficient. If the speaker is inherently identified in the speech pattern, so much the better.

Similarly, tonal dialogue tags should be used sparingly: *he said with relish; she added limply.* Such phrases are blatant "telling," and the chances are that good dialogue will convey its own tone. *"Get off my case!" she said angrily.* We do not need to be told that she said this angrily. If she said it sweetly, then we would probably need to be told. If the dialogue does not give us a clue to the manner in which it is said, an action will often do so better than an adverb. *"I'll have a word with Mr. Ritter about it," he said with finality* is weaker than *"I'll have a word with Mr. Ritter about it," he said, and picked up his hat.*

If human character is the center of fiction, it follows inevitably that you must master dialogue. People speak; they confront each other with speech;

they change through speech. It is by hearing your characters speak that we experience them. There may be times when a summary of speech is justified—when, for example, one character has to inform another of events that we already know, or when the emotional point of a conversation is that it has become tedious.

> Carefully, playing down the danger, Len filled her in on the events of the long night.

> After that, Samantha told us everything we had never wanted to know about the lost art of ormolu, and Marlene gave us a play-by-play account of her last bridge game.

But nothing is more frustrating to a reader than to be told that significant events are taking place in talk and to be denied the drama of the dialogue.

> They whispered to each other all night long, and as he told her all about his past, she began to realize that she was falling in love with him.

Such a summary—it's *telling*—is a stingy way of treating the reader, who wants the chance to fall in love, too: give me *me*!

ACTION

The significant characters of a fiction must be both capable of causing an action and capable of being changed by it.

It is important to understand the difference between action and movement, which are not synonymous. Physical movement is generally necessary to the action, but it is not adequate to ensure that there will be an action. Much movement in a story—the way he crosses his legs, the way she charges down the hall—is actually part of appearance and characterizes without necessarily moving the plot forward. When a book or film is advertised as "action-packed," it is also likely that what is being touted is movement rather than action—lots of sword fights, karate chops, or bombs away—but not necessarily that meaningful arrangement of events in which a character is convincingly compelled to pursue a goal, to make decisions along the way, and to find herself or himself subtly or dramatically altered in the process. It's particularly important to keep this in mind when writing dialogue, because talk is not action unless it contains the possibility of change. *To discuss* is not of itself a dramatic action; *to realize* is. The words *motive*, *motion*, and *emotion* have the same root, and this is neither accidental nor irrelevant to the way the human drama unfolds.

Take another look at the scene from *A Book of Common Prayer* on pages 162–163 and notice how the action counterpoints the dialogue to reveal what is *not* said. Victor's deliberate gazing at the sky and Elena's fretful leafing through the magazine while Antonio shoots at lizards on the creche; Antonio's thrusting the pistol at Isabel and Isabel's closing her eyes—these actions reveal tensions among characters and, in some cases, the tension within characters.

In this scene from Raymond Carver's short story "Neighbors," ordinary, trivial, and domestic actions take on menace as Bill Miller dawdles in the apartment of a neighbor whose cat he has agreed to feed.

> When he returned to the kitchen the cat was scratching in her box. She looked at him steadily for a minute before she turned back to the litter. He opened all the cupboards and examined the canned goods, the cereals, the packaged foods, the cocktail and wine glasses, the china, the pots and pans. He opened the refrigerator. He sniffed some celery, took two bites of cheddar cheese, and chewed on an apple as he walked into the bedroom. The bed seemed enormous, with a fluffy white bedspread draped to the floor. He pulled out a nightstand drawer, found a half-empty package of cigarettes and stuffed them into his pocket. Then he stepped to the closet and was opening it when the knock sounded at the front door.

There is hardly grand larceny being committed here, but the actions build toward tension through two distinct techniques. The first is that they do actually "build": at first Bill only "examines." The celery he only sniffs, whereas he takes two bites of the cheese, then a whole apple, then half a pack of cigarettes. He moves from the kitchen to the bedroom, which is a clearer invasion of privacy, and from cupboard to refrigerator to nightstand to closet, each a more intimate intrusion than the last.

The second technique is that the narrative subtly hints at Bill's own sense of stealth. It would be easy to imagine a vandal who performed the same actions with complete indifference. But Bill thinks the cat looks "steadily" at him, which is hardly of any importance except that he feels it to be. His awareness of the enormous white bed hints at sexual guilt. When the knock at the front door sounds, we start, as he must, in a clear sense of getting caught. As action counterpoints dialogue in the passage from *A Book of Common Prayer*, here thought counterpoints action, revealing Bill's character through his guilt.

THOUGHT

Aristotle is helpful at clarifying the relationship among desire, thought, and action. Aristotle says, as we have seen, that a man "is his desire." That is, his character is defined by his ultimate purpose, good or bad. *Thought,* says Aristotle, is the process by which a person works backward in his mind from his goal to determine what *action* he can take toward that goal at a given moment.

It is not, for example, your ultimate desire to read this book. Very likely you don't even "want" to read it; you'd rather be asleep or jogging or making love. But your ultimate goal is, say, to be a rich, respected, and famous writer. In order to attain this goal, you reason, you must know as much about the craft as you can learn. To do this, you would like to take a graduate degree at the Writer's Workshop in Iowa. To do that, you must take an undergraduate degree in _____, where you now find yourself, and must get an A in Ms. or Mr. _____'s creative writing course. To do that, you must produce a character sketch from one of the assignments at the end of this chapter by a week from Tuesday. To do so, you must sit here reading this chapter now instead of sleeping, jogging, or making love. Your ultimate motive has led you logically backward to a deliberate "moral" decision on the action you can take at this minor crossroads. In fact, it turns out that you want to be reading after all.

The pattern that Aristotle perceives in this relation among desire, thought, and action seems to me a very fruitful one for an author both in the structuring of plot and in the creation of character. What does this protagonist want to happen in the last paragraph of this story? What is the particular thought process by which this person works backward to determine what he or she will do now, in the situation that presents itself in the first paragraph on page one?

The action, of course, may be the wrong one. Thought thwarts us, either because the thought process itself is mistaken (if only you'd gone to sleep, you would now be having a dream that would give you the most brilliant idea for a short story you've ever had); or because thought is full of conflicting desires and consistent inconsistencies (actually you *are* no longer reading this paragraph; someone knocked on your door and suggested a pizza and you couldn't resist); or because there is enormous human tension between suppressed thought and expressed thought (you didn't want a pizza, and certainly not in the company of that bore, but you'd turned him down twice this week already).

"Ever have any bizarre thoughts?" asks the psychiatrist at the opening of "The Second Tree from the Corner." Mr. Trexler has come to the doctor, in fact, precisely because he wants to be rid of his bizarre thoughts, and the logical thing to do at this moment (Trexler does try) is to trust the doctor's expertise and answer the question. But a bizarre thought about a lizard and a bug intervenes, and Trexler realizes that the next question will be "unanswerable." His personal timidity is at odds with his desire to be rid of his fears, and in this consistent inconsistency, thought, at least apparently, thwarts him.

At the opening of "Everything That Rises Must Converge," Julian wants to be free of his mother's tedious demands, but he is also financially dependent upon her, so he wants to meet those demands as minimally as possible. He will take her to the Y, then, but he'll do it in bad grace. At the end of the story he is free of her; but it turns out that his thought processes were faulty, his desire unattainable, and his "dependency" is deeper than he understood.

A person, a character, can't do much about what he or she wants; it just is (which is another way of saying that character is desire). What we can deliberately choose is our behavior, the action we take in a given situation. Achievement of our desire would be easy if the thought process between desire and act were not so faulty and so wayward, or if there were not such an abyss between the thoughts we think and those which we are willing and able to express.

This being so, the conflict that is the essence of character can be effectively (and, if it doesn't come automatically, quite consciously) achieved in fiction by producing a conflict between methods of presentation. A character can be directly revealed to us through *appearance, speech, action,* and *thought.* If you set one of these methods at odds with the others (it is in narrative practice most frequently *thought*), then dramatic tension will be produced. Imagine, for example, a character who is impeccably and expensively dressed, who speaks eloquently, who acts decisively, and whose mind is revealed to us as full of order and determination. He is inevitably a flat character. But suppose that he is impeccable, eloquent, decisive and that his mind is a *mess* of wounds and panic. He is at once interesting.

Here is the opening passage of Saul Bellow's *Seize the Day,* in which appearance and action are thus blatantly at odds with thought. Notice that it is the tension between suppressed thought and what is expressed through appearance and action that produces the rich character conflict.

> When it came to concealing his troubles, Tommy Wilhelm was not less capable than the next fellow. So at least he thought, and there was a certain amount of evidence to back him up. He had once been an actor—no, not quite, an extra—and he knew what acting should be. Also, he was smoking a cigar, and when a man is smoking a cigar, wearing a hat, he has an advantage: it is harder to find out how he feels. He came from the twenty-third floor down to the lobby on the mezzanine to collect his mail before breakfast, and he believed—he hoped—he looked passably well: doing all right.

Tommy Wilhelm is externally composed but mentally anxious, mainly anxious about looking externally composed. By contrast, in the next passage from Samuel Beckett's *Murphy,* the landlady Miss Carridge, who has just discovered a suicide in one of her rooms, is anxious in speech and action but is mentally composed.

She came speeding down the stairs one step at a time, her feet going so fast that she seemed on little caterpillar wheels, her forefinger sawing horribly at her craw for Celia's benefit. She slithered to a stop on the steps of the house and screeched for the police. She capered in the street like a consternated ostrich, with strangled distracted rushes towards the York and Caledonian Roads in turn, embarrassingly equidistant from the tragedy, tossing up her arms, undoing the good work of the samples, screeching for police aid. Her mind was so collected that she saw clearly the impropriety of letting it appear so.

I have said that thought is most frequently at odds with one or more of the other three methods of direct presentation—reflecting the difficulty we have expressing ourselves openly or accurately—but this is by no means always the case. A character may be successfully, calmly, even eloquently expressing fine opinions, betraying himself by pulling at his ear, or herself by crushing her skirt. Captain Queeg of Herman Wouk's *The Caine Mutiny* is a memorable example of this, maniacally clicking the steel balls in his hand as he defends his disciplinary code. Often we are not privy to the thoughts of a character at all, so that the conflicts must be expressed in a contradiction between the external methods of direct presentation, appearance, speech, and action. Character A may be speaking floods of friendly welcome, betraying his real feeling by backing steadily away. Character B, dressed in taffeta ruffles and ostrich plumes, may wax pitying over the miseries of the poor. Notice that the notion of "betraying oneself" is important here: we're more likely to believe the evidence unintentionally given than deliberate expression.

A classic example of such self-betrayal is found in Leo Tolstoy's *The Death of Ivan Ilyich*, where the widow confronts her husband's colleague at the funeral.

> . . . Noticing that the table was endangered by his cigarette ash, she immediately passed him an ashtray, saying as she did so: "I consider it an affectation to say that my grief prevents my attending to practical affairs. On the contrary, if anything can—I won't say console me, but—distract me, it is seeing to everything concerning him." She again took out her handkerchief as if preparing to cry, but suddenly, as if mastering her feeling, she shook herself and began to speak calmly. "But there is something I want to talk to you about."

It is no surprise either to the colleague or to us that Praskovya Federovna wants to talk about getting money.

Finally, character conflict can be expressed by creating a tension between the direct and the indirect methods of presentation, and this is a source of much irony. The author presents us with a judgment of the character, then lets him or her speak, appear, act, and/or think in contradiction of this judgment.

Sixty years had not dulled his responses; his physical reactions, like his moral ones, were guided by his will and strong character, and these could be seen plainly in his features. He had a long tube-like face with a long rounded open jaw and a long depressed nose.

FLANNERY O'CONNOR, *The Artificial Nigger*

Here what we see in the details of Mr. Head's features are not will and strong character but grimly unlikable qualities. "Tube-like" is an ugly image; an "open jaw" suggests stupidity; and "depressed" connotes more than shape, while the dogged repetition of "long" stretches the face grotesquely.

Jane Austen is a master of this ironic method, the authorial voice often having a naive goodwill toward the characters while the characters themselves prevent the reader from sharing it.

> Mr. Woodhouse was fond of society in his own way. He liked very much to have his friends come and see him; and from various united causes, from his long residence at Hartfield, and his good nature, from his fortune, his house, and his daughter, he could command the visits of his own little circle in a great measure as he liked. He had not much intercourse with any families beyond that circle; his horror of late hours and large dinner parties made him unfit for any acquaintance but such as would visit him on his own terms. . . . Upon such occasions poor Mr. Woodhouse's feelings were in sad warfare. He loved to have the cloth laid, because it had been the fashion of his youth; but his conviction of suppers being very unwholesome made him rather sorry to see anything put on it; and while his hospitality would have welcomed his visitors to everything, his care for their health made him grieve that they would eat.
>
> *Emma*

Here all the authorial generalizations about Mr. Woodhouse are generous and positive, whereas his actions and the "sad warfare" of his mind lead us to the conviction that we would just as soon not sup with this good-natured and generous man.

Character: A Summary

It may be helpful to summarize such practical advice on character as this chapter and the previous chapter contain:

1. Keep a journal and use it to explore and build ideas for characters.
2. Know all the influences that go into the making of your character's type: age, gender, race, nationality, marital status, region, education, religion, profession.

3. Know the details of your character's life: what he or she does during every part of the day, thinks about, remembers, wants, likes and dislikes, eats, says, means.

4. Identify, heighten, and dramatize consistent inconsistencies. What does your character want that is at odds with whatever else the character wants? What patterns of thought and behavior work against the primary goal?

5. If the character is based on a real model, including yourself, make a dramatic external alteration.

6. If the character is imaginary or alien to you, identify a mental or emotional point of contact.

7. Focus sharply on how the character looks, on what she or he wears and owns, and on how she or he moves. Let us focus on it, too.

8. Examine the character's speech to make sure it does more than convey information. Does it characterize, accomplish exposition, and reveal emotion, intent, or change? Does it advance the conflict through *no-dialogue*? Speak it aloud: does it "say"?

9. Make the character act and let the action build. Let it reveal or betray in counterpoint to dialogue and thought.

10. Know what your character wants, both generally, out of life, and specifically, in the context of the story. Keeping that desire in mind, "think backward" with the character to decide what he or she would do in any situation presented.

11. Be aware of the five methods of presentation of character: authorial interpretation, appearance, speech, action, and thought; present the character differently in at least one of these ways than you do in the others.

Shiloh

BOBBIE ANN MASON

Leroy Moffitt's wife, Norma Jean, is working on her pectorals. She lifts three-pound dumbbells to warm up, then progresses to a twenty-pound barbell. Standing with her legs apart, she reminds Leroy of Wonder Woman.

"I'd give anything if I could just get these muscles to where they're real hard," says Norma Jean. "Feel this arm. It's not as hard as the other one."

"That's 'cause you're right-handed," says Leroy, dodging as she swings the barbell in an arc.

"Do you think so?"

"Sure."

Leroy is a truckdriver. He injured his leg in a highway accident four months ago, and his physical therapy, which involves weights and a pulley, prompted Norma Jean to try building herself up. Now she is attending a body-building class. Leroy has been collecting temporary disability since his tractor-trailer jackknifed in Missouri, badly twisting his left leg in its socket. He has a steel pin in his hip. He will probably not be able to drive his rig again. It sits in the backyard, like a gigantic bird that has flown home to roost. Leroy has been home in Kentucky for three months, and his leg is almost healed, but the accident frightened him and he does not want to drive any more long hauls. He is not sure what to do next. In the meantime, he makes things from craft kits. He started by building a miniature log cabin from notched Popsicle sticks. He varnished it and placed it on the TV set, where it remains. It reminds him of a rustic Nativity scene. Then he tried string art (sailing ships on black velvet), a macramé owl kit, a snap-together B-17 Flying Fortress, and a lamp made out of a model truck, with a light fixture screwed in the top of the cab. At first the kits were diversions, something to kill time, but now he is thinking about building a full-scale log house from a kit. It would be considerably cheaper than building a regular house, and besides, Leroy has grown to appreciate how things are put together. He has begun to realize that in all the years he was on the road he never took time to examine anything. He was always flying past scenery.

"They won't let you build a log cabin in any of the new subdivisions," Norma Jean tells him.

"They will if I tell them it's for you," he says, teasing her. Ever since they were married, he has promised Norma Jean he would build her a new home one day. They have always rented, and the house they live in is small and nondescript. It does not even feel like a home, Leroy realizes now.

Norma Jean works at the Rexall drugstore, and she has acquired an amazing amount of information about cosmetics. When she explains to Leroy the three stages of complexion care, involving creams, toners, and moisturizers, he thinks happily of other petroleum products—axle grease, diesel fuel. This is a connection between him and Norma Jean. Since he has been home, he has felt unusually tender about his wife and guilty over his long absences. But he can't tell what she feels about him. Norma Jean has never complained about his traveling; she has never made hurt remarks, like calling his truck a "widow-maker." He is reasonably certain she has been faithful to him, but he wishes she would celebrate his permanent homecoming more happily. Norma Jean is often startled to find Leroy at home, and he thinks she seems a little disappointed about it. Perhaps he reminds her too much of the early days of their marriage, before he went on the road. They had a child who died as an infant, years ago. They never speak about their memories of Randy, which have almost faded, but now that Leroy is home all the time, they sometimes feel awkward around each other, and Leroy wonders if one of them should mention the child. He has the feeling that they are waking up out of a dream together — that they must create a new marriage, start afresh. They are lucky they are still married. Leroy has read that for most people losing a child destroys the marriage — or else he heard this on *Donahue*. He can't always remember where he learns things anymore.

At Christmas, Leroy bought an electric organ for Norma Jean. She used to play the piano when she was in high school. "It don't leave you," she told him once. "It's like riding a bicycle."

The new instrument had so many keys and buttons that she was bewildered by it at first. She touched the keys tentatively, pushed some buttons, then pecked out "Chopsticks." It came out in an amplified fox-trot rhythm, with marimba sounds.

"It's an orchestra!" she cried.

The organ had a pecan-look finish and eighteen preset chords, with optional flute, violin, trumpet, clarinet, and banjo accompaniments. Norma Jean mastered the organ almost immediately. At first she played Christmas songs. Then she bought *The Sixties Songbook* and learned every tune in it, adding variations to each with the rows of brightly colored buttons.

"I didn't like these old songs back then," she said. "But I have this crazy feeling I missed something."

"You didn't miss a thing," said Leroy.

Leroy likes to lie on the couch and smoke a joint and listen to Norma Jean play "Can't Take My Eyes Off You" and "I'll Be Back." He is back again. After fifteen years on the road, he is finally settling down with the woman he loves. She is still pretty. Her skin is flawless. Her frosted curls resemble pencil trimmings.

Now that Leroy has come home to stay, he notices how much the town has changed. Subdivisions are spreading across western Kentucky like an oil slick. The sign at the edge of town says "Pop: 11,500" — only seven hundred more than it said twenty years before. Leroy can't figure out who is living in all the new houses. The farmers who used to gather around the courthouse square on Saturday afternoons to play checkers and spit tobacco juice have gone. It has been years since Leroy has thought about the farmers, and they have disappeared without his noticing.

Leroy meets a kid named Stevie Hamilton in the parking lot at the new shopping center. While they pretend to be strangers meeting over a stalled car, Stevie tosses an ounce of marijuana under the front seat of Leroy's car. Stevie is wearing orange jogging shoes and a T-shirt that says CHATTAHOOCHEE SUPER-RAT. His father is a prominent doctor who lives in one of the expensive subdivisions in a new white-columned brick house that looks like a funeral parlor. In the phone book under his name there is a separate number, with the listing "Teenagers."

"Where do you get this stuff?" asks Leroy. "From your pappy?"

"That's for me to know and you to find out," Stevie says. He is slit-eyed and skinny.

"What else you got?"

"What you interested in?"

"Nothing special. Just wondered."

Leroy used to take speed on the road. Now he has to go slowly. He needs to be mellow. He leans back against the car and says, "I'm aiming to build me a log house, soon as I get time. My wife, though, I don't think she likes the idea."

"Well, let me know when you want me again," Stevie says. He has a cigarette in his cupped palm, as though sheltering it from the wind. He takes a long drag, then stomps it on the asphalt and slouches away.

Stevie's father was two years ahead of Leroy in high school. Leroy is thirty-four. He married Norma Jean when they were both eighteen, and their child Randy was born a few months later, but he died at the age of four months and three days. He would be about Stevie's age now. Norma Jean and Leroy were at the drive-in, watching a double feature (*Dr. Strangelove* and *Lover Come Back*), and the baby was sleeping in the back seat. When the first movie ended, the baby was dead. It was the sudden infant death syndrome. Leroy remembers handing Randy to a nurse at the emergency room, as though he were offering her a large doll as a present. A dead baby feels like a sack of flour. "It just happens sometimes," said the doctor, in what Leroy always recalls as a nonchalant tone. Leroy can hardly remember the child anymore, but he still sees vividly a scene from *Dr. Strangelove* in which the President of the United States was talking in a folksy voice on the hot line to the Soviet premier about the bomber accidentally headed toward Russia. He was in the War Room, and the world map was lit up. Leroy remembers Norma Jean standing catatonically beside him in the hospital and himself thinking: Who is this strange girl? He had forgotten who she was. Now scientists are saying that crib death is caused by a virus. Nobody knows anything, Leroy thinks. The answers are always changing.

When Leroy gets home from the shopping center, Norma Jean's mother, Mabel Beasley, is there. Until this year, Leroy has not realized how much time she spends with Norma Jean. When she visits, she inspects the closets and then the plants, informing Norma Jean when a plant is droopy or yellow. Mabel calls the plants "flowers," although there are never any blooms. She always notices if Norma Jean's laundry is piling up. Mabel is a short, overweight woman whose tight, brown-dyed curls look more like a wig than the actual wig she sometimes wears. Today she has brought

Norma Jean an off-white dust ruffle she made for the bed; Mabel works in a custom-upholstery shop.

"This is the tenth one I made this year," Mabel says. "I got started and couldn't stop."

"It's real pretty," says Norma Jean.

"Now we can hide things under the bed," says Leroy, who gets along with his mother-in-law primarily by joking with her. Mabel has never really forgiven him for disgracing her by getting Norma Jean pregnant. When the baby died, she said that fate was mocking her.

"What's that thing?" Mabel says to Leroy in a loud voice, pointing to a tangle of yarn on a piece of canvas.

Leroy holds it up for Mabel to see. "It's my needlepoint," he explains. "This is a *Star Trek* pillow cover."

"That's what a woman would do," says Mabel. "Great day in the morning!"

"All the big football players on TV do it," he says.

"Why, Leroy, you're always trying to fool me. I don't believe you for one minute. You don't know what to do with yourself—that's the whole trouble. Sewing!"

"I'm aiming to build us a log house," says Leroy. "Soon as my plans come."

"Like *heck* you are," says Norma Jean. She takes Leroy's needlepoint and shoves it into a drawer. "You have to find a job first. Nobody can afford to build now anyway."

Mabel straightens her girdle and says, "I still think before you get tied down y'all ought to take a little run to Shiloh."

"One of these days, Mama," Norma Jean says impatiently.

Mabel is talking about Shiloh, Tennessee. For the past few years, she has been urging Leroy and Norma Jean to visit the Civil War battleground there. Mabel went there on her honeymoon—the only real trip she ever took. Her husband died of a perforated ulcer when Norma Jean was ten, but Mabel, who was accepted into the United Daughters of the Confederacy in 1975, is still preoccupied with going back to Shiloh.

"I've been to kingdom come and back in that truck out yonder," Leroy says to Mabel, "but we never yet set foot in that battleground. Ain't that something? How did I miss it?"

"It's not even that far," Mabel says.

After Mabel leaves, Norma Jean reads to Leroy from a list she has made. "Things you could do," she announces. "You could get a job as a guard at Union Carbide, where they'd let you set on a stool. You could get on at the lumberyard. You could do a little carpenter work, if you want to build so bad. You could—"

"I can't do something where I'd have to stand up all day."

"You ought to try standing up all day behind a cosmetics counter. It's amazing that I have strong feet, coming from two parents that never had strong feet at all." At the moment Norma Jean is holding on to the kitchen counter, raising her knees one at a time as she talks. She is wearing two-pound ankle weights.

"Don't worry," says Leroy. "I'll do something."

"You could truck calves to slaughter for somebody. You wouldn't have to drive any big old truck for that."

"I'm going to build you this house," says Leroy. "I want to make you a real home."

"I don't want to live in any log cabin."

"It's not a cabin. It's a house."

"I don't care. It looks like a cabin."

"You and me together could lift those logs. It's just like lifting weights."

Norma Jean doesn't answer. Under her breath, she is counting. Now she is marching through the kitchen. She is doing goose steps.

Before his accident, when Leroy came home he used to stay in the house with Norma Jean, watching TV in bed and playing cards. She would cook fried chicken, picnic ham, chocolate pie — all his favorites. Now he is home alone much of the time. In the mornings, Norma Jean disappears, leaving a cooling place in the bed. She eats a cereal called Body Buddies, and she leaves the bowl on the table, with the soggy tan balls floating in a milk puddle. He sees things about Norma Jean that he never realized before. When she chops onions, she stares off into a corner, as if she can't bear to look. She puts on her house slippers almost precisely at nine o'clock every evening and nudges her jogging shoes under the couch. She saves bread heels for the birds. Leroy watches the birds at the feeder. He notices the peculiar way goldfinches fly past the window. They close their wings, then fall, then spread their wings to catch and lift themselves. He wonders if they close their eyes when they fall. Norma Jean closes her eyes when they are in bed. She wants the lights turned out. Even then, he is sure she closes her eyes.

He goes for long drives around town. He tends to drive a car rather carelessly. Power steering and an automatic shift make a car feel so small and inconsequential that his body is hardly involved in the driving process. His injured leg stretches out comfortably. Once or twice he has almost hit something, but even the prospect of an accident seems minor in a car. He cruises the new subdivisions, feeling like a criminal rehearsing for a robbery. Norma Jean is probably right about a log house being inappropriate here in the new subdivisions. All the houses look grand and complicated. They depress him.

One day when Leroy comes home from a drive he finds Norma Jean in tears. She is in the kitchen making a potato and mushroom-soup casserole, with grated-cheese topping. She is crying because her mother caught her smoking.

"I didn't hear her coming. I was standing here puffing away pretty as you please," Norma Jean says, wiping her eyes.

"I knew it would happen sooner or later," says Leroy, putting his arm around her.

"She don't know the meaning of the word 'knock,' " says Norma Jean. "It's a wonder she hadn't caught me years ago."

"Think of it this way," Leroy says. "What if she caught me with a joint?"

"You better not let her!" Norma Jean shrieks. "I'm warning you, Leroy Moffitt!"

"I'm just kidding. Here, play me a tune. That'll help you relax."

Norma Jean puts the casserole in the oven and sets the timer. Then she plays a ragtime tune, with horns and banjo, as Leroy lights up a joint and lies on the couch, laughing to himself about Mabel's catching him at it. He thinks of Stevie Hamilton—a doctor's son pushing grass. Everything is funny. The whole town seems crazy and small. He is reminded of Virgil Mathis, a boastful policeman Leroy used to shoot pool with. Virgil recently led a drug bust in a back room at a bowling alley, where he seized ten thousand dollars' worth of marijuana. The newspaper had a picture of him holding up the bags of grass and grinning widely. Right now, Leroy can imagine Virgil breaking down the door and arresting him with a lungful of smoke. Virgil would probably have been alerted to the scene because of all the racket Norma Jean is making. Now she sounds like a hard-rock band. Norma Jean is terrific. When she switches to a Latin-rhythm version of "Sunshine Superman," Leroy hums along. Norma Jean's foot goes up and down, up and down.

"Well, what do you think?" Leroy says, when Norma Jean pauses to search through her music.

"What do I think about what?"

His mind has gone blank. Then he says, "I'll sell my rig and build us a house." That wasn't what he wanted to say. He wanted to know what she thought—what she *really* thought—about them.

"Don't start in on that again," says Norma Jean. She begins playing "Who'll Be the Next in Line?"

Leroy used to tell hitchhikers his whole life story—about his travels, his hometown, the baby. He would end with a question: "Well, what do you think?" It was just a rhetorical question. In time, he had the feeling that he'd been telling the same story over and over to the same hitchhikers. He quit talking to hitchhikers when he realized how his voice sounded—

whining and self-pitying, like some teenage-tragedy song. Now Leroy has the sudden impulse to tell Norma Jean about himself, as if he had just met her. They have known each other so long they have forgotten a lot about each other. They could become reacquainted. But when the oven timer goes off and she runs to the kitchen, he forgets why he wants to do this.

The next day, Mabel drops by. It is Saturday and Norma Jean is cleaning. Leroy is studying the plans of his log house, which have finally come in the mail. He has them spread out on the table — big sheets of stiff blue paper, with diagrams and numbers printed in white. While Norma Jean runs the vacuum, Mabel drinks coffee. She sets her coffee cup on a blueprint.

"I'm just waiting for time to pass," she says to Leroy, drumming her fingers on the table.

As soon as Norma Jean switches off the vacuum, Mabel says in a loud voice, "Did you hear about the datsun dog that killed the baby?"

Norma Jean says, "The word is 'dachshund.'"

"They put the dog on trial. It chewed the baby's legs off. The mother was in the next room all the time." She raises her voice. "They thought it was neglect."

Norma Jean is holding her ears. Leroy manages to open the refrigerator and get some Diet Pepsi to offer Mabel. Mabel still has some coffee and she waves away the Pepsi.

"Datsuns are like that," Mabel says. "They're jealous dogs. They'll tear a place to pieces if you don't keep an eye on them."

"You better watch out what you're saying, Mabel," says Leroy.

"Well, facts is facts."

Leroy looks out the window at his rig. It is like a huge piece of furniture gathering dust in the backyard. Pretty soon it will be an antique. He hears the vacuum cleaner. Norma Jean seems to be cleaning the living room rug again.

Later, she says to Leroy, "She just said that about the baby because she caught me smoking. She's trying to pay me back."

"What are you talking about?" Leroy says, nervously shuffling blueprints.

"You know good and well," Norma Jean says. She is sitting in a kitchen chair with her feet up and her arms wrapped around her knees. She looks small and helpless. She says, "The very idea, her bringing up a subject like that! Saying it was neglect."

"She didn't mean that," Leroy says.

"She might not have *thought* she meant it. She always says things like that. You don't know how she goes on."

"But she didn't really mean it. She was just talking."

Leroy opens a king-sized bottle of beer and pours it into two glasses, dividing it carefully. He hands a glass to Norma Jean and she takes it from him mechanically. For a long time, they sit by the kitchen window watching the birds at the feeder.

Something is happening. Norma Jean is going to night school. She has graduated from her six-week body-building course and now she is taking an adult-education course in composition at Paducah Community College. She spends her evenings outlining paragraphs.

"First you have a topic sentence," she explains to Leroy. "Then you divide it up. Your secondary topic has to be connected to your primary topic."

To Leroy, this sounds intimidating. "I never was any good in English," he says.

"It makes a lot of sense."

"What are you doing this for, anyhow?"

She shrugs. "It's something to do." She stands up and lifts her dumbbells a few times.

"Driving a rig, nobody cared about my English."

"I'm not criticizing your English."

Norma Jean used to say, "If I lose ten minutes' sleep, I just drag all day." Now she stays up late, writing compositions. She got a B on her first paper—a how-to theme on soup-based casseroles. Recently Norma Jean has been cooking unusual foods—tacos, lasagna, Bombay chicken. She doesn't play the organ anymore, though her second paper was called "Why Music Is Important to Me." She sits at the kitchen table, concentrating on her outlines, while Leroy plays with his log house plans, practicing with a set of Lincoln Logs. The thought of getting a truckload of notched, numbered logs scares him, and he wants to be prepared. As he and Norma Jean work together at the kitchen table, Leroy has the hopeful thought that they are sharing something, but he knows he is a fool to think this. Norma Jean is miles away. He knows he is going to lose her. Like Mabel, he is just waiting for time to pass.

One day, Mabel is there before Norma Jean gets home from work, and Leroy finds himself confiding in her. Mabel, he realizes, must know Norma Jean better than he does.

"I don't know what's got into that girl," Mabel says. "She used to go to bed with the chickens. Now you say she's up all hours. Plus her a-smoking. I like to died."

"I want to make her this beautiful home," Leroy says, indicating the Lincoln Logs. "I don't think she even wants it. Maybe she was happier with me gone."

"She don't know what to make of you, coming home like this."

"Is that it?"

Mabel takes the roof off his Lincoln Log cabin. "You couldn't get *me* in a log cabin," she says. "I was raised in one. It's no picnic, let me tell you."

"They're different now," says Leroy.

"I tell you what," Mabel says, smiling oddly at Leroy.

"What?"

"Take her on down to Shiloh. Y'all need to get out together, stir a little. Her brain's all balled up over them books."

Leroy can see traces of Norma Jean's features in her mother's face. Mabel's worn face has the texture of crinkled cotton, but suddenly she looks pretty. It occurs to Leroy that Mabel has been hinting all along that she wants them to take her with them to Shiloh.

"Let's all go to Shiloh," he says. "You and me and her. Come Sunday."

Mabel throws up her hands in protest. "Oh, no, not me. Young folks want to be by theirselves."

When Norma Jean comes in with groceries, Leroy says excitedly, "Your mama here's been dying to go to Shiloh for thirty-five years. It's about time we went, don't you think?"

"I'm not going to butt in on anybody's second honeymoon," Mabel says.

"Who's going on a honeymoon, for Christ's sake?" Norma Jean says loudly.

"I never raised no daughter of mine to talk that-a-way," Mabel says.

"You ain't seen nothing yet," says Norma Jean. She starts putting away boxes and cans, slamming cabinet doors.

"There's a log cabin at Shiloh," Mabel says. "It was there during the battle. There's bullet holes in it."

"When are you going to *shut up* about Shiloh, Mama?" asks Norma Jean.

"I always thought Shiloh was the prettiest place, so full of history," Mabel goes on. "I just hoped y'all could see it once before I die, so you could tell me about it." Later, she whispers to Leroy, "You do what I said. A little change is what she needs."

"Your name means 'the king,'" Norma Jean says to Leroy that evening. He is trying to get her to go to Shiloh, and she is reading a book about another century.

"Well, I reckon I ought to be right proud."

"I guess so."

"Am I still king around here?"

Norma Jean flexes her biceps and feels them for hardness. "I'm not fooling around with anybody, if that's what you mean," she says.

"Would you tell me if you were?"

"I don't know."

"What does *your* name mean?"

"It was Marilyn Monroe's real name."

"No kidding!"

"Norma comes from the Normans. They were invaders," she says. She closes her book and looks hard at Leroy. "I'll go to Shiloh with you if you'll stop staring at me."

On Sunday, Norma Jean packs a picnic and they go to Shiloh. To Leroy's relief, Mabel says she does not want to come with them. Norma Jean drives, and Leroy, sitting beside her, feels like some boring hitchhiker she has picked up. He tries some conversation, but she answers him in monosyllables. At Shiloh, she drives aimlessly through the park, past bluffs and trails and steep ravines. Shiloh is an immense place, and Leroy cannot see it as a battleground. It is not what he expected. He thought it would look like a golf course. Monuments are everywhere, showing through the thick clusters of trees. Norma Jean passes the log cabin Mabel mentioned. It is surrounded by tourists looking for bullet holes.

"That's not the kind of log house I've got in mind," says Leroy apologetically.

"I know *that*."

"This is a pretty place. Your mama was right."

"It's O.K.," says Norma Jean. "Well, we've seen it. I hope she's satisfied."

They burst out laughing together.

At the park museum, a movie on Shiloh is shown every half hour, but they decide that they don't want to see it. They buy a souvenir Confederate flag for Mabel, and then they find a picnic spot near the cemetery. Norma Jean has brought a picnic cooler, with pimiento sandwiches, soft drinks, and Yodels. Leroy eats a sandwich and then smokes a joint, hiding it behind the picnic cooler. Norma Jean has quit smoking altogether. She is picking cake crumbs from the cellophane wrapper, like a fussy bird.

Leroy says, "So the boys in gray ended up in Corinth. The Union soldiers zapped 'em finally. April 7, 1862."

They both know that he doesn't know any history. He is just talking about some of the historical plaques they have read. He feels awkward, like a boy on a date with an older girl. They are still just making conversation.

"Corinth is where Mama eloped to," says Norma Jean.

They sit in silence and stare at the cemetery for the Union dead and, beyond, at a tall cluster of trees. Campers are parked nearby, bumper to bumper, and small children in bright clothing are cavorting and squealing. Norma Jean wads up the cake wrapper and squeezes it tightly in her hand. Without looking at Leroy, she says, "I want to leave you."

Leroy takes a bottle of Coke out of the cooler and flips off the cap. He holds the bottle poised near his mouth but cannot remember to take a drink. Finally he says, "No, you don't."

"Yes, I do."

"I won't let you."

"You can't stop me."

"Don't do me that way."

Leroy knows Norma Jean will have her own way. "Didn't I promise to be home from now on?" he says.

"In some ways, a woman prefers a man who wanders," says Norma Jean. "That sounds crazy, I know."

"You're not crazy."

Leroy remembers to drink from his Coke. Then he says, "Yes, you *are* crazy. You and me could start all over again. Right back at the beginning."

"We *have* started all over again," says Norma Jean. "And this is how it turned out."

"What did I do wrong?"

"Nothing."

"Is this one of those women's lib things?" Leroy asks.

"Don't be funny."

The cemetery, a green slope dotted with white markers, looks like a subdivision site. Leroy is trying to comprehend that his marriage is breaking up, but for some reason he is wondering about white slabs in a graveyard.

"Everything was fine till Mama caught me smoking," says Norma Jean, standing up. "That set something off."

"What are you talking about?"

"She won't leave me alone—*you* won't leave me alone." Norma Jean seems to be crying, but she is looking away from him. "I feel eighteen again. I can't face that all over again." She starts walking away. "No, it *wasn't* fine. I don't know what I'm saying. Forget it."

Leroy takes a lungful of smoke and closes his eyes as Norma Jean's words sink in. He tries to focus on the fact that thirty-five hundred soldiers died on the grounds around him. He can only think of that war as a board game with plastic soldiers. Leroy almost smiles, as he compares the Confederates' daring attack on the Union camps and Virgil Mathis's raid on the bowling alley. General Grant, drunk and furious, shoved the Southerners back to Corinth, where Mabel and Jet Beasley were married years later, when Mabel was still thin and good-looking. The next day, Mabel and Jet visited the battleground, and then Norma Jean was born, and then she married Leroy and they had a baby, which they lost, and now Leroy and Norma Jean are here at the same battleground. Leroy knows he is leaving out a lot. He is leaving out the insides of history. History was always just names and dates to him. It occurs to him that building a house out of logs is similarly empty—too simple. And the real inner workings of a marriage, like most of history, have escaped him. Now he sees that building a log house is the dumbest idea he could have had. It was clumsy of him to think Norma Jean would want a log house. It was a crazy idea. He'll have to think of something else, quickly. He will wad the blueprints into tight balls and fling them into the lake. Then he'll get moving again. He opens his eyes. Norma Jean has moved away and is walking through the cemetery, following a serpentine brick path.

Leroy gets up to follow his wife, but his good leg is asleep and his bad leg still hurts him. Norma Jean is far away, walking rapidly toward the bluff by the river, and he tries to hobble toward her. Some children run past him, screaming noisily. Norma Jean has reached the bluff, and she is looking out over the Tennessee River. Now she turns toward Leroy and waves her arms. Is she beckoning to him? She seems to be doing an exercise for her chest muscles. The sky is unusually pale — the color of the dust ruffle Mabel made for their bed.

Suggestions for Discussion

1. What does it contribute to Norma Jean's characterization that she is first introduced as "Leroy Moffit's wife"? How does it signal the reversal and resolution of the story?

2. What does the detailing of Leroy's craft kits tell us about the fundamentals of type in this story? What do these details suggest about the conflict? What judgments are invited?

3. How are these judgments qualified or changed by what we know of Leroy's thoughts?

4. Examine the dialogue among Norma Jean, Leroy, and Mabel on page 176. Where and how does it do more than one thing at a time? How often, and how, are the characters saying *no* to each other?

5. We are privy to Leroy's thoughts, but Norma Jean and Mabel are presented externally. How much can we infer about their thoughts? How does each of them feel about Shiloh? The log cabin? The dead baby? How do we know?

6. Where in the story does a physical action reveal more than the dialogue?

7. Show how dialogue, action, and appearance make "round" characters out of the two very minor characters of Stevie Hamilton and Virgil Mathis.

8. What specific details having to do with cooking, music, and English composition let us know that Norma Jean is changing mentally and emotionally? How does her dialogue let us know, even before she admits, "I want to leave you"?

9. Consider the penultimate paragraph of the story. How does the contrast between external events and Leroy's mental image of them contribute to the emotional effect?

The Only Way to Make It in New York

ROSELLEN BROWN

She had caught him going through her jewelry. She stood on the threshold in her slick raincoat, balancing on her toes, looking casual, almost, as though she were coming in to tell him, "Dinner is served." It was faintly amusing—he would pick up a necklace, hold it toward the ceiling light critically, then fling it down. She was embarrassed, it was like being in an accident and worrying in the ambulance about your dirty underwear. There was so little there, only a ring or two of sentimental value, if that. (Grandma gave her a sapphire at graduation, but Grandma was a shrew in Palm Beach who had chewed her mouth away—or so it had always looked—and had sharpened her voice till it was a pointed stick to skewer the world with. When she'd been eighteen and stayed out late, Grandma had taken to calling her "Chippie," so what was her ring supposed to be worth?) Oh—Martin's watch with the good expanding band. Into his lumpy pocket it went. Her good pearls were hanging out like a dirty hanky.

She was waiting to be frightened. But she wouldn't be. He had no gun that she could see. He was not the man she was expecting, anyway, so she was not about to be intimidated. In fact he was pathetic by comparison. That was funny enough to make her smile and she was sure he would turn around at that; the mock-bitter movement of her lips had sent a million hairline cracks through the air as though it were ice.

She'd been sure, after the first robbery, that it was Tony Aguilar's brother-in-law. Together he and Tony had been building closets and a room divider between the front bedroom and Wendy's little L. The lousy apartment with its painted-over marble fireplaces (styles change but then, dammit, they change back again and you're left with a gallon of paint stripper. She tended to think of it as a fifty-buck-a-month place. Too bad the landlord didn't). Tony was a wide, brown, rough, sweet man with miles of kinky hair, raised around the corner and making good, good enough, with his carpentry. He was a daddy, and respected. His wife's brother was a junkie. Willie came to work and took off his shirt first thing, showing muscles that made her stomach sink. It was a disgusting reaction, adolescent, but she couldn't help it. He had a clean face, sharply cut, Aztec, with a distant vulnerability in the eyes which could only have been the drugs. Something about him was like cream, maple cream, incredibly inviting to touch, where it dipped and flowed over his shoulder blades as he hammered boards inexpertly. She got out fast, later to work each day: she saw his back all the way to the subway. She'd have thought a junkie would look unhealthy. Martin, seamy and mustard-yellow under his tee shirt, looked unhealthy.

Well, the junkie didn't look good when he came around at dinnertime, worse at two in the morning, banging angrily as though they ought to have been expecting him. Money, money, just an advance against more nailing, more sawing so they would have closets for their nice nice clothes. Lady listen. My grandmother, I need it. Near tears, those eyes racing all around ready for escape, his knuckles white, fingertips biting palms cruelly. Martin had asked why Tony couldn't help, or his sister. There was a muttered reply. From where she lay, Martin looked like the heavy. He breathed hard in his maroon robe, laboring at saying no, making it a whole moral business, who cared, who wanted speeches, explanations, truth? Martin was always giving quarters to beggars on the street after he'd extracted the name of the wine they were going to spend it on. A quarter was cheap for that song and dance. He came back to bed shaking his head.

"Don't you think he wanted a fix?" She had lit a cigarette and pushed the smoke out with the force of her irritation.

"Well, I wasn't going to let him have it."

"What will he do?"

"Do you really want to concern yourself with that? What do you care what a dope addict does? He must have friends in some alley somewhere. Let him get his assistance elsewhere."

He took off his robe and sat on the edge of the bed, looking perplexed, his pale flesh gathering in dewlaps around his middle. They were so deep there was true shadow under them, she thought idly. Can you hold a pencil under your breasts? Under your flaps of fat, my dear, you can hold a candle.

Tony's brother came back the next two nights, banging and threatening, but apologetic when they opened the door, as though passion had unmanned him, then let him go. He was a small animal, a ferret, in the mouth of a predator, and one of these days it wasn't going to spit him out alive. Then he stopped coming. But at the end of the week they let themselves in after a party and found all their electrical appliances gone. Wendy had been staying with a friend that night or she'd have been home alone; this was her first season baby-sitting herself.

She had walked around picking things up and dropping them. She felt strangely like a mother cat—no, what animal was it? A mouse?—that loses interest in its babies once they've been handled by someone else. Her underwear, Martin's, lying in a twisted heap, was dishonored, as if by a voyeur. Books lay in a blasted mountain where they'd been tipped off the mantel. Her one poor fur was gone, an antique muskrat that would get the thief a dollar on a good day. The silver was still there—she opened and closed the drawer with astonishing indifference; none of the details mattered much. All the cupboard doors were open in the kitchen and there was one mug, soiled at the lip, in the middle of the floor, a root-beer bottle tipped over beside it. She picked it up gingerly as if by the tail and dropped it in the wastebasket. The mail drawer was rifled, letters perhaps read. She felt incredibly dirty, but that was all. It came as a shock to realize that she cared not one little bit about what had been taken.

The question then was, reporting to the police, should they implicate Aguilar's wife's brother? Willie—whatever his name was. He could have made a key so easily, both of them out all day, Wendy in school. How much trust it took to get through a single day in the world. . . . But she felt queasy about that, on what she called "moral grounds." Martin, angry, dismissed morality.

"Your grandiloquence could find a better cause. I don't want to get sued for false arrest. Accusation. Whatever the hell it is."

"Oh, he'd never *sue* you."

"Who knows what he'd do, a desperate man?" Martin had been going around making an inventory of their losses for his tax return. He seemed mildly elated by the coincidence that would bring them next year's models of solid-state this and automatic-refraction-tuning that, with a tax write-off at current resale values.

"The hundred dollars deductible is deplorable," he was saying—he said it three times—while she picked up a pair of pantyhose that was twined around the bodice of a slip, saw a greasy fingerprint on the daisy embroidery, and dropped it again.

"Who are you?" was all she could think to say now, stupid as it sounded. He was compact, dark, dirty, and concentrating hard on the pathetic cache of jewelry like a competent workman puzzling over shoddy goods.

She was still in the doorway. She could run, she had calculated, if he turned on her. But she didn't think he would.

He looked at her levelly.

"Who are you?"

"Why do you want to know my name? I just took a couple of your rings, that's all you got to know, right?"

He was wearing a red-checked shirt too heavy for late spring, and he was sweating. "You got a lot of junk, you know?"

She smiled her coolest smile. "Am I supposed to apologize?"

"Do what you want." He was deciding whether to get out the same way he got in, his eyes were traveling over the walls, the moldings, the ceiling.

"Take it easy," she said, almost maternally, "I'm not calling the police. I just—I wish you'd wash your hands before you go around fingering everything." She was relieved he wasn't Willie, who would have terrified her.

He nodded gravely, then laughed. "Oh, lady. Clean your fence out there—" He gestured to the back window with his head. The curtains in Wendy's room were gusting out lazily and she could see the inky handprints on the jamb all the way to the front. The cops said they couldn't lift them off that kind of paint; he must know that.

She approached a step. "Well, I wasn't expecting you."

Who did he look like—Yogi Berra? Some baseball player, PeeWee Reese? She had rooted for the Yankees when she was little; California didn't have a single major league team of its own back then. Now she could vaguely see their faces, the swarthy ones with five-o'clock shadow explaining how they had met the ball on the 3-2 pitch. Hank Bauer with her pearls in his pocket.

He sat down on the couch gingerly; suddenly his clothes must have felt very dirty to him, she saw him hunch as though to make himself lighter. She handed him a beer.

"So—you always entertain guys who come in the back window and swipe your stuff?"

She shrugged. "Doesn't happen so often. We probably haven't been here long enough."

"You don't look so mad."

She looked at him with what she knew was an inscrutable face. She felt very good; a funny kind of power it gave you to catch someone right in the middle of a compromising act. Martin did nothing compromising. In all things he did the equivalent of undressing in the closet.

"You look like you have a family, you could have a regular job, if you wanted." His dirty hands made him look as though he was on his way home from work with a lunch box and thermos. Maybe he was. Certainly he didn't have the knife-eyed desperation of an addict.

"Lady—" He spread those hands wide. She was asking him what kind of wine he liked.

She shook her head at herself impatiently. "Well, I suppose you're what we had to have next."

He raised one eyebrow politely. How much should a caught burglar talk? A problem for Amy Vanderbilt.

She looked off. Surviving—the cost of it was going up like the price of milk. She began, patiently. "We moved here from Los Angeles because we were in the earthquake."

In it? Like being in the war? In a play? Yes, in. Among the objects tossed and plummeted. Or within range. Yes, like in the war. The Blitz. Whatever.

"San Fernando, actually. Our house—the back of it, you know—the garage and sun porch and my kitchen, I was in my kitchen—were hanging over a cliff. In about a second—" She snapped her fingers. "My daughter, she's nine? She was playing out back and she came in to get something, a glass of milk, I don't remember, and before she could go back out again there was no back yard."

He was looking at her with steady eyes, keeping quiet.

"Every other thing broke—glass and pictures and a stone vase I had? And things kept tumbling, falling downhill. I close my eyes and everything turns over like—I don't know." She laughed to disparage it. "You know those rides in the amusement park?"

"Yeah, that turn all the way over? You sit on them?"

"It's like that, I get dizzy when I close my eyes so I don't sleep any more. A little, it's getting a little better."

He blinked. "You ought to go to a doctor or something, get some pills, they'll put you out."

"Did you ever go without a lot of sleep?"

He looked up from his beer, considering the question slowly, like a taste. "During the war I did, yeah, in the foxholes. You figured you went to sleep you'd never wake up."

"That's true," she said distantly; she didn't really want to share it, it couldn't have been the same, the suddenness. He probably enlisted, went looking for trouble. She could see him in khakis, his dark hair clipped, his obedient small-dog face snapping to attention, saluting. "That's true. A soldier would . . . "

She had slipped so far, so deep in her dreaming, she had become part of the landslide forever, she held one of the timbers of the porch like someone thrown clear of a wrecked ship and she fell over and over, neat as a hoop, she must have been curled in a ball, a baby, knees up, bumping over stones and boulders, into the center where the earth was hot. Everyone was there, her neighbors were being stirred, heads bobbed out of the stew, popped up like bubbles all around, boiling, then sank back and it closed over. It was all silent, silence seemed right, it went with the suddenness; faster than sound, all of it. What was the broth made of? Molten bones and rock and blood and the earth's own spring water. Top soil, bottom soil, granite shoulders, sand and grass. A dog bone flew past and vanished. Men and women and animals and the roots of trees were thrown up embracing and fell back in slow motion; still tangled they made an opening in the soup and vanished, leaving circles in circles in circles. She skimmed across the surface—a rock skimming, once, three times, seven times, good! —feeling her scraped side, raw, and sank into darkness, and breathed one time only and her lungs were black, charred, gone. She had to scream and felt them try to inflate. But they were full of holes, burst balloons, blood balloons gone lacy and dark. Each time it ended there, like a movie. Nothing more till she started it up again. It made her infinitely weary.

"So my husband said we'd better leave. I was very upset. Coming apart, kind of." She laughed, pulling hard on the fingers of one hand with the other, tugging at herself as though she were a scarf. "You don't have earthquakes here," she said simply.

He had listened very carefully, his hands in his lap looking cut loose, nothing to do with them, company posture. His beer was finished.

"No earthquakes, no tornadoes I don't think. Hurricanes once in a while. Snowstorms . . . " It was a tone he would use on his children, if he had children: full of tact and the distance of years, of small wisdom out of which even a two-bit second-story man could fashion small assurances.

"Robberies," she said, smiling bitterly. "Muggings." Rapes.

She would not tell him how she was closed up by it, cauterized. Here and there her skin puckered with memory. She got through the day. She got through the night. Martin asked her one night, turning from her, taking his hand off her shoulder, "Where the hell are you anyway?"

So she played it out, denial, reassurance, careful kisses applied to his neck where he liked them, put in place just so, like a salve. But she was gone off by herself, going nowhere she couldn't keep an eye on everything she owned. And yet she let it go so easily, her rings, her radio . . . The earth wasn't solid. "We could all do with a little less passion," she said once, sharply, just as he was moving into her, and Martin — proud of what he called his "regularity" in bed as though it had something to do with prunes — had gone slack, furiously, and rolled her away roughly like a stone in the garden. It was like being closed tight, sewn by the heat at the center of the earth. Isn't plastic sewn up that way? Then she was plastic, flesh-colored, clean, and everything stayed either outside or inside. Martin had suggested "Getting Help." But she was not guilty and God knows there was nothing to analyze because she was not to blame. Even his damn insurance policies exempted acts of God.

She looked at her caught man coolly. He was shaking his head. Pitying her?

"Don't you believe me?"

"Sure I do. Why not? I saw all that on the news, the six-o'clock news. All them bodies, listen. You're damn lucky."

She sipped her beer. Wendy would be coming home soon. She had to get dinner. "So now you come along."

"Listen, nobody ever said I was a earthquake. You don't watch out I'm gonna be flattered." He laughed, still looking at her strangely, as though from behind something. "I mean, I crowbar your window, I take a couple things out, most of it ain't much good to me anyway—"

"You sell it? Take it to somebody?"

He picked up his empty beer can and looked under it. "You got your friendly neighborhood fence right down there, don't you know Anthony's?" The dark little store where everything lay sunk under years of dust. She had wondered what moved through those bleak aisles, since it clearly wasn't groceries. "Come on, everybody knows Anthony," he said firmly. She bought milk there, expecting it to be sour.

"You shouldn't have told me that."

"Oh lady you couldn't of been here long, like you say. No secret! Tony does a good business, the cops deal down there too, so, you know—no sweat."

No, she didn't want to know. Strike it from the record.

Now, how do you get rid of a burglar nicely, she wondered, and felt like a schoolteacher. Something about her dispassionate slightly disapproving face; she felt thin-lipped, as though she were someone she'd known once and hadn't especially liked. That and her indifference at the core: Only till three, then I go home. She was very tired; breathing was hard under this damn dirty sky.

So she stood, feeling strong in her indifference. "Well, what do I do with you now? What you took was worth a lot."

"You don't look too stung."

She felt scolded. "That doesn't matter. That stuff is expensive to replace." He had probably looked in their bankbook.

He smiled. "So don't replace it."

"Is that what we have to expect from now on? Strangers walking through our house putting their dirty hands on everything?"

"Jesus, that dirt really gets you, don't it? You ought to meet my mother, you'd get along."

She stood up and paced like some woman on a soap opera, distraught on a small stage. "God, every place I turn. I feel like the apocalypse is coming, bit by bit dribbling away . . ."

"Take it easy, I ain't no earthquake, I ain't a member of the apocalypse. I live in Red Hook, I'm a little hard up, O.K.? I don't even do this regular, so relax."

She gave him a sour look. "Why don't you just go? Only give me what you've taken today. I want that back."

He looked at her, head to foot, as he stood up. "Thanks for the beer," he said quietly in an ordinary voice, a bank teller asking if she'd take singles. "Hey, try to relax a little. You'll make it better. There ain't gonna be no earthquake, you better believe it. Mayor don't allow it." He turned and walked to the front door, unhurried, leaving the footprints of his heavy work shoes on the rug. The cops couldn't get those either. He turned both locks casually, without the usual scrutiny that distracted her visitors from their good-bys. "I'll wash my hands next time." He closed the door exactly as Martin did, sturdily, with one quick push from outside to make sure the lock had clicked.

She sat down on the couch where he'd been sitting. It was so warm it was almost damp. Evisceration, she said to herself, turning the word over, thinking of chickens. Some women get their insides plucked out at around her age anyway. Same difference only cheaper, no Blue Cross. Her womb, her guts, all that dark eternally dangerous stuff stolen. Before it explodes. Dried up; out of business; kaput. Even if Willie came in that window with its curtains dancing up and out, and wanted what was left of her, right here and now before dinner, he'd jimmy her open and find her gone. The only way to make it in New York, she said to herself, and stood up wearily to get the chops out of the freezer. Spread the word.

Suggestions for Discussion

1. "The Only Way to Make It in New York" is told through the protagonist's consciousness. She is presented mainly, therefore, through thought, action, and speech. The robber is presented through his appearance, speech, and action. What can we infer about the protagonist's appearance and the robber's thoughts? How?

2. The protagonist is caught in a situation in which we would expect a reaction of fear. But the narrative suggests a series of unexpected emotions: *looking casual, faintly amusing, waiting to be frightened, not about to be intimidated, mock-bitter.* How are these emotions finally explained?

3. After two paragraphs, the story leaves its present conflict for a long flashback in which Willie and Martin are characterized. How does the contrast between them help to characterize each?

4. Do you accept the protagonist's judgment of Martin? Why?

5. Examine the dialogue between the woman and the robber. How do speech pattern and word choice characterize and contrast them in terms of gender, class, and emotion?

6. In the paragraphs on page 189 beginning, "So my husband said we'd better leave," and in the following three paragraphs, action and appearance counterpoint the dialogue. What is revealed by each?

7. Throughout the story, how is the protagonist's mental state at odds with her external action, including speech? How does each element of character presentation reveal the others?

8. What is the resolution? What is the only way to make it in New York?

RETROSPECT

1. Consider how thought is at odds with appearance and speech and/or action in the narrator of "The Persistence of Memory." In Trexler of "The

Second Tree from the Corner." In Bobby, his mother, and his father in "Cutting Edge."

2. In "Everything That Rises Must Converge," Julian and his mother are sometimes unwilling, sometimes unable to say exactly what they mean. How do these limitations help the dialogue do more than one thing at a time?

WRITING ASSIGNMENTS

1. Write a character sketch employing the four elements of direct presentation: appearance, action, speech, and thought. Use no authorial interpretation. Put one element in conflict with the other three.

2. Write a scene in which the central character does something palpably outrageous—violent, cruel, foolhardy, obscene. Let us, because we see into her or his mind, know that the character is behaving justly, kindly, or reasonably.

3. Write a character sketch describing the character both in generalizations (authorial interpretation) and in specific details. Let the details contradict the generalizations. ("Larry was the friendliest kid on the block. He had a collection of brass knucks he would let you see for fifty cents, and he would let you cock his BB gun for him as long as you were willing to hold the target.")

4. Write a scene in which a man (or boy) questions a woman (or girl) about her mother. Characterize all three.

5. Two friends are in love with the same person. One describes her/his feelings honestly and well; the other is unwilling or unable to do so, but betrays her/his feelings through appearance and action. Write the scene.

6. At the end of the story, Character A wants a great deal of money from Character B, but now, on the first page, Character A must deal with Character B's dog. Write the page; characterize A, B, and the dog.

7. Nearly every writer under pressure of a deadline at some point succumbs to the temptation of writing a story about writing a story. These stories are rarely successful, because they offer so few possibilities of external conflict and lively characterization. (The story in this book by Gabriel Josipovici is a notable exception.) So write this story: You must write a short story, and you must therefore get your major character to do whatever he or she is to do in the story. But the character is too lazy, irritable, sick, suicidal, cruel, stupid, frivolous, or having too good a time. You must trick, cajole, or force the character into the story. Do you succeed?

6

CLIMATE CONTROL
Atmosphere

Narrative Place: Setting
Narrative Time: Scene and Summary

Your fiction must have an atmosphere because without it your characters will be unable to breathe.

Like many of the terms that relate to the elements of fiction, *atmosphere* has more than one meaning, sometimes referring to subject matter, sometimes to technique. Part of the atmosphere of a scene or story is its setting, which includes the locale, period, weather, and time of day. Part of the atmosphere is its *tone*, an attitude taken by the narrative voice that can be described, not in terms of time and place, but as a quality—sinister, facetious, formal, solemn, wry, and so on. There is difficulty in discussing a term that has both a content meaning and a technical meaning: the two meanings need to be kept distinct for the sake of clarity; yet at the same time they are often inextricably mixed in the ultimate effect. A sinister atmosphere in a story might be partly achieved by syntax, rhythm, and word choice; partly by night, dampness, and a desolated landscape. We'll encounter the same difficulty discussing *point of view*, where complex literary techniques also include and make use of the mundane meaning of the phrase as "opinion." This chapter deals primarily with atmosphere as setting, the fictional boundaries in space and time, though it will not be possible to deal with those elements without reference to tone. Since tone, however, implies an attitude, not only toward the setting, but also toward the characters and the reader, it will be more fully discussed in chapter 8 on point of view, under the heading "At What Distance?"

Narrative Place: Setting

HARMONY AND CONFLICT
BETWEEN CHARACTER AND BACKGROUND

If character is the foreground of fiction, setting is the background, and as in a painting's composition, the foreground may be in harmony or in conflict with the background. If we think of the impressionist paintings of the late nineteenth century, we think of the harmony of, say, women with light-scattering parasols strolling against summer landscapes of light-scattering trees. By contrast, the Spanish painter José Cortijo has a portrait of a girl on her communion day; she sits curled and ruffled, in a lace mantilla, on an ornately carved Mediterranean throne—against a backdrop of stark, harshly lit, poverty-stricken shacks. It will be clear from this illustration that where there is a conflict between background and foreground, between character and setting, there is already "narrative content," or the makings of a story.

But whether there is conflict between character and setting or the conflict takes place entirely in the foreground, within, between, or among the characters, the setting is important to our understanding of type and of what to expect as well as to the emotional value that arises from the conflict. As we need to know a character's gender, race, and age, we need to know in what atmosphere she or he operates to understand the significance of the action.

The world and its creatures are essentially materialistic—composed of *matter* and in constant relation to matter. Our relation to place, time, and weather, like our relation to clothes and other objects, is charged with emotion more or less subtle, more or less profound. It is filled with judgment mellow or harsh. And it alters according to what happens to us. In some rooms you are always trapped; you enter them with grim purpose and escape them as soon as you can. Others invite you to settle in, to nestle or carouse. Some landscapes lift your spirits, others depress you. Cold weather gives you energy and bounce, or else it clogs your head and makes you huddle, struggling. You describe yourself as a "night person" or a "morning person." The house you loved as a child now makes you, precisely because you were once happy there, think of loss and death.

All such emotion can be used or heightened (or invented) to dramatic effect in fiction. Just as significant detail calls up a sense impression and also an abstraction, so the setting of a story imparts both information and emotion. Likewise, just as the rhythm of your prose may be more or less important but must work with and not against your intention, so the use of setting may be more or less vital, but it must work with and not against your ultimate meaning. In the Cortijo painting previously described, the communicant in the foreground is in disharmony with the houses in the background; but the contrast is part of the harmony of the composition as a whole: it is the point of the painting.

As I write, part of me is impatient with these speculations. Dully aware that every discussion of the elements of fiction includes of necessity the notions of atmosphere, setting, and tone, I have an impulse to deal with the matter summarily and get on to the next chapter: events occur in the time and through time, people move in space and through space. Therefore, let your story occur some time and some place and take some attitude or other.

But part of me is aware of a dull March day outside my window, a stubbled field of muddy snow, the students' heels sucked by the thawing path, the rubble of winter without any sign that the contract for spring is in the mail. The river is frozen to the bridge and breaking up fitfully below; ice fidgets at the bank. This morning, stretching too far in a series of sit-ups, I pulled my back out of joint, and now my movements are confined; my spine reaches cautiously for the back of the chair, and my hand moves gingerly toward my tea. The dullness in myself looks for dullness in the day, finds it, and creates it there.

And so, observing this, part of me is impelled toward awe at the boundaries of time and space, imposed on human beings and on their fictions and yet always pulling them toward a wider context. *Why* must a story be set during some time and in some place, and why does the choice inevitably matter? Psychologists have determined that one of the earliest processes of a child's mental development is the differentiation between self and other. Until the infant discovers that its mother is not itself, it has no sense of self as we know it. Yet even before this discovery it has instinctive reactions to the elements, to warmth, cold, damp. As the mind develops it becomes aware of its environment, both social and physical, and hard on the heels of this awareness comes the attempt to control and manipulate: crying for mama, grasping the bars of the crib.

Biologists point out that the cells of our blood and bodies change according to the season, like the sap of trees, so that "spring fever" is a physical fact. The blood will thin and thicken in response to climate on the zones of the globe. The pupils of our eyes expand at night, contract by day. The new science of bioecology posits the theory that people adapt over generations to their habitat and that what we call nervous, mental, and emotional disorders may in fact be allergies of the blood and brain to food grown in alien soil.

Some linguists posit the theory that language itself originates in prepositions — that is, that spatial relationships are the primary function of the mind, and our perceptions of *above, below, toward, beyond,* and so on precede any other element in the structure of logical expression.

SYMBOLIC AND SUGGESTIVE SETTING

Whether or not these linguists are right, it is certainly so that since the rosy-fingered dawn came over the battlefield of Homer's *Iliad* (and no doubt well before that), poets and writers have used the context of history, night, storm, stars, sea, city, and plain to give their stories a sense of reaching out toward the universe. Sometimes the universe resonates with an answer. In his plays Shakespeare consistently drew parallels between the conflicts of the heavenly bodies and the conflicts of nations and characters. Whether or not an author deliberately uses this correspondence to suggest the influence of the macrocosm on the microcosm, a story's setting can give the significant sense of other without which, as in an infant's consciousness, there is no valid sense of self.

In "The Life You Save May Be Your Own," Flannery O'Connor uses the elements in a conscious Shakespearian way, letting the setting reflect and effect the theme.

> The old woman and her daughter were sitting on their own porch when Mr. Shiflet came up their road for the first time. The old woman slid to the edge of her chair and leaned forward, shading her eyes from the piercing sunset with her hand. The daughter could not see far in front of her and continued to play with her fingers. Although the old woman lived in this desolate spot with only her daughter, and she had never seen Mr. Shiflet before, she could tell, even from a distance, that he was a tramp and no one to be afraid of. His left coat sleeve was folded up to show there was only half an arm in it and his gaunt figure listed lightly to the side as if the breeze were pushing him. He had on a black town suit and a brown felt hat that was turned up in the front and down in the back and he carried a tin tool box by a handle. He came on at an amble, up her road, his face turned toward the sun which appeared to be balancing itself on the peak of a small mountain.

The focus in this opening paragraph of the story is on the characters and their actions, and the setting is economically, almost incidentally established: *porch, road, sunset, breeze, peak, small mountain.* What the passage gives us is a "type" of landscape, rural and harsh; the only adjectives in the description of the setting are "piercing," "desolate," and "small." But this general background works together with details of action, thought, and appearance to establish a great deal more that is both informational and emotional. The old woman's peering suggests that people on the road are not only unusual but suspicious. On the other hand, that she is reassured to see a tramp suggests both a period and a set of assumptions about country life. That Mr. Shiflet wears a "town suit" establishes him as a stranger to this set of assumptions. That the sun "appeared to be balancing itself" (we are not sure whether it is the old woman's observation or the author's) leaves us, at the end of the paragraph, with a sense of anticipation, tension.

Now, what happens in the story is this: Mr. Shiflet repairs the old woman's car and (in order to get the car) marries her retarded daughter. He abandons the daughter on their "honeymoon" and picks up a hitchhiker who insults both Mr. Shiflet and the memory of his mother. The hitchhiker jumps out. Mr. Shiflet curses and drives on.

Throughout the story, as in the first paragraph, the focus remains on the characters and their actions. Yet the landscape and the weather make their presence felt, subtly commenting on attitudes and actions. As Mr. Shiflet's fortunes wax promising, and he expresses satisfaction with his own morality, "A fat yellow moon appeared in the branches of the fig tree as if it were going to roost there with the chickens." When, hatching his plot, he sits on the steps with the mother and daughter, "The old woman's three mountains were black against the sky." Once he has abandoned the girl, the weather grows "hot and sultry, and the country had flattened out. Deep in the sky a storm was preparing very slowly and without thunder." Once more there is a sunset, but this time the sun "was a reddening ball that through his windshield was slightly flat on the bottom and top," and this deflated sun reminds us of the "balanced" one about to be punctured by the peak in its inevitable decline. When the hitchhiker has left him, a cloud covers the sun, and Mr. Shiflet in his fury prays for the Lord to "break forth and wash the slime from this earth!" His prayer is apparently answered.

> After a few minutes there was a guffawing peal of thunder from behind and fantastic raindrops, like tin-can tops, crashed over the rear of Mr. Shiflet's car. Very quickly he stepped on the gas and with his stump sticking out the window he raced the galloping shower to Mobile.

The setting in this story, as this bald summary emphasizes, is deliberately used as a comment on the actions. The behavior of the elements, in ironic juxtaposition to the title, "The Life You Save May Be Your Own," makes clear that the "slime" Mr. Shiflet has damned may be himself. Yet the reader is never aware of this as a symbolic intrusion. The setting remains natural and realistically convincing, as incidental backdrop, until the heavens are ready to make their guffawing comment.

Robert Coover's settings rarely present a symbolic or sentient universe, but they produce in us an emotionally charged expectation of what is likely to happen here. The following passages are the opening paragraphs of three short stories from a single collection, *Pricksongs and Descants*. Notice how the three different settings are achieved, not only by imagery and content, but by the very different rhythms of the sentence structure.

A pine forest in the midafternoon. Two children follow an old man, dropping breadcrumbs, singing nursery tunes. Dense earthy greens seep into the darkening distance, flecked and streaked with filtered sunlight. Spots of red, violet, pale blue, gold, burnt orange. The girl carries a basket for gathering flowers. The boy is occupied with the crumbs. Their song tells of God's care for little ones.

"The Gingerbread House"

Situation: television panel game, live audience. Stage strobelit and cameras insecting about. Moderator, bag shape corseted and black suited behind desk/rostrum, blinking mockmodesty at lens and lamps, practised pucker on his soft mouth and brows arched in mild goodguy astonishment. Opposite him, the panel: Aged Clown, Lovely Lady and Mr. America, fat as the continent and bald as an eagle. There is an empty chair between Lady and Mr. A, which is now filled, to the delighted squeals of all, by a spectator dragged protesting from the Audience, nondescript introduced as Unwilling Participant, or more simply, Bad Sport. Audience: same as ever, docile, responsive, good-natured, terrifying. And the Bad Sport, you ask, who is he? fool! thou art!

"Panel Game"

She arrives at 7:40, ten minutes late, but the children, Jimmy and Bitsy, are still eating supper, and their parents are not ready to go yet. From the other rooms come the sounds of a baby screaming, water running, a television musical (no words: probably a dance number—patterns of gliding figures come to mind). Mrs. Tucker sweeps into the kitchen, fussing with her hair, and snatches a baby bottle full of milk out of a pan of warm water, rushes out again. "Harry!" she calls. "The babysitter's here already!"

"The Babysitter"

Here are three quite familiar places: a fairy-tale forest, a television studio, and a suburban house. In at least the first two selections, the locale is more consciously and insistently set than in the O'Connor opening, yet all three remain suggestive backdrops rather than active participants. Coover directs our attitude toward these places through imagery and tone. The forest is a neverland, and the time is "once upon a time," though there are grimmer than Grimm hints of violence about it. The TV studio is a place of hysteria, chaos, and hypocrisy, whereas the American suburbia where presumably such TV shows are received is boring rather than chaotic, not hysterical but merely hassled in a predictable sort of way.

In "The Gingerbread House," simple sentence structure helps establish the childlike quality appropriate to a fairy tale. But a more complex sentence intervenes, with surprising intensity of imagery: *dense, earthy, seep, darkening, flecked, streaked, filtered*. Because of this, the innocence of the tone is set askew, so that by the time we hear of "God's care for little ones," we fully and accurately expect a brutal disillusionment.

Note that although all fiction is bounded by place and time, the "place" and "time" may perfectly well be "no place" and "outside time." The failure to create an atmosphere, to bore or confuse us because we have no sense of where or when the story takes place, is always a fault. But an intensely created fantasy world makes new boundaries for the mind. *Once upon a time, long ago and far away, a dream, hell, heaven, time warp, black hole*, and the *subconscious* all have been the settings of excellent fiction. "Outer space" is an exciting setting precisely because its physical boundary is the outer edge of our familiar world. Obviously this does not absolve the writer from the necessity of giving "outer space" its own characteristics, atmosphere, and logic. If anything, these must be more intensely realized within the fiction, since we have less to borrow from in our own experience.

Setting can often, and in a variety of ways, arouse reader expectation and foreshadow events to come. In "The Gingerbread House," there is an implied conflict between character and setting, between the sentimentality of the children's flowers and nursery tunes and the threatening forest, so that we are immediately aware of the central conflict of the story: innocence versus violence.

But anticipation can also be aroused by an insistent single attitude toward setting, and in this case the reader, being a contrary sort of person, is likely to anticipate a change or paradox. The opening pages of E. M. Forster's *A Passage to India*, for instance, create an unrelenting portrait of the muddy dreariness of Chadrapore: *nothing extraordinary, rubbish, mean, ineffective, alleys, filth, made of mud, mud moving, abased, monotonous, rotting, swelling, shrinking, low but indestructible form of life*. The images are a little too one-sided, and as we might protest in life against a too fanatical condemnation of a place—isn't there anything good about it?—so we are led to expect (accurately again) that in the pages that follow, somehow beauty and mystery will break forth from the dross. Likewise—but in the opposite way—the opening pages of Woolf's *Mrs. Dalloway* burst with affirmation, the beauty of London and spring, love of life and love of life and love of life again! We suspect (accurately once more) that death and hatred lurk.

Where conflict between character and setting is immediately introduced, as it is in both "The Gingerbread House" and "Panel Game," it is usually because the character is unfamiliar with, or uncomfortable in, the setting. In "Panel Game" it's both. The TV studio, which is in fact a familiar and unthreatening place to most of us, has been made mad. Partly, this is achieved by violating expected grammar. The sentences are not sentences. They are missing vital verbs and logical connectives, so that the images are squashed against each other. The prose is cluttered, effortful, negative; as a result, as reader you know the "delighted squeals of all" do not include your own, and you're ready to sympathize with the unwilling central character (you!).

ALIEN AND FAMILIAR SETTING

Many poets and novelists have observed that the function of literature is to make the ordinary fresh and strange. F. Scott Fitzgerald, on the other hand, advised a young writer that reporting extreme things as if they were ordinary was the starting point of fiction. Both of these views are true, and they are particularly true of setting. Whether a place is familiar or unfamiliar, comfortable or discomfiting in fiction has nothing to do with whether the reader actually knows the place and feels good there. It is an attitude taken, an assumption made. In his detective novels, Ross MacDonald assumes a familiarity toward California that is perfectly translatable into Japanese ("I turned left off the highway and down an old switchback blacktop to a dead end"), whereas even the natives of North Hollywood must feel alien on Tom Wolfe's version of their streets:

> . . . endless scorched boulevards lined with one-story stores, shops, bowling alleys, skating rinks, taco drive-ins, all of them shaped not like rectangles but like trapezoids, from the way the roofs slant up from the back and the plate-glass fronts slant out as if they're going to pitch forward on the sidewalk and throw up.
>
> *The Kandy-Kolored Tangerine-Flake Streamline Baby*

The prose of Tom Wolfe, whether about rural North Carolina, Fifth Avenue, or Cape Kennedy, lives in a tone of constant astonishment. Ray Bradbury's outer space is pure down-home:

> It was quiet in the deep morning of Mars, as quiet as a cool black well, with stars shining in the canal waters, and, breathing in every room, the children curled with their spiders in closed hands.
>
> *Martian Chronicles*

The setting of the passage from Coover's "The Babysitter" is ordinary and is presented as ordinary. The sentences have standard and rather leisurely syntax; neither form nor image startles. In fact, there are few details of the sort that produce interesting individuality: the house is presented without a style; the children are named but not seen; Mrs. Tucker behaves in a way predictable and familiar to anyone in late-twentieth-century America. What Coover has in fact done is to present us with a setting so usual that (in the contrary way of readers) we begin to suspect that something unusual is afoot.

I have said of characterization that if the character is presented as typical we would judge that character to be stupid or evil. The same is true of setting, but with results more varied and fruitful for an author's ultimate purpose. At the center of a fiction is a consciousness, one as individual and vital as the author can produce. If the setting remains dull and damnable, then there is conflict between character and setting, and this conflict can throw that individuality and vitality into relief. Many great stories and novels have relied on setting as a means of showing the intensity and variety of human consciousness by contrasting consciousness with a social or physical world that is rule-hampered, insincere, and routine. Gustave Flaubert's *Madame Bovary* comes instantly to mind: the fullness and exactitude of the portrait is partly achieved by the provinciality of the background. This provinciality, which is French and nineteenth century, remains typical to American readers of the 1980s, who are much more likely to have grown up in Coover's suburban house. It is Flaubert's tone that creates a sense of the familiar and the typical.

Much the same thing happens in "The Babysitter." The Tuckers, their house, their children, their car, their night out, and their babysitter remain unvaryingly typical through all the external actions in the course of the evening. Against this backdrop the individual fantasies of the characters play—brilliant, brutal, sexual, dangerous, and violent—which is the conflict of the story.

One great advantage of being a writer is that you may create the world. Places and the elements have the significance and the emotional effect you choose, provided that you make them do so. As a person you may be depressed by rain, but as an author you are free to make rain "mean" freshness, growth, bounty, and God. You may choose; the only thing you are not free to do is not to choose.

As with character, the first requisite of effective setting is to know it fully, to experience it mentally; the second is to create it through significant detail. What sort of place is this, and what are its peculiarities? What is the weather like, the light, the season, the time of day? What are the contours of the land and architecture? What are the social assumptions of the inhabitants, and how familiar and comfortable are the characters with this place and its life-style? These things are not less important in fiction than in life, but more, since their selection inevitably takes on significance.

AN EXERCISE IN SETTING

There follows a series of passages about war, set in various periods and places. The first is in Russia during the campaign of Napoleon, the second in Italy during World War I, the third on the island of Pianosa during World War II, the fourth during the Vietnam War, the fifth in a post-holocaust future.

Compare the settings. How do climate, period, imagery, and language contribute to each? To what degree is setting a sentient force? Is there conflict between character and setting? How does setting affect and/or reveal the attitude taken toward the war?

> Several tens of thousands of the slain lay in diverse postures and various uniforms. . . . Over the whole field, previously so gaily beautiful with the glitter of bayonets and cloudlets of smoke in the morning sun, there now spread a mist of damp and smoke and a strange acid smell of saltpeter and blood. Clouds gathered and drops of rain began to fall on the dead and wounded, on the frightened, exhausted, and hesitating men, as if to say: "Enough, men! Enough! Cease . . . bethink yourselves! What are you doing?"
>
> LEO TOLSTOY, *War and Peace*

> In the late summer of that year we lived in a house in a village that looked across the river and plain to the mountains. In the bed of the river there were pebbles and boulders, dry and white in the sun, and the water was clear and swiftly moving and blue in the channels. Troops went by the house and down the road and the dust they raised powdered the leaves of the trees. The trunks of the trees too were dusty and the leaves fell early that year and we saw the troops marching along the road and the dust rising and leaves, stirred by the breeze, falling and the soldiers marching and afterward the road bare and white except for the leaves.
>
> ERNEST HEMINGWAY, *A Farewell to Arms*

Their only hope was that it would never stop raining, and they had no hope because they all knew it would. When it did stop raining in Pianosa, it rained in Bologna. When it stopped raining in Bologna, it began again in Pianosa. If there was no rain at all, there were freakish, inexplicable phenomena like the epidemic of diarrhea or the bomb line that moved. Four times during the first six days they were assembled and briefed and then sent back. Once, they took off and were flying in formation when the control tower summoned them down. The more it rained, the worse they suffered. The worse they suffered, the more they prayed that it would continue raining.

JOSEPH HELLER, *Catch-22*

The rain fed fungus that grew in the men's boots and socks, and their socks rotted, and their feet turned white and soft so that the skin could be scraped off with a fingernail, and Stink Harris woke up screaming one night with a leech on his tongue. When it was not raining, a low mist moved across the paddies, blending the elements into a single gray element, and the war was cold and pasty and rotten. Lieutenant Corson, who came to replace Lieutenant Sidney Martin, contracted the dysentery. The trip-flares were useless. The ammunition corroded and the foxholes filled with mud and water during the nights, and in the mornings there was always the next village and the war was the same.

TIM O'BRIEN, *Going After Cacciato*

She liked the wild, quatrosyllabic lilt of the word, "Barbarian." Then, looking beyond the wooden fence, she saw a trace of movement in the fields beyond. It was not the wind among the young corn; or, if it was wind among the young corn, it carried her the whinny of a raucous horse. It was too early for poppies but she saw a flare of scarlet. She ceased to watch the Soldiers; instead she watched the movement flow to the fences and crash through them and across the tender wheat. Bursting from the undergrowth came horseman after horseman. . . . They flashed with curious curved plates of metal dredged up from the ruins. Their horses were bizarrely caparisoned with rags, small knives, bells and chains dangling from manes and tails, and man and horse together, unholy centaurs crudely daubed with paint, looked twice as large as life. They fired long guns. Confronted with the terrors of the night in the freshest hours of the morning, the gentle crowd scattered, wailing.

ANGELA CARTER, *Heroes and Villains*

Narrative Time: Scene and Summary

Literature is, by virtue of its nature and subject matter, tied to time in a way the other arts are not. A painting represents a frozen instant in time, and the "viewing time" is a matter of the viewer's choice; no external limits are imposed in order to say that you have seen the painting. Music takes a certain time to hear, and the timing of the various parts is of utmost importance, but the time scheme is self-enclosed and makes no reference to time in the world outside itself. A book takes time to read, but the reader chooses his or her rate and may put it down and take it up at will. Its vital relationship to time is content time, the period covered in the story. It is quite possible to write a story that takes about twenty minutes to read and covers about twenty minutes of action (Jean-Paul Sartre performed experiments in this "durational realism"), but no one has suggested it as a fictional requirement. Sometimes the period covered is telescoped, sometimes stretched. The history of the world up until now can be covered in a sentence; four seconds of crisis may take a chapter. It's even possible to do both at once: William Golding's entire novel *Pincher Martin* takes place between the time the drowning protagonist begins to take off his boots and the moment he dies with his boots still on. But when asked by a student, "How long does it *really* take?" Golding replied, "Eternity."

Scene and *summary* are methods of treating time in fiction. A summary covers a relatively long period of time in relatively short compass; a scene deals with a relatively short period of time at length. Summary is a useful and often necessary device: to give information, fill in a character's background, let us understand a motive, alter pace, create a transition, leap moments or years. *Scene is always necessary to fiction.* A confrontation, a turning point, or a crisis occurs at given moments that take on significance *as moments* and cannot be summarized. The form of a story requires confrontation, turning points, and crises, and therefore requires scenes. It is quite possible to write a short story in a single scene, without any summary at all. It is not possible to write a successful story entirely in summary. One of the most common errors beginning fiction writers make is to summarize events rather than to realize them as moments.

In the following paragraph from Margaret Atwood's *Lady Oracle,* the narrator has been walking home from her Brownie troop with older girls who tease and terrify her with threats of a "bad man."

> The snow finally changed to slush and then to water, which trickled down the hill of the bridge in two rivulets, one on either side of the path; the path itself turned to mud. The bridge was damp, it smelled rotten, the willow branches turned yellow, the skipping ropes came out. It was light again in the afternoons, and on one of them, when for a change Elizabeth hadn't run off but was merely discussing the possibilities with the others, a real man actually appeared.
>
> He was standing at the far side of the bridge, a little off the path, holding a bunch of daffodils in front of him. He was a nice-looking man, neither old nor young, wearing a good tweed coat, not at all shabby or disreputable. He didn't have a hat on, his taffy-colored hair was receding and the sunlight gleamed on his high forehead.

The first paragraph of this quotation covers the way things were over a period of a few months, then makes a transition to one of the afternoons; the second paragraph specifies a particular moment. Notice that although summary sets us at a distance from the action, sense details remain necessary to its life: *snow, path, bridge, willow branches, skipping ropes.* These become more sharply focused as we concentrate on the particular moment. More important, the scene is introduced when an element of conflict and confrontation occurs. That the threatened "bad man" does appear and that he is surprisingly innocuous promises a turn of events and a change in the relationship among the girls. We need to see the moment when this change occurs.

Throughout *Lady Oracle,* which is by no means unusual in this respect, the pattern recurs: a summary leading up to, and followed by, a scene that represents a turning point.

> My own job was fairly simple. I stood at the back of the archery range, wearing a red leather change apron, and rented out the arrows. When the barrels of arrows were almost used up, I'd go down to the straw targets. . . . The difficulty was that we couldn't make sure all the arrows had actually been shot before we went down to clear the targets. Rob would shout, "Bows DOWN, please, arrows OFF the string," but occasionally someone would let an arrow go, on purpose or by accident. This was how I got shot. We'd pulled the arrows and the men were carrying the barrels back to the line; I was replacing a target face, and I'd just bent over.

The summaries in these two passages are of the two most common types, which I would call *sequential* and *circumstantial,* respectively. The summary in the first passage is sequential; it relates events in their sequence but compresses them: *snow to slush to water, willow branches turned yellow,* then *skipping ropes came out;* the transition from winter to spring is made in a paragraph. The summary in the second excerpt is circumstantial because it describes the general circumstances during a period of time: this is how things were, this is what usually or frequently happened. The narrator in the second passage describes her job in such a way: *I stood at the back of the archery range. . . . I'd go down to the straw targets. . . . Rob would shout.* Again, when the narrator arrives at an event that changes her circumstance (*I got shot*), she focuses on a particular moment: *I was replacing a target face, and I'd just bent over. . . .*

These two types of summary accurately represent two methods of the memory, which also drastically condenses. You might think of your past as a movement through time: *I was born in Arizona and lived there with my parents until I was eighteen, then I spent three years in New York before going on to England.* Or you might remember the way things were during a period of that time: *In New York we used to go down Broadway for a midnight snack, and Judy would always dare us to some nonsense or other before we got back.* But when you think of the events that significantly altered either the sequence or the circumstances of your life, your mind will present you with a scene: *Then one afternoon Professor Bovie stopped me in the hall after class and wagged his glasses at me. "Had you thought about studying in England?"*

Examining your own mind for these kinds of memory — sequential summary, circumstantial summary, and scene — will help make evident the necessity of scene in fiction. The moments that altered your life you remember at length and in detail; your memory tells you your story, and it is a great natural story teller.

How Far She Went

MARY HOOD

They had quarreled all morning, squalled all summer about the incidentals: how tight the girl's cut-off jeans were, the "Every Inch a Woman" T-shirt, her choice of music and how loud she played it, her practiced inattention, her sullen look. Her granny wrung out the last boiled dishcloth, pinched it to the line, giving the basin a sling and a slap, the water flying out in a scalding arc onto the Queen Anne's lace by the path, never mind if it bloomed, that didn't make it worth anything except to chiggers, but the girl would cut it by the everlasting armload and cherish it in the old churn, going to that much trouble for a weed but not bending once—unbegged—to pick the nearest bean; she was sulking now. Bored. Displaced.

"And what do you think happens to a chigger if nobody ever walks by his weed?" her granny asked, heading for the house with that sidelong uneager unanswered glance, hoping for what? The surprise gift of a smile? Nothing. The woman shook her head and said it. "Nothing." The door slammed behind her. Let it.

"I hate it here!" the girl yelled then. She picked up a stick and broke it and threw the pieces—one from each hand—at the laundry drying in the noon. Missed. Missed.

Then she turned on her bare, haughty heel and set off high-shouldered into the heat, quick but not far, not far enough—no road was *that* long—only as far as she dared. At the gate, a rusty chain swinging between two lichened posts, she stopped, then backed up the raw drive to make a run at the barrier, lofting, clearing it clean, her long hair wild in the sun. Triumphant, she looked back at the house where she caught at the dark window her granny's face in its perpetual eclipse of disappointment, old at fifty. She stepped back, but the girl saw her.

"You don't know me!" the girl shouted, chin high, and ran till her ribs ached.

As she rested in the rattling shade of the willows, the little dog found her. He could be counted on. He barked all the way, and squealed when she pulled the burr from his ear. They started back to the house for lunch. By then the mailman had long come and gone in the old ruts, leaving the one letter folded now to fit the woman's apron pocket.

If bad news darkened her granny's face, the girl ignored it. Didn't talk at all, another of her distancings, her defiances. So it was as they ate that the woman summarized, "Your daddy wants you to cash in the plane ticket and buy you something. School clothes. For here."

Pale, the girl stared, defenseless only an instant before blurting out, "You're lying."

The woman had to stretch across the table to leave her handprint on that blank cheek. She said, not caring if it stung or not, "He's been planning it since he sent you here."

"I could turn this whole house over, dump it! Leave you slobbering over that stinking jealous dog in the dust!" The girl trembled with the vision, with the strength it gave her. It made her laugh. "Scatter the Holy Bible like confetti and ravel the crochet into miles of stupid string! I could! I will! I won't stay here!" But she didn't move, not until her tears rose to meet her color, and then to escape the shame of minding so much she fled. Just headed away, blind. It didn't matter, this time, how far she went.

The woman set her thoughts against fretting over their bickering, just went on unalarmed with chores, clearing off after the uneaten meal, bringing in the laundry, scattering corn for the chickens, ladling manure tea onto the porch flowers. She listened though. She always had been a listener. It gave her a cocked look. She forgot why she had gone into the girl's empty room, that ungirlish, tenuous lodging place with its bleak order, its ready suitcases never unpacked, the narrow bed, the contested radio on the windowsill. The woman drew the cracked shade down between the radio and the August sun. There wasn't anything else to do.

It was after six when she tied on her rough oxfords and walked down the drive and dropped the gate chain and headed back to the creosoted shed where she kept her tools. She took a hoe for snakes, a rake, shears to trim the grass where it grew, and seed in her pocket to scatter where it never had grown at all. She put the tools and her gloves and the bucket in the trunk of the old Chevy, its prime and rust like an Appaloosa's spots through the chalky white finish. She left the trunk open and the tool handles sticking out. She wasn't going far.

The heat of the day had broken, but the air was thick, sultry, weighted with honeysuckle in second bloom and the Nu-Grape scent of kudzu. The maple and poplar leaves turned over, quaking, silver. There wouldn't be any rain. She told the dog to stay, but he knew a trick. He stowed away when she turned her back, leaped right into the trunk with the tools, then gave himself away with exultant barks. Hearing him, her court jester, she stopped the car and welcomed him into the front seat beside her. Then they went on. Not a mile from her gate she turned onto the blue gravel of the cemetery lane, hauled the gearshift into reverse to whoa them, and got out to take the idle walk down to her buried hopes, bending all along to rout out a handful of weeds from between the markers of old acquaintance. She stood there and read, slow. The dog whined at her hem; she picked him up and rested her chin on his head, then he wriggled and whined to run free, contrary and restless as a child.

The crows called strong and bold MOM! MOM! A trick of the ear to hear it like that. She knew it was the crows, but still she looked around. No one called her that now. She was done with that. And what was it worth anyway? It all came to this: solitary weeding. The sinful fumble of flesh, the fear, the listening for a return that never came, the shamed waiting, the unanswered prayers, the perjury on the certificate—hadn't she lain there weary of the whole lie and it only beginning? and a voice telling her, "Here's your baby, here's your girl," and the swaddled package meaning no more to her than an extra anything, something store-bought, something she could take back for a refund.

"Tie her to the fence and give her a bale of hay," she had murmured, drugged, and they teased her, excused her for such a welcoming, blaming the anesthesia, but it went deeper than that; *she* knew, and the *baby* knew: there was no love in the begetting. That was the secret, unforgivable, that not another good thing could ever make up for, where all the bad had come from, like a visitation, a punishment. She knew that was why Sylvie had been wild, had gone to earth so early, and before dying had made this child in sudden wedlock, a child who would be just like her, would carry the hurting on into another generation. A matter of time. No use raising her hand. But she *had* raised her hand. Still wore on its palm the memory of the sting of the collision with the girl's cheek; had she broken her jaw? Her heart? Of course not. She said it aloud: "Takes more than that."

She went to work then, doing what she could with her old tools. She pecked the clay on Sylvie's grave, new-looking, unhealed after years. She tried again, scattering seeds from her pocket, every last possible one of them. Off in the west she could hear the pulpwood cutters sawing through another acre across the lake. Nearer, there was the racket of motorcycles laboring cross-country, insect-like, distracting.

She took her bucket to the well and hung it on the pump. She had half filled it when the bikers roared up, right down the blue gravel, straight at her. She let the bucket overflow, staring. On the back of one of the machines was the girl. Sylvie's girl! Her bare arms wrapped around the shirtless man riding between her thighs. They were first. The second biker rode alone. She studied their strangers' faces as they circled her. They were the enemy, all of them. Laughing. The girl was laughing too, laughing like her mama did. Out in the middle of nowhere the girl had found these two men, some moth-musk about her drawing them (too soon!) to what? She shouted it: "What in God's—" They roared off without answering her, and the bucket of water tipped over, spilling its stain blood-dark on the red dust.

The dog went wild barking, leaping after them, snapping at the tires, and there was no calling him down. The bikers made a wide circuit of the churchyard, then roared straight across the graves, leaping the ditch and landing upright on the road again, heading off toward the reservoir.

Furious, she ran to her car, past the barking dog, this time leaving him behind, driving after them, horn blowing nonstop, to get back what was not theirs. She drove after them knowing what they did not know, that all the roads beyond that point dead-ended. She surprised them, swinging the Impala across their path, cutting them off; let them hit it! They stopped. She got out, breathing hard, and said, when she could, "She's underage." Just that. And put out her claiming hand with an authority that made the girl's arms drop from the man's insolent waist and her legs tremble.

"I was just riding," the girl said, not looking up.

Behind them the sun was heading on toward down. The long shadows of the pines drifted back and forth in the same breeze that puffed the distant sails on the lake. Dead limbs creaked and clashed overhead like the antlers of locked and furious beasts.

"Sheeeut," the lone rider said. "I told you." He braced with his muddy boot and leaned out from his machine to spit. The man the girl had been riding with had the invading sort of eyes the woman had spent her lifetime bolting doors against. She met him now, face to face.

"Right there, missy," her granny said, pointing behind her to the car.

The girl slid off the motorcycle and stood halfway between her choices. She started slightly at the poosh! as he popped another top and chugged the beer in one uptilting of his head. His eyes never left the woman's. When he was through, he tossed the can high, flipping it end over end. Before it hit the ground he had his pistol out and, firing once, winged it into the lake.

"Freaking lucky shot," the other one grudged.

"I don't need luck," he said. He sighted down the barrel of the gun at the woman's head. "POW!" he yelled, and when she recoiled, he laughed. He swung around to the girl; he kept aiming the gun, here, there, high, low, all around. "Y'all settle it," he said, with a shrug.

The girl had to understand him then, had to know him, had to know better. But still she hesitated. He kept looking at her, then away.

"She's fifteen," her granny said. "You can go to jail."

"You can go to hell," he said.

"Probably will," her granny told him. "I'll save you a seat by the fire." She took the girl by the arm and drew her to the car; she backed up, swung around, and headed out the road toward the churchyard for her tools and dog. The whole way the girl said nothing, just hunched against the far door, staring hard-eyed out at the pines going past.

The woman finished watering the seed in, and collected her tools. As she worked, she muttered, "It's your own kin buried here, you might have the decency to glance this way one time. . . ." The girl was finger-tweezing her eyebrows in the side mirror. She didn't look around as the dog and the woman got in. Her granny shifted hard, sending the tools clattering in the trunk.

When they came to the main road, there were the men. Watching for them. Waiting for them. They kicked their machines into life and followed, close, bumping them, slapping the old fenders, yelling. The girl gave a wild glance around at the one by her door and said, "Gran'ma?" and as he drew his pistol, "Gran'ma!" just as the gun nosed into the open window. She frantically cranked the glass up between her and the weapon, and her granny, seeing, spat, "Fool!" She never had been one to pray for peace or rain. She stamped the accelerator right to the floor.

The motorcycles caught up. Now she braked, hard, and swerved off the road into an alley between the pines, not even wide enough for the school bus, just a fire scrape that came out a quarter mile from her own house, if she could get that far. She slewed on the pine straw, then righted, tearing along the dark tunnel through the woods. She had for the time being bested them; they were left behind. She was winning. Then she hit the wallow where the tadpoles were already five weeks old. The Chevy plowed in and stalled. When she got it cranked again, they were stuck. The tires spattered mud three feet up the near trunks as she tried to spin them out, to rock them out. Useless. "Get out and run!" she cried, but the trees were too close on the passenger side. The girl couldn't open her door. She wasted precious time having to crawl out under the steering wheel. The woman waited but the dog ran on.

They struggled through the dusky woods, their pace slowed by the thick straw and vines. Overhead, in the last light, the martins were reeling free and sure after their prey.

"Why? Why?" the girl gasped, as they lunged down the old deer trail. Behind them they could hear shots, and glass breaking as the men came to the bogged car. The woman kept on running, swatting their way clear through the shoulder-high weeds. They could see the Greer cottage, and made for it. But it was ivied-over, padlocked, the woodpile dry-rotting under its tarp, the electric meterbox empty on the pole. No help there.

The dog, excited, trotted on, yelping, his lips white-flecked. He scented the lake and headed that way, urging them on with thirsty yips. On the clay shore, treeless, deserted, at the utter limit of land, they stood defenseless, listening to the men coming on, between them and home. The woman pressed her hands to her mouth, stifling her cough. She was exhausted. She couldn't think.

"We can get under!" the girl cried suddenly, and pointed toward the Greers' dock, gap-planked, its walkway grounded on the mud. They splashed out to it, wading in, the woman grabbing up the telltale, tattletale dog in her arms. They waded out to the far end and ducked under. There was room between the foam floats for them to crouch neck-deep.

The dog wouldn't hush, even then; never had yet, and there wasn't time to teach him. When the woman realized that, she did what she had to do. She grabbed him whimpering; held him; held him under till the struggle ceased and the bubbles rose silver from his fur. They crouched there then, the two of them, submerged to the shoulders, feet unsteady on the slimed lake bed. They listened. The sky went from rose to ocher to violet in the cracks over their heads. The motorcycles had stopped now. In the silence there was the glissando of locusts, the dry crunch of boots on the flinty beach, their low man-talk drifting as they prowled back and forth. One of them struck a match.

"—they in these woods we could burn 'em out."

The wind carried their voices away into the pines. Some few words eddied back.

"—lippy old smartass do a little work on her knees besides praying—"

Laughter. It echoed off the deserted house. They were getting closer.

One of them strode directly out to the dock, walked on the planks over their heads. They could look up and see his boot soles. He was the one with the gun. He slapped a mosquito on his bare back and cursed. The carp, roused by the troubling of the waters, came nosing around the dock, guzzling and snorting. The girl and her granny held still, so still. The man fired his pistol into the shadows, and a wounded fish thrashed, dying. The man knelt and reached for it, chuffing out his beery breath. He belched. He pawed the lake for the dead fish, cursing as it floated out of reach. He shot it again, firing at it till it sank and the gun was empty. Cursed that too. He stood then and unzipped and relieved himself of some of the beer. They had to listen to that. To know that about him. To endure that, unprotesting.

Back and forth on shore the other one ranged, restless. He lit another cigarette. He coughed. He called, "Hey! They got away, man, that's all. Don't get your shorts in a wad. Let's go."

"Yeah." He finished. He zipped. He stumped back across the planks and leaped to shore, leaving the dock tilting amid widening ripples. Underneath, they waited.

The bike cranked. The other ratcheted, ratcheted, then coughed, caught, roared. They circled, cut deep ruts, slung gravel, and went. Their roaring died away and away. Crickets resumed and a near frog bic-bic-bicked.

Under the dock, they waited a little longer to be sure. Then they ducked below the water, scraped out from under the pontoon, and came up into free air, slogging toward shore. It had seemed warm enough in the water. Now they shivered. It was almost night. One streak of light still stood reflected on the darkening lake, drew itself thinner, narrowing into a final cancellation of day. A plane winked its way west.

The girl was trembling. She ran her hands down her arms and legs, shedding water like a garment. She sighed, almost a sob. The woman held the dog in her arms; she dropped to her knees upon the random stones and murmured, private, haggard, "Oh, honey," three times, maybe all three times for the dog, maybe once for each of them. The girl waited, watching. Her granny rocked the dog like a baby, like a dead child, rocked slower and slower and was still.

"I'm sorry," the girl said then, avoiding the dog's inert, empty eye.

"It was him or you," her granny said, finally, looking up. Looking her over. "Did they mess with you? With your britches? Did they?"

"No!" Then, quieter, "No, ma'am."

When the woman tried to stand up she staggered, lightheaded, clumsy with the freight of the dog. "No, ma'am," she echoed, fending off the girl's "Let me." And she said again, "It was him or you. I know that. I'm not going to rub your face in it." They saw each other as well as they could in that failing light, in any light.

The woman started toward home, saying, "Around here, we bear our own burdens." She led the way along the weedy shortcuts. The twilight bleached the dead limbs of the pines to bone. Insects sang in the thickets, silencing at their oncoming.

"We'll see about the car in the morning," the woman said. She bore her armful toward her own moth-ridden dusk-to-dawn security light with that country grace she had always had when the earth was reliably progressing underfoot. The girl walked close behind her, exactly where *she* walked, matching her pace, matching her stride, close enough to put her hand forth (if the need arose) and touch her granny's back where the faded voile was clinging damp, the merest gauze between their wounds.

Suggestions for Discussion

1. Observe how scene and summary alternate in the first paragraph. What does each contribute?

2. What details help create in the reader a sense of familiarity with a setting that is in fact probably unfamiliar to most of us?

3. In what ways is each of the characters in harmony or conflict with the setting?

4. The girl tells us directly that she hates this place, but we are never directly given an image of the place she comes from. What do we know about it, and how?

5. In the two paragraphs on page 209 beginning, "The crows called strong. . . ," identify elements of scene, sequential summary, and circumstantial summary.

6. Apart from the bikers, what elements of the modern world seem to violate the setting?

7. Explain the irony of the refrains to do with leaving the place: "not far enough— no road was *that* long—only as far as she dared," "It didn't matter, this time, how far she went," "She wasn't going far," ". . . if she could get that far."

8. In the last three paragraphs of the story, how do elements of the setting symbolize reversal and resolution?

August 2002: Night Meeting

RAY BRADBURY

Before going on up into the blue hills, Tomás Gomez stopped for gasoline at the lonely station.

"Kind of alone out here, aren't you, Pop?" said Tomás.

The old man wiped off the windshield of the small truck. "Not bad."

"How do you like Mars, Pop?"

"Fine. Always something new. I made up my mind when I came here last year I wouldn't expect nothing, nor ask nothing, nor be surprised at nothing. We've got to forget Earth and how things were. We've got to look at what we're in here, and how *different* it is. I get a hell of a lot of fun out of just the weather here. It's *Martian* weather. Hot as hell daytimes, cold as hell nights. I get a big kick out of the different flowers and different rain. I came to Mars to retire and I wanted to retire in a place where everything is different. An old man needs to have things different. Young people don't want to talk to him, other old people bore hell out of him. So I thought the best thing for me is a place so different that all you got to do is open your eyes and you're entertained. I got this gas station. If business picks up too much, I'll move on back to some other old highway that's not so busy, where I can earn just enough to live on and still have time to feel the *different* things here."

"You got the right idea, Pop," said Tomás, his brown hands idly on the wheel. He was feeling good. He had been working in one of the new colonies for ten days straight and now he had two days off and was on his way to a party.

"I'm not surprised at anything any more," said the old man. "I'm just looking. I'm just experiencing. If you can't take Mars for what she is, you might as well go back to Earth. Everything's crazy up here, the soil, the air, the canals, the natives (I never saw any yet, but I hear they're around), the clocks. Even my clock acts funny. Even *time* is crazy up here. Sometimes I feel I'm here all by myself, no one else on the whole damn planet. I'd take bets on it. Sometimes I feel about eight years old, my body squeezed up and everything else tall. Jesus, it's just the place for an old man. Keeps me alert and keeps me happy. You know what Mars is? It's like a thing I got for Christmas seventy years ago—don't know if you ever had one—they called them kaleidoscopes, bits of crystal and cloth and beads and pretty junk. You held it up to the sunlight and looked in through at it, and it took your breath away. All the patterns! Well, that's Mars. Enjoy it. Don't ask it to be nothing else but what it is. Jesus, you know that highway right there, built by the Martians, is over sixteen centuries old and still in good condition? That's one dollar and fifty cents, thanks and good night."

Tomás drove off down the ancient highway, laughing quietly.

It was a long road going into darkness and hills and he held to the wheel, now and again reaching into his lunch bucket and taking out a piece of candy. He had been driving steadily for an hour, with no other car on the road, no light, just the road going under, the hum, the roar, and Mars out there, so quiet. Mars was always quiet, but quieter tonight than any other. The deserts and empty seas swung by him, and the mountains against the stars.

There was a smell of Time in the air tonight. He smiled and turned the fancy in his mind. There was a thought. What did Time smell like? Like dust and clocks and people. And if you wondered what Time sounded like it sounded like water running in a dark cave and voices crying and dirt dropping down upon hollow box lids, and rain. And, going further, what did Time *look* like? Time looked like snow dropping silently into a black room or it looked like a silent film in an ancient theater, one hundred billion faces falling like those New Year balloons, down and down into nothing. That was how Time smelled and looked and sounded. And tonight—Tomás shoved a hand into the wind outside the truck—tonight you could almost *touch* Time.

He drove the truck between hills of Time. His neck prickled and he sat up, watching ahead.

He pulled into a little dead Martian town, stopped the engine, and let the silence come in around him. He sat, not breathing, looking out at the white buildings in the moonlight. Uninhabited for centuries. Perfect, faultless, in ruins, yes, but perfect, nevertheless.

He started the engine and drove on another mile or more before stopping again, climbing out, carrying his lunch bucket, and walking to a little promontory where he could look back at that dusty city. He opened his thermos and poured himself a cup of coffee. A night bird flew by. He felt very good, very much at peace.

Perhaps five minutes later there was a sound. Off in the hills, where the ancient highway curved, there was a motion, a dim light, and then a murmur.

Tomás turned slowly with the coffee cup in his hand.

And out of the hills came a strange thing.

It was a machine like a jade-green insect, a praying mantis, delicately rushing through the cold air, indistinct, countless green diamonds winking over its body, and red jewels that glittered with multifaceted eyes. Its six legs fell upon the ancient highway with the sounds of a sparse rain which dwindled away, and from the back of the machine a Martian with melted gold for eyes looked down at Tomás as if he were looking into a well.

Tomás raised his hand and thought Hello! automatically but did not move his lips, for this *was* a Martian. But Tomás had swum in blue rivers on Earth, with strangers passing on the road, and eaten in strange houses with strange people, and his weapon had always been his smile. He did not carry a gun. And he did not feel the need of one now, even with the little fear that gathered about his heart at this moment.

The Martian's hands were empty too. For a moment they looked across the cool air at each other.

It was Tomás who moved first.

"Hello!" he called.

"Hello!" called the Martian in his own language.

They did not understand each other.

"Did you say hello?" they both asked.

"What did you say?" they said, each in a different tongue.

They scowled.

"Who are you?" said Tomás in English.

"What are you doing here?" In Martian; the stranger's lips moved.

"Where are you going?" they said, and look bewildered.

"I'm Tomás Gomez."

"I'm Muhe Ca."

Neither understood, but they tapped their chests with the words and then it became clear.

And then the Martian laughed. "Wait!" Tomás felt his head touched, but no hand had touched him. "There!" said the Martian in English. "That is better!"

"You learned my language, so quick!"

"Nothing at all!"

They looked, embarrassed with a new silence, at the steaming coffee he had in one hand.

"Something different?" said the Martian, eying him and the coffee, referring to them both, perhaps.

"May I offer you a drink?" said Tomás.

"Please."

The Martian slid down from his machine.

A second cup was produced and filled, steaming. Tomás held it out.

Their hands met and—like mist—fell through each other.

"Jesus Christ!" cried Tomás, and dropped the cup.

"Name of the Gods!" said the Martian in his own tongue.

"Did you see what happened?" they both whispered.

They were very cold and terrified.

The Martian bent to touch the cup but could not touch it.

"Jesus!" said Tomás.

"Indeed." The Martian tried again and again to get hold of the cup, but could not. He stood up and thought for a moment, then took a knife from his belt. "Hey!" cried Tomás. "You misunderstand, catch!" said the Martian, and tossed it. Tomás cupped his hands. The knife fell through his flesh. It hit the ground. Tomás bent to pick it up but could not touch it, and he recoiled, shivering.

Now he looked at the Martian against the sky.

"The stars!" he said.

"The stars!" said the Martian, looking, in turn, at Tomás.

The stars were white and sharp beyond the flesh of the Martian, and they were sewn into his flesh like scintillas swallowed into the thin, phosphorescent membrane of a gelatinous sea fish. You could see stars flickering like violet eyes in the Martian's stomach and chest, and through his wrists, like jewelry.

"I can see through you!" said Tomás.

"And I through you!" said the Martian, stepping back.

Tomás felt his own body and, feeling the warmth, was reassured. *I am real*, he thought.

The Martian touched his own nose and lips. "*I have flesh*," he said, half aloud. "*I am alive*."

Tomás stared at the stranger. "And if *I* am real, then you must be dead."

"No, you!"

"A ghost!"

"A phantom!"

They pointed at each other, with starlight burning in their limbs like daggers and icicles and fireflies, and then fell to judging their limbs again, each finding himself intact, hot, excited, stunned, awed, and the other, ah yes, that other over there, unreal, a ghostly prism flashing the accumulated light of distant worlds.

I'm drunk, thought Tomás. I won't tell anyone of this tomorrow, no, no.

They stood there on the ancient highway, neither of them moving.

"Where are you from?" asked the Martian at last.

"Earth."

"What is that?"

"There." Tomás nodded to the sky.

"When?"

"We landed over a year ago, remember?"

"No."

"And all of you were dead, all but a few. You're rare, don't you *know* that?"

"That's not true."

"Yes, dead. I saw the bodies. Black, in the rooms, in the houses, dead. Thousands of them."

"That's ridiculous. We're *alive!*"

"Mister, you're invaded, only you don't know it. You must have escaped."

"I haven't escaped; there was nothing to escape. What do you mean? I'm on my way to a festival now at the canal, near the Eniall Mountains. I was there last night. Don't you see the city there?" The Martian pointed.

Tomás looked and saw the ruins. "Why, that city's been dead thousands of years."

The Martian laughed. "Dead. I slept there yesterday!"

"And I was in it a week ago and the week before that, and I just drove through it now, and it's a heap. See the broken pillars?"

"Broken? Why, I see them perfectly. The moonlight helps. And the pillars are upright."

"There's dust in the streets," said Tomás.

"The streets are clean!"

"The canals are empty right there!"

"The canals are full of lavender wine!"

"It's dead."

"It's alive!" protested the Martian, laughing more now. "Oh, you're quite wrong. See all the carnival lights? There are beautiful boats as slim as women, beautiful women as slim as boats, women the color of sand, women with fire flowers in their hands. I can see them, small, running in the streets there. That's where I'm going now, to the festival; we'll float on the waters all night long; we'll sing, we'll drink, we'll make love. Can't you *see* it?"

"Mister, that city is dead as a dried lizard. Ask any of our party. Me, I'm on my way to Green City tonight; that's the new colony we just raised over near Illinois Highway. You're mixed up. We brought in a million board feet of Oregon lumber and a couple dozen tons of good steel nails and hammered together two of the nicest little villages you ever saw. Tonight we're warming one of them. A couple rockets are coming in from Earth, bringing our wives and girl friends. There'll be barn dances and whisky—"

The Martian was now disquieted. "You say it is over *that* way?"

"There are the rockets." Tomás walked him to the edge of the hill and pointed down. "See?"

"No."

"Damn it, there they *are!* Those long silver things."

"No."

Now Tomás laughed. "You're blind!"

"I see very well. You are the one who does not see."

"But you see the new *town*, don't you?"

"I see nothing but an ocean, and water at low tide."

"Mister, that water's been evaporated for forty centuries."

"Ah, now, now, that *is* enough."

"It's true, I tell you."

The Martian grew very serious. "Tell me again. You do not see the city the way I describe it? The pillars very white, the boats very slender, the festival lights—oh, I see them *clearly*! And listen! I can hear them singing. It's no space away at all."

Tomás listened and shook his head. "No."

"And I, on the other hand," said the Martian, "cannot see what you describe. Well."

Again they were cold. An ice was in their flesh.

"Can it be . . . ?"

"What?"

"You say 'from the sky'?"

"Earth."

"Earth, a name, nothing," said the Martian. "*But* . . . as I came up the pass an hour ago. . . ." He touched the back of his neck. "I felt . . ."

"Cold?"

"Yes."

"And now?"

"Cold again. Oddly. There was a thing to the light, to the hills, the road," said the Martian. "I felt the strangeness, the road, the light, and for a moment I felt as if I were the last man alive on this world. . . ."

"So did I!" said Tomás, and it was like talking to an old and dear friend, confiding, growing warm with the topic.

The Martian closed his eyes and opened them again. "This can only mean one thing. It has to do with Time. Yes. You are a figment of the Past!"

"No, you are from the Past," said the Earth Man, having had time to think of it now.

"You are so *certain*. How can you prove who is from the Past, who from the Future? What year is it?"

"Two thousand and one!"

"What does that mean to *me*?"

Tomás considered and shrugged. "Nothing."

"It is as if I told you that it is the year 4462853 S.E.C. It is nothing and more than nothing! Where is the clock to show us how the stars stand?"

"But the ruins prove it! They prove that *I* am the Future, *I* am alive, *you* are dead!"

"Everything in me denies this. My heart beats, my stomach hungers, my mouth thirsts. No, no, not dead, not alive, either of us. More alive than anything else. Caught between is more like it. Two strangers passing in the night, that is it. Two strangers passing. Ruins, you say?"

"Yes. You're afraid?"

"Who wants to see the Future, who *ever* does? A man can face the Past, but to think—the pillars *crumbled*, you say? And the sea empty, and the canals dry, and the maidens dead, and the flowers withered?" The Martian was silent, but then he looked on ahead. "But there they *are*. I *see* them. Isn't that enough for me? They wait for me now, no matter *what* you say."

And for Tomás the rockets, far away, waiting for *him*, and the town and the women from Earth. "We can never agree," he said.

"Let us agree to disagree," said the Martian. "What does it matter who is Past or Future, if we are both alive, for what follows will follow, tomorrow or in ten thousand years. How do you know that those temples are not the temples of your own civilization one hundred centuries from now, tumbled and broken? You do not know. Then don't ask. But the night is very short. There go the festival fires in the sky, and the birds."

Tomás put out his hand. The Martian did likewise in imitation.

Their hands did not touch; they melted through each other.

"Will we meet again?"

"Who knows? Perhaps some other night."

"I'd like to go with you to that festival."

"And I wish I might come to your new town, to see this ship you speak of, to see these men, to hear all that has happened."

"Good-by," said Tomás.

"Good night."

The Martian rode his green metal vehicle quietly away into the hills. The Earth Man turned his truck and drove it silently in the opposite direction.

"Good lord, what a dream that was," sighed Tomás, his hands on the wheel, thinking of the rockets, the women, the raw whisky, the Virginia reels, the party.

How strange a vision was that, thought the Martian, rushing on, thinking of the festival, the canals, the boats, the women with golden eyes, and the songs.

The night was dark. The moons had gone down. Starlight twinkled on the empty highway where now there was not a sound, no car, no person, nothing. And it remained that way all the rest of the cool dark night.

Suggestions for Discussion

1. The gas station owner, Pop, keeps insisting on how different Mars is from Earth. We as readers are perversely struck with how much the same it is. How does Bradbury accomplish this result?

2. Why is it necessary to the story that the atmosphere of Mars should be established as familiar and comfortable before Tomás meets the Martian?

3. On page 215, Tomás speculates about the smell, sound, and look of Time. How does this prepare us for what follows?

4. The paragraph beginning, "He started the engine . . . ," on page 215, introduces a sequential summary. Where and why does this summary give way to scene?

5. Examine the Martian's dialogue. Although he has learned English at a touch, his use of it is slightly stilted and old-fashioned. How does this contribute to his characterization? To the atmosphere?

6. Though Tomás has driven off "laughing quietly" at the gas station owner, now he and the Martian are amazed at the distortion of time they discover. Are they more amazed than the reader? Why?

7. At the end of the story each rides off convinced that the other is a dream. In what way is this a resolution?

RETROSPECT

1. Contrast the rural atmosphere of "Girl" and "How Far She Went." To what extent is setting an element of conflict in each story?

2. Contrast the atmosphere of New York City as presented in "The Second Tree from the Corner" and "The Only Way to Make It in New York." Where do the two atmospheres of the city coincide, and where do they diverge?

3. Reread "Shiloh," focusing on the alternation of scene, sequential summary, and circumstantial summary.

WRITING ASSIGNMENTS

1. Write a scene, involving only one character, who is uncomfortable in his or her surroundings: socially inadequate, frightened, revolted, painfully

nostalgic, or the like. Using active verbs in your description of the setting, build forceful conflict between the person and the place.

2. Write a scene with two characters in conflict over the setting: one wants to go, and one wants to stay. The more interesting the setting you choose, the more interesting the conflict will inevitably be.

3. Write a scene in a setting that is likely to be quite familiar to your readers (supermarket, dormitory, classroom, movie theater, suburban house, etc.) but that is unfamiliar, strange, outlandish, or outrageous to the central character. Let us feel the strangeness through the character's eyes.

4. Write a scene set in a strange, exotic place or a time far distant either in the past or the future, in which the setting is quite familiar to the central character. Convince us of the ordinariness of the place.

5. Write a scene in which the character's mood is at odds with the weather and make the weather nevertheless express her or his mood: the rain is joyful, the clear skies are threatening, the snow is comforting, the summer beach is chilling.

6. Identify the place you have most hated in your life. Then write a scene set in that place, about a character who loves it.

7. Write a passage that begins with a sequential summary of the central character's life, then moves to a crucial scene, goes on to a circumstantial summary, and ends with a scene of crisis.

7

CALL ME ISHMAEL
Point of View, Part I

Who Speaks?
To Whom?
In What Form?

Point of view is the most complex element of fiction. Although it lends itself to analysis, definitions, and diagrams, it is finally a question of relationship among writer, characters, and reader—subject like any relationship to organic subtleties. We can discuss person, omniscience, narrative voice, tone, authorial distance, and reliability; but none of these things will ever pigeonhole a work in such a way that any other work may be placed in the exact same pigeonhole.

The first thing to do is to set aside the common use of the phrase "point of view" as being synonymous with "opinion," as in *It's my point of view that they all ought to be shot.* An author's view of the world as it is and as it ought to be will ultimately be revealed by his or her manipulation of the technique of point of view, but not vice versa—identifying the author's beliefs will not describe the point of view of the work. Rather than thinking of point of view as an opinion or belief, begin with the more literal synonym of "vantage point." *Who* is standing *where* to watch the scene?

Better, since we are dealing with a verbal medium, these questions might be translated: Who speaks? To whom? In what form? At what distance from the action? With what limitations? All these issues go into the determination of the point of view. Because *the author inevitably wants to convince us to share the same perspective*, the answers will also help reveal her or his final opinion, judgment, attitude, or message.

This chapter deals with the first three questions: Who speaks? To whom? In what form? Distance and limitations are considered in chapter 8.

Who Speaks?

The primary point-of-view decision that you as author must make before you can set down the first sentence of the story is *person*. This is the simplest and crudest subdivision that must be made in deciding who speaks. The story can be told in the third person (*She walked out into the harsh sunlight*), the second person (*You walked out into the harsh sunlight*), or the first person (*I walked out into the harsh sunlight*). Third- and second-person stories are "told" by an author; first-person stories, by a character.

THIRD PERSON

Third person, in which the author is telling the story, can be subdivided again according to the degree of knowledge, or *omniscience* the author assumes. Notice that since this is a matter of degree, the subdivisions are again only a crude indication of the variations possible. As an author you are free to decide how much you know. You may know every universal and eternal truth; you may know what is in the mind of one character but not what is in the mind of another; or you may know only what can be externally observed. You decide, and very early in the story you signal to the reader what degree of omniscience you have chosen. Once given, this signal constitutes a "contract" between author and reader, and it will be difficult to break the contract gracefully. If you have restricted yourself to the mind of James Lordly for five pages, as he observes the actions of Mrs. Grumms and her cats, you will violate the contract by suddenly dipping into Mrs. Grumms's mind to let us know what she thinks of James Lordly. We are likely to feel misused, and likely to cancel the contract altogether, if you suddenly give us the thoughts of the cats.

The omniscient author, sometimes referred to as the *editorial omniscient author*, because she or he tells us directly what we are supposed to think, has total knowledge. As omniscient author you are God. You can—

Who Speaks?		
The Author	**The Author**	**Character**
In: Third Person	In: Second Person	In: First Person
Editorial Omniscient	"You" as character	Central Narrator
Limited Omniscient	"You" as reader-turned-	Peripheral Narrator
Objective	character	

To Whom?		
The Reader	**Another Character**	**The Self**
Characterized or	**or Characters**	
Uncharacterized		

In What Form?

"Written Story," "Spoken Story," Reportage, Oratory, Monologue, Confessional, Journal, Diary, Interior Monologue, Stream of Consciousness, etc. . . .

At What Distance?

Reader and Author ◄────────► Narrator ◄────────► Characters
Complete Identification ◄────────────────────────► Complete Opposition
Temporal, Spatial, Moral, Intellectual, Aesthetic, Physical, Educational, Experiential

With What Limitations?

Reliable Narrator (or "Author") ◄────────► Unreliable Narrator (or "Author")
on any of values listed above

1. Objectively report what is happening;
2. Go into the mind of any character;
3. Interpret for us that character's appearance, speech, actions, and thoughts, even if the character cannot do so;
4. Move freely in time or space to give us a panoramic, telescopic, microscopic, or historical view; tell us what has happened elsewhere or in the past or what will happen in the future;
5. Provide general reflections, judgments, and truths.

In all these aspects, we will accept what the omniscient author tells us. If you tell us that Ruth is a good woman, that Jeremy doesn't really understand his own motives, that the moon is going to explode in four hours, and that everybody will be better off for it, we will believe you. Here is a paragraph that blatantly exhibits all five of these areas of knowledge.

(1) Joe glared at the screaming baby. (2) Frightened by his scowl, the baby gulped and screamed louder. I hate that thing, Joe thought. (3) But it was not really hatred that he felt. (4) Only two years ago he himself had screamed like that. (5) Children can't tell hatred from fear.

This illustration is awkwardly compressed, but an author well in control of his craft can move easily from one area of knowledge to another. In the first scene of *War and Peace*, Tolstoy describes Anna Scherer.

> To be an enthusiast had become her social vocation, and sometimes even when she did not feel like it, she became enthusiastic in order not to disappoint the expectations of those who knew her. The subdued smile which, though it did not suit her faded features, always played around her lips, expressed as in a spoiled child, a continual consciousness of her charming defect, which she neither wished, nor could, nor considered it necessary to correct.

Here in two sentences Tolstoy tells us what is in Anna's mind and the expectations of her acquaintances, what she looks like, what suits her, what she can and cannot do; and he offers a general reflection on spoiled children.

The omniscient voice is the voice of the classical epic (*And Meleager, far-off, knew nothing of this, but felt his vitals burning with fever*), of the Bible (*So the Lord sent a pestilence upon Israel; and there fell seventy thousand men*), and of most nineteenth-century novels (*Tito put out his hand to help him, and so strangely quick are men's souls that in this moment, when he began to feel that his atonement was accepted, he had a darting thought of the irksome efforts it entailed.*). But it is one of the manifestations of literature's movement downward in class from heroic to common characters, inward from action to the mind, that authors of the twentieth century have largely avoided the godlike stance of the omniscient author and chosen to restrict themselves to fewer areas of knowledge.

The limited omniscient viewpoint is one in which the author may move with some, but not all, of the omniscient author's freedom. You may grant yourself the right, for example, to know what the characters in a scene are thinking but not to interpret their thoughts. You may interpret one character's thoughts and actions but see the others only externally. You may see with microscopic accuracy but not presume to reach any universal truths. The most commonly used form of the limited omniscient point of view is one in which the author can see events objectively and also grants himself or herself access to the mind of one character, but not to the minds of the others, nor to any explicit powers of judgment. This point of view is particularly useful for the short story because it very quickly establishes the point-of-view character or *means of perception*. The short story is so compressed a form that there is rarely time or space to develop more than one consciousness. Staying with external observation and one character's thoughts helps control the focus and avoid *awkward point-of-view shifts*.

But the form is also frequently used for the novel, as in Gail Godwin's *The Odd Woman*.

> It was ten o'clock on the evening of the same day, and the permanent residents of the household on the mountain were restored to routines and sobriety. Jane, on the other hand, sat by herself in the kitchen, a glass of Scotch before her on the cleanly wiped table, going deeper and deeper into a mood she could recognize only as unfamiliar. She could not describe it; it was both frightening and satisfying. It was like letting go and being taken somewhere. She tried to trace it back. When, exactly, had it started?

It is clear here that the author has limited her omniscience. She is not going to tell us the ultimate truth about Jane's soul, nor is she going to define for us the "unfamiliar mood" that the character herself cannot define. The author has the facts at her disposal, and she has Jane's thoughts, and that is all.

The advantage of the limited omniscient over the omniscient voice is immediacy. Here, because we are not allowed to know more than Jane does about her own thoughts and feelings, we grope *with* her toward understanding. In the process, a contract has been made between the author and the reader, and this contract must not now be broken. If at this point the author should step in and answer Jane's question, "When, exactly, had it started?" with, "Jane was never to remember this, but in fact it had started one afternoon when she was two years old," we would feel it as an abrupt and uncalled-for *authorial intrusion*.

Nevertheless, within the limits the author has set herself, there is fluidity and a range of possibilities. Notice that the passage begins with a panoramic observation (*ten o'clock, permanent residents, routines*) and moves to the tighter focus of a view, still external, of Jane (*sat by herself in the kitchen*), before moving into her mind. The sentence "She tried to trace it back" is a relatively factual account of her mental process, whereas in the next sentence, "When, exactly, had it started?" we are in Jane's mind, overhearing her question to herself.

Although this common form of the limited omniscient (objective reporting plus one mind) may seem very restricted, given all the possibilities of omniscience, it has a freedom that no human being has. In life you have full access to only one mind, your own; and you are also the one person you may not externally observe. As a fiction writer you can do what no human being can do, be simultaneously inside and outside a given character; it is this that E.M. Forster describes in *Aspects of the Novel* as "the fundamental difference between people in daily life and people in books."

In daily life we never understand each other, neither complete clairvoyance nor complete confessional exists. We know each other approximately, by external signs, and these serve well enough as a basis for society and even for intimacy. But people in a novel can be understood completely by the reader, if the novelist wishes; their inner as well as their outer life can be exposed. And this is why they often seem more definite than characters in history, or even our own friends.

The *objective author.*   Sometimes the novelist or short-story writer does not wish to expose any more than the external signs. The *objective* author is not omniscient but impersonal. As an objective author, you restrict your knowledge to the facts that might be observed by a human being; to the senses of sight, sound, smell, taste, and touch. In the story "Hills Like White Elephants," Ernest Hemingway reports what is said and done by a quarreling couple, both without any direct revelation of the characters' thoughts and without comment.

> The American and the girl with him sat at a table in the shade, outside the building. It was very hot and the express from Barcelona would come in forty minutes. It stopped at this junction for two minutes and went on to Madrid.
> "What should we drink?" the girl asked. She has taken off her hat and put it on the table.
> "It's pretty hot," the man said.
> "Let's drink beer."
> "Dos cervezas," the man said into the curtain.
> "Big ones?" a woman asked from the doorway.
> "Yes. Two big ones."
> The woman brought two glasses of beer and two felt pads. She put the felt pads and the beer glasses on the table and looked at the man and the girl. The girl was looking off at the line of hills. They were white in the sun and the country was brown and dry.

In the course of this story we learn, entirely by inference, that the girl is pregnant and that she feels herself coerced by the man into having an abortion. Neither pregnancy nor abortion is ever mentioned. The narrative remains clipped, austere, and external. What does Hemingway gain by this pretense of objective reporting? The reader is allowed to discover what is really happening. The characters avoid the subject, prevaricate, and pretend, but they betray their real meanings and feelings through gestures, repetitions, and slips of the tongue. The reader, focus directed by the author, learns by inference, as in life, so that we finally have the pleasure of knowing the characters better than they know themselves.

For the sake of clarity, the possibilities of third-person narration have been divided into the editorial omniscient, limited omniscient, and objective authors, but between the extreme stances of the editorial omniscient (total knowledge) and the objective author (external observation only), the powers of the limited omniscient are immensely variable. Because you are most likely to choose your authorial voice in this range, you need to be aware that you make your own rules and that, having made them, you must stick to them. Your position as a writer is analogous to that of a poet who may choose whether to write free verse or a ballad stanza. If the poet chooses the stanza, then he or she is obliged to rhyme. Beginning writers of prose fiction are often tempted to shift viewpoint when it is both unnecessary and disturbing.

> Leo's neck flushed against the prickly weave of his uniform collar. He concentrated on his buttons and tried not to look into the face of the bandmaster, who, however, was more amused than angry.

This is an awkward point-of-view shift because, having felt Leo's embarrassment with him, we are suddenly asked to leap into the bandmaster's feelings. The shift can be corrected by moving instead from Leo's mind to an observation that he might make.

> Leo's neck flushed against the prickly weave of his uniform collar. He concentrated on his buttons and tried not to look into the face of the bandmaster, who, however, was astonishingly smiling.

The rewrite is easier to follow because we remain with Leo's mind as he observes that the bandmaster is not angry. It further serves the purpose of implying that Leo fails to concentrate on his buttons, and so intensifies his confusion.

SECOND PERSON

First and third persons are most common in literature; the second person remains an idiosyncratic and experimental form, but it is worth mentioning because several twentieth-century authors have been attracted to its possibilities.

Person refers to the basic mode of a piece of fiction. In the third person, all the characters will be referred to as *he, she,* and *they.* In the first person, the character telling the story will refer to himself or herself as *I* and to other characters as *he, she,* and *they.* The second person is the basic mode of the story *only when a character* is referred to as *you.* When an omniscient author addresses the reader as *you* (*You will remember that John Doderring was left dangling on the cliff at Dover*), this does not alter the basic mode of the piece from third to second person. Only when "you" become an actor in the drama is the story or novel written in second person.

In *Even Cowgirls Get the Blues*, Tom Robbins exhibits both of these uses of the second person.

> If you could buckle your Bugs Bunny wristwatch to a ray of light, your watch would continue ticking but its hands wouldn't move.

The *you* involved here is a generalized reader, and the passage is written in the stance of an omniscient author delivering a general "truth."

But when the author turns to address his central character, Sissy Hankshaw, the basic mode of the narration becomes that of the second person.

> You hitchhike. Timidly at first, barely flashing your fist, leaning almost imperceptibly in the direction of your imaginary destination. A squirrel runs along a tree limb. You hitchhike the squirrel. A blue jay flies by. You flag it down.

The effect of this second-person narration is odd and original; the author observes Sissy Hankshaw, and yet his direct address implies an intimate and affectionate relationship that makes it easy to move further into her mind.

> Your thumbs separate you from other humans. You begin to sense a presence about your thumbs. You wonder if there is not magic there.

In this example it is a character clearly delineated and distinguished from the reader who is the *you* of the narrative. But the second person can also be used as a means of making the reader into a character, as in Robert Coover's story, "Panel Game," quoted in chapter 6.

> You squirm, viced by Lady (who excites you) and America (who does not, but bless him all the same), but your squirms are misread: Lovely Lady lifts lashes, crosses eyes, and draws breath excitedly. . . . Audience howls happily the while and who can blame them? You, Sport, resign yourself to pass the test in peace and salute them with a timid smile, squirm no more.

Here again the effect of the second person is unusual and complex. The author assigns you, the reader, specific characteristics and reactions and thereby—assuming that you go along with his characterization of you—pulls you deeper and more intimately into the story.

It is unlikely that the second person will ever become a major mode of narration as the first and third are, but for precisely that reason you may find it an attractive experiment. It is startling and relatively unexplored.

FIRST PERSON

A story is told in the first person when it is a character who speaks. The term "narrator" is sometimes loosely used to refer to any teller of a tale, but strictly speaking a story "has a narrator" only when it is told in the first person by one of the characters. This character may be the protagonist, the *I* telling *my* story, in which case that character is a *central narrator*; or the character may be telling a story about someone else, in which case he or she is a *peripheral narrator*.

In either case it's important to indicate early which kind of narrator we have so that we know who the story's protagonist is, as in the first paragraph of Alan Sillitoe's "The Loneliness of the Long-Distance Runner."

> As soon as I got to Borstal they made me a long-distance cross-country runner. I suppose they thought I was just the build for it because I was long and skinny for my age (and still am) and in any case I didn't mind it much, to tell you the truth, because running had always been made much of in our family, especially running away from the police.

The focus here is immediately thrown on the *I* of the story, and we expect that *I* to be the central character whose desires and decisions impel the action. But from the opening lines of R. Bruce Moody's *The Decline and Fall of Daphne Finn*, it is Daphne who is brought alive by attention and detail, while the narrator is established as an observer and recorder of his subject.

> "Is it really you?"
> Melodious and high, this voice descended to me from behind and above — as it seemed it was always to do — indistinct as bells in another country.
> Unable to answer in the negative, I turned from my desk, looked up, and smiled sourly.
> "Yes," I said, startling a face which had been peering over my shoulder, a face whose beauty it was apparent at the outset had made no concession to convention. It retreated as her feet staggered back.

The central narrator is always, as the term implies, at the center of the action; the peripheral narrator may be in virtually any position that is not the center. He or she may be the second most important character in the story, or may not be involved in the action at all but merely placed in a position to observe. The narrator may characterize himself or herself in detail or may remain detached and scarcely identifiable. It is even possible to make the first-person narrator plural, as William Faulkner does in "A Rose for Emily," where the story is told by a narrator identified only as one of "us," the people of the town in which the action has taken place.

That a narrator may be either central or peripheral, that a character may tell either his own story or someone else's, is both commonly assumed and obviously logical. But the author and editor Rust Hills, in his book *Writing in General and the Short Story in Particular*, takes interesting and persuasive exception to this idea. When point of view fails, Hills argues, it is always because the perception we are using for the course of the story is different from that of the character who is moved or changed by the action. Even when a narrator seems to be a peripheral observer and the story is "about" someone else, in fact it is the narrator who is changed, and must be, in order for us to be satisfied by our emotional identification with him or her.

> This, I believe, is what will always be the case in successful fiction: that either the character moved by the action will be the point-of-view character, or else the point-of-view character will *become* the character moved by the action. Call it Hills' Law.

Obviously, this view does not mean that we have to throw out the useful fictional device of the peripheral narrator. Hills uses the familiar examples of *The Great Gatsby* and *Heart of Darkness* to illustrate his meaning. In the former, Nick Carroway as a peripheral narrator observes and tells the story of Jay Gatsby, but by the end of the book it is Nick's life that has been changed by what he has observed. In the latter, Marlow purports to tell the tale of the ivory hunter Kurtz, even protesting that "I don't want to bother you much with what happened to me personally." By the end of the story, Kurtz (like Gatsby) is dead, but it is not the death that moves us so much as what, "personally," Marlow has learned *through* Kurtz and his death. The same can be said of *The Decline and Fall of Daphne Finn*; the focus of the action is on Daphne, but the pain, the passion, and the loss are those of her biographer. Even in "A Rose for Emily," where the narrator is a collective "we," it is the implied effect of Miss Emily on the town that moves us, the emotions of the townspeople that we share. Because we tend to identify with the means of perception in a story, we are moved with that perception; even when the overt action of the story is elsewhere, it is often the act of observation itself that provides the epiphany.

The thing to recognize about a first-person narrator is that because she or he is a character, she or he has all the limitations of a human being and cannot be omniscient. The narrator is confined to reporting what she or he could realistically know. More than that, although the narrator may certainly interpret actions, deliver dictums, and predict the future, these remain the fallible opinions of a human being, we are not bound to accept them as we are bound to accept the interpretations, truths, and predictions of the omniscient author. You may want us to accept the narrator's word, and then the most difficult part of your task, and the touchstone of your story's success, will be to convince us to trust and believe the narrator. On the other hand, it may be an important part of your purpose that we should reject the narrator's opinions and form our own. In the latter case, the narrator is "unreliable," a phenomenon that will be taken up in chapter 8.

To Whom?

In choosing a point of view, the author implies an identity, not only for the teller of the tale, but for the audience as well.

THE READER

Most fiction is addressed to a literary convention, "*the reader*." When we open a book, we tacitly accept our role as a member of this unspecified audience. If the story begins, "I was born of a drunken father and an illiterate mother in the peat bogs of Galway during the Great Potato Famine," we are not, on the whole, alarmed. We do not face this clearly deceased Irishman who has crossed the Atlantic to take us into his confidence and demand, "Why are you telling me all this?"

Notice that the tradition of "the reader" assumes the universality of the audience. Most stories do not specifically address themselves to a segment or period of humanity, and they make no concessions to such difference as might exist between reader and author; they assume that anyone who reads the story can be brought around to the same understanding of it the author has. In practice most writers, though they do not acknowledge it in the text and may not admit it to themselves, are addressing someone *who can* be brought around to the same understanding as themselves. The author of a "Harlequin Romance" addresses the story to a generalized "reader" but knows that his or her likely audience is trained by repetition of the formula to expect certain Gothic features—rich lover, virtuous heroine, threatening house, colorful costume. Slightly less formulaic is the notion of "a *New Yorker* story," which is presumably what the author perceives that the editors perceive will be pleasing to the people who buy *The New Yorker*. Anyone who pens or types what he or she hopes is "literature" is assuming that his audience is literate, which leaves out better than half the world. My mother, distressed at the difficulty of my fictional style, used to urge me to write for "the masses," by which she meant subscribers to the *Reader's Digest*, whom she thought to be in need of cheering and escape. I considered this a very narrow goal until I realized that my own ambition to be "universal" was more exclusive still: I envisioned my audience as made up of people who *would not* subscribe to the *Reader's Digest*.

Nevertheless, the most common assumption of the tale-teller, whether omniscient author or narrating character, is that the reader is an amenable and persuasible Everyman, and that the telling needs no justification.

But there are various exceptions to this tendency which can be used to dramatic effect and which always involve a more definite characterizing of the receiver of the story. The author may address "the reader" but assign that reader specific traits that we, the actual readers, must then accept as our own if we are to accept the fiction. Nineteenth-century novelists had a tradition of addressing "You, gentle reader," "Dear reader," and the like, and this minimal characterization was a technique for implying mutual understanding. In "The Loneliness of the Long-Distance Runner," by Alan Sillitoe, on the other hand, the narrator divides the world into "us" and "you." *We*, the narrator and his kind, are the outlaws, all those who live by their illegal wits; and *you*, the readers, are by contrast law-abiding, prosperous, educated, and rather dull. To quote again from "The Loneliness of the Long-Distance Runner":

> I suppose you'll laugh at this, me saying the governor's a stupid bastard when I know hardly how to write and he can read and write and add-up like a professor. But what I say is true right enough. He's stupid and I'm not, because I can see further into the likes of him than he can see into the likes of me.

The clear implication here is that the narrator can see further into the likes of us readers than we can see into the likes of him, and much of the effective irony of the story rests in the fact that the more we applaud and identify with the narrator, the more we must accept his condemning characterization of "us."

ANOTHER CHARACTER

More specifically still, the story may be told to *another character or characters*, in which case we as readers "overhear" it; the teller of the tale does not acknowledge us even by implication. Just as the third-person author telling "her story" is theoretically more impersonal than the first-person character telling "my story," so "the reader" is theoretically a more impersonal receiver of the tale than another character. I insert the word *theoretically* because, with regard to point of view more than any other element of fiction, any rule laid down seems to be an invitation to rule breaking by some original and inventive author.

In the *epistolary* novel or story, the narrative consists entirely of letters written from one character to another, or between characters.

> I, Mukhail Ivanokov, stone mason in the village of Ilba in the Ukranian Soviet Socialist Republic, greet you and pity you, Charles Ashland, petroleum merchant in Titusville, Florida, in the United States of America. I grasp your hand.
>
> KURT VONNEGUT, "The Manned Missiles"

Or the convention of the story may be that of a monologue, spoken aloud by one character to another.

> May I, *monsieur*, offer my services without running the risk of intruding? I fear you may not be able to make yourself understood by the worthy ape who presides over the fate of this establishment. In fact, he speaks nothing but Dutch. Unless you authorize me to plead your case, he will not guess that you want gin.
>
> ALBERT CAMUS, *The Fall*

Again, the possible variations are infinite; the narrator may speak in intimate confessional to a friend or lover, or may present his case to a jury or a mob; she may be writing a highly technical report of the welfare situation, designed to hide her emotions; he may be pouring out his heart in a love letter he knows (and we know) he will never send.

In any of these cases, the convention employed is the opposite of that employed in a story told to "the reader." The listener as well as the teller is involved in the action; the assumption is not that we readers are there but that we are not. We are eavesdroppers, with all the ambiguous intimacy that position implies.

THE SELF

An even greater intimacy is implied if the character's story is as secret as a diary or as private as a mind, addressed to *the self* and not intended to be heard by anyone inside or outside the action.

November 6

Something has got into the Chief of my Division. When I arrived at the office he called me and began as follows: "Now then, tell me. What's the matter with you? . . . I know you're trailing after the Director's daughter. Just look at yourself—what are you? Just nothing. You haven't a penny to your name. Look in the mirror. How can you even think of such things?" The hell with him! Just because he's got a face like a druggist's bottle and that quiff of hair on his head all curled and pomaded.

NIKOLAI GOGOL, *The Diary of a Madman*

The protagonist here is clearly using his diary to vent his feelings and does not intend it to be read by anyone else. Still, he has deliberately externalized his secret thoughts in a journal. Because the author has the power to enter a character's mind, the reader also has the power to eavesdrop on thoughts, read what is "not written," hear what is "not spoken," and share what cannot be shared.

Interior Monologue. Overheard thoughts are generally of two kinds, of which the most common is *interior monologue*, the convention being that we follow that character's thoughts in their sequence, though in fact the author, for our convenience, sets out those thoughts with a coherence and logic that no human mind ever possessed.

I must organize myself. I must, as they say, pull myself together, dump this cat from my lap, stir—yes, resolve, move, do. But do what? My will is like the rosy dustlike light in this room: soft, diffuse, and gently comforting. It lets me do . . . anything . . . nothing. My ears hear what they happen to; I eat what's put before me; my eyes see what blunders into them; my thoughts are not thoughts, they are dreams. I'm empty or I'm full . . . depending; and I cannot choose. I sink my claws in Tick's fur and scratch the bones of his back until his rear rises amorously. Mr. Tick, I murmur, I must organize myself, I must pull myself together. And Mr. Tick rolls over on his belly, all ooze.

WILLIAM H. GASS, "In the Heart of the Heart of the Country"

This interior monologue ranges, as human thoughts do, from sense impression to self-admonishment, from cat to light to eyes and ears, from specific to general and back again. But the logical connections between these things are all provided; the mind "thinks" logically and grammatically as if the character *were* trying to express himself.

Stream of Consciousness. In fact the human mind does not operate with the order and clarity of the monologue just quoted. Even what little we know of its operations makes clear that it skips, elides, makes and breaks images, leaps faster and further than any mere sentence can suggest. Any mind at any moment is simultaneously accomplishing dozens of tasks that cannot be conveyed simultaneously. As you read this sentence part of your mind is following the sense of it; part of your mind is directing your hand to hold the book open; part of it twisting your spine into a more comfortable position; part of it still lingering on the last interesting image of this text, Mr. Tick rolling over on his belly, which reminds you of a cat you had once that was also *all ooze*, which reminds you that you're nearly out of milk and have to finish this chapter before the store closes . . . and so forth.

In *Ulysses*, James Joyce tried to catch the speed and multiplicity of the mind with a technique that has come to be known as *stream of consciousness*. The device is difficult and in many ways thankless: since the speed of thought is so much faster than that of writing or speaking, and stream of consciousness tries to suggest the process as well as the content of the mind, it requires a more, not less, rigorous selection and arrangement than ordinary grammar requires. But Joyce and a very few other writers have handled stream of consciousness as an ebullient and exciting way of capturing the mind.

> Yes because he never did a thing like that before as ask to get his breakfast in bed with a couple of eggs since the *City Arms* hotel when he used to be pretending to be laid up with a sick voice doing his highness to make himself interesting to that old faggot Mrs. Riordan that he thought he had a great leg of and she never left us a farthing all for masses for herself and her soul greatest miser ever was actually afraid to lay out 4d for her methylated spirit telling me all her ailments she had too much old chat in her about politics and earthquakes and the end of the world let us have a bit of fun first God help the world if all the women were her sort. . . .
>
> JAMES JOYCE, *Ulysses*

The preceding two examples, of interior monologue and stream of consciousness, respectively, are written in the first person, so that we overhear the minds of narrator characters. Through the omniscient and limited omniscient authors we may also overhear the thoughts of the characters, and when this is the case there is a curious doubling or crossing of literary conventions. Say that the story is told by a limited omniscient author, who is therefore speaking "to the reader." But this author may also enter the mind of a character, who is speaking to him- or herself. The passage from *The Odd Woman* on page 227 is of this sort. Here is a still more striking example.

> Dusk was slowly deepening. Somewhere, he could not tell exactly where, a cricket took up a fitful song. The air was growing soft and heavy. He looked over the fields, longing for Bobo. . . .

He shifted his body to ease the cold damp of the ground, and thought back over the day. Yeah, he'd been damn right about not wanting to go swimming. If he had followed his right mind he'd never have gotton into all this trouble.

RICHARD WRIGHT, "Big Boy Leaves Home"

Though this story, first published in 1938, makes use of an old style of dialect misspelling, Wright moves gracefully between the two voices. An authorial voice—educated, eloquent, and mature—tells us what is in Big Boy's mind: *he could not tell exactly where, longing for Bobo*; and a dialect voice lets us overhear Big Boy's thoughts, adolescent and uneducated: *Yeah, hed been dam right*. If either of these voices were absent, the passage would be impoverished; it needs the scope of the author and the immediacy of the character to achieve its effect.

In What Form?

The form of the story, like the teller and the listener, can be more or less specified as part of the total point of view. The form may announce itself without justification as a generalized *story*, either *written* or *spoken*; or it may suggest *reportage, confessional, interior monologue,* or *stream of consciousness*; or it may be overtly identified as *monologue, oratory, journal,* or *diary*. The relationship between the teller of a tale and its receiver often automatically implies a form for the telling, so that most of the forms above have already been mentioned. The list is not exhaustive; you can tell your story in the form of a catalogue or a TV commercial as long as you can devise a way to do so that also has the form of a story.

Form is important to point of view because the form in which a story is told indicates the degree of self-consciousness on the part of the teller; this will in turn affect the language chosen, the intimacy of the relationship, and the honesty of the telling. A written account will imply less spontaneity, on the whole, than one that appears to be spoken aloud, which suggests less spontaneity than thought. A narrator writing a letter to his grandmother may be less honest than he is when he tells the same facts aloud to his friend.

Certain relationships established by the narrative between teller and audience make certain forms more likely than others, but almost any combination of answers is possible to the questions: *Who speaks? To whom? In what form?* If you are speaking as an omniscient author to the literary convention of "the reader," we may assume that you are using the convention of "written story" as your form. But you might say:

Wait, step over here a minute. What's this in the corner, stuffed down between the bedpost and the wall?

If you do this, you slip at least momentarily into the different convention of the spoken word—the effect is that we are drawn more immediately into the scene—and the point of view of the whole is slightly altered. A central narrator might be thinking, and therefore "talking to herself," while actually angrily addressing her thoughts to another character. Conversely, one character might be writing a letter to another but letting the conscious act of writing deteriorate into a betrayal of his own secret thoughts. Any complexities such as these will alter and inform the total point of view.

Here are the opening passages from a student short story in which the point of view is extremely complex. An adequate analysis of it will require, more than a definition or a diagram, a series of *yes but's* and *but also's*.

Report: He is the light-bringer, the peerless one. She is the dark-water creature, the Queen of Fishes. I don't know why I say that except sometimes I get desperate for sheer sound. You would too if you went to St. Katherine's Day Academy where the D.H. Lawrence is in a locked cabinet in the library. I used to wonder why Tom sends me there except now I know it's his notion of a finishing school. "It's what your mother would have wanted," he says, tragic-eyed. But I know he's thinking about Vivian.

I started my journal to show you what she's doing to him. He doesn't know. He wouldn't. But I sit in on the seminar. I read the Eliot, the Rhys, the Muir, the MacDiarmid with them. They think I'm amusing, these long tall girls in *Rive Gauche* jeans and velour with Parker chrome mechanical pencils—engraved initials—and notebooks written all over: "Bring *The Green Helmet* to class Tues." and "talk to Dr. Johnson about Parents' Day Brunch" and phone numbers everywhere. I am a sort of mascot. They'd be surprised to know that I, their Tom's daughter, knows what they are at when they talk of regional sensibility in Muir and the mythic fallacy. Especially Vivian who comes to class early and stays late and comes for dinner and once "took Elaine shopping, isn't that nice?" God, I hated it. "Look, Elaine, that grey would just match your eyes. I'll bet Tom, I mean your father, would like that." I went home that day and cast a Mars number square against her for discord, discord, discord. But still she came back—back for Tom.

DIANE ROBERTS, *"Lamia"*

Who speaks? The passage is written in the first person—so much is easy. So it is a narrator who speaks, and this narrator tells us that she is peripheral: "I started my journal to show you what she's doing to him." But against this statement of the narrator's intention, we feel so much personal grief and bottled fury, and the focus of the narrative returns so insistently to what the *I* of the story is doing and feeling, that we are inclined to believe the real subject is not "what she's doing to him" but *what they're doing to me* and, therefore, to feel that we're dealing with a central narrator.

To whom? The narrator addresses a *you* who is clearly the convention of "the reader." Yet on several counts this notion doesn't bear pursuing. She is revealing bitter attitudes that couldn't be confessed to her father, so the *you* to whom she reveals them can scarcely include a reader sitting with printed pages. The reader who is the *you* of the narrative becomes so abstract that it might be the spirit of justice she addresses, or God. Yet the narrator makes little attempt to present a coherent account of background facts, which come out obliquely, subsidiary to the pent-up emotion—*I am a sort of mascot; They'd be surprised to know*—which suggests that she's really talking to herself.

In what form? She tells us twice: this is "a report" and "my journal." Neither is quite possible. The opening word "Report" is immediately contradicted by the dramatic imagery of "light-bringer" and "dark-water creature," so that we understand the word itself is an ironic attempt to claim logic and objectivity for an emotion that admits of neither. It's a journal, then, a diary of great intimacy. That's what it feels like; but how can a diary be addressed to a reader?

The amazing thing about all this is that we are not in the least confused! The paradoxes and contradictions of the narrative do not make us feel that the author is inept but, on the contrary, that she has captured with great precision the paradoxes and contradictions of the narrator's emotional state. We feel no awkward point-of-view shift because all the terms of the contract—those same paradoxes and contradictions—are laid out for us in the opening paragraph.

Clearly there is an author somewhere, who is not the same person as this narrator, and who is directing us moment by moment to accept or reject, to believe or disbelieve, what the narrator tells us.

In order to deal with a viewpoint as complex as this, it will be necessary to deal, not only with who speaks to whom in what form, but with *distance* and *limitation*, subjects treated in chapter 8.

The Bella Lingua

JOHN CHEEVER

Wilson Streeter, like many Americans who live in Rome, was divorced. He worked as a statistician for the F.R.U.P.C. agency, lived alone, and led a diverting social life with other expatriates and those Romans who were drawn into expatriate circles, but he spoke English all day long at his office and the Italians he met socially spoke English so much better than he spoke

Italian that he could not bring himself to converse with them in their language. It was his feeling that in order to understand Italy he would have to speak Italian. He did speak it well enough when it was a question of some simple matter of shopping or making arrangements of one kind or another, but he wanted to be able to express his sentiments, to tell jokes, and to follow overheard conversations on trolley cars and buses. He was keenly conscious of the fact that he was making his life in a country that was not his own, but this sense of being an outsider would change, he thought, when he knew the language.

For the tourist, the whole experience of traveling through a strange country is on the verge of the past tense. Even as the days are spent, these *were* the days in Rome, and everything—the sightseeing, souvenirs, photographs, and presents—is commemorative. Even as the traveler lies in bed waiting for sleep, these *were* the nights in Rome. But for the expatriate there is no past tense. It would defeat his purpose to think of this time in another country in relation to some town or countryside that was and might again be his permanent home, and he lives in a continuous and unrelenting present. Instead of accumulating memories, the expatriate is offered the challenge of learning a language and understanding a people. So they catch a glimpse of one another in the Piazza Venezia—the expatriates passing through the square on their way to their Italian lessons, the tourists occupying, by prearrangement, all the tables at a sidewalk café and drinking Campari, which they have been told is a typical Roman *aperitivo*.

Streeter's teacher was an American woman named Kate Dresser, who lived in an old palace near the Piazza Firenze, with an adolescent son. Streeter went there for his lessons on Tuesday and Friday evenings and on Sunday afternoons. He enjoyed the walk in the evening from his office, past the Pantheon, to his Italian lesson. Among the rewards of his expatriation were a heightened awareness of what he saw and an exhilarating sense of freedom. Mixed with the love we hold for our native country is the fact that it is the place where we were raised, and, should anything have gone a little wrong in this process, we will be reminded of this fault, by the scene of the crime, until the day we die. Some such unhappiness may have accounted for Streeter's sense of freedom, and his heightened awareness may have been nothing but what is to be expected of a man with a good appetite walking through the back streets of a city in the autumn. The air was cold and smelled of coffee—sometimes of incense, if the doors to a church stood open—and chrysanthemums were for sale everywhere. The sights were exciting and confusing—the ruins of Republican and Imperial Rome, and the ruins of what the city had been the day before yesterday—but the whole thing would be revealed to him when he could speak Italian.

It was not easy, Streeter knew, for a man his age to learn anything, and he had not been fortunate in his search for a good Italian teacher. He had first gone to the Dante Alighieri Institute, where the classes were so large that he made no progress. Then he had taken private lessons from an old lady. He was supposed to read and translate Collodi's *Pinocchio*, but when he had done a few sentences the teacher would take the book out of his hands and do the reading and translating herself. She loved the story so much that she laughed and cried, and sometimes whole lessons passed in which Streeter did not open his mouth. It disturbed his sense of fitness that he, a man of fifty, should be sitting in a cold flat at the edge of Rome, being read a children's tale by a woman of seventy, and after a dozen lessons he told his teacher that he had to go to Perugia on business. After this he enrolled in the Tauchnitz School and had private lessons. His teacher was an astonishingly pretty young woman who wore the tight-waisted clothes that were in fashion that year, and a wedding ring—a prop, he guessed, because she seemed so openly flirtatious and gay. She wore a sharp perfume, rattled her bracelets, pulled down her jacket, swung her hips when she walked to the blackboard, and gave Streeter, one evening, such a dark look that he took her in his arms. What she did then was to shriek, kick over a little desk, and run through three intervening classrooms to the lobby, screaming that she had been attacked by a beast. After all his months of study, "beast" was the only word in her tirade that Streeter understood. The whole school was alerted, of course, and all he could do was to wipe the sweat off his forehead and start through the classrooms toward the lobby. People stood on chairs to get a better look at him, and he never went back to Tauchnitz.

His next teacher was a very plain woman with gray hair and a lavender shawl that she must have knitted herself, it was so full of knots and tangles. She was an excellent teacher for a month, and then one evening she told him that her life was difficult. She waited to be encouraged to tell him her troubles, and when he did not give her any encouragement, she told them to him anyhow. She had been engaged to be married for twenty years, but the mother of her betrothed disapproved of the match and, whenever the subject was raised, would climb up onto the window sill and threaten to jump into the street. Now her betrothed was sick, he would have to be cut open (she gestured) from the neck to the navel, and if he died she would go to her grave a spinster. Her wicked sisters had got pregnant in order to force their marriages—one of them had walked down the aisle eight months gone (more gestures)—but she would rather (with a hitch at her lavender shawl) solicit men in the street than do that. Streeter listened helplessly to her sorrow, as we will listen to most human troubles, having some of our own, but she was still talking when her next student, a Japanese, came in for his lesson, and Streeter had learned no Italian that night. She had not told Streeter all of the story, and she continued it when he came again. The fault might have been his—he should have discouraged her rudely—but now that she had made him her confidant, he saw that he could not change this relationship. The force he had to cope with was the loneliness that is to be found in any large city, and he invented another trip to Perugia. He had two more teachers, two more trips to Perugia, and then, in the late autumn of his second year in Rome, someone from the Embassy recommended Kate Dresser.

An American woman who teaches Italian in Rome is unusual, but then all arrangements in Rome are so complicated that lucidity and skepticism give way when we try to follow the description of a scene in court, a lease, a lunch, or anything else. Each fact or detail breeds more questions than it answers, and in the end we lose sight of the truth, as we were meant to do. Here comes Cardinal Micara with the True Finger of Doubting Thomas— that much is clear—but is the man beside us in church asleep or dead, and what are all the elephants doing in the Piazza Venezia?

The lessons took place at one end of a huge *sala*, by the fireplace. Streeter spent an hour and sometimes two hours preparing for them. He finished *Pinocchio* and began to read *I Promessi Sposi*. After this would come the *Divine Comedy*. He was as proud as a child of his completed homework, loved to be given tests and dictation, and usually came into Kate's apartment with a big, foolish smile on his face, he was so pleased with himself. She was a very good teacher. She understood his fatuousness, the worn condition of his middle-aged memory, and his desire to learn. She spoke an Italian that he could almost always understand, and by keeping a wristwatch on the table to mark the period, by sending him bills through the mail, and by never speaking of herself, she conducted the lessons in an atmosphere that was practical and impersonal. He thought she was a good-looking woman—intense, restless, overworked, perhaps, but charming.

Among the things that Kate Dresser did not tell him, as they sat in this part of the room that she had staked out for herself with a Chinese screen and some rickety gold chairs, was the fact that she was born and raised in the little town of Krasbie, Iowa. Her father and mother were both dead. In a place where almost everybody worked in the chemical-fertilizer factory, her father had happened to be a trolley conductor. When she was growing up, Kate could never bring herself to admit that her father took fares in a trolley car. She could never even admit that he was her father, although she had inherited his most striking physical feature—a nose that turned up so spectacularly at the tip that she was called Roller Coaster and Pug. She had gone from Krasbie to Chicago, from Chicago to New York, where she married a man in the Foreign Service. They lived in Washington and then Tangier. Shortly after the war, they moved to Rome, where her husband died of food poisoning, leaving her with a son and very little money. So she made her home in Rome. The only preparation Krasbie had given her for Italy was the curtain in the little movie theatre where she had spent her Saturday afternoons when she was a girl. Skinny then, dressed no better than most rebellious children and smelling no sweeter, her hair in braids, her pockets full of peanuts and candy and her mouth full of chewing gum, she had put down her quarter every Saturday afternoon, rain or shine, and spread herself out in a seat in the front row. There were shouts of "Roller Coaster!" and "Pug!" from all over the theatre, and, what with the high-heeled shoes (her sister's) that she sometimes wore and the five-and-ten-cent-store diamonds on her fingers, it was no wonder that people made fun of her. Boys dropped chewing gum into her hair and shot spitballs at the back of her skinny neck, and, persecuted in body and spirit, she would raise her eyes to the curtain and see a remarkably precise vision of her future. It was painted on canvas, very badly cracked from having been rolled and unrolled so many times—a vision of an Italian garden, with cypress trees, a terrace, a pool and fountain, and a marble balustrade with roses spilling from marble urns. She seemed literally to have risen up from her seat and to have entered the cracked scene, for it was almost exactly like the view from her window into the courtyard of the Palazzo Tarominia, where she lived.

Now, you might ask why a woman who had so little money was living in the Palazzo Tarominia, and there was a Roman answer. The Baronessa Tramonde—the Duke of Rome's sister—lived in the west wing of the palace, in an apartment that had been built for Pope Andros X and that was reached by a great staircase with painted walls and ceilings. It had pleased the Baronessa, before the war, to stand at the head of this staircase and greet her friends and relations, but things had changed. The Baronessa had grown old, and so had her friends; they could no longer climb the stairs. Oh, they tried. They had straggled up to her card parties like a patrol under machine-gun fire, the gentlemen pushing the ladies and sometimes vice versa, and old marchesas and princesses—the cream of Europe— huffing and puffing and sitting down on the steps in utter exhaustion. There was a lift in the other wing of the palace—the wing Kate lived in—but a lift could not be installed in the west wing, because it would ruin the paintings. The only other way to enter the Baronessa's quarters was to take the lift to Kate's apartment and walk through it and out a service door that led into the other wing. By giving the Duke of Rome, who also had an apartment in the Palazzo, a kind of eminent domain, Kate had a palace apartment at a low rent. The Duke usually passed through twice a day to visit his sister, and on the first Thursday of every month, at five minutes after eight, a splendid and elderly company would troop through Kate's rooms to the Baronessa's card party. Kate did not mind. In fact, when she heard the doorbell ring on Thursdays her heart would begin a grating beat of the deepest excitement. The old Duke always led the procession. His right hand had been chopped off at the wrist by one of Mussolini's public executioners, and now that the old man's enemies were dead, he carried the stump proudly. With him would come Don Fernando Marchetti, the Duke of Treno, the Duke and Duchess Ricotto-Sproci, Count Ambro di Albentiis, Count and Countess Fabrizio Daromeo, Princess Urbana Tessoro, Princess Isabella Tessoro, and Federico Cardinal Baldova. They had all distinguished themselves in one way or another. Don Fernando had driven a car from Paris to Peking, via the Gobi Desert. Duke Ricotto-Sporci had broken most of his bones in a steeplechase accident, and the Countess Daromeo had operated an Allied radio station in the middle of Rome during the German Occupation. The old Duke of Rome would present Kate with a little bouquet of flowers, and then he and his friends would file through the kitchen and go out the service door.

Kate spoke an admirable Italian, and had done some translating and given lessons, and for the past three years she had supported herself and her son by dubbing parts of English dialogue into old Italian movies, which were then shown over British TV. With her cultivated accent, she played mostly dowagers and the like, but there seemed to be plenty of work, and she spent much of her time in a sound studio near the Tiber. With her salary and the money her husband had left her, she had barely enough to get by on. Her elder sister, in Krasbie, wrote her a long lament two or three times a year: "Oh, you lucky, lucky dog, Kate! Oh, how I envy you being away from all the tiresome, nagging, stupid, petty details of life at home." Kate Dresser's life was not lacking in stupid and nagging details, but instead of mentioning such things in her letters, she inflamed her sister's longing to travel by sending home photographs of herself in gondolas, or cards from Florence, where she always spent Easter with friends.

Streeter knew that under Kate Dresser's teaching he was making progress with his Italian, and usually when he stepped out of the Palazzo Tarominia into the street after his lesson, he was exhilarated at the thought that in another month—at the end of the season, anyhow—he would understand everything that was going on and being said. But his progress had its ups and downs.

The beauty of Italy is not easy to come by any longer, if it ever was, but, driving to a villa below Anticoli for a weekend with friends, Streeter saw a country of such detail and loveliness that it could not be described. They had reached the villa early on a rainy night. Nightingales sang in the trees, the double doors of the villa stood open, and in all the rooms there were bowls of roses and olivewood fires. It had seemed, with the servants bowing and bringing in candles and wine, like some gigantic and princely homecoming in a movie, and, going out onto the terrace after dinner to hear the nightingales and see the lights of the hill towns, Streeter felt that he had never been put by dark hills and distant lights into a mood of such tenderness. In the morning, when he stepped out onto his bedroom balcony, he saw a barefoot maid in the garden, picking a rose to put in her hair. Then she began to sing. It was like a flamenco—first guttural and then falsetto—and poor Streeter found his Italian still so limited that he couldn't understand the words of the song, and this brought him around to the fact that he couldn't quite understand the landscape, either. His feeling about it was very much what he might have felt about some excellent resort or summer place—a scene where, perhaps as children, we have thrown ourselves into a temporary relationship with beauty and simplicity that will be rudely broken off on Labor Day. It was the evocation of a borrowed, temporary, bittersweet happiness that he rebelled against— but the maid went on singing, and Streeter did not understand a word.

When Streeter took his lessons at Kate's, her son, Charlie, usually passed through the *sala* at least once during the hour. He was a baseball fan, and had a bad complexion and an owlish laugh. He would say hello to Streeter and pass on some sports news from the Rome *Daily American*. Streeter had a son of his own of about the same age, and was enjoined by the divorce settlement from seeing the boy, and he never looked at Charlie without a pang of longing for his own son. Charlie was fifteen, and one of those American boys you see waiting for the school bus up by the Embassy, dressed in black leather jackets and Levi's, and with sideburns or duck-tail haircuts, and fielder's mitts—anything that will stamp them as American. These are the real expatriates. On Saturdays after the movies they go into one of those bars called Harry's or Larry's or Jerry's, where the walls are covered with autographed photographs of unknown electric-guitar players and unknown soubrettes, to eat bacon and eggs and talk baseball and play American records on the jukebox. They are Embassy children, and the children of writers and oil-company and airline employees and divorcées and Fulbright Fellows. Eating bacon and eggs, and listening to the jukebox, they have a sense of being far, far from home that is a much sweeter and headier distillation than their parents ever know. Charlie had spent five years of his life under a ceiling decorated with gold that had been brought from the New World by the first Duke of Rome, and he had seen old marchesas with diamonds as big as acorns slip the cheese parings into their handbags when the lunch was finished. He had ridden in gondolas and played softball on the Palatine. He had seen the Palio at Siena, and had heard the bells of Rome and Florence and Venice and Ravenna and Verona. But it wasn't about these things that he wrote in a letter to his mother's Uncle George in Krasbie toward the middle of March. Instead, he asked the old man to take him home and let him be an American boy. The timing was perfect. Uncle George had just retired from the fertilizer factory and had always wanted to bring Kate and her son home. Within two weeks he was on board a ship bound for Naples.

Streeter, of course, knew nothing of this. But he had suspected that there was some tension between Charlie and his mother. The boy's hoe-down American clothes, the poses he took as a rail splitter, pitcher, and cowboy, and his mother's very Italianate manners implied room for sizable disagreement, at least, and, going there one Sunday afternoon, Streeter stepped into a quarrel. Assunta, the maid, let him in, but he stopped at the door of the *sala* when he heard Kate and her son shouting at one another in anger. Streeter could not retreat. Assunta had gone on ahead to say he was there, and all he could do was wait in the vestibule. Kate came out to him then—she was crying—and said, in Italian, that she could not give him a lesson that afternoon. She was sorry. Something had come up, and there had not been time to telephone him. He felt like a fool, confronted with her tears, holding his grammar, his copybook, and *I Promessi Sposi* under one arm. He said it didn't matter about the lesson, it was nothing, and could he come on Tuesday? She said yes, yes, would he come on Tuesday—and would he come on Thursday, not for a lesson but to do her a favor? "My father's brother—my Uncle George—is coming, to try and take Charlie home. I don't know what to do. I don't know what I *can* do. But I would appreciate it if there was a man here; I would feel so much better if I weren't alone. You don't have to say anything or do anything but sit in a chair and have a drink, but I would feel so much better if I weren't alone."

Streeter agreed to come, and went away then, wondering what kind of a life it was she led if she had to count in an emergency on a stranger like him. With his lesson canceled and nothing else that he had to do, he took a walk up the river as far as the Ministry of the Marine, and then came back through a neighborhood that was neither new nor old nor anything else you could specify. Because it was Sunday afternoon, the houses were mostly shut. The streets were deserted. When he passed anyone, it was usually a family group returning from an excursion to the zoo. There were also a few of those lonely men and women carrying pastry boxes that you see everywhere in the world at dusk on Sunday—unmarried aunts and uncles going out to tea with their relations and bringing a little pastry to sweeten the call. But mostly he was alone, mostly there was no sound but his own footsteps and, in the distance, the iron ringing of iron trolley-car wheels on iron tracks—a lonely sound on Sunday afternoons for many Americans; a lonely one for him, anyhow, and reminding him of some friendless, loveless, galling Sunday in his youth. As he came closer to the city, there were more lights and people—flowers and the noise of talk—and under the gate of Santa Maria del Popolo a whore spoke to him. She was a beautiful young woman, but he told her, in his broken Italian, that he had a friend, and walked on.

Crossing the Piazza, he saw a man struck by a car. The noise was loud— that surprising loudness of our bones when they are dealt a mortal blow.

The driver of the car slipped out of his seat and ran up the Pincian Hill. The victim lay in a heap on the paving, a shabbily dressed man but with a lot of oil in his black, wavy hair, which must have been his pride. A crowd gathered—not solemn at all, although a few women crossed themselves—and everyone began to talk excitedly. The crowd, garrulous, absorbed in its own opinions and indifferent, it seemed, to the dying man, was so thick that when the police came they had to push and struggle to reach the victim. With the words of the whore still in his ears, Streeter wondered why it was that they regarded a human life as something of such dubious value.

He turned away from the Piazza then, toward the river, and, passing the Tomb of Augustus, he noticed a young man calling to a cat and offering it something to eat. The cat was one of those thousands of millions that live in the ruins of Rome and eat leftover spaghetti, and the man was offering the cat a piece of bread. Then, as the cat approached him, the man took a firecracker out of his pocket, put it into the piece of bread, and lit the fuse. He put the bread on the sidewalk, and just as the cat took it the powder exploded. The animal let out a hellish shriek and leaped into the air, its body all twisted, and then it streaked over the wall and was lost in the darkness of Augustus' Tomb. The man laughed at his trick, and so did several people who had been watching.

Streeter's first instinct was to box the man's ears and teach him not to feed lighted firecrackers to stray cats. But, with such an appreciative audience, this would have amounted to an international incident, and he realized there wasn't anything he could do. The people who had laughed at the prank were good and kind—most of them affectionate parents. You might have seen them earlier in the day on the Palatine, picking violets.

Streeter walked on into a dark street and heard at his back the hoofs and trappings of horses—it sounded like cavalry—and stepped aside to let a hearse and a mourner's carriage pass. The hearse was drawn by two pairs of bays with black plumes. The driver wore funerary livery, with an admiral's hat, and had the brutish red face of a drunken horse thief. The hearse banged, slammed, and rattled over the stones in such a loose-jointed way that the poor soul it carried must have been in a terrible state of disarrangement, and the mourner's carriage that followed was empty. The friends of the dead man had probably been too late or had got the wrong date or had forgotten the whole thing, as was so often the case in Rome. Off the hearse and carriage rattled toward the Servian Gate.

Streeter knew one thing then: He did not want to die in Rome. He was in excellent health and had no reason to think about death; nevertheless, he was afraid. Back at his flat, he poured some whiskey and water into a glass and stepped out onto his balcony. He watched the night fall and the street lights go on with complete bewilderment at his own feelings. He did not want to die in Rome The power of this idea could only stem from igno-rance and stupidity, he told himself—for what could such a fear represent but the inability to respond to the force of life? He reproached himself with arguments and consoled himself with whiskey, but in the middle of the night he was waked by the noise of a carriage and horses' hoofs, and again he sweated with fear. The hearse, the horse thief, and the empty mourner's carriage, he thought, were rattling back, under his balcony. He got up out of bed and went to the window to see, but it was only two empty carriages going back to the stables.

When Uncle George landed in Naples, on Tuesday, he was excited and in a good humor. His purpose in coming abroad was twofold—to bring Charlie and Kate home, and to take a vacation, the first in forty-three years. A friend of his in Krasbie who had been to Italy had written an itinerary for him: "Stay at the Royal in Naples. Go to the National Museum. Have a drink in the Galleria Umberto. Eat supper at the California. Good Ameri-can food. Take the Roncari *auto-pullman* in the morning for Rome. This goes through two interesting villages and stops at Nero's villa. In Rome stay at the Excelsior. Make reservations in advance. . . ."

On Wednesday morning, Uncle George got up early and went down to the hotel dining room. "Orange juice and ham and eggs," he said to the waiter. The waiter brought him orange juice, coffee, and a roll. "Where's my ham and eggs?" Uncle George asked, and then realized, when the waiter bowed and smiled, that the man did not understand English. He got out his phrase book, but there was nothing about ham and eggs. "You gotta no hamma?" he asked loudly. "You gotta no eggsa?" The waiter went on smiling and bowing, and Uncle George gave up. He ate the breakfast he hadn't ordered, gave the waiter a twenty-lira tip, cashed four hundred dollars' worth of traveler's checks at the desk, and checked out. All this money in lire made a bump in his suit jacket, and he held his left hand over his wallet as if he had a pain there. Naples, he knew, was full of thieves. He took a cab to the bus station, which was in a square near the Galleria Umberto. It was early in the morning, the light was slanting, and he enjoyed the smell of coffee and bread and the stir of people hurrying along the streets to work. A fine smell of the sea rose up the streets from the bay. He was early and was shown his seat in the bus by a red-faced gentleman who spoke English with a British accent. This was the guide—one of those who, whatever conveyance you take and wherever you go, make travel among the monuments bizarre. Their command of languages is extraordinary, their knowledge of antiquity is impressive, and their love of beauty is passionate, but when they separate themselves from the party for a moment it is to take a pull from a hip flask or to pinch a young pilgrim. They praise the ancient world in four languages, but their clothes are threadbare, their linen is dirty, and their hands tremble with thirst and lechery. While the guide chatted about the weather with Uncle George, the whiskey could already be smelled on his breath. Then the guide left Uncle George to greet the rest of the party, now coming across the square.

There were about thirty—they moved in a flock, or mass, understandably timid about the strangeness of their surroundings—and they were mostly old women. As they came into the bus, they cackled (as we all will when we grow old), and made the fussy arrangements of elderly travelers. Then, with the guide singing the praises of ancient Naples, they started on their way.

They first went along the coast. The color of the water reminded Uncle George of postcards he had received from Honolulu, where one of his friends had gone for a vacation. It was green and blue. He had never seen anything like it himself. They passed some resorts only half open and sleepy, where young men sat on rocks in their bathing trunks, waiting patiently for the sun to darken their skins. What did they think about? Uncle George wondered. During all those hours that they sat on rocks, what on earth did they think about? They passed a ramshackle colony of little bathhouses no bigger than privies, and Uncle George remembered—how many years ago—the thrill of undressing in such briny sea chambers as these when he had been taken to the seashore as a boy. As they turned inland, he craned his neck to get a last look at the sea, wondering why it should seem, shining and blue, like something that he remembered in his bones. Then they went into a tunnel and came out in farmland. Uncle George was interested in farming methods and admired the way that vines were trained onto trees. He admired the terracing of the land, and was troubled by the traces of soil erosion that he saw. And he recognized that he was separated only by a pane of glass from a life that was as strange to him as life on the moon.

The bus, with its glass roof and glass windows, was like a fishbowl, and the sunlight and cloud shadows of the day fell among the travelers. Their way was blocked by a flock of sheep. Sheep surrounded the bus, isolated this little island of elderly Americans, and filled the air with dumb, harsh bleating. Beyond the sheep they saw a girl carrying a water jug on her head. A man lay sound asleep in the grass by the side of the road. A woman sat on a doorstep, suckling a child. Within the dome of glass the old ladies discussed the high price of airplane luggage. "Grace got ringworm in Palermo," one of them said. "I don't think she'll ever be cured."

The guide pointed out fragments of old Roman road, Roman towers and bridges. There was a castle on a hill—a sight that delighted Uncle George, and no wonder, for there had been castles painted on his supper plate when he was a boy, and the earliest books that had been read to him and that he had been able to read had been illustrated with castles. They had meant everything that was exciting and strange and wonderful in life, and now, by raising his eyes, he could see one against a sky as blue as the sky in his picture books.

After traveling for an hour or two, they stopped in a village where there were a coffee bar and toilets. Coffee cost one hundred lire a cup, a fact that filled the ladies' conversation for some time after they had started again. Coffee had been sixty lire at the hotel. Forty at the corner. They took pills and read from their guidebooks, and Uncle George looked out of the windows at this strange country, where the spring flowers and the autumn flowers seemed to grow side by side in the grass. It would be miserable weather in Krasbie, but here everything was in bloom—fruit trees, mimosa—and the pastures were white with flowers and the vegetable gardens already yielding crops.

They came into a town or city then—an old place with crooked and narrow streets. He didn't catch the name. The guide explained that there was a *festa*. The bus driver had to blow his horn continuously to make any progress, and two or three times came to a full stop, the crowd was so dense. The people in the streets looked up at this apparition—this fish-bowl of elderly Americans—with such incredulity that Uncle George's feelings were hurt. He saw a little girl take a crust of bread out of her mouth to stare at him. Women held their children up in the air to see the strangers. Windows were thrown open, bars were emptied, and people pointed at the curious tourists and laughed. Uncle George would have liked to address them, as he so often addressed the Rotary. "Don't stare," he wanted to say to them. "We are not so queer and rich and strange. Don't stare at us."

The bus turned down a side street, and there was another stop for coffee and toilets. Most of the travelers scattered to buy postcards. Uncle George, seeing an open church across the street, decided to go inside. The air smelled of spice when he pushed the door open. The stone walls inside were bare—it was like an armory—and only a few candles burned in the chapels at the sides. Then Uncle George heard a loud voice and saw a man kneeling in front of one of the chapels, saying his prayers. He carried on in a way that Uncle George had never seen before. His voice was strong, supplicatory, sometimes angry. His face was wet with tears. He was be-seeching the Cross for something—an explanation or an indulgence or a life. He waved his hands, he wept, and his voice and his sobs echoed in the barny place. Uncle George went out and got back into his seat on the bus.

They left the city for the country again, and a little before noon they stopped at the gates to Nero's villa, bought their tickets, and went in. It was a large ruin, fanciful, and picked clean of everything but its brick supports. The place had been vast and tall, and now the walls and archways of roofless rooms, the butts of towers, stood in a stretch of green pasture, with nothing leading anywhere any more except to nothing, and all the many staircases mounting and turning stopped in midair. Uncle George left the party and wandered happily through these traces of a palace. The atmosphere seemed to him pleasant and tranquil—a little like the feeling in a forest—and he heard a bird singing and the noise of water. The forms of the ruins, all bristling with plants like the hair in an old man's ears, seemed pleasantly familiar, as if his unremembered dreams had been played out against a scene like this. He found himself then in a place that was darker than the rest. The air was damp, and the senseless brick rooms, opening onto one another, were full of brush. It might have been a dungeon or a guardhouse or a temple where obscene rites were performed, for he was suddenly stirred licentiously by the damp. He turned back, looking for the sun, the water, and the bird, and found a guide standing in his path.

"You wish to see the special place?"

"What do you mean?"

"Very special," the guide said. "For men only. Only for strong men. Such pictures. Very old."

"How much?"

"Two hundred lire."

"All right." Uncle George took two hundred lire out of his change pocket.

"Come," the guide said. "This way." He walked on briskly—so briskly that Uncle George nearly had to run to keep up with him. He saw the guide go through a narrow opening in the wall, a place where the brick had crumbled, but when Uncle George followed him the guide seemed to have disappeared. It was a trap. He felt an arm around his throat, and his head was thrown back so violently that he couldn't call for help. He felt a hand lift the wallet out of his pocket—a touch as light as the nibble of a fish on a line—and then he was thrown brutally to the ground. He lay there dazed for a minute or two. When he sat up, he saw that he had been left his empty wallet and his passport.

Then he roared with anger at the thieves, and hated Italy, with its thieving population of organ grinders and bricklayers. But even during this outburst his anger was not as strong as a feeling of weakness and shame. He was terribly ashamed of himself, and when he picked up his empty wallet and put it in his pocket, he felt as if his heart had been plucked out and broken. Who could he blame? Not the damp ruins. He had asked for something that was by his lights all wrong, and he could only blame himself. The theft might happen every day—some lecherous old fool like him might be picked clean each time the bus stopped. He got to his feet, weary and sick of the old bones that had got him into trouble. He dusted the dirt off his clothes. Then he realized that he might be late. He might have missed the bus and be stranded in the ruins without a cent. He began to walk and run through the rooms, until he came out into a clearing and saw in the distance the flock of old ladies, still clinging to one another.

The guide came out from behind a wall, and they all got in the bus and started off again.

Rome was ugly; at least, the outskirts were: trolley cars and cut-rate furniture stores and torn-up streets and the sort of apartment houses that nobody every really wants to live in. The old ladies began to gather their guidebooks and put on their coats and hats and gloves. Journey's end is the same everywhere. Then, dressed for their destination, they all sat down again, with their hands folded in their laps, and the bus was still. "Oh, I wish I'd never come," one old lady said to another. "I just wish I'd never left home." She was not the only one.

"*Ecco, ecco Roma,*" the guide said, and so it was.

Streeter went to Kate's at seven on Thursday. Assunta let him in, and, for the first time, he walked down the *sala* without his copy of *I Promessi Sposi*, and sat down by the fireplace. Charlie came in then. He had on the usual outfit—the tight Levi's, with cuffs turned up, and a pink shirt. When he moved, he dragged or banged the leather heels of his loafers on the marble floor. He talked about baseball and exercised his owlish laugh, but he didn't mention Uncle George. Neither did Kate, when she came in, nor did she offer Streeter a drink. She seemed to be in the throes of an emotional storm, with all her powers of decision suspended. They talked about the weather. At one point, Charlie came and stood by his mother, and she took both of his hands in one of hers. Then the doorbell rang, and Kate went down the room to meet her uncle. They embraced very tenderly—the members of a family—and when this was over he said, "I was robbed, Katie. I was robbed yesterday of four hundred dollars. Coming up from Naples on the bus."

"Oh, I'm so sorry!" she said. "Wasn't there anything you could do, George? Wasn't there anyone you could speak to?"

"Speak to, Katie? There hasn't been anyone I could speak to since I got off the boat. No speaka da English. If you cut off their hands, they wouldn't be able to say anything. I can afford to lose four hundred dollars—I'm not a poor man—but if I could only have given it to some worthwhile cause."

"I'm terribly sorry."

"You've got quite a place here, Katie."

"And, Charlie, this is Uncle George."

If she had counted on their not getting along, this chance was lost in a second. Charlie forgot his owlish laugh and stood so straight, so in need of what America could do for him that the rapport between the man and the boy was instantaneous, and Kate had to separate them in order to introduce Streeter. Uncle George shook hands with her student and came to a likely but erroneous conclusion.

"Speaka da English?" he asked.

"I'm an American," Streeter said.

"How long is your sentence?"

"This is my second year," Streeter said. "I work at F.R.U.P.C."

"It's an immoral country," Uncle George said, sitting down in one of the golden chairs. "First they rob me of four hundred dollars, and then, walking around the streets here, all I see is statues of men without any clothes on. Nothing."

Kate rang for Assunta, and when the maid came in she ordered whiskey and ice, in very rapid Italian. "It's just another way of looking at things, Uncle George," she said.

"No, it isn't," Uncle George said. "It isn't natural. Not even in locker rooms. There's very few men who'd choose to parade around a locker room stark naked if a towel was handy. It's not natural. Everywhere you look. Up on the roofs. At the main traffic intersections. When I was coming over here, I passed through a little garden—playground, I guess you'd say—and right in the middle of it, right in the middle of all these little children, is one of these men without anything on."

"Will you have some whiskey?"

"Yes, please. . . . The boat sails on Saturday, Katie, and I want you and the boy to come home with me."

"I don't want Charlie to leave," Kate said.

"He wants to leave—don't you, Charlie? He wrote me a nice letter. Nicely worded, and he's got a nice handwriting. That was a nice letter, Charlie. I showed it to the high-school superintendent, and he said you can enter the Krasbie high school whenever you want. And I want you to come too, Kate. It's your home, and you've only got one. The trouble with you, Katie, is that when you were a kid they used to make fun of you in Krasbie, and you just started running, that's all, and you never stopped."

"If that's true—and it may be," she said quickly, "why should I want to go back to a place where I will seem ridiculous."

"Oh, Katie, you won't seem ridiculous. I'll take care of that."

"I want to go home, Mama," Charlie said. He was sitting on a stool by the fireplace—not so straight-backed any more. "I'm homesick all the time."

"How could you possibly be homesick for America?" Her voice was very sharp. "You've never seen it. This is your home."

"How do you mean?"

"Your home is with your mother."

"There's more to it than that, Mama. I feel strange here all the time. Everybody on the street speaking a different language."

"You've never even tried to learn Italian."

"Even if I had, it wouldn't make any difference. It would still sound strange. I mean, it would still remind me that it wasn't my language. I just don't understand the people, Mama. I like them all right, but I just don't understand them. I never know what they're going to do next."

"Why don't you try and understand them?"

"Oh, I do, but I'm no genius, and you don't understand them, either. I've heard you say so, and sometimes you're homesick, too, I know. I can tell by the way you look."

"Homesickness is nothing," she said angrily. "It is absolutely nothing. Fifty percent of the people in the world are homesick all the time. But I don't suppose you're old enough to understand. When you're in one place and long to be in another, it isn't as simple as taking a boat. You don't really long for another country. You long for something in yourself that you don't have, or haven't been able to find."

"Oh, I don't mean that, Mama. I just mean if I was with people who spoke my language, people who understood me, I'd be more comfortable."

"If comfort is all you expect to get out of life, God help you."

Then the doorbell rang and Assunta answered it. Kate glanced at her watch and saw that it was five after eight. It was also the first Thursday in the month. Before she could get out an explanation, they had started down the *sala*, with the old Duke of Rome in the lead, holding some flowers in his left hand. A little behind him was the Duchess, his wife—a tall, willowy, gray-haired woman wearing a lot of jewelry that had been given to the family by Francis I. An assortment of nobles brought up the rear, looking like a country circus, gorgeous and travel-worn. The Duke gave Kate her flowers. They all bowed vaguely to her company and went out through the kitchen, with its smell of gas leaks, to the service door.

"Oh, Giuseppe the barber he gotta the cash," Uncle George sang loudly. "He gotta the bigga the blacka mustache." He waited for someone to laugh, and when no one did he asked, "What was that?"

Kate told him, but her eyes were brighter, and he noticed this.

"You like that kind of thing, don't you?" he said.

"Possibly," she said.

"It's crazy, Katie," he said. "It's crazy, it's crazy. You come home with me and Charlie. You and Charlie can live in the other half of my house, and I'll have a nice American kitchen put in for you."

Streeter saw that she was touched by this remark, and he thought she was going to cry. She said quickly, "How in hell do you think America would have been discovered if everybody stayed home in places like Krasbie?"

"You're not discovering anything, Katie."

"I am. I am."

"We'll all be happier, Mama," Charlie said. "We'll all be happier if we have a nice clean house and lots of nice friends and a nice garden and kitchen and stall shower."

She stood with her back to them, by the mantelpiece, and said loudly, "No nice friends, no kitchen, no garden, no shower bath or anything else will keep me from wanting to see the world and the different people who live in it." Then she turned to her son and spoke softly. "You'll miss Italy, Charlie."

The boy laughed his owlish laugh. "I'll miss the black hairs in my food," he said. She didn't make a sound. She didn't even sigh. Then the boy went to her and began to cry. "I'm sorry, Mummy," he said. "I'm sorry. That was a dumb thing to say. It's just an old joke." He kissed her hands and the tears on her cheeks, and Streeter got up and left.

"*Tal era ciò che di meno deforme e di men compassionevole si faceva vedere intorno, i sani, gli agiati,*" Streeter read when he went again for his lesson Sunday. "*Chè, dopo tante immagini di miseria, e pensando a quella ancor più grave, per mezzo alla quale dovrem condurre il lettore, no ci fermeremo ora a dir qual fosse lo spettacolo degli appestati che si strascicavano o giacevano per le strade, de' poveri, de' fanciulli, delle donne.*"*

The boy had gone, he could tell—not because she said so but because the place seemed that much bigger. In the middle of his lesson, the old Duke of Rome came through in his bathrobe and slippers, carrying a bowl of soup to his sister, who was sick. Kate looked tired, but then she always did, and when the lesson ended and Streeter stood up, wondering if she would mention Charlie or Uncle George, she complimented him on the progress he had made and urged him to finish *I Promessi Sposi* and to buy a copy of the *Divine Comedy* for next week.

Suggestions for Discussion

1. Who speaks in "The Bella Lingua"? To whom? In what form?

2. How many options of the omniscient author listed on page 225 does Cheever employ in the first three paragraphs?

3. The early pages of the narrative repeatedly refer to "us." Who are "we?" Who is "you" in the paragraph beginning, "Now, you might ask . . . ," on page 244?

4. With the sentence beginning, "Among the things that Kate Dresser did not tell him . . ." (page 243), the narrative switches from the mind of Streeter to that of his teacher. How has this shift in point of view been prepared for?

5. In the course of the paragraph beginning, "When Streeter took his lessons at Kate's . . . " (page 246), we move from Streeter's point of view so intimately into Charlie's that the next paragraph must begin, "Streeter, of course, knew nothing of this." How is the transition accomplished?

*"Such were the less deformed and less pitiable that could be seen all around, the healthy and wealthy . . . for after so many images of misery, and keeping in mind the still greater ones we will have to present to the reader, we will not now stop to describe the plague-ridden who dragged themselves through the street, or lay there; the poor, the children, the women."

6. A vignette of "the guide" is presented in a paragraph on the bottom of page 249. From what point of view is this character type presented? Why is he presented as a type rather than as an individual?

7. Why does the narrative provide us with Uncle George's consciousness? What would be lost if he were presented only externally?

8. The most dramatic overt change in this story takes place in the lives of Kate and Charlie. Yet Streeter is clearly the major means of perception. In what sense is Streeter the one who is moved or changed at the resolution?

The Masked Marvel's Last Toehold

RICHARD SELZER

Morning Rounds.

On the fifth floor of the hospital, in the west wing, I know that a man is sitting up in his bed, waiting for me. Elihu Koontz is seventy-five, and he is diabetic. It is two weeks since I amputated his left leg just below the knee. I walk down the corridor, but I do not go straight into his room. Instead, I pause in the doorway. He is not yet aware of my presence, but gazes down at the place in the bed where his leg used to be, and where now there is the collapsed leg of his pajamas. He is totally absorbed, like an athlete apprais-ing the details of his body. What is he thinking, I wonder. Is he dreaming the outline of his toes? Does he see there his foot's incandescent ghost? Could he be angry? Feel that I have taken from him something for which he yearns now with all his heart? Has he forgotten so soon the pain? It was a pain so great as to set him apart from all other men, in a red-hot place where he had no kith or kin. What of those black gorilla toes and the soupy mess that was his heel? I watch him from the doorway. It is a kind of spying, I know.

Save for a white fringe open at the front, Elihu Koontz is bald. The hair has grown too long and is wilted. He wears it as one would wear a day-old laurel wreath. He is naked to the waist, so that I can see his breasts. They are the breasts of Buddha, inverted triangles from which the nipples swing, dark as garnets.

I have seen enough. I step into the room, and he sees that I am there.

"How did the night go, Elihu?"

He looks at me for a long moment. "Shut the door," he says.

I do, and move to the side of the bed. He takes my left hand in both of his, gazes at it, turns it over, then back, fondling, at last holding it up to his cheek. I do not withdraw from this loving. After a while he relinquishes my hand, and looks up at me.

"How is the pain?" I ask.

He does not answer, but continues to look at me in silence. I know at once that he has made a decision.

"Ever hear of The Masked Marvel?" He says this in a low voice, almost a whisper.

"What?"

"The Masked Marvel," he says. "You never heard of him?"

"No."

He clucks his tongue. He is exasperated.

All at once there is a recollection. It is dim, distant, but coming near.

"Do you mean the wrestler?"

Eagerly, he nods, and the breasts bob. How gnomish he looks, oval as the huge helpless egg of some outlandish lizard. He has very long arms, which, now and then, he unfurls to reach for things—a carafe of water, a get-well card. He gazes up at me, urging. He *wants* me to remember.

"Well . . . yes," I say. I am straining backward in time. "I saw him wrestle in Toronto long ago."

"Ha!" He smiles. "You saw *me*." And his index finger, held rigid and upright, bounces in the air.

The man has said something shocking, unacceptable. It must be challenged.

"You?" I am trying to smile.

Again that jab of the finger. "You saw *me*."

"No," I say. But even then, something about Elihu Koontz, those prolonged arms, the shape of his head, the sudden agility with which he leans from his bed to get a large brown envelope from his nightstand, something is forcing me toward a memory. He rummages through his papers, old newspaper clippings, photographs, and I remember . . .

It is almost forty years ago. I am ten years old. I have been sent to Toronto to spend the summer with relatives. Uncle Max has bought two tickets to the wrestling match. He is taking me that night.

"He isn't allowed," says Aunt Sarah to me. Uncle Max has angina.

"He gets too excited," she says.

"I wish you wouldn't go, Max," she says.

"You mind your own business," he says.

And we go. Out into the warm Canadian evening. I am not only abroad, I am abroad in the *evening*! I have never been taken out in the evening. I am terribly excited. The trolleys, the lights, the horns. It is a bazaar. At the

Maple Leaf Gardens, we sit high and near the center. The vast arena is dark except for the brilliance of the ring at the bottom.

It begins.

The wrestlers circle. They grapple. They are all haunch and paunch. I am shocked by their ugliness, but I do not show it. Uncle Max is exhilarated. He leans forward, his eyes unblinking, on his face a look of enormous happiness. One after the other, a pair of wrestlers enter the ring. The two men join, twist, jerk, tug, bend, yank, and throw. Then they leave and are replaced by another pair. At last it is the main event. "The Angel vs. The Masked Marvel."

On the cover of the program notes, there is a picture of The Angel hanging from the limb of a tree, a noose of thick rope around his neck. The Angel hangs just so for an hour every day, it is explained, to strengthen his neck. The Masked Marvel's trademark is a black stocking cap with holes for the eyes and mouth. He is never seen without it, states the program. No one knows who The Masked Marvel really is!

"Good," says Uncle Max. "Now you'll see something." He is fidgeting, waiting for them to appear. They come down separate aisles, climb into the ring from opposite sides. I have never seen anything like them. It is The Angel's neck that first captures the eye. The shaved nape rises in twin columns to puff into the white hood of a sloped and bosselated skull that is too small. As though, strangled by the sinews of that neck, the skull had long since withered and shrunk. The thing about The Angel is the absence of any mystery in his body. It is simply *there*. A monosyllabic announcement. A grunt. One looks and knows everything at once, the fat thighs, the gigantic buttocks, the great spine from which hang knotted ropes and pale aprons of beef. And that prehistoric head. He is all of a single hideous piece, The Angel is. No detachables.

The Masked Marvel seems dwarfish. His fingers dangle kneeward. His short legs are slightly bowed as if under the weight of the cask they are forced to heft about. He has breasts that swing when he moves! I have never seen such breasts on a man before.

There is a sudden ungraceful movement, and they close upon one another. The Angel stoops and hugs The Marvel about the waist, locking his hands behind The Marvel's back. Now he straightens and lifts The Marvel as though he were uprooting a tree. Thus he holds him, then stoops again, thrusts one hand through The Marvel's crotch, and with the other grabs him by the neck. He rears and . . . The Marvel is aloft! For a long moment, The Angel stands as though deciding where to make the toss. Then throws. Was that board or bone that splintered there? Again and again, The Angel hurls himself upon the body of The Masked Marvel.

Now The Angel rises over the fallen Marvel, picks up one foot in both of his hands, and twists the toes downward. It is far beyond the tensile strength of mere ligament, mere cartilage. The Masked Marvel does not hide his agony, but pounds and slaps the floor with his hand, now and then reaching up toward The Angel in an attitude of supplication. I have never seen such suffering. And all the while his black mask rolls from side to side, the mouth pulled to a tight slit through which issues an endless hiss that I can hear from where I sit. All at once, I hear a shouting close by.

"Break it off! Tear off a leg and throw it up here!"

It is Uncle Max. Even in the darkness I can see that he is gray. A band of sweat stands upon his upper lip. He is on his feet now, panting, one fist pressed at his chest, the other raised warlike toward the ring. For the first time I begin to think that something terrible might happen here. Aunt Sarah was right.

"Sit down, Uncle Max," I say. "Take a pill, please."

He reaches for the pillbox, gropes, and swallows without taking his gaze from the wrestlers. I wait for him to sit down.

"That's not fair," I say, "twisting his toes like that."

"It's the toehold," he explains.

"But it's not *fair*," I say again. The whole of the evil is laid open for me to perceive. I am trembling.

And now The Angel does something unspeakable. Holding the foot of The Marvel at full twist with one hand, he bends and grasps the mask where it clings to the back of The Marvel's head. And he pulls. He is going to strip if off! Lay bare an ultimate carnal mystery! Suddenly it is beyond mere physical violence. Now I am on my feet, shouting into the Maple Leaf Gardens.

"Watch out," I scream. "Stop him. Please, somebody, stop him."

Next to me, Uncle Max is chuckling.

Yet The Masked Marvel hears me, I know it. And rallies from his bed of pain. Thrusting with his free heel, he strikes The Angel at the back of the knee. The Angel falls. The Masked Marvel is on top of him, pinning his shoulders to the mat. One! Two! Three! And it is over. Uncle Max is strangely still. I am gasping for breath. All this I remember as I stand at the bedside of Elihu Koontz.

Once again, I am in the operating room. It is two years since I amputated the left leg of Elihu Koontz. Now it is his right leg which is gangrenous. I have already scrubbed. I stand to one side wearing my gown and gloves. And . . . *I am masked*. Upon the table lies Elihu Koontz, pinned in a fierce white light. Spinal anesthesia has been administered. One of his arms is taped to a board placed at a right angle to his body. Into this arm, a needle has been placed. Fluid drips here from a bottle overhead. With his other hand, Elihu Koontz beats feebly at the side of the operating table. His head rolls from side to side. His mouth is pulled into weeping. It seems to me that I have never seen such misery.

An orderly stands at the foot of the table, holding Elihu Koontz's leg aloft by the toes so that the intern can scrub the limb with antiseptic solutions. The intern paints the foot, ankle, leg, and thigh, both front and back, three times. From a corner of the room where I wait, I look down as from an amphitheater. Then I think of Uncle Max yelling, "Tear off a leg. Throw it up here." And I think that forty years later I am making the catch.

"It's not fair," I say aloud. But no one hears me. I step forward to break The Masked Marvel's last toehold.

Suggestions for Discussion

1. Who speaks in "The Masked Marvel's Last Toehold?" To whom? In what form?

2. Is the surgeon a peripheral or a central narrator? It is Elihu Koontz who loses his legs; how can the surgeon be said to be the one who is changed in the story?

3. How does the contrast between the surgeon's thoughts and his professional demeanor help characterize him?

4. The flashback beginning on page 258 moves back and forth between summary and scene. What is the function of each?

5. In the flashback the narrator re-creates his consciousness as a boy. How might the description differ if he were telling of the wrestling match from his adult perspective? What would be lost?

6. Suppose that the story were told from the point of view of The Masked Marvel. Could it be the same story?

RETROSPECT

1. Identify the *person* employed in each of the stories read up to now. Which are told from the viewpoint of the omniscient, the limited omniscient, the objective, the central, and the peripheral narrator?

2. In Jamaica Kincaid's "Girl," who speaks to whom in what form? Would you describe this as a first- or second-person narration? Would you call it a list, reprimand, imperative, lecture, catechism, summary, condensation, argument? None or all of these?

3. Compare "The Bella Lingua" to "Cutting Edge," which also explores the thoughts of several characters. Which of these stories is written from the more omniscient point of view?

WRITING ASSIGNMENTS

1. Write a short scene about the birth or death of anything. (You may interpret "anything" liberally—the birth or death of a person, plant, animal, machine, scheme, passion, etc.) Use all five areas of knowledge of the *editorial omniscient author*. Be sure to do the following: give us the thoughts of more than one character, tell us something about at least one character that he or she doesn't know or realize, include some exposition from the past or the future, and provide at least one universal "truth."

2. Write a love scene, serious or comic, from the *limited omniscient* viewpoint, confining yourself to objective observation and the thoughts of one character. Make this character believe that the other loves her or him, while the external actions make clear to the reader that this is not so.

3. Write about your most interesting recent dream, using the viewpoint of the *objective author*. Without any comment or interpretation whatever, report the events (the more bizarre, the better) as they occur.

4. Write a scene from the point of view of a *peripheral narrator* who is not at all involved in the events he or she describes but who is placed in a position from which to observe them. Nevertheless, make the observing narrator the character who is moved by the action.

5. Write a letter from a *central narrator* to another character from whom the narrator wants a great deal of money. Convince us as readers that the money is deserved.

6. Place your character in an uncomfortable social situation and write a passage in which the character's thoughts are presented both in an *interior monologue* and aloud. Nothing else. Contrast the expressed with the unexpressed thoughts.

7. Write a scene in the *second person*, in which the reader is drawn into identifying with the protagonist.

8

ASSORTED LIARS
Point of View, Part II

At What Distance?
With What Limitations?

At What Distance?

As with the chemist at her microscope and the lookout in his tower, fictional point of view always involves the *distance*, close or far, of the perceiver from the thing perceived. Point of view in fiction, however, is immensely complicated by the fact that distance is not only, though it may be partly, spatial. It may also be temporal. Or the distance may be intangible and involve a judgment moral, intellectual, and/or emotional. More complicated still, the narrator or characters or both may view the action from one distance, the author and reader from another.

In any reading experience there is an implied dialogue among author, narrator, the other characters and the reader. Each of the four can range, in relation to each of the others, from identification to complete opposition, on any axis of value, moral, intellectual, aesthetic and even physical. . . . From the author's

viewpoint, a successful reading of his book must eliminate all distance between [his] essential norms . . . and the norms of the postulated reader.

WAYNE C. BOOTH, The Rhetoric of Fiction

Booth means that the author may ask us to identify completely with one character and totally condemn another. One character may judge another harshly while the author suggests that we should qualify that judgment. Author, characters, and reader are always in the dialogue, but if there is also a narrator, that narrator may think himself morally superior while the author behind his back makes sure that we will think him morally defi- cient. Further, the four members of the dialogue may operate differently in various areas of value: the character calls the narrator stupid and ugly; the narrator thinks herself ugly but clever; the author and the reader know that she is both intelligent and beautiful.

Any complex or convolution of judgments among author, narrator, and characters can make successful fiction. The one relationship in the dialogue in which there must not be any opposition is between author and reader. We may find the characters and/or the narrator bad, stupid, and tasteless and still applaud the book as just, brilliant, and beautiful. But if the hero's agony strikes us as ridiculous, if the comedy leaves us cold—if we say that the *book* is bad, stupid, or tasteless—then we are in opposition to the author on some axis of value and reject his "point of view" in the sense of "opinion." Ultimately, the reader must accept the "essential norms"—the attitudes and judgments—of the author, even if only provisionally, whether these are the norms of the characters or not, if the fiction is going to work.

I can think of no exception to this rule, and it is not altered by experi- mental plays and stories in which the writer's purpose is to embarrass, anger, or disgust us. Our acceptance of such experiments rests on our understanding that the writer did want to embarrass, anger, or disgust us, just as we accept being frightened by a horror story because we know that the writer set out to frighten us. If we think the writer is disgusting by accident, ineptitude, or moral depravity, then we are "really" disgusted and the fiction does not work.

It is a frustrating experience for many beginning (and established) au- thors to find that, whereas they meant the protagonist to appear sensitive, their readers find him self-pitying; whereas he meant her to be witty, the readers find her vulgar. When this happens there is a failure of *authorial distance*: the author did not have sufficient perspective on the character to convince us to share his or her judgment. I recall one class in which a student author had written, with excellent use of image and scene, the story of a young man who fell in love with an exceptionally beautiful young woman, and whose feelings turned to revulsion when he found out she had had a mastectomy. The most vocal feminist in the class loved this story, which she described as "the exposé of a skuzzwort." This was not, from the author's point of view, a successful reading of his story.

The notion of authorial distance may be clarified by a parallel with acting. Assume that you go to see Jack Nicholson on successive nights in *One Flew Over the Cuckoo's Nest* and *The Shining*. In both, you are aware of Nicholson-the-actor: his face, voice, idiosyncrasies, and the mannerisms he brings to both roles. At the same time you're willing to accept his identity now as the buoyantly sane Randle P. McMurphy, now as the murdering monster Jack Torrence. While McMurphy springs a motley crew of asylum inmates for a fishing trip, you identify with McMurphy, his goals and his values, and you also understand that Nicholson-the-actor wishes you to so identify. While Torrence chases his son with an ax, you hate and fear the character, and you understand that Nicholson-the-actor wishes you to so hate and fear him. In both films, other characters pronounce the protagonist "mad." In one of them, you judge with the actor that he is sane; in the other, you judge with the actor that he is mad. Neither judgment makes you question the sanity of Nicholson-the-actor.

The same phenomenon occurs between writer and reader of the novels from which these films were adapted, or any other fiction. We may judge Moll Flanders to be materialistic; the Godfather, brutal; and Popeye, psychotic. But we understand that the author has directed us toward these judgments and do not think Defoe materialistic, Puzo brutal, or Faulkner psychotic. A significant difference is that the actor has various physical and vocal means to direct our judgment; the writer's resources are the selection and arrangement of words alone. Only as an omniscient author may you "tell" us what your attitude is—and even then you may opt not to. If you purport to be objective, or if you are speaking through the mouth or mind of a character or narrator, then you must show us by implication, through your *tone*.

The word *tone*, applied to fiction, is a metaphor derived from music and also commonly—also metaphorically—used to describe color and speech. When we speak of a "tone of voice" we mean, as in fiction, that an attitude is conveyed, and this attitude is determined by the situation and by the relation of the persons involved in the situation. Tone can match, emphasize, alter, or contradict the meaning of the words.

The situation is that Louise stumbles into her friend Judy's apartment, panting, hair disheveled, coat torn, and face blanched. Judy rushes to support her. "You look awful! What happened?" Here the tone conveys alarm, openness, and a readiness to sympathize.

Judy's son wheels in grinning, swinging a baseball bat, shirt torn, mud splattered, and missing a shoe. "You look awful! What happened?" Judy's tone is angry, exasperated.

Louise's ex-boyfriend drops by that night decked out in a plaid polyester sports coat and an electric blue tie. "You look awful! What happened?" Louise says, her tone light, but cutting, so that he knows she means it.

Judy's husband comes back from a week in Miami and takes off his shirt to model his tan. "You look awful! What happened?" she teases, playful and flirting, so that he knows she means he looks terrific.

In each of these situations the attitude is determined by the situation and the emotional relationships of the persons involved, and in life as in acting the various tones would be conveyed by vocal means—pitch, tempo, plosion, nasality—reinforced by posture, gesture, and facial expression. When we apply the word *tone* to fiction, we tacitly acknowledge that we must do without these helpful signs. The author, of course, may describe pitch, posture, and the like, or may identify a tone as "cutting" or "playful," but these verbal and adverbial aids describe only the tone used among characters, whereas the fictional relationship importantly includes an author who must also convey identification or distance, sympathy or judgment, and who must choose and arrange words so that they match, emphasize, alter, or contradict their inherent meaning.

SPATIAL AND TEMPORAL DISTANCE

The author's or narrator's attitude may involve distance in time or space or both. When a story begins, "Long ago and far away," we are instantly transported by a tone we recognize as belonging to fairy tale, fantasy, and neverland. The year 1890 may be long ago, and the Siberian saltmines far away, but if the author is going to expose prison conditions in tsarist Russia, he had better take another tone.

Anytime you (or your narrator) begin by telling us that the events you are relating took place in the far past, you distance us, making a submerged promise that the events will come to an end, since they "already have." This, of course, may be a device to lure us into the story, and you may—almost certainly do—want to draw us into closer and deeper involvement as the story progresses.

That spring, when I had a great deal of potential and no money at all, I took a job as a janitor. That was when I was still very young and spent money very freely, and when, almost every night, I drifted off to sleep lulled by sweet anticipation of that time when my potential would suddenly be realized and there would be capsule biographies of my life on the dust jackets of many books.

JAMES ALAN McPHERSON, "Gold Coast"

Here a distance in time indicates the attitude of the narrator toward his younger self, and his indulgent, self-mocking tone (*lulled by sweet anticipation of that time when my potential would suddenly be realized*) invites us as readers to identify with the older, narrating self. We know that he is no longer lulled by such fantasies, and, at least for the duration of the story, neither are we. That is, we are close to the narrator, distanced from him as a young man, so that the distance in time also involves distance in attitude. The story "Gold Coast" continues to reinforce this distance, the temporal involving us in the emotional.

> I then became very rich, with my own apartment, a sensitive girl, a stereo, two speakers, one tattered chair, one fork, a job, and the urge to acquire . . . .

Now, all of us either know, or are, people who would consider a job, an apartment, and a sensitive girl very real prosperity. But the author forces us to take a longer perspective than we might in life by including the contrast between "very rich" and "one fork" and "the urge to acquire." Only toward the end of the story, when the narrator himself is moved by his memory, does he let us share the emotion of the younger self.

In the next passage, the author makes use of space to establish an impersonal and authoritative tone.

> An unassuming young man was traveling, in midsummer, from his native city of Hamburg, to Davos-Platz in the Canton of Grisons, on a three week visit.
>
> From Hamburg to Davos is a long journey — too long, indeed, for so brief a stay. It crosses all sorts of country; goes up hill and down dale, descends from the plateau of Southern Germany to the shore of Lake Constance, over its bounding waves and on across marshes once thought to be bottomless.
>
> THOMAS MANN, *The Magic Mountain*

Here Mann distances us from the young man by characterizing him perfunctorily, not even naming him, and describes the place travelogue style, inviting us to take a panoramic view. This choice of tone establishes a remoteness emotional as well as geographical, and would do so even if the reader happened to be a native of Grisons Canton. Again, we will eventually become intimately involved with Davos and the unassuming young man, who is in for a longer stay than he expects.

By closing the literal distance between the reader and the subject, the intangible distance can be closed as well.

> Her face was half an inch from my face. The curtain flapped at the open window and her pupils pulsed with the coming and going of the light. I know

Jill's eyes; I've painted them. They're violent and taciturn, a ring of gas-blue points like cold explosion to the outside boundary of iris, the whole held back with its brilliant lens. A detonation under glass.

JANET BURROWAY, Raw Silk

In the extreme closeness of this focus, we are brought emotionally close, invited to share the narrator's perspective of Jill's explosive eyes.

It will be obvious that using time and space as a means of controlling the reader's emotional closeness or distance involves all the elements of atmosphere discussed in chapter 6. This is true of familiarity, which invites identification with a place, and of strangeness, which alienates. And it is true of summary, which distances, and of scene, which draws us close. If you say, "There were twelve diphtheria outbreaks in Coeville over the next thirty years," you invite us to take a detached historical attitude. But if you say, "He forced his finger into her throat and tilted her toward the light to see, as he'd expected, the grayish membrane reaching toward the roof of her mouth and into her nose," the doctor may remain detached, but we as readers cannot.

There is a grammatical technique involving distance and the use of time as *tense*, which is very often misused. Most fiction in English is written in the *past tense*. (*She put her foot on the shovel and leaned all her weight against it.*) The author's constant effort is to give this past the immediacy of the present. A story may be written in the *present tense (She puts her foot on the shovel and leans all her weight against it)*, and the effect of the present tense, somewhat self-consciously, is to reduce distance and increase immediacy: we are there. Generally speaking, the tense once established *should not be changed.*

> Danforth got home about five o'clock in the morning and fixed himself a peanut butter sandwich. He eats it over the sink, washing it down with half a carton of chocolate milk. He left the carton on the sink and stumbled up to bed.

The change of tense in the second sentence is pointless; it violates the reader's sense of time to have the action skip from past to present and back again and produces no compensating effect.

There are times, however, when a change of tense can be functional and effective. In the story "Gold Coast," we are dealing with two time frames, one having to do with the narrator's earlier experiences as a janitor, and one in which he acknowledges the telling.

> I left the rug on the floor because it was dirty and too large for my new apartment. I also left the two plates given me by James Sullivan, for no

reason at all. Sometimes I want to go back to get them, but I do not know how to ask for them or explain why I left them in the first place.

The tense change here is logical and functional: it acknowledges the past of the "story" and the present of the "telling"; it also incidentally reinforces our emotional identification with the older, narrating self.

Sometimes, however, a shift into the present tense without a strictly logical justification can achieve the effect of intensity and immediacy, so that the emotional distance between reader and character is diminished.

When alone he had a dreadful and distressing desire to call someone, but he knew beforehand that with others present it would be still worse. "Another dose of morphine—to lose consciousness. I will tell him, the doctor, that he must think of something else. It's impossible, impossible, to go on like this."

An hour and another pass like that. But now there's a ring at the doorbell. Perhaps it's the doctor? It is. He comes in fresh, hearty, plump and cheerful.

LEO TOLSTOY,   *The Death of Ivan Ilyich*

This switch from the past to the present draws us into the character's anguish and makes the doctor's arrival more intensely felt. Notice that Ivan Ilyich's thoughts—"Another dose of morphine"—which occur naturally in the present tense, serve as a transition from past to present so that we are not jolted by the change. In *The Death of Ivan Ilyich*, Tolstoy keeps the whole scene of the doctor's visit in the present tense, while Ivan Ilyich's consciousness is at a pitch of pain, contempt for the doctor, and hatred for his wife; then, as the focus moves to the wife, the tense slips back into the past.

The thrill of hatred he feels for her makes him suffer from her touch.

Her attitude towards him and his disease is still the same. Just as the doctor had adopted a certain relation to his patient which he could not abandon, so had she formed one toward him . . . and she could not now change that attitude.

The present tense can be effectively employed to depict moments of special intensity, but it needs both to be saved for those crucial moments and to be controlled so carefully in the transition that the reader is primarily aware of the intensity, rather than the tense.

INTANGIBLE DISTANCE

Spatial and temporal distance, then, can imply distance in the attitude of the teller toward his or her material. But authorial distance may also be implied through tone without any tangible counterpart.

Tone itself is an intangible, and there are probably as many possible tones as there are possible situations, relationships, and sentences. But in a very general way, we will trust, in literature as in life, a choice of words that seems appropriate in intensity or value to the meaning conveyed. If the intensity or value seems inappropriate, we will start to read between the lines. If a woman putting iodine on a cut says "Ouch," we don't have to search for her meaning. But if the cut is being stitched up without anesthetic, then "Ouch" may convey courage, resignation, and trust. If she says "Ouch" when her lover strokes her cheek, then we read anger and recoil into the word.

In the same way, you as author manipulate intensity and value in your choice of language, sometimes matching meaning, sometimes contradicting, sometimes overstating, sometimes understating, to indicate your attitude to the reader.

> She was a tall woman of imperious mien, handsome, with definite black eyebrows. Her smooth black hair was parted exactly. For a few moments she stood steadily watching the miners as they passed along the railway; then she turned toward the brook course. Her face was calm and set, her mouth was closed with disillusionment.
>
> D. H. LAWRENCE, "Odor of Chrysanthemums"

There is in this passage no discrepancy between the thing conveyed and the intensity with which it is conveyed, and we take the words at a face value, accepting that the woman is as the author says she is. The phrase "imperious mien" has itself an imperious tone about it (I doubt one would speak of a *real cool mien*). The syntax is as straightforward as the woman herself. (Notice how the rhythm alters with "For a few moments," so that the longest and most flowing clause follows the passing miners.) You might describe the tone of the passage as a whole as "calm and set."

The next example is quite different.

> Mrs. Herriton did not believe in romance, nor in transfiguration, nor in parallels from history, nor in anything that may disturb domestic life. She adroitly changed the subject before Philip got excited.
>
> E. M. FORSTER, *Where Angels Fear to Tread*

This is clearly also a woman of "imperious mien," and the author purports, like the first, to be informing us of her actions and attitudes. But unlike the first example, the distance here between the woman's attitude and the author's is apparent. It is possible to "believe in" both romance and transfiguration, which are concepts. If Lawrence should say of the woman in "Odor of Chrysanthemums" that "she did not believe in romance, nor in transfiguration," we would accept it as a straightforward part of her characterization. But how can one believe in parallels? *Belief* is too strong a word for *parallels*, and the discrepancy makes us suspicious. Not to "believe" in "anything that may disturb domestic life" is a discrepancy of a severer order, unrealistic and absurd. The word "adroitly" presents a value judgment, one of praise. But placed as it is between "anything that may disturb domestic life" and "before Philip got excited," it shows us that Mrs. Herriton is manipulating the excitement out of domestic life.

Irony. Discrepancies of intensity and value are *ironic*. Any time there is a discrepancy between what is said and what we are to accept as the truth, we are in the presence of an *irony*. There are three basic types of irony.

Verbal irony is a rhetorical device in which the author (or character) says one thing and means another. Mrs. Herriton "adroitly changed the subject" is a form of verbal irony. When the author goes on to say, "Lilia tried to assert herself, and said that she should go to take care of [her mother]. It required all Mrs. Herriton's kindness to prevent her," there is further verbal irony in the combination of "required" and "kindness."

Dramatic irony is a device of plot in which the reader or audience knows more than the character does. The classical example of dramatic irony is *Oedipus Rex*, where the audience knows that Oedipus himself is the murderer he seeks. There is a dramatic irony in *The Death of Ivan Ilyich*, as Ilyich persists in ignoring the pain from his fall, protesting to himself that it's nothing, while the reader knows that it will lead to his death.

Cosmic irony is an all-encompassing attitude toward life, which takes into account the contradictions inherent in the human condition. The story "Cutting Edge" exemplifies cosmic irony when Mrs. Zeller's attempts to force her son into being the person she can love and recognize as her own inevitably drive him from her.

Any of these types of irony will inform the author's attitude toward the material and will be reflected in his or her tone. Any of them will involve authorial distance, since the author means, knows, or wishes to take into account—and also intends the reader to understand—something not wholly conveyed by the literal meaning of the words.

In the two passages quoted above, we may say that the first, from Lawrence, is without irony; the second, from Forster, contains an irony presented by the author, understood by the reader, and directed against the character described.

The following passage, again about a woman of imperious mien, is more complex because it introduces the fourth possible member of the narrative dialogue, the narrator; and it also contains temporal distance.

> She was a tall woman with high cheekbones, now more emphasized than ever by the loss of her molar teeth. Her lips were finer than most of her tribe's and wore a shut, rather sour expression. Her eyes seemed to be always fixed

on the distance, as though she didn't "see" or mind the immediate, but dwelt in the eternal. She was not like other children's grandmothers we knew, who would spoil her grandchildren and had huts "just outside the hedge" of their sons' homesteads. Grandmother lived three hills away, which was inexplicable.

JONATHAN KARIARA,   "Her Warrior"

This paragraph begins, like Lawrence's, without irony, as a strong portrait of a strong woman. Because we trust the consistent tone of the first two sentences, we also accept the teller's smile "as though she didn't 'see' or mind the immediate," which emphasizes without contradicting. Up to this point the voice seems to have the authority of an omniscient author, but in the fourth sentence the identity of the narrator is introduced — one of the woman's grandchildren. Because the past tense is used, and even more, because the language is measured and educated, we instantly understand that the narrator is telling of his childhood perceptions from an adult, temporally distanced perspective. Curiously, the final word of the final sentence presents us with a contradiction of everything we have just found convincing. It cannot be "inexplicable" that this woman lived three hills away, because it has already been explained to us that she lived in deep and essential remoteness.

This irony is not directed primarily against the character of the grandmother but by the narrator against himself as a child. Author, narrator, and reader all concur in an intellectual distance from the child's mind and its faulty perceptions. At the same time, there is perhaps a sympathetic identification with the child's hurt, and therefore there results a residual judgment of the grandmother.

With What Limitations?

In each of the passages excerpted in the section "Intangible Distance" we trust the teller of the tale. We may find ourselves in opposition to characters perceived or perceiving, but we identify with the attitudes, straightforward or ironic, of the authors and narrators who present us these characters. We share, at least for the duration of the narrative, their norms.

THE UNRELIABLE NARRATOR

It is also possible to mistrust the teller. Authorial distance may involve not a deliberate attitude taken by the speaker, but distance on the part of the author from the narrator. The answer to the question "Who speaks?"

may itself necessitate a judgment, and again this judgment may imply opposition of the author (and reader) on any scale of value—moral, intellectual, aesthetic, or physical—and to these I would add educational and experiential (probably the list can be expanded further).

If the answer to "Who speaks?" is *a child, a bigot, a jealous lover, an animal, a schizophrenic, a murderer, a liar,* any of these may imply that the narrator speaks with *limitations* we do not necessarily share. To the extent that the narrator displays and betrays such limitations, she or he is an *unreliable narrator*; and the author, without a word to call his own, must let the reader know that the story is not to be trusted.

Here is a fourth woman imperious and sour, who tells her own story.

> But that's why I have an understanding of the girl Ginny downstairs and her kids. They're runty, underdeveloped. No sun, no beef. Noodles, beans, cabbage. Well, my mother off the boat knew better than that. . . .
>
> Five ladies on the block, old friends, nosy, me not included, got up a meeting and wrote a petition to Child Welfare. I already knew it was useless, as the requirement is more than dirt, drunkenness, and a little once-in-a-way whoring. That is probably something why the children in our city are in such a state. I've noticed it for years, though it's not my business. Mothers and fathers get up when they wish, half being snuggled in relief, go to bed in the afternoon with their rumpy bumpy sweethearts pumping away before 3 p.m. (So help me.) Child Welfare does not show its concern. No matter who writes them. People of influence, known in the district, even the district leader, my cousin Leonie . . .
>
> GRACE PALEY, "Distance"

We mistrust every judgment this woman makes, but we are also aware of an author we do trust, manipulating the narrator's tone to expose her. The outburst is fraught with ironies (including perhaps the title, "Distance"), but because the narrator is unaware of them they are directed against herself. She claims "understanding" and "concern" for what she exhibits as invective. She claims respectability, which she lamely bolsters by name-dropping her mother and her cousin, while her own language is "rumpy bumpy" lascivious. Her syntax betrays ignorance and her bristling intensity is spent on the wrong values, and "that is probably something why" author and reader side with Ginny and her kids in direct opposition to the narrator.

In this case the narrator is wholly unreliable, and we're unlikely to accept any judgment she could make. But it is also possible for a narrator to be reliable in some areas of value and unreliable in others. Mark Twain's Huckleberry Finn is a famous case in point. Here Huck has decided to free his friend Jim, and he is astonished that Tom Sawyer is going along with the plan.

Well, one thing was dead sure; and that was, that Tom Sawyer was in earnest and was actly going to help steal that nigger out of slavery. That was the thing that was too many for me. Here was a boy that was respectable, and well brung up; and had a character to lose; and folks at home that had characters; and he was bright and not leather-headed; and knowing and not ignorant; and not mean, but kind; and yet here he was, without any more pride, or rightness, or feeling, than to stoop to this business, and make himself a shame, and his family a shame, before everybody. I *couldn't* understand it, no way at all.

The extended irony in this excerpt is that slavery should be defended by the respectable, the bright, the knowing, the kind, and those of character. We reject Huck's assessment of Tom as well as the implied assessment of himself as worth so little that he has nothing to lose by freeing a slave. Huck's moral instincts are better than he himself can understand. (Notice, incidentally, how Huck's lack of education is communicated by word choice and syntax and how sparse the misspellings are.) So author and reader are in intellectual opposition to Huck the narrator, but morally identify with him.

The unreliable narrator—who has become one of the most popular characters in modern fiction—is far from a newcomer to literature and in fact predates fiction. Every drama contains characters who speak for themselves and present their own cases, and from whom we are partly or wholly distanced in one area of value or another. So we identify with Othello's morality but mistrust his logic, trust Faust's intellect but not his ethics, admire Barney Fife's heart of gold but not his courage. As these examples suggest, the unreliable narrator always presents us with dramatic irony, because we always "know" more than he or she does about the characters, the events, and the significance of both.

AN EXERCISE IN UNRELIABILITY

The following five passages—one a lyric and four prose fiction—represent narrations by five relatively mad madmen. How mad is each? To whom does each speak? In what form? Which of their statements are reliable? Unreliable? Which of them admit to madness? Is the admission reliable? What ironies can you identify, and against whom is each directed? What is the attitude of the author behind the narrator? By what choice and arrangement of words do you know this?

I met my old lover
  On the street last night
  She seemed so glad to see me

I just smiled
And we talked about some old times
And we drank ourselves some beers
Still crazy after all these years . . .

I'm not the kind of man
Who tends to socialize
I seem to lean on
Old familiar ways
And I ain't no fool for love songs
That whisper in my ears
Still crazy after all these years . . .

Now I sit by the window
And I watch the stars
I fear I'll do some damage
One fine day
But I would not be convicted
By a jury of my peers . . .
Still crazy after all these years.

PAUL SIMON, "Still Crazy After All These Years"

The doctor advised me not to insist too much on looking so far back. Recent events, he says, are equally valuable for him, and above all my fancies and dreams of the night before. But I like to do things in their order, so directly I left the doctor (who was going to be away from Trieste for some time). I bought and read a book on psychoanalysis, so that I might begin from the very beginning, and make the doctor's task easier. It is not difficult to understand, but very boring. I have stretched myself out after lunch in an easy chair, pencil and paper in hand. All the lines have disappeared from my forehead as I sit here with mind completely relaxed. I seem to be able to see my thoughts as something quite apart from myself. I can watch them rising, falling, their only form of activity. I seize my pencil in order to remind them that it is the duty of thought to manifest itself. At once the wrinkles collect on my brow as I think of the letters that make up every word.

ITALO SVEVO, *Confessions of Zeno*

Madrid, Februarius the thirtieth

So I'm in Spain. It all happened so quickly that I hardly had time to realize it. This morning the Spanish delegation finally arrived for me and we all got into the carriage. I was somewhat bewildered by the extraordinary speed at which we traveled. We went so fast that in half an hour we reached the Spanish border. But then, nowadays there are railroads all over Europe and the ships go so fast too. Spain is a strange country. When we entered the first room, I saw a multitude of people with shaven heads. I soon realized, though, that these must be Dominican or Capuchin monks because they always shave their heads. I also thought that the manners of the King's Chancellor, who was leading me by the hand, were rather strange. He pushed me into a small room and said: "You sit quiet and don't you call yourself King Ferdinand again or I'll beat the nonsense out of your head." But I knew that I was just being tested and refused to submit.

NIKOLAI GOGOL, The Diary of a Madman

Pushed back into sleep as I fight to emerge, pushed back as they drown a kitten, or a child fighting to wake up, pushed back by voices and lullabies and bribes and bullies, punished by tones of voices and by silences, gripped into sleep by medicines and syrups and dummies and dope.

Nevertheless I fight, desperate, like a kitten trying to climb out of the slippysided zinc pail it has been flung in, an unwanted, unneeded cat to drown, better dead than alive, better asleep than awake, but I fight, up and up into the light, greeting dark now as a different land, a different texture, a different state of the Light.

DORIS LESSING, Briefing for a Descent into Hell

Come into my cell. Make yourself at home. Take the chair; I'll sit on the cot. No? You prefer to stand by the window? I understand. You like my little view. Have you noticed that the narrower the view the more you can see? For the first time I understand how old ladies can sit on their porches for years.

Don't I know you? You look very familiar. I've been feeling rather depressed and I don't remember things very well. I think I am here because of that or because I committed a crime. Perhaps it's both. Is this a prison or a hospital or a prison hospital? A Center for Aberrant Behavior? So that's it. I have behaved aberrantly. In short, I'm in the nuthouse.

WALKER PERCY, Lancelot

UNRELIABILITY IN OTHER VIEWPOINTS

I have said that a narrator cannot be omniscient, although he or she may be reliable. It may seem equally plausible that the phenomenon of unreliability can apply only to a narrator, who is by definition a fallible human being. But the subtleties of authorial distance are such that it is possible to indicate unreliability through virtually any point of view. If, for example, you have chosen a limited omniscient viewpoint including only external observation and the thoughts of one character, then it may be that the character's thoughts are unreliable and that he or she misinterprets external facts. Then you must make us aware through tone that you know more than you have chosen to present. William Golding, in *The Inheritors*, tells his story in the third person, but through the eyes and thoughts of a Neanderthal who has not yet developed the power of deductive reasoning.

The man turned sideways in the bushes and looked at Lok along his shoulder. A stick rose upright and there was a lump of bone in the middle .... Suddenly Lok understood that the man was holding the stick out to him but neither he nor Lok could reach across the river. He would have laughed if it were not for the echo of screaming in his head. The stick began to grow shorter at both ends. Then it shot out to full length again.

The dead tree by Lok's ear acquired a voice.

"Clop!"

His ears twitched and he turned to the tree. By his face there had grown a twig: a twig that smelt of other, and of goose, and of the bitter berries that Lok's stomach told him he must not eat.

The imaginative problem here, imaginatively embraced, is that we must supply the deductive reasoning of which our point-of-view character is incapable. Lok has no experience of bows or poison arrows, nor of "men" attacking each other, so his conclusions are unreliable. "Suddenly Lok understood" is an irony setting us in opposition to the character's intellect; at the same time, his innocence makes him morally sympathetic. Since the author does not intervene to interpret for us, the effect is very near that of an unreliable narrator.

Other experiments abound. Isaac Loeb Peretz tells the story of "Bontsha the Silent" from the point of view of the editorial omniscient, privy to the deliberations of the angels, but with Yiddish syntax and "universal truths" so questionable that the omniscient voice itself is unreliable. Conversely, Faulkner's *The Sound and the Fury* is told through several unreliable narrators, each with an idiosyncratic and partial perception of the story, so that the cumulative effect is of an omniscient author able not only to penetrate many minds but also to perceive the larger significance.

I'm conscious that this discussion of point of view contains more analysis than advice, and this is because very little can be said to be right or wrong about point of view as long as the reader ultimately identifies with the author; as long, that is, as you make it work. In *Aspects of the Novel* E.M. Forster speaks vaguely, but with undeniable accuracy, of "the power of the writer to bounce the reader into accepting what he says." He then goes on to prove categorically that Dickens's *Bleak House* is a disaster, "Logically . . . all to pieces, but Dickens bounces us, so that we do not mind the shiftings of the view-point."

The one imperative is that the reader must bounce with, not against, the author. Virtually any story can be told from virtually any point of view and convey the same attitude of the author.

Suppose, for example, that you are going to write this story: Two American soldiers in a Far Eastern "police action," one a seasoned corporal and the other a newly arrived private, are sent on a mission to kill a sniper. They track, find, and capture the Oriental, who turns out to be a fifteen-year-old boy. The corporal offers to let the private pull the trigger, but he cannot. The corporal kills the sniper and triumphantly cuts off his ear for a trophy. The young soldier vomits; ashamed of himself, he pulls himself together and vows to do better next time.

Your attitude as author of this story is that war is inhumane and dehumanizing.

You may write the story from the point of view of the editorial omniscient, following the actions of the hunters and the hunted, going into the minds of corporal, private, and sniper, ranging the backgrounds of each and knowing the ultimate pointlessness of the death, telling us, in effect, that war is inhumane and dehumanizing.

Or you may write it from the point of view of the corporal as an unreliable narrator, proud of his toughness and his expertise, condescending to the private, certain the Orientals are animals, glorying in his trophy, betraying his inhumanity.

Between these two extremes of total omniscience and total unreliability, you may take any position of the middle ground. The story might be written in the limited omniscient, presenting the thoughts only of the anxious private and the external actions of the others. It might be written objectively, with a cold and detached accuracy of military detail. It might be written by a peripheral narrator, a war correspondent, from interviews and documents; as a letter home from the private to his girl; as a field report from the corporal; as an interior monologue of the young sniper during the seconds before his death.

Any of these modes could contain your meaning, any of them fulfill your purpose. Your central problem as a writer might prove to be the choosing. But whatever your final choice of point of view in the technical sense, your point of view in the sense of *opinion* would remain that war is inhumane and dehumanizing, and could be suggested.

Battle Royal

RALPH ELLISON

It goes a long way back, some twenty years. All my life I had been looking for something, and everywhere I turned someone tried to tell me what it was. I accepted their answers too, though they were often in contradiction and even self-contradictory. I was naïve. I was looking for myself and asking everyone except myself questions which I, and only I, could answer. It took me a long time and much painful boomeranging of my expectations to achieve a realization everyone else appears to have been born with: That I am nobody but myself. But first I had to discover that I am an invisible man!

And yet I am no freak of nature, nor of history. I was in the cards, other things having been equal (or unequal) eighty-five years ago. I am not ashamed of my grandparents for having been slaves. I am only ashamed of myself for having at one time been ashamed. About eighty-five years ago they were told that they were free, united with others of our country in everything pertaining to the common good, and, in everything social, separate like the fingers of the hand. And they believed it. They exulted in it. They stayed in their place, worked hard, and brought up my father to do the same. But my grandfather is the one. He was an odd old guy, my grandfather, and I am told I take after him. It was he who caused the trouble. On his deathbed he called my father to him and said, "Son, after I'm gone I want you to keep up the good fight. I never told you, but our life is a war and I have been a traitor all my born days, a spy in the enemy's country ever since I give up my gun back in the Reconstruction. Live with your head in the lion's mouth. I want you to overcome 'em with yeses, under-mine 'em with grins, agree 'em to death and destruction, let 'em swoller you till they vomit or bust wide open." They thought the old man had gone out of his mind. He had been the meekest of men. The younger children were rushed from the room, the shades drawn and the flame of the lamp turned so low that it sputtered on the wick like the old man's breathing. "Learn it to the younguns," he whispered fiercely; then he died.

But my folks were more alarmed over his last words than over his dying. It was as though he had not died at all, his words caused so much anxiety. I was warned emphatically to forget what he had said and, indeed, this is the first time it has been mentioned outside the family circle. It had a tremen-dous effect upon me, however. I could never be sure of what he meant. Grandfather had been a quiet old man who never made any trouble, yet on his deathbed he had called himself a traitor and a spy, and he had spoken of his meekness as a dangerous activity. It became a constant puzzle which lay unanswered in the back of my mind. And whenever things went well for me I remembered my grandfather and felt guilty and uncomfort-able. It was as though I was carrying out his advice in spite of myself. And to make it worse, everyone loved me for it. I was praised by the most lily-white men of the town. I was considered an example of desirable conduct—just as my grandfather had been. And what puzzled me was that the old man had defined it as *treachery*. When I was praised for my conduct I felt a guilt that in some way I was doing something that was really against the wishes of the white folks, that if they had understood they would have desired me to act just the opposite, that I should have been sulky and mean, and that that really would have been what they wanted, even though they were fooled and thought they wanted me to act as I did. It made me afraid that some day they would look upon me as a traitor and I would be lost. Still I was more afraid to act any other way because they didn't like that at all. The old man's words were like a curse. On my graduation day I delivered an oration in which I showed that humility was the secret, indeed, the very essence of progress. (Not that I believed this—how could I, remembering my grandfather?—I only believed that it worked.) It was a great success. Everyone praised me and I was invited to give the speech at a gathering of the town's leading white citizens. It was a triumph for our whole community.

It was the main ballroom of the leading hotel. When I got there I discovered that it was on the occasion of a smoker, and I was told that since I was to be there anyway I might as well take part in the battle royal to be fought by some of my schoolmates as part of the entertainment. The battle royal came first.

All of the town's big shots were there in their tuxedoes, wolfing down the buffet foods, drinking beer and whiskey and smoking black cigars. It was a large room with a high ceiling. Chairs were arranged in neat rows around three sides of a portable boxing ring. The fourth side was clear, revealing a gleaming space of polished floor. I had some misgivings over the battle royal, by the way. Not from a distaste for fighting, but because I didn't care too much for the other fellows who were to take part. They were tough guys who seemed to have no grandfather's curse worrying their minds. No one could mistake their toughness. And besides, I suspected that fighting a battle royal might detract from the dignity of my speech. In those pre-invisible days I visualized myself as a potential Booker T. Washington. But the other fellows didn't care too much for me either, and there were nine of them. I felt superior to them in my way, and I didn't like the manner in which we were all crowded together into the servants' elevator. Nor did they like my being there. In fact, as the warmly lighted floors flashed past the elevator we had words over the fact that I, by taking part in the fight, had knocked one of their friends out of a night's work.

We were led out of the elevator through a rococo hall into an anteroom and told to get into our fighting togs. Each of us was issued a pair of boxing gloves and ushered out into the big mirrored hall, which we entered looking cautiously about us and whispering, lest we might accidentally be heard above the noise of the room. It was foggy with cigar smoke. And already the whiskey was taking effect. I was shocked to see some of the most important men of the town quite tipsy. They were all there—bankers, lawyers, judges, doctors, fire chiefs, teachers, merchants. Even one of the more fashionable pastors. Something we could not see was going on up front. A clarinet was vibrating sensuously and the men were standing up and moving eagerly forward. We were a small tight group, clustered together, our bare upper bodies touching and shining with anticipatory sweat; while up front the big shots were becoming increasingly excited over something we still could not see. Suddenly I heard the school superintendent, who had told me to come, yell, "Bring up the shines, gentlemen! Bring up the little shines!"

We were rushed up to the front of the ballroom, where it smelled even more strongly of tobacco and whiskey. Then we were pushed into place. I almost wet my pants. A sea of faces, some hostile, some amused, ringed around us, and in the center, facing us, stood a magnificent blond—stark naked. There was dead silence. I felt a blast of cold air chill me. I tried to back away, but they were behind me and around me. Some of the boys stood with lowered heads, trembling. I felt a wave of irrational guilt and fear. My teeth chattered, my skin turned to goose flesh, my knees knocked. Yet I was strongly attracted and looked in spite of myself. Had the price of looking been blindness, I would have looked. The hair was yellow like that of a circus kewpie doll, the face heavily powdered and rouged, as though to form an abstract mask, the eyes hollow and smeared a cool blue, the color of a baboon's butt. I felt a desire to spit upon her as my eyes brushed slowly over her body. Her breasts were firm and round as the domes of East Indian temples, and I stood so close as to see the fine skin texture and beads of pearly perspiration glistening like dew around the pink and erected buds of her nipples. I wanted at one and the same time to run from the room, to sink through the floor, or go to her and cover her from my eyes and the eyes of the others with my body; to feel the soft thigh, to caress her and destroy her, to love her and murder her, to hide from her, and yet to stroke where below the small American flag tattooed upon her belly her thighs formed a capital V. I had a notion that of all in the room she saw only me with her impersonal eyes.

And then she began to dance, a slow sensuous movement; the smoke of a hundred cigars clinging to her like the thinnest of veils. She seemed like a fair bird-girl girdled in veils calling to me from the angry surface of some gray and threatening sea. I was transported. Then I became aware of the clarinet playing and the big shots yelling at us. Some threatened us if we looked and others if we did not. On my right I saw one boy faint. And now a man grabbed a silver pitcher from a table and stepped close as he dashed ice water upon him and stood him up and forced two of us to support him as his head hung and moans issued from his thick bluish lips. Another boy began to plead to go home. He was the largest of the group, wearing dark red fighting trunks much too small to conceal the erection which projected from him as though in answer to the insinuating low-registered moaning of the clarinet. He tried to hide himself with his boxing gloves.

And all the while the blonde continued dancing, smiling faintly at the big shots who watched her with fascination, and faintly smiling at our fear. I noticed a certain merchant who followed her hungrily, his lips loose and drooling. He was a large man who wore diamond studs in a shirtfront which swelled with the ample paunch underneath, and each time the blonde swayed her undulating hips he ran his hand through the thin hair of his bald head and, with his arms upheld, his posture clumsy like that of an intoxicated panda, wound his belly in a slow and obscene grind. This creature was completely hypnotized. The music had quickened. As the dancer flung herself about with a detached expression on her face, the men began reaching out to touch her. I could see their beefy fingers sink into the soft flesh. Some of the others tried to stop them and she began to move around the floor in graceful circles, as they gave chase, slipping and sliding over the polished floor. It was mad. Chairs went crashing, drinks were spilt, as they ran laughing and howling after her. They caught her just as she reached the door, raised her from the floor, and tossed her as college boys are tossed at a hazing, and above her red, fixed-smiling lips I saw the terror and disgust in her eyes, almost like my own terror and that which I saw in some of the other boys. As I watched, they tossed her twice and her soft breasts seemed to flatten against the air and her legs flung wildly as she spun. Some of the more sober ones helped her to escape. And I started off the floor, heading for the anteroom with the rest of the boys.

Some were still crying and in hysteria. But as we tried to leave we were stopped and ordered to get into the ring. There was nothing to do but what we were told. All ten of us climbed under the ropes and allowed ourselves to be blindfolded with broad bands of white cloth. One of the men seemed to feel a bit sympathetic and tried to cheer us up as we stood with our backs against the ropes. Some of us tried to grin. "See that boy over there?" one of the men said. "I want you to run across at the bell and give it to him right in the belly. If you don't get him, I'm going to get you. I don't like his looks." Each of us was told the same. The blindfolds were put on. Yet even then I had been going over my speech. In my mind each word was as bright as flame. I felt the cloth pressed into place, and frowned so that it would be loosened when I relaxed.

But now I felt a sudden fit of blind terror. I was unused to darkness. It was as though I had suddenly found myself in a dark room filled with poisonous cottonmouths. I could hear the bleary voices yelling insistently for the battle royal to begin.

"Get going in there!"

"Let me at that big nigger!"

I strained to pick up the school superintendent's voice, as though to squeeze some security out of that slightly more familiar sound.

"Let me at those black sonsabitches!" someone yelled.

"No, Jackson, no!" another voice yelled. "Here, somebody, help me hold Jack."

"I want to get at that ginger-colored nigger. Tear him limb from limb," the first voice yelled.

I stood against the ropes trembling. For in those days I was what they called ginger-colored, and he sounded as though he might crunch me between his teeth like a crisp ginger cookie.

Quite a struggle was going on. Chairs were being kicked about and I could hear voices grunting as with a terrific effort. I wanted to see, to see more desperately than ever before. But the blindfold was as tight as a thick skin-puckering scab and when I raised my gloved hands to push the layers of white aside a voice yelled, "Oh, no you don't, black bastard! Leave that alone!"

"Ring the bell before Jackson kills him a coon!" someone boomed in the sudden silence. And I heard the bell clang and the sound of feet scuffling forward.

A glove smacked against my head. I pivoted, striking out stiffly as someone went past, and felt the jar ripple along the length of my arm to my shoulder. Then it seemed as though all nine of the boys had turned upon me at once. Blows pounded me from all sides while I struck out as best I could. So many blows landed upon me that I wondered if I were not the only blindfolded fighter in the ring, or if the man called Jackson hadn't succeeded in getting me after all.

Blindfolded, I could no longer control my emotions. I had no dignity. I stumbled about like a baby or a drunken man. The smoke had become thicker and with each new blow it seemed to sear and further restrict my lungs. My saliva became like hot bitter glue. A glove connected with my head, filling my mouth with warm blood. It was everywhere. I could not tell if the moisture I felt upon my body was sweat or blood. A blow landed hard against the nape of my neck. I felt myself going over, my head hitting the floor. Streaks of blue light filled the black world behind the blindfold. I lay prone, pretending that I was knocked out, but felt myself seized by hands and yanked to my feet. "Get going, black boy! Mix it up!" My arms were like lead, my head smarting from blows. I managed to feel my way to the ropes and held on, trying to catch my breath. A glove landed in my mid-section and I went over again, feeling as though the smoke had become a knife jabbed into my guts. Pushed this way and that by the legs milling around me I finally pulled erect and discovered that I could see the black, sweat-washed forms weaving in the smoky-blue atmosphere like drunken dancers weaving to the rapid drum-like thuds of blows.

Everyone fought hysterically. It was complete anarchy. Everybody fought everybody else. No group fought together for long. Two, three, four, fought one, then turned to fight each other, were themselves attacked. Blows landed below the belt and in the kidney, with the gloves open as well as closed, and with eye partly opened now there was not so much terror. I moved carefully, avoiding blows, although not too many to attract attention, fighting from group to group. The boys groped about like blind, cautious crabs crouching to protect their mid-sections, their heads pulled in short against their shoulders, their arms stretched nervously before them, with their fists testing the smoke-filled air like the knobbed feelers of hypersensitive snails. In one corner I glimpsed a boy violently punching the air and heard him scream in pain as he smashed his hand against a ring post. For a second I saw him bent over holding his hand, then going down as a blow caught his unprotected head. I played one group against the other, slipping in and throwing a punch then stepping out of range while pushing the others into the melee to take the blows blindly aimed at me. The smoke was agonizing and there were no rounds, no bells at three minute intervals to relieve our exhaustion. The room spun round me, a swirl of lights, smoke, sweating bodies surrounded by tense white faces. I bled from both nose and mouth, the blood spattering upon my chest.

The men kept yelling, "Slug him, black boy! Knock his guts out!"

"Uppercut him! Kill him! Kill that big boy!"

Taking a fake fall, I saw a boy going down heavily beside me as though we were felled by a single blow, saw a sneaker-clad foot shoot into his groin as the two who had knocked him down stumbled upon him. I rolled out of range, feeling a twinge of nausea.

The harder we fought the more threatening the men became. And yet, I had begun to worry about my speech again. How would it go? Would they recognize my ability? What would they give me?

I was fighting automatically when suddenly I noticed that one after another of the boys was leaving the ring. I was surprised, filled with panic; as though I had been left alone with an unknown danger. Then I understood. The boys had arranged it among themselves. It was the custom for the two men left in the ring to slug it out for the winner's prize. I discovered this too late. When the bell sounded two men in tuxedoes leaped into the ring and removed the blindfold. I found myself facing Tatlock, the biggest of the gang. I felt sick at my stomach. Hardly had the bell stopped ringing in my ears than it clanged again and I saw him moving swiftly toward me. Thinking of nothing else to do I hit him smash on the nose. He kept coming, bringing the rank sharp violence of stale sweat. His face was a black blank of a face, only his eyes alive—with hate of me and aglow with a feverish terror from what had happened to us all. I became anxious. I wanted to deliver my speech and he came at me as though he meant to beat it out of me. I smashed him again and again, taking his blows as they came. Then on a sudden impulse I struck him lightly and as we clinched, I whispered, "Fake like I knocked you out, you can have the prize."

"I'll break your behind," he whispered hoarsely.

"For *them?*"

"For *me*, sonofabitch!"

They were yelling for us to break it up and Tatlock spun me half around with a blow, and as a joggled camera sweeps in a reeling scene, I saw the howling red faces crouching tense beneath the cloud of bluegray smoke.

For a moment the world wavered, unraveled, flowed, then my head cleared and Tatlock bounced before me. That fluttering shadow before my eyes was his jabbing left hand. Then falling forward, my head against his damp shoulder, I whispered.

"I'll make it five dollars more."

"Go to hell!"

But his muscles relaxed a trifle beneath my pressure and I breathed, "Seven?"

"Give it to your ma," he said, ripping me beneath the heart.

And while I still held him I butted him and moved away. I felt myself bombarded with punches. I fought back with hopeless desperation. I wanted to deliver my speech more than anything else in the world, because I felt that only these men could judge truly my ability, and now this stupid clown was ruining my chances. I began fighting carefully now, moving in to punch him and out again with my greater speed. A lucky blow to his chin and I had him going too—until I heard a loud voice yell, "I got my money on the big boy."

Hearing this, I almost dropped my guard. I was confused: Should I try to win against the voice out there? Would not this go against my speech, and was not this a moment for humility, for nonresistance? A blow to my head as I danced about sent my right eye popping like a jack-in-the-box and settled my dilemma. The room went red as I fell. It was a dream fall, my body languid and fastidious as to where to land, until the floor became impatient and smashed up to meet me. A moment later I came to. An hypnotic voice said FIVE emphatically. And I lay there, hazily watching a dark red spot of my own blood shaping itself into a butterfly, glistening and soaking into the soiled gray world of the canvas.

When the voice drawled TEN I was lifted up and dragged to a chair. I sat dazed. My eye pained and swelled with each throb of my pounding heart and I wondered if now I would be allowed to speak. I was wringing wet, my mouth still bleeding. We were grouped along the wall now. The other boys ignored me as they congratulated Tatlock and speculated as to how much they would be paid. One boy whimpered over his smashed hand. Looking up front, I saw attendants in white jackets rolling the portable ring away and placing a small square rug in the vacant space surrounded by chairs. Perhaps, I thought, I will stand on the rug to deliver my speech.

Then the M.C. called to us, "Come on up here boys and get your money."

We ran forward to where the men laughed and talked in their chairs, waiting. Everyone seemed friendly now.

"There it is on the rug," the man said. I saw the rug covered with coins of all dimensions and a few crumpled bills. But what excited me, scattered here and there, were the gold pieces.

"Boys, it's all yours," the man said. "You get all you grab."

"That's right, Sambo," a blond man said, winking at me confidentially.

I trembled with excitement, forgetting my pain. I would get the gold and the bills, I thought. I would use both hands. I would throw my body against the boys nearest me to block them from the gold.

"Get down around the rug now," the man commanded, "and don't anyone touch it until I give the signal."

"This ought to be good," I heard.

As told, we got around the square rug on our knees. Slowly the man raised his freckled hand as we followed it upward with our eyes.

I heard, "These niggers look like they're about to pray!"

Then, "Ready," the man said. "Go!"

I lunged for a yellow coin lying on the blue design of the carpet, touching it and sending a surprised shriek to join those rising around me. I tried frantically to remove my hand but could not let go. A hot, violent force tore through my body, shaking me like a wet rag. The rug was electrified. The hair bristled up on my head as I shook myself free. My muscles jumped, my nerves jangled, writhed. But I saw that this was not stopping the other boys. Laughing in fear and embarrassment, some were holding back and scooping up the coins knocked off by the painful contortions of the others. The men roared above us as we struggled.

"Pick it up, goddammit, pick it up!" someone called like a bass-voiced parrot. "Go on, get it!"

I crawled rapidly around the floor, picking up the coins, trying to avoid the coppers and to get greenbacks and the gold. Ignoring the shock by laughing, as I brushed the coins off quickly, I discovered that I could contain the electricity—a contradiction, but it works. Then the men began to push us onto the rug. Laughing embarrassedly, we struggled out of their hands and kept after the coins. We were all wet and slippery and hard to hold. Suddenly I saw a boy lifted into the air, glistening with sweat like a circus seal, and dropped, his back landing flush upon the charged rug, heard him yell and saw him literally dance upon his back, his elbows beating a frenzied tattoo upon the floor, his muscles twitching like the flesh of a horse stung by many flies. When he finally rolled off, his face was gray and no one stopped him when he ran from the floor amid booming laughter.

"Get the money," the M.C. called. "That's good hard American cash!"

And we snatched and grabbed, snatched and grabbed. I was careful not to come too close to the rug now, and when I felt the hot whiskey breath descend upon me like a cloud of foul air I reached out and grabbed the leg of a chair. It was occupied and I held on desperately.

"Leggo, nigger! Leggo!"

The huge face wavered down to mine as he tried to push me free. But my body was slippery and he was too drunk. It was Mr. Colcord, who owned a chain of movie houses and "entertainment palaces." Each time he grabbed me I slipped out of his hands. It became a real struggle. I feared the rug more than I did the drunk, so I held on, surprising myself for a moment by trying to topple *him* upon the rug. It was such an enormous idea that I found myself actually carrying it out. I tried not to be obvious, yet when I grabbed his leg, trying to tumble him out of the chair, he raised up roaring with laughter, and, looking at me with soberness dead in the eye, kicked me viciously in the chest. The chair leg flew out of my hand and I felt myself going and rolled. It was as though I had rolled through a bed of hot coals. It seemed a whole century would pass before I would roll free, a century in which I was seared through the deepest levels of my body to the fearful breath within me and the breath seared and heated to the point of explosion. It'll all be over in a flash, I thought as I rolled clear. It'll all be over in a flash.

But not yet, the men on the other side were waiting, red faces swollen as though from apoplexy as they bent forward in their chairs. Seeing their fingers coming toward me I rolled away as a fumbled football rolls off the receiver's fingertips, back into the coals. That time I luckily sent the rug sliding out of place and heard the coins ringing against the floor and the boys scuffling to pick them up and the M.C. calling, "All right, boys, that's all. Go get dressed and get your money."

I was limp as a dish rag. My back felt as though it had been beaten with wires.

When we had dressed the M.C. came in and gave us each five dollars, except Tatlock, who got ten for being last in the ring. Then he told us to leave. I was not to get a chance to deliver my speech, I thought. I was going out into the dim alley in despair when I was stopped and told to go back. I returned to the ballroom, where the men were pushing back their chairs and gathering in groups to talk.

The M.C. knocked on a table for quiet. "Gentlemen," he said, "we almost forgot an important part of the program. A most serious part, gentlemen. This boy was brought here to deliver a speech which he made at his graduation yesterday . . ."

"Bravo!"

"I'm told that he is the smartest boy we've got out there in Greenwood. I'm told that he knows more big words than a pocket-sized dictionary."

Much applause and laughter.

"So now, gentlemen, I want you to give him your attention."

There was still laughter as I faced them, my mouth dry, my eye throbbing. I began slowly, but evidently my throat was tense, because they began shouting, "Louder! Louder!"

"We of the younger generation extol the wisdom of that great leader and educator," I shouted, "who first spoke these flaming words of wisdom: 'A ship lost at sea for many days suddenly sighted a friendly vessel. From the mast of the unfortunate vessel was seen a signal: "Water, water; we die of thirst!" The answer from the friendly vessel came back: "Cast down your bucket where you are." The captain of the distressed vessel, at last heeding the injunction, cast down his bucket, and it came up full of fresh sparkling water from the mouth of the Amazon River.' And like him I say, and in his words, 'To those of my race who depend upon bettering their condition in a foreign land, or who underestimate the importance of cultivating friendly relations with the Southern white man, who is his next-door neighbor, I would say: "Cast down your bucket where you are"—cast it down in making friends in every manly way of the people of all races by whom we are surrounded . . .' "

I spoke automatically and with such fervor that I did not realize that the men were still talking and laughing until my dry mouth, filling up with blood from the cut, almost strangled me. I coughed, wanting to stop and go to one of the tall brass, sand-filled spittoons to relieve myself, but a few of the men, especially the superintendent, were listening and I was afraid. So I gulped it down, blood, saliva and all, and continued. (What powers of endurance I had during those days! What enthusiasm! What a belief in the rightness of things!) I spoke even louder in spite of the pain. But still they talked and still they laughed, as though deaf with cotton in dirty ears. So I spoke with greater emotional emphasis. I closed my ears and swallowed blood until I was nauseated. The speech seemed a hundred times as long as before, but I could not leave out a single word. All had to be said, each memorized nuance considered, rendered. Nor was that all. Whenever I uttered a word of three or more syllables a group of voices would yell for me to repeat it. I used the phrase "social responsibility" and they yelled:

"What's that word you say, boy?"

"Social responsibility," I said.

"What?"

"Social . . ."

"Louder."

". . . responsibility."

"More!"

"Respon—"

"Repeat!"

"—sibility."

The room filled with the uproar of laughter until, no doubt, distracted by having to gulp down my blood, I made a mistake and yelled a phrase I had often seen denounced in newspaper editorials, heard debated in private.

"Social . . ."

"What?" they yelled.

"... equality—"

The laughter hung smokelike in the sudden stillness. I opened my eyes, puzzled. Sounds of displeasure filled the room. The M.C. rushed forward. They shouted hostile phrases at me. But I did not understand.

A small dry mustached man in the front row blared out, "Say that slowly, son!"

"What sir?"

"What you just said!"

"Social responsibility, sir," I said.

"You weren't being smart, were you, boy?" he said, not unkindly.

"No, sir!"

"You sure that about 'equality' was a mistake?"

"Oh, yes, sir", I said. "I was swallowing blood."

"Well, you had better speak more slowly so we can understand. We mean to do right by you, but you've got to know your place at all times. All right, now, go on with your speech."

I was afraid. I wanted to leave but I wanted also to speak and I was afraid they'd snatch me down.

"Thank you, sir," I said, beginning where I had left off, and having them ignore me as before.

Yet when I finished there was a thunderous applause. I was surprised to see the superintendent come forth with a package wrapped in white tissue paper, and, gesturing for quiet, address the men.

"Gentlemen, you see that I did not overpraise this boy. He makes a good speech and some day he'll lead his people in the proper paths. And I don't have to tell you that that is important in these days and times. This is a good, smart boy, and so to encourage him in the right direction, in the name of the Board of Education I wish to present him a prize in the form of this ..."

He paused, removing the tissue paper and revealing a gleaming calfskin brief case.

"... in the form of this first-class article from Shad Whitmore's shop."

"Boy," he said, addressing me, "take this prize and keep it well. Consider it a badge of office. Prize it. Keep developing as you are and some day it will be filled with important papers that will help shape the destiny of your people."

I was so moved that I could hardly express my thanks. A rope of bloody saliva forming a shape like an undiscovered continent drooled upon the leather and I wiped it quickly away. I felt an importance that I had never dreamed.

"Open it and see what's inside," I was told.

My fingers a-tremble, I complied, smelling the fresh leather and finding an official-looking document inside. It was a scholarship to the state college for Negroes. My eyes filled with tears and I ran awkwardly off the floor.

I was overjoyed; I did not even mind when I discovered that the gold pieces I had scrambled for were brass pocket tokens advertising a certain make of automobile.

When I reached home everyone was excited. Next day the neighbors came to congratulate me. I even felt safe from grandfather, whose deathbed curse usually spoiled my triumphs. I stood beneath his photograph with my brief case in hand and smiled triumphantly into his stolid black peasant's face. It was a face that fascinated me. The eyes seemed to follow everywhere I went.

That night I dreamed I was at a circus with him and that he refused to laugh at the clowns no matter what they did. Then later he told me to open my brief case and read what was inside and I did, finding an official envelope stamped with the state seal; and inside the envelope I found another and another, endlessly, and I thought I would fall of weariness. "Them's years," he said. "Now open that one." And I did and in it I found an engraved document containing a short message in letters of gold. "Read it," my grandfather said. "Out loud."

"To Whom It May Concern," I intoned. "Keep This Nigger-Boy Running."

I awoke with the old man's laughter ringing in my ears.

(It was a dream I was to remember and dream again for many years after. But at that time I had no insight into its meaning. First I had to attend college.)

Suggestions for Discussion

1. Ellison begins the story by insisting, "It goes a long way back. . . ." Why? What is gained by this temporal distancing?

2. There are two time frames in the story: one for the events recalled, one for the telling. Yet when the narrator describes the smoker, he does so from the viewpoint of himself as a boy, without any adult comment on his memory. Why? How does this alter the distance? What limitations are implied in the boy's perceptions?

3. The narrator tells us that the grandfather's dying words "became a constant puzzle" and that he "had no insight" into the meaning of his dream about his grandfather. How do we as readers understand so clearly what the narrator claims not to have understood and does not explain?

4. Describe the distance, tangible or intangible, of the narrator from each of the following: himself as a boy, the grandfather, the town's leading white citizens, the dancer, and the other boys.

5. Show how the narrator's graduation speech is an extended irony.

6. What is our perspective on the boy's gratitude for the scholarship? How does Ellison manipulate tone to reveal the irony?

7. "Battle Royal" was conceived, not as a short story, but as a chapter in a novel, *Invisible Man*. To what extent does it have the form of a short story, and in what ways is it unresolved?

The Gift
of the Prodigal

PETER TAYLOR

There's Ricky down in the washed river gravel of my driveway. I had my yardman out raking it before 7 A.M.—the driveway. It looks nearly perfect. Ricky also looks nearly perfect down there. He looks extremely got up and cleaned up, as though he had been carefully raked over and smoothed out. He is wearing a three-piece linen suit, which my other son, you may be sure, wouldn't be seen wearing on any occasion. And he has on an expensive striped shirt, open at the collar. No tie, of course, His thick head of hair, parted and slicked down, is just the same tan color as the gravel. Hair and gravel seem equally clean and in order. The fact is, Ricky looks this morning as though he belongs nowhere else in the world but out there in that smooth spread of washed river gravel (which will be mussed up again before noon, of course—I'm resigned to it), looks as though he feels perfectly at home in that driveway of mine that was so expensive to install and that requires so much upkeep.

Since one can't see his freckles from where I stand at this second-story window, his skin looks very fair—almost transparent. (Ricky just misses being a real redhead, and so never lets himself get suntanned. Bright sunlight tends to give him skin cancers.) From the window directly above him, I am able to get the full effect of his outfit. He looks very masculine standing down there, which is no doubt the impression his formfitting clothes are meant to give. And Ricky *is* very masculine, no matter what else he is or isn't. Peering down from up here, I mark particularly that where his collar stands open, and with several shirt buttons left carelessly or carefully undone, you can see a triangle of darker hair glistening on his chest. It isn't hard to imagine just how recently he has stepped out of the shower. In a word, he *is* looking what he considers his very best. And this says to me that Ricky is coming to me *for* something, or *because of* something.

His little sports car is parked in the turnaround behind this house, which I've built since he and the other children grew up and since their mother died. I know of course that, for them, coming here to see me can never really be like coming home. For Rick it must be like going to see any other old fellow who might happen to be his boss and who is ailing and is staying away from the office for a few days. As soon as I saw him down there, though, I knew something was really seriously wrong. From here I could easily recognize the expression on his face. He has a way, when he is concerned about something, of knitting his eyebrows and at the same time opening his eyes very wide, as though his eyes are about to pop out of his head and his eyebrows are trying to hold them in. It's a look that used to give him away even as a child when he was in trouble at school. If his mother and I saw that expression on his face, we would know that we were apt to be rung up by one of his teachers in a day or so or maybe have a house call from one of them.

Momentarily Ricky massages his face with his big right hand, as if to wipe away the expression. And clearly now he is headed for the side door that opens on the driveway. But before actually coming over to the door he has stopped in one spot and keeps shuffling his suede shoes about, roughing up the smooth gravel, like a young bull in a pen. I almost call out to him not to *do* that, not to muss up my gravel, which even his car wheels haven't disturbed—or not so much as he is doing with his suede shoes. I *almost* call out to him. But of course I don't really. For Ricky is a man twenty-nine years old, with two divorces already and no doubt another coming up soon. He's been through all that, besides a series of live-ins between marriages that I don't generally speak of, even.

For some time before coming on into the house, Ricky remains there in that spot in the driveway. While he stands there, it occurs to me that he may actually be looking the place over, as though he'd never noticed what this house is like until now. The old place on Wertland Street, where he and the other children grew up, didn't have half the style and convenience of this one. It had more room, but the room was mostly in pantries and hallways, with front stairs and back stairs and third-floor servants' quarters in an age when no servant would be caught dead living up there in the attic—or staying anywhere else on the place, for that matter. I am not unaware, of course, how much better that old house on Wertland was than this one. You couldn't have replaced it for twice what I've poured into this compact and well-appointed habitation out here in Farmington. But its neighborhood had gone bad. Nearly all of Charlottesville proper has, as a matter of fact, either gone commercial or been absorbed by the university.

You can no longer live within the shadow of Mr. Jefferson's Academical Village. And our old Wertland Street house is now a funeral parlor. Which is what it ought to have been five years before I left it. From the day my wife, Cary, died, the place seemed like a tomb. I wandered up and down the stairs and all around, from room to room, sometimes greeting myself in one of Cary's looking glasses, doing so out of loneliness or out of thinking *that* couldn't be *me* still in my dresing gown and slippers at midday, or fully dressed—necktie and all—at 3 A.M. I knew well enough it was time to sell. And, besides, I wanted to have the experience at last of making something new. You see, we never built a house of our own, Cary and I. We always bought instead of building, wishing to be in an established neighborhood, you know, where there were good day schools for the girls (it was before St. Anne's moved to the suburbs), where there were streetcars and buses for the servants, or, better still, an easy walk for them to Ridge Street.

My scheme for building a new house after Cary died seemed a harebrained idea to my three older children. They tried to talk me out of it. They said I was only doing it out of idleness. They'd laugh and say I'd chosen a rather expensive form of entertainment for myself in my old age. That's what they *said*. That wasn't all they *thought*, however. But I never held against them what they thought. All motherless children—regardless of age—have such thoughts. They had in mind that I'd got notions of marrying again. Me! Why, I've never looked at another woman since the day I married. Not to this very hour. At any rate, one night when we were having dinner and they were telling me how they worried about me, and making it plainer than usual what they thought my plans for the future were or might be, Ricky spoke up—Ricky who never gave a thought in his life to what happened to anybody except himself—and he came out with just what was on the others' minds. "What if you should take a notion to marry again?" he asked. And I began shaking my head before the words were out of his mouth, as did all the others. It was an unthinkable thought for them as well as for me. "Why not?" Ricky persisted, happy of course that he was making everyone uncomfortable. "Worse things have happened, you know. And I nominate the handsome Mrs. Capers as a likely candidate for bride."

I *think* he was referring to a certain low sort of woman who had recently moved into the old neighborhood. You could depend upon Ricky to know about her and know her name. As he spoke he winked at me. Presently he crammed his wide mouth full of food, and as he chewed he made a point of drawing back his lips and showing his somewhat overlarge and overly white front teeth. He continued to look straight at me as he chewed, but looking with only one eye, keeping the eye he'd winked at me squinched up tight. He looked for all the world like some old tomcat who's found a nasty morsel he likes the taste of and *is* not going to let go of. I willingly would have knocked him out of his chair for what he'd said, even more for that common look he was giving me. I knew he knew as well as the others that I'd never looked at any woman besides his mother.

Yet I laughed with the others as soon as I realized they were laughing. You don't let a fellow like Ricky know he's got your goat—especially when he's your own son, and has been in one bad scrape after another ever since he's been grown, and seems always just waiting for a chance to get back at you for something censorious you may have said to him while trying to help him out of one of his escapades. Since Cary died, I've tried mostly just to keep lines of communication open with him. I think that's the thing she would have wanted of me—that is, not to shut Rick out, to keep him talking. Cary used to say to me, "You may be the only person he can talk to about the women he gets involved with. He can't talk to me about such things." Cary always thought it was the women he had most on his mind and who got him into scrapes. I never used to think so. Anyway, I believe that Cary would have wished above all else for me to keep lines open with Rick, would have wanted it even more than she would have wanted me to go ahead in whatever way I chose with schemes for a new house for my old age.

The house was *our* plan originally, you see, hers and mine. It was something we never told the children about. There seemed no reason why we should. Not talking about it except between ourselves was part of the pleasure of it, somehow. And that night when Ricky came out with the speculation about my possibly marrying again, I didn't tell him or the others that actually I had already sold the Wertland Street house and already had blueprints for the new house here in Farmington locked away in my desk drawer, and even a contractor all set to break ground.

Well, my new house was finished the following spring. By that time all the children, excepting Rick, had developed a real enthusiasm for it. (Rick didn't give a damn one way or the other, of course.) They helped me dispose of all the superfluous furniture in the old house. The girls even saw to the details of moving and saw to it that I got comfortably settled in. They wanted me to be happy out here. And soon enough they saw I was. There was no more they could do for me now than there had been in recent years. They had their good marriages to look after (that's what Cary would have wished for them), and they saw to it that I wasn't left out of whatever of their activities I wanted to be in on. In a word, they went on with their busy lives, and my own life seemed busy enough for any man my age.

What has vexed the other children, though, during the five years since I built my house, is their brother Ricky's continuing to come to me at almost regular intervals with new ordeals of one kind or another that he's been going through. They have thought he ought not to burden me with his outrageous and sometimes sordid affairs. I think they have especially resented his troubling me here at home. I still go to the office, you see, two or three days a week—just whenever I feel like it or when I'm not playing golf or bridge or am not off on a little trip to Sarasota (I stay at the same inn Cary and I used to go to). And so I've always seen Ricky quite regularly at the office. He's had every chance to talk to me there. But the fact is Rick was never one for bringing his personal problems to the office. He has always brought them home.

Even since I've moved, he has always come *here,* to the house, when he's really wanted to talk to me about something. I don't know whether it's the two servants I still keep or some of the young neighbors hereabouts who tell them, but somehow the other children always know when Ricky has been here. And they of course can put two and two together. It will come out over Sunday dinner at one of their houses or at the Club—in one of those little private dining rooms. It is all right if we eat in the big dining room, where everybody else is. I know I'm safe there. But as soon as I see they've reserved a private room I know they want to talk about Ricky's latest escapade. They will begin by making veiled references to it among themselves. But at last it is I who am certain to let the cat out of the bag. For I can't resist joining in when they get onto Rick, as they all know very well I won't be able to. You see, often they will have the details wrong—maybe they get them wrong on purpose—and I feel obliged to straighten them out. Then one of them will turn to me, pretending shocked surprise: "How ever did you know about it? Has *he* been bringing his troubles to *you* again? At his age you'd think he'd be ashamed to! Someone ought to remind him he's a grown man now!" At that point one of the girls is apt to rest her hand on mine. As they go on, I can hear the love for me in their voices and see it in their eyes. I know then what a lucky man I am. I want to say to them that their affection makes up for all the unhappiness Ricky causes me. But I have never been one to make speeches like that. Whenever I have managed to say such things, I have somehow always felt like a hypocrite afterward. Anyway, the talk will go on for a while till I remember a bridge game I have an appointment for in the Club lounge, at two o'clock. Or I recall that my golf foursome is waiting for me in the locker room.

I've never tried to defend Rick from the others. The things he does are really quite indefensible. Sometimes I've even found myself giving details about some escapade of his that the others didn't already know and are genuinely shocked to hear—especially coming from me. He was in a shooting once that everybody in Farmington and in the whole county set knew about—or knew about, that is, in a general way, though without knowing the very thing that would finally make it a public scandal. It's an ugly story, I warn you, as, indeed, nearly all of Ricky's stories are.

He had caught another fellow in bed with a young married woman with whom he himself was running around. Of course it was a scandalous business, all of it. But the girl, as Rick described her to me afterward, was a real beauty of a certain type and, according to Rick, as smart as a whip. Rick even showed me her picture, though I hadn't asked to see it, naturally. She had a tight little mouth, and eyes that—even in that wallet-sized picture—burned themselves into your memory. She was the sort of intense and reckless-looking girl that Ricky has always gone for. I've sometimes looked at pictures of his other girls, too, when he wanted to show them to me. And of course I know what his wives have looked like. All three of his wives have been from good families. For, bad as he is, Ricky is not the sort of fellow who would embarrass the rest of us by *marrying* some slut. Yet even his wives have tended to dress themselves in a way that my own daughters wouldn't. They have dressed, that is to say, in clothes that seemed designed to call attention to their female forms and not, as with my daughters, to call attention to the station and the affluence of their husbands. Being the timid sort of man I am, I used to find myself whenever I talked with his wife—whichever one—carefully looking out the window or looking across the room, away from her, at some inanimate object or other over there or out there. My wife, Cary, used to say that Ricky had bad luck in his wives, that each of them turned out to have just as roving an eye as Ricky himself. I can't say for certain whether this was true for each of them in the beginning or whether it was something Ricky managed to teach them all.

Anyway, the case of the young married woman in whose bed—or apartment—Ricky found that other fellow came near to causing Ricky more trouble than any of his other escapades. The fellow ran out of the apartment, with Rick chasing him into the corridor and down the corridor to a door of an outside stairway. It was not here in Farmington, you see, but out on Barracks Road, where so many of Rick's friends are—in a development that's been put up on the very edge of where the horse farms begin. The fellow scurried down the outside stairs and across a parking lot toward some pastureland beyond. And Rick, as he said, couldn't resist taking a shot at him from that upstairs stoop where he had abandoned the chase. He took aim just when the fellow reached the first pasture fence and was about to climb over. Afterward, Rick said that it was simply too good to miss. But Rick rarely misses a target when he takes aim. He hit the fellow with a load of rat shot right in the seat of the pants.

I'll never know how Rick happened to have the gun with him. He told me that he was deeply in love with the young woman and would have married her if her husband had been willing to give her a divorce. The other children maintain to this day that it was the husband Rick meant to threaten with the gun, but the husband was out of town and Rick lost his head when he found the other fellow there in his place. Anyhow, the story got all over town. I suppose Ricky himself helped to spread it. He thought it all awfully funny at first. But before it was over, the matter came near to getting into the courts and into the paper. And that was because there was something else involved, which the other children and the people in the Barracks Road set didn't know about and I did. In fact, it was something that I worried about from the beginning. You see, Rick naturally took that fellow he'd blasted with the rat shot to a doctor — a young doctor friend of theirs — who removed the shot. But, being a friend, the doctor didn't report the incident. A certain member of our judiciary heard the details and thought perhaps the matter needed looking into. We were months getting it straightened out. Ricky went out of town for a while, and the young doctor ended by having to move away permanently — to Richmond or Norfolk, I think. I only give this incident in such detail in order to show the sort of low company Ricky has always kept, even when he seemed to be among our own sort.

His troubles haven't all involved women, though. Or not primarily. And that's what I used to tell Cary. Like so many people in Charlottesville, Rick has always had a weakness for horses. For a while he fancied himself a polo player. He bought a polo pony and got cheated on it. He bought it at a stable where he kept another horse he owned — bought it from the man who ran the stable. After a day or so, he found that the animal was a worthless, worn-out nag. It couldn't even last through the first chukker, which was humiliating of course for Ricky. He daren't try to take it onto the field again. It had been all doped up when he bought it. Ricky was outraged. Instead of simply trying to get his money back, he wanted to have his revenge upon the man and make an even bigger fool of *him*. He persuaded a friend to dress himself up in a turtleneck sweater and a pair of yellow jodhpurs and pretend just to be passing by the stall in the same stable where the polo pony was still kept. His friend played the role, you see, of someone only just taking up the game and who thought he *had* to have that particular pony. He asked the man whose animal it was, and before he could get an answer he offered more than twice the price that Rick had paid. He even put the offer into writing — using an assumed name, of course. He said he was from up in Maryland and would return in two days' time. Naturally, the stable-man telephoned Ricky as soon as the stranger in jodhpurs had left the stable. He said he had discovered, to his chagrin, that the pony was not in as good condition as he had thought it was. And he said that in order that there be no bad feeling between them he was willing to buy it back for the price Ricky had paid.

Ricky went over that night and collected his money. But when the stranger didn't reappear and couldn't be traced, the stableman of course knew what had happened. Rick didn't return to the stable during the following several days. I suppose, being Ricky, he was busy spreading the story all over town. His brother and sisters got wind of it. And I did soon enough. On Sunday night, two thugs and some woman Ricky knew but would never identify—not even to me—came to his house and persuaded him to go out and sit in their car with them in front of his house. And there they beat him brutally. He had to be in the hospital for five or six days. They broke his right arm, and one of them—maybe it was the woman— was trying to bite off the lobe of his left ear when Ricky's current wife, who had been out to some party without the favor of his company, pulled into the driveway beside his house. The assailants shoved poor Ricky, bruised and bleeding and with his arm broken, out onto the sidewalk. And then of course they sped away down the street in their rented car. Ricky's wife and the male friend who was with her got the license number, but the car had been rented under an assumed name—the same name, actually, as some kind of joke, I suppose, that Ricky's friend in jodhpurs had used with the stablekeeper.

Since Ricky insisted that he could not possibly recognize his two male assailants in a lineup, and since he refused to identify the woman, there was little that could be done about his actual beating. I don't know that he ever confessed to anyone but me that he knew the woman. It was easy enough for me to imagine what *she* looked like. Though I would not have admitted it to Ricky or to anyone else, I would now and then during the following weeks see a woman of a certain type on the streets downtown—with one of those tight little mouths and with burning eyes—and imagine that she might be the very one. All we were ever able to do about the miserable fracas was to see to it finally that that stable was put out of business and that the man himself had to go elsewhere (he went down into North Carolina) to ply his trade.

There is one other scrape of Ricky's that I must mention, because it remains particularly vivid for me. The nature and the paraphernalia of this one will seem even more old-fashioned than those of the other incidents. Maybe that's why it sticks in my mind so. It's something that might have happened to any number of rough fellows I knew when I was coming along.

Ricky, not surprising to say, likes to gamble. From the time he was a young boy he would often try to inveigle one of the other children into making wagers with him on how overdone his steak was at dinner. He always liked it very rare and when his serving came he would hold up a bite on his fork and, for a decision on the bet, would ask everyone what shade of brown the meat was. He made all the suggestions of color himself. And one night his suggestions got so coarse and vile his mother had to send him from the dining room and not let him have a bite of supper. Sometimes he would try to get the other children to bet with him on the exact number of minutes the parson's sermon would last on Sunday or how many times the preacher would use the word "Hell" or "damnation" or "adultery." Since he has got grown, it's the races, of course, he likes—horse races, it goes without saying, but also such low-life affairs as dog races and auto races. What catches his fancy above all else, though, are the chicken fights we have always had in our part of the country. And a few years ago he bought himself a little farm a dozen miles or so south of town where he could raise his own game chickens. I saw nothing wrong with that at the time. Then he built an octagonal barn down there, with a pit in it where he could hold the fights. I worried a little when he did that. But we've always had cockfights hereabouts. The birds are beautiful creatures, really, though they have no brains, of course. The fight itself is a real spectacle and no worse than some other things people enjoy. At Ricky's urging, I even went down to two or three fights at his place. I didn't bet, because I knew the stakes were very high. (Besides, it's the betting that's illegal.) And I didn't tell the other children about my going. But this was after Cary was dead, you see, and I thought maybe she would have liked my going for Ricky's sake, though she would never have acknowledged it. Pretty soon, sizable crowds began attending the fights on weekend nights. Cars would be parked all over Ricky's front pasture and all around the yard of the tenant house. He might as well have put up a sign down at the gate where his farm road came off the highway.

The point is, everyone knew that the cockfights went on. And one of his most regular customers and biggest bettors was one of the county sheriff's right-hand men. I'm afraid Rick must have bragged about that in advertising his fights to friends—friends who would otherwise have been a little timid about coming. And during the fights he would move about among the crowd, winking at people and saying to them under his breath, "The deputy's here tonight." I suppose it was his way of reassuring them that everything was all right. I don't know whether or not his spreading the word so widely had anything to do with the raid, but nevertheless the deputy was present the night the federal officers came stealing up the farm road, with their car lights off and with search warrants in their pockets. And it was the deputy who first got wind of the federal officers' approach. He had one of his sidekicks posted outside the barn. Maybe he had somebody watching out there every night that he came. Maybe all along he had had a plan for his escape in such an emergency. Rick thought so afterward. Anyhow, the deputy's man outside knew at once what those cars moving up the lane with their lights off meant. The deputy got the word before anyone else, but, depend upon Ricky, he saw the first move the deputy made to leave. And he was not going to have it. He took out after him.

The deputy's watchman was prepared to stay on and take his chances. (He wasn't even a patrolman. He probably only worked in the office.) I imagine he was prepared to spend a night in jail if necessary, and pay whatever fine there might be, because his presence could explain one of the sheriff's cars' being parked in the pasture. But the deputy himself took off through the backwoods on Ricky's property and toward a county road on the back of the place. Ricky, as I've said, was not going to have that. Since the cockfight was on his farm, he knew there was no way out of trouble for himself. But he thought it couldn't, at least, do him any harm to have the deputy caught along with everybody else. Moreover, the deputy had lost considerable amounts of money there at the pit in recent weeks and had insinuated to Ricky that he suspected some of the cocks had been tampered with. (I, personally, don't believe Ricky would stand for that.) Ricky couldn't be sure there wasn't some collusion between the deputy and the feds. He saw the deputy's man catch the deputy's eye from the barn doorway and observed the deputy's departure. He was right after him. He overtook him just before he reached the woods. Fortunately, the deputy wasn't armed. (Ricky allowed no one to bring a gun inside the barn.) And fortunately Ricky wasn't armed, either, that night. They scuffled a little near the gate to the woods lot. The deputy, being a man twice Rick's age, was no match for him and was soon overpowered. Ricky dragged him back to the barn, himself resisting—as he later testified—all efforts at bribery on the deputy's part, and turned in both himself and his captive to the federal officers.

Extricating Ricky from that affair and setting matters aright was a long and complicated undertaking. The worst of it really began for Ricky after the court proceedings were finished and all fines were paid (there were no jail terms for anyone), because from his last appearance in the federal courthouse Ricky could drive his car scarcely one block through that suburb where he lives without receiving a traffic ticket of some kind. There may not have been anything crooked about it, for Ricky is a wild sort of driver at best. But, anyhow, within a short time his driving license was revoked for the period of a year. Giving up driving was a great inconvenience for him and a humiliation. All we could do about the deputy, who, Ricky felt sure, had connived with the federal officers, was to get him out of his job after the next election.

The outcome of the court proceedings was that Rick's fines were very heavy. Moreover, efforts were made to confiscate all the livestock on his farm, as well as the farm machinery. But he was saved from the confiscation by a special circumstance, which, however, turned out to produce for him only a sort of Pyrrhic victory. It turned out, you see, that the farm was not in Ricky's name but in that of his young tenant farmer's wife. I never saw her, or didn't know it if I did. Afterward, I used to try to recall if I hadn't seen some such young woman when I was down watching the cockfights—one who would have fitted the picture in my mind. My imagination played tricks on me, though. I would think I remembered the face or figure of some young girl I'd seen there who could conceivably be the one. But then suddenly I'd recall another and think possibly it might be she who had the title to Ricky's farm. I never could be sure.

When Ricky appeared outside my window just now, I'd already had a very bad morning. The bursitis in my right shoulder had waked me before dawn. At last I got up and dressed, which was an ordeal in itself. (My right hip was hurting somewhat, too.) When finally the cook came in, she wanted to give me a massage before she began fixing breakfast even. Cary would never have allowed her to make that mistake. A massage, you see, is the worst thing you can do for my sort of bursitis. What I wanted was some breakfast. And I knew it would take Meg three quarters of an hour to put breakfast on the table. And so I managed to get out of my clothes again and ease myself into a hot bath, groaning so loud all the while that Meg came up to the door twice and asked if I was all right. I told her just to go and get my breakfast ready. After breakfast, I waited till a decent hour and then telephoned one of my golf foursome to tell him I couldn't play today. It's this damp fall weather that does us in worst. All you can do is sit and think how you've got the whole winter before you and wonder if you'll be able to get yourself off to someplace like Sarasota.

While I sat at a front window, waiting for the postman (he never brings anything but circulars and catalogs on Saturday; besides, all my serious mail goes to the office and is opened by someone else), I found myself thinking of all the things I couldn't do and all the people who are dead and that I mustn't think about. I tried to do a little better—that is, to think of something cheerful. There was lots I *could* be cheerful about, wasn't there? At least three of my children were certain to telephone today—all but Ricky, and it was sure to be bad news if he did! And a couple of the grandchildren would likely call, too. Then tomorrow I'd be going to lunch with some of them if I felt up to it. Suddenly I thought of the pills I was supposed to have taken before breakfast and had forgotten to: the Inderal and the potassium and the hydrochlorothiazide. I began to get up from my chair and then I settled down again. It didn't really matter. There was no ailment I had that could really be counted on to be fatal if I missed one day's dosage. And then I wholeheartedly embraced the old subject, the old speculation: How many days like this one, how many years like this one lay ahead for me? And finally, irresistibly, I descended to lower depths still, thinking of past times not with any relish but remembering how in past times I had always *told* myself I'd someday look back with pleasure on what would seem good old days, which was an indication itself that they hadn't somehow been good enough—not good enough, that is, to stand on their own as an end in themselves. If the old days were so damned good, why had I had to think always how good they would someday seem in retrospect? I had just reached the part where I think there was nothing *wrong* with them and that I ought to be satisfied, had just reached that point at which I recall that I loved and was loved by my wife, that I love and am loved by my children, that it's not them or my life but *me* there's something wrong with!—had just reached that inevitable syllogism that I always come to, when I was distracted by the arrival of Saturday morning's late mail delivery. It was brought in, it was handed to me by a pair of black hands, and of course it had nothing in it. But I took it upstairs to my sitting room. (So that even the servant wouldn't see there was nothing worth having in it.) I had just closed my door and got out my pills when I heard Ricky's car turn into the gravel driveway.

He was driving so slowly that his car wheels hardly disturbed the gravel. That in itself was an ominous phenomenon. He was approaching slowly and quietly. He didn't want me to know ahead of time what there was in store for me. My first impulse was to lock my door and refuse to admit him. I simply did not feel up to Rick this morning! But I said to myself, "That's something I've never done, though maybe ought to have done years ago no matter what Cary said. He's sure to send my blood pressure soaring." I thought of picking up the telephone and phoning one of the other children to come and protect me from this monster of a son and from whatever sort of trouble he was now in.

But it was just then that I caught my first glimpse of him down in the driveway. I had the illusion that he was admiring the place. And then of course I was at once disillusioned. He was only hesitating down there because he dreaded seeing me. But he was telling himself he *had* to see me. There would be no other solution to his problem but to see his old man. I knew what he was thinking by the gesture he was making with his left hand. It's strange how you get the notion that your children are like you just because they have the same facial features and the same gestures when talking to themselves. None of it means a thing! It's only an illusion. Even now I find myself making gestures with my hands when I'm talking to myself that I used to notice my own father making sometimes when we were out walking together and neither of us had spoken a word for half an hour or so. It used to get on my nerves when I saw Father do it, throwing out his hand almost imperceptibly, with his long fingers spread apart. I don't know why it got on my nerves so. But, anyhow, I never dreamed that I could inherit such a gesture—or much less that one of my sons would. And yet there Ricky is, down in the driveway, making that same gesture precisely. And there never were three men with more different characters than my father and me and my youngest child. I watch Ricky make the gesture several times while standing in the driveway. And now suddenly he turns as if to go back to his car. I step away from the window, hoping he hasn't seen me and will go on off. But, having once seen him down there, I can't, of course, do that. I have to receive him and hear him out. I open the sash and call down to him, "Come on up, Ricky."

He looks up at me, smiles guiltily, and shrugs. Then he comes on in the side entrance. As he moves through the house and up the stairs, I try to calm myself. I gaze down at the roughed-up gravel where his suede shoes did their damage and tell myself it isn't so bad and even manage to smile at my old-maidishness. Presently, he comes into the sitting room. We greet each other with the usual handshake. I can smell his shaving lotion. Or maybe it is something he puts on his hair. We go over and sit down by the fireplace, where there is a fire laid but not lit in this season, of course. He begins by talking about everything under the sun except what is on his mind. This is standard procedure in our talks at such times. Finally, he begins looking into the fireplace as though the fire were lit and as though he were watching low-burning flames. I barely keep myself from smiling when he says, "I've got a little problem — not so damned little, in fact. It's a matter that's got out of hand."

And then I say, "I supposed as much."

You can't give Ricky an inch at these times, you see. Else he'll take advantage of you. Pretty soon he'll have shifted the whole burden of how he's to be extricated onto your shoulders. I wait for him to continue, and he is about to, I think. But before he can get started he turns his eyes away from the dry logs and the unlit kindling and begins looking about the room, just as he looked about the premises outside. It occurs to me again that he seem to be observing my place for the very first time. But I don't suppose he really is. His mind is, as usual, on himself. Then all at once his eyes do obviously come to focus on something over my shoulder. He runs his tongue up under his upper lip and then under his lower lip, as though he were cleaning his teeth. I, involuntarily almost, look over my shoulder. There on the library table behind me, on what I call my desk, are my cut-glass tumbler and three bottles of pills — my hydrochlorothiazide, my Inderal, and my potassium. Somehow I failed to put them back in my desk drawer earlier. I was so distracted by my morbid thoughts when I came upstairs that I forgot to stick them away in the place where I keep them out of sight from everybody. (I don't even like for the servants to see what and how much medicine I take.) Without a word passing between us, and despite the pains in my shoulder and hip, I push myself up out of my chair and sweep the bottles, and the tumbler, too, into the desk drawer. I keep my back to Ricky for a minute or so till I can overcome the grimacing I never can repress when these pains strike. Suddenly, though, I do turn back to him and find he has come to his feet. I pay no special attention to that. I ease myself back into my chair saying, "Yes, Ricky." Making my voice rather hard, I say, "You've got a problem?" He looks at me coldly, without a trace of the sympathy any one of the other children would have shown — knowing, that is, as he surely does, that I am having pains of some description. And he speaks to me as though I were a total stranger toward whom he feels nothing but is just barely human enough to wish not to torture. "Man," he says—the idea of his addressing *me* that way!—"Man, you've got problems enough of your own. Even the world's greatest snotface can see that. One thing sure, you don't need to hear *my* crap."

I am on my feet so quick you wouldn't think I have a pain in my body. "Don't you use that gutter language with me, Ricky!" I say. "You weren't brought up in some slum over beyond Vinegar Hill!" He only turns and looks into the fireplace again. If there were a fire going I reckon he would have spat in it at this point. Then he looks back at me, running his tongue over his teeth again. And then, without any apology or so much as a by-your-leave, he heads for the door. "Come back here, Ricky!" I command. "Don't you dare leave the room!" Still moving toward the closed door, he glances back over his shoulder at me, with a wide, hard grin on his face, showing his mouthful of white teeth, as though my command were the funniest thing he has ever heard. At the door, he puts his big right hand on the glass knob, covering it entirely. Then he twists his upper body, his torso, around—seemingly just from the hips—to face me. And simultaneously he brings up his left hand and scratches that triangle of dark hair where his shirt is open. It is like some kind of dirty gesture he is making. I say to myself, "He really is like something not quite human. For all the jams and scrapes he's been in, he's never suffered any second thoughts or known the meaning of remorse. I ought to have let him hang," I say to myself, "by his own beautiful locks."

But almost simultaneously what I hear myself saying aloud is "Please don't go, Rick. Don't go yet, son." Yes, I am pleading with him, and I mean what I say with my whole heart. He still has his right hand on the doorknob and has given it a full turn. Our eyes meet across the room, directly, as they never have before in the whole of Ricky's life or mine. I think neither of us could tell anyone what it is he sees in the other's eyes, unless it is a need beyond any description either of us is capable of.

Presently Rick says, "You don't need to hear my crap."

And I hear my bewildered voice saying, "I do . . . I do." And "Don't go, Rick, my boy." My eyes have even misted over. But I still meet his eyes across the now too silent room. He looks at me in the most compassionate way imaginable. I don't think any child of mine has ever looked at me so before. Or perhaps it isn't really with compassion he is viewing me but with the sudden, gratifying knowledge that it is not, after all, such a one-sided business, the business between us. He keeps his right hand on the doorknob a few seconds longer. Then I hear the latch click and know he has let go. Meanwhile, I observe his left hand making that familiar gesture, his fingers splayed, his hand tilting back and forth. I am out of my chair by now. I go to the desk and bring out two Danlys cigars from another desk drawer, which I keep locked. He is there ready to receive my offering when I turn around. He accepts the cigar without smiling, and I give it without smiling, too. Seated opposite each other again, each of us lights his own.

And then Ricky begins. What will it be this time, I think. I am wild with anticipation. Whatever it will be, I know it is all anyone in the world can give me now—perhaps the most anyone has ever been able to give a man like me. As Ricky begins, I try to think of all the good things the other children have done for me through the years and of their affection, and of my wife's. But it seems this was all there ever was. I forget my pains and my pills, and the canceled golf game, and the meaningless mail that morning. I find I can scarcely sit still in my chair for wanting Ricky to get on with it. Has he been brandishing his pistol again? Or dragging the sheriff's deputy across a field at midnight? And does he have in his wallet perhaps a picture of some other girl with a tight little mouth, and eyes that burn? Will his outrageous story include her? And perhaps explain it, leaving her a blessed mystery? As Ricky begins, I find myself listening not merely with fixed attention but with my whole being. . . . I hear him beginning. I am listening. I am listening gratefully to all he will tell me about himself, about any life that is not my own.

Suggestions for Discussion

1. Describe the spatial and temporal distance of "The Gift of the Prodigal." What function does the present tense serve? Try recasting a passage here and there in the past tense ("Ricky was down there in the washed river gravel of my driveway. I had had my yardman out raking it before 7 a.m.—the driveway. It looked nearly perfect.") How would using the past tense alter the reversal and resolution of this story?

2. If spatial and temporal distance are very close here, authorial distance is not. Consider the distance between the narrator and the author. What do you infer that the author would say about the relationship between father and son that the narrator does not and would not say?

3. At what point do you begin to anticipate that you will not quite share the narrator's assessment of his son? How does Taylor accomplish this?

4. The narrator says, "As soon as I saw him down there, though, I knew something was really seriously wrong." Apparently this judgment is quite accurate, as it turns out. How and why, then, do we feel that the narrator is nevertheless limited in his judgment?

5. Does the narrator contradict himself? Does he ever actually lie?

6. What details of the rat shot, polo pony, and cockfight incidents incline you to admire Ricky, which to condemn him?

7. Analyze the three paragraphs beginning "Even since I've moved ..." on pages 295-296. How does the narrator feel about Ricky's brother, sisters, and wives? How do you feel? How does Taylor direct you toward these judgments?

8. How complex is your ultimate view of Ricky? The narrator?

RETROSPECT

1. How many time periods are involved in "The Masked Marvel's Last Toehold"? To what extent does the narrator retain an adult perspective on the child's experience? To what extent does he enter that experience and see it from the child's viewpoint?

2. How would you describe the authorial distance of "The Bella Lingua"? How do time, place, and tone affect and inform that distance?

3. "The Power" is written in the third person limited omniscient; therefore, it is an "author" telling the story. Nevertheless, because we are seeing through Medea's eyes, the language is largely hers. Try to describe the authorial distance that this technique achieves. What does the author report as fact, for instance, that he does not necessarily accept as fact?

WRITING ASSIGNMENTS

1. Choose a crucial incident from a child's life (your own or invented) and write about it from the temporally distanced perspective of an adult narrator.

2. Rewrite the same incident in the child's language from the point of view of the child as narrator.

3. Write a passage from the point of view of a central narrator who is spatially distanced from the events she or he describes. Make the contrast significant—write of a sea voyage from prison, of home from an alien country, of a closet from a mountaintop, or the like.

4. Write a short scene from the point of view of anything nonhuman (a plant, object, animal, Martian, angel). We may sympathize or not with the perceptions of the narrator, but try to imagine yourself into the terms, logic, and frame of reference this character would use.

5. Write from the point of view of a narrator who passes scathing judgments on another character, but let us know that the narrator really loves or envies the other.

6. Let your narrator begin with a totally unacceptable premise—illogical, ignorant, bigoted, insane. In the passage, let us gradually come to sympathize with his or her view.

7. Take any assignment you have previously done and recast it from another point of view. This may (but will not simply) involve changing the person in which it is written. Alter the means of perception or point-of-view character so that we have an entirely different perspective on the events. But let your attitude as author remain the same.

9

IS AND IS NOT
Comparison

Types of Metaphor and Simile
Metaphoric Faults to Avoid
Allegory
Symbol
The Objective Correlative

As the concept of distance implies, every reader reading is a self-deceiver. We simultaneously "believe" a story and know that it is a fiction, a fabrication. Our belief in the reality of the story may be so strong that it produces physical reactions—tears, trembling, sighs, gasps, a headache. At the same time, as long as the fiction is working for us, we know that our submission is voluntary; that we have, as Samuel Taylor Coleridge pointed out, suspended disbelief. "It's just a *movie*," says the exasperated father as he takes his shrieking six-year-old out to the lobby. For the father the fiction is working; for the child it is not.

The necessity of disbelief was demonstrated for me some years ago with the performance of a play that ended with too "good" a hanging. The harness was too well hidden, the actor too adept at purpling and bloating his face when the trap fell. Consternation rippled through the audience:

my God, they've hanged the *actor*. Because the illusion was too like reality the illusion was destroyed, and the audience was jolted from its belief in the story back into the real world of the performance.

Simultaneous belief and awareness of illusion are present in both the content and the craft of literature, and what is properly called artistic pleasure derives from the tension of this *is and is not*.

The content of a plot tells us that something happens that does not happen, that people who do not exist behave in such a way, and that the events of life — which we know to be random, unrelated, and unfinished — are necessary, patterned, and come to closure. When someone declares interest or pleasure in a story "because it really happened," he or she is expressing an unartistic and antiartistic preference, subscribing to the lie that events can be accurately translated into the medium of words. Pleasure in artistry comes precisely when the illusion rings true without, however, destroying the knowledge that it is an illusion.

In the same way, the techniques of every art offer us the tension of things that are and are not *alike*. This is true of poetry, in which rhyme is interesting because *tend* sounds like *mend* but not exactly like; it is true of music, whose interest lies in variations on a theme; of composition, where shapes and colors are balanced in asymmetry. And it is the fundamental nature of metaphor, from which literature derives.

Just as the content of a work must not be too like life to destroy the knowledge that it is an illusion, so the likenesses in the formal elements of art must not be too much alike. Rich rhyme, in which *tend* rhymes with *contend* and *pretend*, is boring and restrictive, and virtually no poet chooses to write a whole poem in it. Repetitive tunes jingle; symmetrical compositions tend toward decor.

Metaphor is the literary device by which we are told that something is, or is like, something that it clearly is not, or is not exactly like. What a good metaphor does is surprise us with the unlikeness of the two things compared, while at the same time convincing us of the aptness or truth of the likeness. A bad metaphor fails to surprise or to convince or both.

Types of Metaphor and Simile

The simplest distinction between types of comparison, and usually the first one grasped by beginning students of literature, is between *metaphor* and *simile*. A simile makes a comparison with the use of *like* or *as*, a metaphor without. Though this distinction is technical, it is not entirely trivial, for a metaphor demands a more literal acceptance. If you say, "a woman is a rose," you ask for an extreme suspension of disbelief, whereas "a woman is like a rose" is a more sophisticated form, acknowledging the artifice in the statement.

Historically, metaphor preceded simile, originating in a purely sensuous comparison. When we speak of "the eyes of a potato," or "the eye of a needle," we mean simply that the leafbud and the thread hole *look like* eyes. We don't mean to suggest that the potato or the needle can *see*. The comparisons do not suggest any essential or abstract quality to do with sight.

Both metaphor and simile have developed, however, so that the resonance of comparison is precisely in the essential or abstract quality that the two objects share. When a writer speaks of "the eyes of the houses" or "the windows of the soul," the comparison of eyes to windows does contain the idea of transmitting vision between the inner and the outer. When we speak of "the king of beasts," we don't mean that a lion wears a crown or sits on a throne (though it is relevant that in children's stories the lion often does precisely that, in order to suggest a primitive physical likeness); we mean that king and lion share abstract qualities of power, position, pride, and bearing.

In both metaphor and simile a physical similarity can yield up a characterizing abstraction. So "a woman" may be either "a rose" or "like a rose." The significance of either lies not in the physical similarity but in the essential qualities that such similarity implies: slenderness, suppleness, fragrance, beauty, color—and perhaps the hidden threat of thorns.

Every metaphor and simile I have used so far is either a cliché or a dead metaphor (both of which will be discussed later): each of them may at one time have surprised by their aptness, but by now each has been used so often that the surprise is gone. I wished to use familiar examples in order to clarify that *the resonance of comparison depends on the abstractions conveyed in the likeness of the things compared.* A good metaphor reverberates with the essential; this is the writer's principle of choice.

So Flannery O'Connor, in "A Good Man Is Hard to Find," describes the mother as having "a face as round and innocent as a cabbage." A soccer ball is also round and innocent; so is a schoolroom globe; so is a streetlamp. But if the mother's face had been as round and innocent as any of these things, she would be a different woman altogether. A cabbage is also rural, heavy, dense, and cheap, and so it conveys a whole complex of abstractions about the woman's class and mentality. There is, on the other hand, no innocence in the face of Shrike, in Nathanael West's *Miss Lonelyhearts*, who "buried his triangular face like a hatchet in her neck."

Sometimes the aptness of a comparison is achieved by taking it from an area of reference relevant to the thing compared. In *Dombey and Son*, Charles Dickens describes the ships' instrument maker Solomon Gills as having "eyes as red as if they had been small suns looking at you through a fog." The simile suggests a seascape, whereas in *One Flew Over the Cuckoo's Nest*, Ken Kesey's Ruckly, rendered inert by shock therapy, has eyes "all smoked up and gray and deserted inside like blown fuses." But the metaphor may range further from its original, in which case the abstraction conveyed must strike us as strongly and essentially appropriate. William Faulkner's Emily Grierson in "A Rose for Emily" has "haughty black eyes in a face the flesh of which was strained across the temple and about the eyesockets as you imagine a lighthouse-keeper's face ought to look." Miss Emily has no connection with the sea, but the metaphor reminds us not only of her sternness and self-sufficiency, but also that she has isolated herself in a locked house. The same character as an old woman has eyes that "looked like two pieces of coal pressed into a lump of dough," and the image domesticates her, robs her of her light.

Both metaphors and similes can be *extended*, meaning that the writer continues to present aspects of likeness in the things compared.

> There was a white fog ... standing all around you like something solid. At eight or nine, perhaps, it lifted as a shutter lifts. We had a glimpse of the towering multitude of trees, of the immense matted jungle, with the blazing little ball of the sun hanging over it—all perfectly still—and then the shutter came down again, smoothly, as if sliding in greased grooves.
>
> JOSEPH CONRAD, *Heart of Darkness*

Notice that Conrad moves from a generalized image of "something solid" to the specific simile "as a shutter lifts"; reasserts the simile as a metaphor, "then the shutter came down again"; and becomes still more specific in the extension "as if sliding in greased grooves." Also note that Conrad emphasizes the dumb solidity of the fog by comparing the larger natural image with the smaller domestic one. Metaphor may equally work when the smaller or more ordinary image is compared with one larger or more intense, as in this example from Katherine Anne Porter's "Flowering Judas."

> Sometimes she wishes to run away, but she stays. Now she longs to fly out of this room, down the narrow stairs, and into the street where the houses lean together like conspirators under a single mottled lamp.

A *conceit*, which can be either metaphor or simile, is a comparison of two things radically and startlingly unlike—in Samuel Johnson's words, "yoked by violence together." A conceit is as far removed as possible from the purely sensuous comparison of "the eyes of the potato." It compares two things that have very little or no immediately apprehensible similarity; and so it is the nature of the conceit to be long. The author must explain to us, sometimes at great length, why these things can be said to be alike. When John Donne compares a flea to the Holy Trinity, the two images have no areas of reference in common, and we don't understand. He must explain to us that the flea, having bitten both the poet and his lover, now has the blood of three souls in its body.

The conceit is more common to poetry than to prose because of the density of its imagery, but it can be used to good effect in fiction. In *The Day of the Locust*, Nathanael West uses a conceit in an insistent devaluation of love. The screenwriter Claude Estee says:

> Love is like a vending machine, eh? Not bad. You insert a coin and press home the lever. There's some mechanical activity inside the bowels of the device. You receive a small sweet, frown at yourself in the dirty mirror, adjust your hat, take a firm grip on your umbrella and walk away, trying to look as though nothing had happened.

"Love is like a vending machine" is a conceit; if the writer didn't explain to us in what way love is like a vending machine, we'd founder trying to figure it out. So he goes on to develop the vending machine in images that suggest not "love," but seamy sex. The last image—"trying to look as though nothing had happened"—has nothing to do with the vending machine; we accept it because by this time we've fused the two ideas in our minds.

Tom Robbins employs conceit in *Even Cowgirls Get the Blues*, in a playfully self-conscious, mock-scientific comparison of Sissy Hankshaw's thumbs to a pearl.

> As for the oyster, its rectal temperature has never been estimated, although we must suspect that the tissue heat of the sedentary bivalve is as far below good old 98.6 as that of the busy bee is above. Nonetheless, the oyster, could it fancy, should fancy its excremental equipment a hot item, for what other among Creation's crapping creatures can convert its bodily wastes to treasure?
>
> There is a metaphor here, however strained. The author is attempting to draw a shaky parallel between the manner in which the oyster, when beset by impurities or disease, coats the offending matter with its secretions—and the manner in which Sissy Hankshaw, adorned with thumbs that many might consider morbid, coated the offending digits with glory.

The vignette of the oyster is a frivolous digression, relevant only in the making of the pearl. The comparison of pearl and thumbs is a conceit because sensuous similarity is not the point: Sissy's thumbs are not necessarily pale or shiny. The similarity is in the abstract idea of converting "impurities" to "glory."

A *dead metaphor* is one so familiar that it has in effect ceased to be a metaphor; has lost the force of the original comparison and acquired a new definition. Fowler's *Modern English Usage* uses the word *sift* to demonstrate the dead metaphor, one that has "been used so often that speaker and hearer have ceased to be aware that the words used are not literal."

> Thus, in *The men were sifting the meal* we have a literal use of *sift*; in *Satan hath desired to have you, that he may sift you as wheat*, *sift* is a live metaphor; in *the sifting of evidence*, the metaphor is so familiar that it is about equal chances whether *sifting* or *examination* will be used, and that a sieve is not present to the thought.

English abounds in dead metaphors. *Abounds* is one, where the overflowing of liquid is not present to the thought. When a man *runs* for office, his legs are not present to the thought, nor is an arrow when we speak of his *aim*, hot stones when we go through an *ordeal*, headgear when someone *caps* a joke. Unlike clichés, dead metaphors enrich the language. There is a residual resonance from the original metaphor but no pointless effort on the part of the mind to resolve the tension of like and unlike. English is fertile with metaphors (including those eyes of the potato and the needle) that have died and been resurrected as *idiom*, a "manner of speaking."

Metaphoric Faults to Avoid

Comparison is not a frivolity. It is, on the contrary, the primary business of the brain. Some eighteenth-century philosophers spoke of the human mind as a *tabula rasa*, a blank sheet on which sense impressions were recorded, compared, and grouped. Now we're more likely to speak of the mind as a "computer" (notice that both images are metaphors), "storing" and "sorting" "data." What both acknowledge is that comparison is the basis of all learning and all reasoning. When a child burns his hand on the stove and his mother says, "It's hot," and then goes toward the radiator and the mother says, "It's hot," the child learns not to burn his fingers. But the goal of reasoning is fact, toward a mode of behavior. When we speak of "the flames of torment," our impulse is comprehension and compassion. The goal of literary comparison is not fact but perception, toward scope of understanding.

Nevertheless, *metaphor* is a dirty word in some critical circles, because of the strain of the pursuit. Clichés, mixed metaphors, similes that are inept, unapt, obscure, or done to death mar good prose and tax the patience of the most willing reader. After eyes have been red suns, burnt-out fuses, lighthouse keepers, and lumps of coal, what else can they be?

The answer is: always something. But because by definition metaphor introduces an alien image into the flow of the story, metaphor is to some degree always self-conscious. Badly handled, it calls attention to the writer rather than the meaning and produces a sort of hiccup in the reader's involvement. A good metaphor fits so neatly that it fuses to and illuminates the meaning; or, like the Robbins passage quoted above, it acknowledges its self-consciousness so as to take the reader into the game. Generally speaking, where metaphors are concerned, less is more and, if in doubt, don't.

(Now I want to analyze the preceding paragraph. It contains at least seven dead metaphors: *alien, flow, handled, calls, fits, fuses,* and *illuminates.* A metaphor is not a foreigner; a story is not water; we do not take comparisons in our fingers; they have no vocal cords; they are not puzzle pieces; they do not congeal; and they give off no light rays. But each of these words has acquired a new definition and so settles into its context without strain. At the same time, the metaphoric echoes of these words make them more interesting than their abstract synonyms: *introduces an image from a different context into the meaning of the story . . . badly written, it makes us aware of the writer . . . a good metaphor is so directly relevant that it makes the meaning more understandable*—these abstract synonyms contain no imagery, and so they make for flatter writing. I have probably used what Fowler speaks of as a "moribund or dormant, but not stone-dead" metaphor when I speak of Robbins "taking the reader into the game." If I were Robbins, I'd probably have said, "inviting the reader to sit down at the literary pinochle table," which is a way of acknowledging that "taking the reader into the game" is a familiar metaphor; that is, it's a way of taking us into the game. I have used one live metaphor—"produces a sort of hiccup in the reader's involvement"—and I think I will leave it there to defend itself.)

There are more *don't*'s than *do*'s to record for the writing of metaphor and simile, because every good comparison is its own justification by virtue of being apt and original.

To study good metaphor, read. In the meantime, avoid the following:

Cliché metaphors are metaphors on their way to being dead. They are inevitably apt comparisons; if they were not, they wouldn't have been repeated often enough to become clichés. But they have not acquired new definitions, and so the reader's mind must make the imaginative leap to an image. The image fails to surprise, and we blame the writer for this expenditure of energy without a payoff. The metaphor is not original. Or, to put it a worse way:

Clichés are *the last word* in bad writing, and it's *a crying shame* to see all you *bright young things* spoiling your *deathless prose* with phrases *as old as the hills*. You must *keep your nose to the grindstone*, because *the sweet smell of success* only comes to those who *march to the tune of a different drummer*.

It's a sad fact that because you have been born into the twentieth century you may not say that eyes are like pools or stars, and you should be very wary of saying that they flood with tears. These have been so often repeated that they've become shorthand for emotions (attractions in the first and second instances, grief in the third) without the felt force of those emotions. Anytime you as writer record an emotion without convincing us to feel that emotion, you introduce a fatal distance between author and reader. Therefore, neither may your characters be hawk-eyed nor eagle-eyed; nor may they have ruby lips or pearly teeth or peaches-and-cream complexions or necks like swans or thighs like hams. I once gave a character spatulate fingers—and have been worrying about it ever since. If you sense—and you may—that the moment calls for the special intensity of metaphor, you may have to sift through a whole stock of clichés that come readily to mind before you find the fresh comparison that is both apt and startling.

Nevertheless, *pools* and *stars* have become clichés for *eyes* because they capture and manifest something essential about the nature of eyes. As long as eyes continue to contain liquid and light, there will be a new way of saying so. And a metaphor freshly pursued can even take advantage of the shared writer-reader consciousness of familiar images. Here William Golding, in *The Inheritors*, describes his Neanderthal protagonist's first tears, which mark his evolution into a human being:

> There was a light now in each cavern, lights faint as the starlight reflected in the crystals of a granite cliff. The lights increased, acquired definition, brightened, lay each sparkling at the lower edge of a cavern. Suddenly, noiselessly, the lights became thin crescents, went out, and streaks glistened on each cheek. The lights appeared again, caught among the silvered curls of the beard. They hung, elongated, dropped from curl to curl and gathered at the lowest tip. The streaks on the cheeks pulsed as the drops swam down them, a great drop swelled at the end of a hair of the beard, shivering and bright. It detached itself and fell in a silver flash.

In this sharply focused and fully extended metaphor of eyes as caverns, Golding asks us to draw on a range of familiar light imagery: starlight, crystal, the crescent moon, silver. The light imagery usually associated with eyes attaches to the water imagery of tears, though neither eyes nor tears are named. There is a submerged acknowledgment of cliché, but there is no cliché; Golding has reinvested the familiar images with their comparative and emotional force.

In both serious and comic writing, the consciousness of the familiar can be a peripheral advantage if you find a new way of exploiting it. It is a cliché to say, "You'll break my heart," but when Linda Ronstadt sings, "Break my mind, break my mind . . . ," the heart is still there, and the old image takes on new force. Although you may not say *her eyes are like pools*, you may probably say *her eyes are like the scummy duck pond out back*, and we'll find it comic partly because we know the cliché is lurking under the scum.

Cliché can also be useful as a device for establishing authorial distance toward a character or narrator. If the author tells us that Rome wasn't built in a day, we're likely to think the author has little to contribute to human insight; but if a character says so, in speech or thought, the judgment attaches to the character rather than to the author.

The door closed and he turned to find the dumpy figure, surmounted by the atrocious hat, coming toward him. "Well," she said, "*you only live once* and paying a little more for it, I at least won't *meet myself coming and going*."

"Some day I'll start making money . . ."

"I think you're doing fine," she said, drawing on her gloves. "You've only been out of school a year. *Rome wasn't built in a day*."

(italics mine)

FLANNERY O'CONNOR, "Everything That Rises Must Converge"

Though you can exploit the familiar by acknowledging it in a new way, it is never sufficient to put a cliché in quotation marks: *They hadn't seen each other for "eons."* Writers are sometimes tempted to do this in order to indicate that they know a cliché when they see one. Unfortunately, quotation marks have no power to renew emotion. All they say is, "I'm being lazy and I know it."

Farfetched metaphors are the opposite of clichés; they surprise but are not apt. As the dead metaphor *farfetched* suggests, the mind must travel too far to carry back the likeness, and too much is lost on the way. When such a comparison does work, we speak laudatorily of a "leap of the imagination." But when it does not, what we face is in effect a failed conceit: the explanation of what is alike about these two things does not convince. Very good writers in the search for originality sometimes fetch too far. Ernest Hemingway's talent was not for metaphor, and on the rare occasions that he used a metaphor, he was likely to strain. In this passage from *A Farewell to Arms*, the protagonist has escaped a firing squad and is fleeing the war:

You had lost your cars and your men as a floorwalker loses the stock of his department in a fire. There was, however, no insurance. You were out of it now. You had no more obligation. If they shot floorwalkers after a fire in the department store because they spoke with an accent they had always had, then certainly the floorwalkers would not be expected to return when the store opened again for business. They might seek other employment; if there was any other employment and the police did not get them.

Well, this doesn't work. We may be willing to see the likeness between stock lost in a department store fire and men and cars lost in a military skirmish; but "they" *don't* shoot floorwalkers as they shoot prisoners of war; and although a foreign accent might be a disadvantage behind enemy lines, it is hard to see how a floorwalker could be killed because of one, although it might make it hard for him to get hired in the first place, if . . . The mind twists trying to find any illuminating or essential logic in the comparison of a soldier to a floorwalker, and fails, so that the protagonist's situation is trivialized in the attempt.

Mixed metaphors are so called because they ask us to compare the original image with things from two or more different areas of reference: *as you walk the path of life, don't founder on the reefs of ignorance*. Life can be a path or a sea, but it cannot be both at the same time. The point of metaphor is to fuse two images in a single tension. The mind is adamantly unwilling to fuse three.

Separate metaphors or similes too close together, especially if they come from areas of reference very different in value or tone, disturb in the same way the mixed metaphor does. The mind doesn't leap; it staggers. The cliché paragraph on page 315 gives an example of metaphors packed too closely. Here is another example, less cliché.

> They fought like rats in a Brooklyn sewer. Nevertheless her presence was the axiom of his heart's geometry, and when she was away you would see him walking up and down the street dragging his cane along the picket fence like an idle boy's stick.

Any of these metaphors or similes might be acceptable by itself, but rats, axioms, and boy's sticks connote three different areas and tones, and two sentences cannot contain them all.

Mixed metaphors and metaphors too close together may be used for comic or characterizing effect. *The New Yorker* has been amusing its readers for decades with a filler item called "Block That Metaphor." But the laugh is always on the writer/speaker, and put-down humor, like a bad pun, is more likely to produce a snicker than an insight. Just as writers are sometimes tempted to put a cliché in quotation marks, they are sometimes tempted to mix metaphors and then apologize for it, in some such phrase as "to mix the metaphor," or, "If I may be permitted a mixed metaphor." It doesn't work. Don't apologize and don't mix.

Obscure and *overdone metaphors* falter because the author has misjudged the difficulty of the comparison. The result is either confusion or an insult to the reader's intelligence. In the case of obscurity, a similarity in the author's mind isn't getting onto the page. One student described the spines on a prickly pear cactus as being "slender as a fat man's fingers." I was completely confused by this. Was it ironic, that the spines weren't slender at all? Ah no, he said, hadn't I noticed how startling it was when someone with a fleshy body had bony fingers and toes? The trouble here was that the author knew what he meant but had left out the essential abstraction in the comparison, the startling quality of the contrast: "the spines of the fleshy prickly pear, like slender fingers on a fat man."

In this case, the simile was underexplained. It's probably a more common impulse—we're so anxious to make sure the reader gets it—to explain the obvious. In the novel *Raw Silk*, I had the narrator describe quarrels with her husband, "which I used to face with my dukes up in high confidence that we'd soon clear the air. The air can't be cleared now. We live in marital Los Angeles. This is the air—polluted, poisoned." A critic friend pointed out to me that anybody who didn't know about LA smog wouldn't get it anyway, and that all the last two words did was ram the comparison down his throat. He was right. "The air can't be cleared now. We live in marital Los Angeles. This is the air." The rewrite is much stronger because it neither explains nor exaggerates; and the reader enjoys supplying the metaphoric link.

Allegory

Allegory is a narrative form in which comparison is structural rather than stylistic. An allegory is a continuous fictional comparison of events, in which the action of the story represents a different action or a philosophical idea. The simplest illustration of an allegory is a fable, in which, for example, the race between the tortoise and the hare is used to illustrate the philosophical notion that "the race is not always to the swift." Such a story can be seen as an extended simile, with the original figure of the comparison suppressed: the tortoise and the hare represent types of human beings, but people are never mentioned and the comparison takes place in the reader's mind. George Orwell's *Animal Farm* is a less naive animal allegory, exploring ideas about corruption in a democratic society. Muriel Spark's *The Abbey* is a historical allegory, representing, without any direct reference to Richard Nixon, the events of Nixon's presidential term, through allegorical machinations in a nunnery. The plots of such stories are self-contained, but their significance lies in the reference to outside events or ideas.

Allegory is a tricky form. In the hands of Dante, John Bunyan, Edmund Spenser, John Keats, Franz Kafka, Henrik Ibsen, and Samuel Beckett, it has yielded works of the highest philosophical insight. But most allegories seem to smirk. A naive philosophical fable leads to a simpleminded idea that can be stated in a single phrase; a historical allegory relies on our familiarity with the Watergate scandal or the tribulations of the local football team, and so appeals to a limited and insular readership.

Symbol

A *symbol* differs from metaphor and simile in that it need not contain a comparison. A symbol is an object or event that, by virtue of association, represents something more or something other than itself. Sometimes an object is invested arbitrarily with such meaning, as a flag represents a nation and patriotism. Sometimes a single event stands for a whole complex of events, as the crucifixion of Christ stands as well for resurrection and redemption. Sometimes an object is invested with a complex of qualities through its association with the event, like the cross itself. These symbols are not metaphors; the cross represents redemption, but is not similar to redemption, which cannot be said to be wooden or T-shaped. The mother's hat in "Everything That Rises Must Converge" is such a symbol; it cannot be said to "resemble" desegregation, but in the course of the story it comes to represent the tenacious nostalgia of gentility and the aspirations of the new black middle class, and therefore the unacknowledged "converging" of equality.

Nevertheless, most literary symbols, including this one, do in the course of the action derive their extra meaning from some sort of likeness on the level of emotional or ideological abstraction. The hat is not "like" desegregation, but the action of the story reveals that both women are able to buy such a hat and choose it; this is a concrete example of equality, and so represents the larger concept of equality.

Margaret Drabble's novel *The Garrick Year* recounts the disillusionment of a young wife and mother who finds no escape from her situation. The book ends with a family picnic in an English meadow and the return home.

> On the way back to the car, Flora dashed at a sheep that was lying in the path, but unlike all the others it did not get up and move: it stared at us instead with a sick and stricken indignation. Flora passed quickly on, pretending for pride's sake that she had not noticed its recalcitrance; but as I passed, walking slowly, supported by David, I looked more closely and I saw curled up and clutching at the sheep's belly a real snake. I did not say anything to David:

I did not want to admit that I had seen it, but I did see it, I can see it still. It is the only wild snake that I have ever seen. In my book on Herefordshire it says that that part of the country is notorious for its snakes. But "Oh, well, so what," is all that one can say, the Garden of Eden was crawling with them too, and David and I managed to lie amongst them for one whole pleasant afternoon. One just has to keep on and to pretend, for the sake of the children, not to notice. Otherwise one might just as well stay at home.

The sheep is a symbol of the young woman's emotional situation. It does resemble her, but only on the level of the abstractions: sickness, indignation, and yet resignation at the fatal dangers of the human condition. There is here a metaphor that could be expressed as such (*she was sick and resigned as the sheep*), but the strength of the symbol is that such literal expression does not take place: we let the sheep stand in the place of the young woman while it reaches out to the larger significance.

A symbol may also begin as and grow from a metaphor, so that it finally contains more qualities than the original comparison. In John Irving's novel *The World According to Garp*, the young Garp mishears the word *undertow* as *under toad* and compares the danger of the sea to the lurking fantasies of his childish imagination. Throughout the novel the "under toad" persists, and it comes symbolically to represent all the submerged dangers of ordinary life, ready to drag Garp under just when he thinks he is swimming under his own power. Likewise the African continent in *Heart of Darkness* is dark like the barbaric reaches of the soul; but in the course of the novella we come to understand that darkness is shot with light and light with darkness, that barbarity and civilization are inextricably intermixed, and that the heart of darkness is the darkness of the heart.

One important distinction in the use of literary symbols is between those symbols of which the character is aware, and therefore "belong" to him or her; and those symbols of which only writer and reader are aware, and that therefore belong to the work. This distinction is often important to characterization, theme, and distance. In the passage quoted from *The Garrick Year*, the narrator is clearly aware of the import of the sheep, and her awareness suggests her intelligence and the final acceptance of her situation, so that we identify with her in recognizing the symbol. But the narrator in "The Gift of the Prodigal" does not recognize the symbolism of his gravel and so distances us from his self-perception. To the father the gravel, river washed, raked, and perfect, represents the orderliness of life as he prefers it, but the author and the reader see it from the first as an expression of over-meticulousness, a source of petty irritation, and finally as a symbol of the empty sameness of his days.

Sometimes the interplay between these types of symbol—those recognized by the characters and those seen only by writer and reader—can enrich the story in scope or irony. In *The Inheritors*, from which I've quoted several times, the Neanderthal tribe has its own religious symbols—a root, a grave, shapes in the ice cap—that represent its life-cycle worship. But in the course of the action, flood, fire, and a waterfall recall biblical symbols that allow the reader to supply an additional religious interpretation, which the characters would be incapable of doing. Again, in "Everything That Rises Must Converge," the mother sees her hat as representing, first, her taste and pride, and later the outrageousness of black presumption. For the reader it has the opposite and ironic significance, as a symbol of equality.

Symbols are subject to all the same faults as metaphor: cliché, strain, obscurity, obviousness, and overwriting. For these reasons, and because the word *Symbolism* also describes a particular late-nineteenth-century movement in French poetry, with connotations of obscurity, dream, and magical incantation, *symbolism* as a method has sometimes been treated with scorn in the hard-nosed twentieth century.

Yet it seems to me incontrovertible that the writing process is inherently and by definition symbolic. In the structuring of events, the creation of character and atmosphere, the choice of object, detail, and language, you are selecting and arranging toward the goal that these elements should signify more than their mute material existence. If this were not so, then you would have no principle of choice, and might just as well write about any other set of events, characters, and objects. If you so much as say, "as innocent as a cabbage," the image is minutely symbolic, not a statement of fact but selected to mean "something more and something other" than itself.

There is another and more mundane reason that symbol cannot be avoided in literature, and should not, which is that people also, constantly, function symbolically. We must do so because we rarely know exactly what we mean, and if we do we are not willing to express it, and if we are willing we are not able, and if we are able we are not heard, and if we are heard we are not understood. Words are unwieldy and unyielding, and we leap them with intuition, body language, tone, and symbol. "Is the oven supposed to be on?" he asks. He is only peripherally curious about whether the oven is supposed to be on. He is really complaining: *You're scatterbrained and extravagant with the money I go out and earn.* "If I don't preheat it, the muffins won't crest," she says, meaning: *You didn't catch me this time! You're always complaining about the food, and God knows I wear myself out trying to please you.* "We used to have *salade niçoise* in the summertime," he recalls, meaning: *Don't be so damn triumphant. You're still extravagant, and you haven't got the class you used to have when we were young.* "We used to keep a garden," she says, meaning: *You're always away on weekends and never have time to do anything with me because you don't love me anymore; I think you have a mistress.* "What do you expect of me!" he explodes, and neither of them is surprised that ovens, muffins, salads, and gardens have erupted. When people say "we quarreled over nothing," this is what they mean. They quarreled over symbols.

The Objective Correlative

But the conflict in a fiction cannot be "over nothing," and as a writer you must search for the concrete external manifestations that are adequate to the inexpressible feeling. T.S. Eliot used the term "objective correlative" to describe this process and this necessity.

> The only way of expressing emotion in the form of art is by finding an "objective correlative"; in other words, a set of objects, a situation, a chain of events which shall be the formula of that particular emotion; such that when the external facts, which must terminate in sensory experience, are given, the emotion is immediately invoked.
>
> *The Sacred Wood*

Some critics have argued that Eliot's *objective correlative* is really no more than a synonym for *symbol*, but the term and its definition make several important distinctions:

1. An "objective correlative" contains and evokes an *emotion*. Unlike many other sorts of symbols—scientific formulae, notes of music, the letters of the alphabet—the purpose of artistic symbol is to invoke emotion.
2. Some kinds of symbol—religious or political, for example—also arouse emotion, but they do so by virtue of one's acceptance of a general community of belief not specific to the context in which that symbol is used. The wine that represents the blood of Christ will evoke the same general emotion in Venice, Buenos Aires, and New York. But an artistic symbol arouses an emotion specific to the work and does not rely on sympathy or belief outside that work. Mentioning the wine of the communion ceremony in a story cannot be relied on to produce religious emotion in the reader; indeed, the author may choose to make it arouse some other emotion entirely.
3. The elements of a story are interrelated in such a way that the specific objects, situation, and events produce a *specific* emotion. The "romance" and "pity" invoked by *Romeo and Juliet* are not the same romance and pity invoked by *Anna Karenina* or *Gone With the Wind*, because the external manifestations in each work (which, being external "terminate in sensory experience") define the nature of the emotion.

4. The objects, situation, and events of a particular work contain its particular effect; conversely, if they do not contain the desired emotional effect, that effect cannot be produced in that work, either by its statement in abstractions or by appeal to outside symbols. The "objective" sensory experience (objects, situation, events) must be "co-relative" to the emotion, each corresponding to the other, for that is *the only way* of expressing emotion in the form of art.

When literary symbols fail, it is most often in this difficult and essential mutuality. In a typical example, we begin the story in a room of a dying woman alone with her collection of perfume bottles. The story ranges back over her rich and sensuous life, and at the end we focus on an empty perfume bottle. It is meant to move us at her death, but it does not. Yet the fault is not in the perfume bottle. Presumably a perfume bottle may express mortality as well as a hat may express racial equality. The fault is in the use of the symbol, which has not been integrated into the texture of the story. We would need to be convinced, perhaps, of the importance this woman placed on perfume as essence, need to know how the collection has played a part in the conflicts of her life, perhaps to see her fumbling now toward her favorite, so that we could emotionally equate the spilling or evaporation of the scent with her own spirit.

Writers of the first rank have had this difficulty dealing with the two holocausts of World War II, the extermination camps and the bombing of Hiroshima and Nagasaki, not because fact is stranger than fiction, but because the two horrors are of such magnitude that it is almost impossible to find a particular series of objects, situations, and events adequate to invoke the emotion of the historical facts. Arthur Miller's play *Incident at Vichy*, Lina Wertmuller's film *Seven Beauties*, and William Styron's novel *Sophie's Choice*—all these seem to some extent to borrow from the emotion invoked by the extermination camps, rather than to co-relate the facts and the emotions.

A symbolic object, situation, or event may err because it is insufficiently integrated into the story, and so seems to exist for its own sake rather than to emanate naturally from the characters' lives. It may err because the objective correlative is inadequate to the emotion it is supposed to evoke. Or it may err because it is too heavy or heavy-handed; that is, the author keeps pushing the symbol at us, nudging us in the ribs to say: Get it? In any of these cases we will say that the symbol is *artificial*—a curious word in the critical vocabulary, analogous to the charge of a *formula* plot, since art, like *form*, is a word of praise. All writing is "artificial," and when we charge it with being so, we mean that it isn't artificial enough, that the artifice has not concealed itself so as to give the illusion of the natural, and that the artificer must go back to work.

Signs and Symbols

VLADIMIR NABOKOV

I

For the fourth time in as many years they were confronted with the problem of what birthday present to bring a young man who was incurably deranged in his mind. He had no desires. Man-made objects were to him either hives of evil, vibrant with a malignant activity that he alone could perceive, or gross comforts for which no use could be found in his abstract world. After eliminating a number of articles that might offend him or frighten him (anything in the gadget line for instance was taboo), his parents chose a dainty and innocent trifle: a basket with ten different fruit jellies in ten little jars.

At the time of his birth they had been married already for a long time; a score of years had elapsed, and now they were quite old. Her drab gray hair was done anyhow. She wore cheap black dresses. Unlike other women of her age (such as Mrs. Sol, their next-door neighbor, whose face was all pink and mauve with paint and whose hat was a cluster of brookside flowers), she presented a naked white countenance to the fault-finding light of spring days. Her husband, who in the old country had been a fairly successful businessman, was now wholly dependent on his brother Isaac, a real American of almost forty years' standing. They seldom saw him and had nicknamed him "the Prince."

That Friday everything went wrong. The underground train lost its life current between two stations, and for a quarter of an hour one could hear nothing but the dutiful beating of one's heart and the rustling of newspapers. The bus they had to take next kept them waiting for ages; and when it did come, it was crammed with garrulous high-school children. It was raining hard as they walked up the brown path leading to the sanitarium. There they waited again; and instead of their boy shuffling into the room as he usually did (his poor face blotched with acne, ill-shaven, sullen, and confused), a nurse they knew, and did not care for, appeared at last and brightly explained that he had again attempted to take his life. He was all right, she said, but a visit might disturb him. The place was so miserably understaffed, and things got mislaid or mixed up so easily, that they decided not to leave their present in the office but to bring it to him next time they came.

She waited for her husband to open his umbrella and then took his arm. He kept clearing his throat in a special resonant way he had when he was upset. They reached the bus-stop shelter on the other side of the street and he closed his umbrella. A few feet away, under a swaying and dripping tree, a tiny half-dead unfledged bird was helplessly twitching in a puddle.

During the long ride to the subway station, she and her husband did not exchange a word; and every time she glanced at his old hands (swollen veins, brown-spotted skin), clasped and twitching upon the handle of his umbrella, she felt the mounting pressure of tears. As she looked around trying to hook her mind onto something, it gave her a kind of soft shock, a mixture of compassion and wonder, to notice that one of the passengers, a girl with dark hair and grubby red toenails, was weeping on the shoulder of an older woman. Whom did that woman resemble? She resembled Rebecca Borisovna, whose daughter had married one of the Soloveichiks—in Minsk, years ago.

The last time he had tried to do it, his method had been, in the doctor's words, a masterpiece of inventiveness; he would have succeeded, had not an envious fellow patient thought he was learning to fly—and stopped him. What he really wanted to do was to tear a hole in his world and escape.

The system of his delusions had been the subject of an elaborate paper in a scientific monthly, but long before that she and her husband had puzzled it out for themselves. "Referential mania," Herman Brink had called it. In these very rare cases the patient imagines that everything happening around him is a veiled reference to his personality and exist-ence. He excludes real people from the conspiracy—because he considers himself to be so much more intelligent than other men. Phenomenal nature shadows him wherever he goes. Clouds in the staring sky transmit to one another, by means of slow signs, incredibly detailed information regarding him. His inmost thoughts are discussed at nightfall, in manual alphabet, by darkly gesticulating trees. Pebbles or stains or sun flecks form patterns representing in some awful way messages which he must inter-cept. Everything is a cipher and of everything he is the theme. Some of the spies are detached observers, such are glass surfaces and still pools; others, such as coats in store windows, are prejudiced witnesses, lynchers at heart; others again (running water, storms) are hysterical to the point of insanity, have a distorted opinion of him and grotesquely misinterpret his actions. He must be always on his guard and devote every minute and module of life to the decoding of the undulation of things. The very air he exhales is indexed and filed away. If only the interest he provokes were limited to his immediate surroundings—but alas it is not! With distance the torrents of wild scandal increase in volume and volubility. The silhouettes of his blood corpuscles, magnified a million times, flit over vast plains; and still farther, great mountains of unbearable solidity and height sum up in terms of granite and groaning firs the ultimate truth of his being.

II

When they emerged from the thunder and foul air of the subway, the last dregs of the day were mixed with the street lights. She wanted to buy some fish for supper, so she handed him the basket of jelly jars, telling him to go home. He walked up to the third landing and then remembered he had given her his keys earlier in the day.

In silence he sat down on the steps and in silence rose when some ten minutes later she came, heavily trudging upstairs, wanly smiling, shaking her head in deprecation of her silliness. They entered their two-room flat and he at once went to the mirror. Straining the corners of his mouth apart by means of his thumbs, with a horrible masklike grimace he removed his new hopelessly uncomfortable dental plate and severed the long tusks of saliva connecting him to it. He read his Russian-language newspaper while she laid the table. Still reading, he ate the pale victuals that needed no teeth. She knew his moods and was also silent.

When he had gone to bed, she remained in the living room with her pack of soiled cards and her old albums. Across the narrow yard where the rain tinkled in the dark against some battered ash cans, windows were blandly alight and in one of them a black-trousered man with his bare elbows raised could be seen lying supine on an untidy bed. She pulled the blind down and examined the photographs. As a baby he looked more surprised than most babies. From a fold in the album, a German maid they had had in Leipzig and her fat-faced fiancé fell out. Minsk, the Revolution, Leipzig, Berlin, Leipzig, a slanting house front badly out of focus. Four years old, in a park: moodily, shyly, with puckered forehead, looking away from an eager squirrel as he would from any other stranger. Aunt Rosa, a fussy, angular, wild-eyed old lady, who had lived in a tremulous world of bad news, bankruptcies, train accidents, cancerous growths—until the Germans put her to death, together with all the people she had worried about. Age six—that was when he drew wonderful birds with human hands and feet, and suffered from insomnia like a grown-up man. His cousin, now a famous chess player. He again, aged about eight, already difficult to understand, afraid of the wallpaper in the passage, afraid of a certain picture in a book which merely showed an idyllic landscape with rocks on a hillside and an old cart wheel hanging from the branch of a leafless tree. Aged ten: the year they left Europe. The shame, the pity, the humiliating difficulties, the ugly, vicious, backward children he was with in that special school. And then came a time in his life, coinciding with a long convalescence after pneumonia, when those little phobias of his which his parents had stubbornly regarded as the eccentricities of a prodigiously gifted child hardened as it were into a dense tangle of logically interacting illusions, making him totally inaccessible to normal minds.

This, and much more, she accepted—for after all living did mean accepting the loss of one joy after another, not even joys in her case—mere possibilities of improvement. She thought of the endless waves of pain that for some reason or other she and her husband had to endure; of the invisible giants hurting her boy in some unimaginable fashion; of the incalculable amount of tenderness contained in the world; of the fate of this tenderness, which is either crushed, or wasted, or transformed into madness; of neglected children humming to themselves in unswept corners; of beautiful weeds that cannot hide from the farmer and helplessly have to watch the shadow of his simian stoop leave mangled flowers in its wake, as the monstrous darkness approaches.

III

It was past midnight when from the living room she heard her husband moan; and presently he staggered in, wearing over his nightgown the old overcoat with astrakhan collar which he much preferred to the nice blue bathrobe he had.

"I can't sleep," he cried.

"Why," she asked, "why can't you sleep? You were so tired."

"I can't sleep because I am dying," he said and lay down on the couch.

"Is it your stomach? Do you want me to call Dr. Solov?"

"No doctors, no doctors," he moaned. "To the devil with doctors! We must get him out of there quick. Otherwise we'll be responsible. Responsible!" he repeated and hurled himself into a sitting position, both feet on the floor, thumping his forehead with his clenched fist.

"All right," she said quietly, "we shall bring him home tomorrow morning."

"I would like some tea," said her husband and retired to the bathroom.

Bending with difficulty, she retrieved some playing cards and a photograph or two that had slipped from the couch to the floor: knave of hearts, nine of spades, ace of spades, Elsa and her bestial beau.

He returned in high spirits, saying in a loud voice:

"I have it all figured out. We will give him the bedroom. Each of us will spend part of the night near him and the other part on this couch. By turns. We will have the doctor see him at least twice a week. It does not matter what the Prince says. He won't have to say much anyway because it will come out cheaper."

The telephone rang. It was an unusual hour for their telephone to ring. His left slipper had come off and he groped for it with his heel and toe as he stood in the middle of the room, and childishly, toothlessly, gaped at his wife. Having more English than he did, it was she who attended to calls.

"Can I speak to Charlie," said a girl's dull little voice.

"What number you want? No. That is not the right number."

The receiver was gently cradled. Her hand went to her old tired heart. "It frightened me," she said.

He smiled a quick smile and immediately resumed his excited monologue. They would fetch him as soon as it was day. Knives would have to be kept in a locked drawer. Even at his worst he presented no danger to other people.

The telephone rang a second time. The same toneless anxious young voice asked for Charlie.

"You have the incorrect number. I will tell you what you are doing: you are turning the letter O instead of the zero."

They sat down to their unexpected festive midnight tea. The birthday present stood on the table. He sipped noisily; his face was flushed; every now and then he imparted a circular motion to his raised glass so as to make the sugar dissolve more thoroughly. The vein on the side of his bald head where there was a large birthmark stood out conspicuously and, although he had shaved that morning, a silvery bristle showed on his chin. While she poured him another glass of tea, he put on his spectacles and re-examined with pleasure the luminous yellow, green, red little jars. His clumsy moist lips spelled out their eloquent labels: apricot, grape, peach plum, quince. He had got to crab apple, when the telephone rang again.

Suggestions for Discussion

1. In the third paragraph of the story we read, "The underground train lost its life current between two stations . . ."; and at the beginning of section II, "they emerged from the thunder and foul air of the subway." How do these metaphors relate to the situation of the story and to its symbolic pattern?

2. Is the "tiny half-dead unfledged bird . . . helplessly twitching in a puddle" at the end of the fourth paragraph of the first section a symbol? Of what?

3. The "referential mania" described on page 325 is the symbolic system of a madman, in which every natural phenomenon means something other and something more than itself. What distance do we take on this system when we first encounter it? How has that distance altered by the end of the story?

4. What place do the following have in the symbolic meaning of the story: The description of Aunt Rosa on page 326? The shadow of the farmer's "simian stoop" at the end of section II on page 327? The old woman's explanation, "you are turning the letter O instead of the zero," on page 328?

5. This is a "Lady or the Tiger" tale, ending with an unanswered and unanswerable question. Why has Nabokov chosen this form for this particular story? Who do *you* think is on the other end of the telephone at the third call? What significance does it have for the symbolic meaning of the story if it should be the wrong-number caller again? The hospital?

Underground Women

JESSE LEE KERCHEVAL

La photographie

I am taking a photograph of a Lavomatic near the Gare du Nord in Paris.
It is a color photograph and so shows the walls sharp yellow, the machines
the shiny white that means clean. The front of the Lavomatic is plate glass.
Glass that lets out into the night the bright fluorescent light of the laundry.
Glass that reflects a red hint of an ambulance beacon. Glass that lets the
photographer catch this scene, this knot of official people grouped casually
around a dark wrinkled shape on the floor. Catch at an angle of extreme
foreshortening the stubby, already almost blue, legs, the one outflung
hand holding one black sock.

It is the photograph of a dead woman.

Le Grand Hotel

It is on the evening of my first day in Paris that I take the photograph of
the dead woman in the Lavomatic and then check into Le Grand Hotel de
l'Univers Nord. At first I am tempted to find the name humorous—do the
East, West, and South quarters of the universe keep separate grand hotels?—
but decide against it. I do not know enough French to have any sense of
humor in it at all.

Madame Desnos crie

And it is the photograph of the Lavomatic or rather my memory of the
dead woman in it that wakes me up so early at Le Grand Hotel. I catch
Madame Denos the proprietaire, in her leopard-spotted robe, still breaking
the baguettes for the guests' breakfasts.

"Mademoiselle . . ." she says, waving me to a seat at the counter. "His
ankles," she remarks pleasantly, cracking off a six-inch hunk of bread. I
think it is something colloquial and smile. "His knees," she adds, breaking
off another piece which I helpfully arrange in its basket. "My husband has
sent me a postcard," Madame Desnos pauses to choose another loaf, "so he
is not dead, and worse still, he says he misses me." She starts on a new loaf.
"His spine." I drop a basket and when I bend to pick it up I see Madame
Desnos's legs beneath her spotted robe. Like the woman in the Lavomatic
Madame Desnos's legs are protected only by hose fallen in wrinkled waves
around her ankles, though hers are pink with only a foreshadowing of
heavy blue veins. I begin to cry. Madame Desnos cries too, taking the scarf
from her hair to wipe our tears. Her hair is the faded red of a very old
dachshund.

"No, no, it's not so bad. I've paid off the loan he took out on the place the last time he came back." She pokes me in the navel with the last loaf of bread. "Smile," she says. "The mails are slow and people die every day." She breaks the bread in two. "His neck."

Le Grand Hotel encore

After breakfast I become the desk clerk at Le Grand Hotel. Perhaps in France people who want jobs as desk clerks always get up early and help with breakfast.

"Remember," says Madame Desnos, "this arrondissment may be filled with hotels run by Algerians for Algerians, Vietnamese for Vietnamese, and Moroccans for Moroccans, but Le Grand Hotel de l'Univers Nord is a French hotel," she waves a fine thin hand at the lobby, "that just happens to be filled with Algerians, Vietnamese, and Moroccans."

Monsieur Peret

I am polishing the big brass room keys the guests leave each morning when they go out to work or to look for work when a small man with very large false teeth appears suddenly at the door and rushes to kiss Madame Desnos on the cheek.

"Ah, Monsieur Peret," she says without looking up.

"Ah, ah, ah . . . " Monsieur Peret moans, "business is so bad, Madame, I have come to beg you to encourage your new desk clerk to mention the closeness of my excellent facilities to your guests." Monsieur Peret slides down the counter towards me and takes one end of the key I am polishing in his very tiny very clean hand. "Surely, Madame, you have already told your new clerk how much more reasonable my coin laundry is than that place over on the Rue de Ste. Marie, and how it is my standard and well honored policy to offer one free wash with every three validated referrals? Surely, Madame, I need not mention these things myself." Monsieur Peret draws the key across the counter with my hand still attached. "Au revoir," he says, pecking me lightly with his dentures.

La photographie encore

I tell Madame Desnos about the photograph I took the night before of a dead woman in Monsieur Peret's Lavomatic and she makes me go with her at once to the developer's.

"It does not surprise me that a dead woman should bring Monsieur Peret's business trouble," says Madame Desnos as we wait for Monsieur Blanc, the developer, to bring out the prints. "Monsieur Peret was not good to his wife," she says, "and such things do not always go unpunished. He worked her so hard in that Lavomatic that to get some rest she went to a doctor and let him remove a part. Ah, but once the doctors start on someone they can never have done with them, and so they kept at poor Madame Peret until there was nothing left at all."

Monsieur Blanc brings out the dripping prints but Madame Desnos refuses to look at them until he leaves the room. She takes my hand and I look again at the round dead shape of the woman in the Lavomatic.

"It's the way the customers are all just doing their wash, not even looking at her, that makes me want to cry," I tell Madame Desnos.

"Ah, but the only way a woman can make a mark on this world," says Madame Desnos, "is with her body, surely not even a dead one should be allowed to go to waste. At least by dying in the Lavomatic she made a friend on the other side in Madame Peret." Madame Desnos puts the woman in the Lavomatic into a brown envelope for safe keeping. "Let us go see Monsieur Peret and let his complaining cheer us up."

Monsieur Peret encore

"Oh, she was not even a regular customer," Monsieur Peret complains before we are even inside the plate glass wall of the Lavomatic. "And these people," he looks over his shoulder at the Moroccans and Algerians who are passing by outside in their dirty clothes, then waves a tiny clean hand at the empty laundry, "they are so superstitious. This picture on the wall," he takes Madame Desnos's sleeve and draws her to a small copy of a woodcut that is hardly noticeable on the bright yellow wall. "It has been here for years—my poor wife picked it out the last time she was ever here—suddenly after this incident, over which I had no control, they complain about this picture. Just to cause me grief. There is nothing as irrational as a woman who has dirty laundry and wants an excuse not to do her wash." Monsieur Peret shakes his head. I move closer to examine the woodcut. It depicts five virgin martyrs being flayed.

Madame Desnos touches a long thin finger to one of the martyrs. "Perhaps if you feel you must replace this thoughtful gift of your wife's— would it not fit in somewhere in your own rooms?—the mademoiselle here could be of some service to you. I have just discovered she is a most accomplished photographer and plan to have some postal cards of the hotel made up expressly to utilize her talents."

"Well," Monsieur Peret looks from the flayed virgins to me, "perhaps a nice shot of myself, in a very white shirt, standing poised and attentive in front of the Lavomatic."

"Ah, well ... perhaps the matter requires some thought," Madame Desnos says, "but I am certain if I talk to the mademoiselle we could all get what we deserve."

"Indeed," says Monsieur Peret.

Madame Desnos takes my arm as we leave. "We must think of something appropriate," she says to me.

Au cinema

"Only every tenth movie shown in France can be made in America," Madame Desnos tells me as I am handing out the room keys to the returning guests. "And only every tenth song played on the radio. But," she says, "there are ways and there are ways; if a song is sung in French it is a French song—no matter if it is 'The Yellow Rose of Texas.' So tonight we shall go to the movies and what we will see will be American movies so old they have become French by default."

After the last guest is in she tells the Algerians playing cards in the lobby where she will be in case the hotel catches fire or her husband returns, and we leave for the cinema.

"This theater has been running the same American serials since I was a young bride," Madame Desnos tells me as we hurry to find our seats before the house lights go down. "I don't come often but slowly I am getting to see the beginning, middle, and end of them all."

We find our seats just in time. The lights go out. The titles come up on the screen. *The Queen of the Underground Women*. It stars Gene Autry as a radio station operator; under his Radio Ranch lives a kingdom of underground Amazons. After the titles the Queen of the Underground Women stands facing the camera and declares:

"Our lives are serene. Our minds are superior. Our achievements are greater than theirs. We must capture Gene Autry."

Madame Desnos pulls my arm and we get up and leave. Outside she shakes her head. "They are making a terrible mistake," she says.

Pere Lachaise

After the keys are turned in the next morning Madame Desnos announces we are going to make a small pilgrimage—"A pilgrimage is a trip that is its own reward," she says—to Pere Lachaise, one of Paris's great cemeteries. On the way to the Metro she stops near the station and buys a stalk of hollyhocks. "For Madame Peret," she explains.

"Is Madame Peret buried at Pere Lachaise then?" I ask.

"No," says Madame Desnos, "there was so little left of her that Monsieur Peret let the doctors have that too, but it is a good place to be buried and a good place to visit the dead. We'll put the flowers on someone else's tomb and if it is important perhaps they will tell Madame Peret we called."

In the Metro on the way to Pere Lachaise we sit in seats marked reserved in descending order for disabled veterans, the civil blind, civil amputees, pregnant women, and women with children in arms.

Madame Desnos shrugs. "So we are pregnant," she says, "that at least they don't make you carry papers to prove. Not important enough for them, I suppose."

We walk from the Metro stop through the gates of the cemetery and then on over the crumbling hills of mausoleums, each family vault the size of an elevator, each with its shards of stained glass and leaf-clogged altar. There are cats everywhere, asleep under brown wreaths, fat and indifferent to the rain.

"Do you know," Madame Desnos asks, "that in Germany they only bury you for just a while—say until your husband remarries or your children move away. Then up you come, tombstone and all, and another German goes in your place. Busy people, the Germans."

We pass the tombs of Molière and La Fontaine, who are probably not really buried there, and the monument to the love of Heloise and Abelard, who most certainly are not, and then the grave of Colette, who is but hidden under her husband's name, and walk on until we reach the columbarium with its tiered drawers of ashes.

"I am sure this is where Madame Peret would have chosen. She was a frugal woman and there really wasn't much of her left." Madame Desnos runs one thin finger down a line of drawers. Names, dates, beloved this and thats—then she stops, her fingertip poised on a drawer with a black and white photograph of a young woman, a flapper, wearing only lipstick and long jet beads, a graceful hand poised beneath her chin and jet, jet eyes. No names, no dates.

Madame Desnos puts the hollyhocks in the flapper's dry vase.

Madame Desnos crie encore

On the way back to Le Grand Hotel we stop to shop at Printemps. Madame Desnos instructs me to buy a black bra.

"You American girls are not safe on the streets," she says to me and to the saleswoman in Lingerie. "Looking innocent is no protection." I remember Madame Peret's flayed virgins and think perhaps Madame Desnos has a point.

We stop at a cafe for coffee and brandy to ward off the rain and then because of this must also stop across the street at an art nouveau underground toilette.

"Madame Desnos!" the attendant cries out when she comes down off the ladder where she has been fixing one of the tanks.

"Marie-Louise!" Madame Desnos squeals back, "I thought you were still in the Place St. Germaine."

"No, no I have been here for almost a month—a promotion."

"Indeed," says Madame Desnos, waving her long fine hand at the stained glass lilies set in the stall doors, the hand-painted lily tiles, the murals of lily-languid young women.

I walk over and examine a beveled glass case behind the attendant's station. It is filled with little momentos of the sort nieces bring back to their favorite aunt. There is a stuffed baby alligator from Florida next to a set of Eiffel tower salt and pepper shakers.

"Those were Madame Galfont's," Marie-Louise says, coming up behind me. "She was here for many years, since before the war, and had many regular clients."

"Madame Galfont has . . ." asks Madame Desnos with another wave of her hand, "passed on?"

"No, well, I usually say that she retired. It is a painful point." Marie-Louise shakes her head. "Did you see the signs on your way down the stairs?" She points up at some black and yellow government posters. "This new government—now they have boarded up all the pissoirs so the men too must pay a franc for a stall. Madame Galfont met a man in this way, and so she left . . ." Marie-Louise spreads her short arms in an encompassing gesture, " . . . this. I trained under Madame Galfont, to me it was as if she had abdicated." Marie-Louise shakes her head. Madame Desnos shakes her head. "So there was a meeting of all the attendants, all the women, and they voted that I should come here and now I must be the one to show the new women how things have always been done, but I am no Madame Galfont." Marie-Louise takes a small Polaroid snapshot out of the beveled case. Madame Galfont smiles out of it, perhaps at some satisfied client, some tourist amazed at this splendid museum toilette. I look closer. I recognize Madame Galfont from another photograph, though in that one she is not smiling. I show Marie-Louise the woman in the Lavomatic. She cries. Madame Desnos cries. I cry.

Marie-Louise touches the printed image of Madame Galfont's outstretched hand. "A man's sock," she says and shakes her head one last time.

Marie-Louise takes the final picture of Madame Galfont and places it in the beveled case near the smiling Galfont, propping it up behind a pencil case from the Swiss Alps. The box cuts off the bottom of the picture—suddenly there is only the Lavomatic. White-coated officials view the Lavomatic with pride as busy customers concentrate on their wash. Madame Galfont is removed from the photograph as abruptly, as thoroughly, as she was from the Lavomatic itself, and yet . . . she is there. Gene Autry walking the hollow soil of his Radio Ranch, hurried Parisians whose footsteps I can hear on the sidewalk above—who cannot feel the presence of the Queen of the Underground Women? I turn to Madame Desnos.

"I have something for Monsieur Peret," I say.

La photographie encore une fois

I go back to Monsieur Blanc with the negative of the death of Madame Galfont.

"Cropped and blown up?" he asks.

"And framed," I say, "as large as possible and framed."

"Ah, well, for a friend of Monsieur Peret's I think it can be arranged."

Monsieur Peret pour la derniere fois

Monsieur Peret straightens the framed photograph on the nail from which he has already exiled Madame Peret's virgin martyrs. "I am overcome," he says, still unable to decide once and for all that the picture is hanging level—he feels a certain unease about it. "Madame Desnos is too generous, too kind—a gift such as this . . ." Monsieur Peret stands lost in admiration for this magic mirror copy of his Lavomatic and does not even notice two women behind him become nervous, take their laundry still damp from the dryers and leave.

Madame Desnos ne crie pas

When I return to Le Grand Hotel I find a telegram for Madame Desnos lying open on the counter.

COMING HOME, BABY. STOP.

It is not signed but I am sure Monsieur Desnos felt there would be no confusion. I go upstairs to pack. When I come back down with my bags Madame Desnos's are standing in the hall.

"One moment!" she calls from behind the counter in the lobby. I watch as she takes each long brass room key and drops it into her net shopping bag. We pick up our bags and she locks the door of Le Grand Hotel de l'Univers Nord behind us and puts that key too in her bag. We check our luggage at the Gare de Nord and then walk slowly toward the Seine.

"I have been Paris a long time, but I was born in Troyes," says Madame Desnos as we draw even with Notre Dame de Paris, Our Lady of Paris. "Troyes too has a cathedral, and in it the columns grow into trees and the arched vaults are draped with grape vines. I think in Troyes they have done kinder things with their stone," she waves her fine hand at Notre Dame's great east front, "than in Paris. In Troyes there are even carved escargot feeding among the marble vines."

We cross to the middle of the bridge from the Île de Cité and stand looking back at the city.

"And in Troyes there is a woman who sits every day in the market and sells vegetables that the other vendors have thrown down on the floor as too old or too rotten, yet from this woman even the mayor must wait in line each day and pay for the privilege of her weighing him out old parsnips." Madame Desnos unties her bag and reaches out the keys, "I think you would have to live in Troyes a long time to know why this is so."

"Perhaps there are places where it is better for a woman to live."

Madame Desnos holds one of the brass keys between her long fingers and lets it drop into the Seine. I watch as one by one they fall, golden beads on a rosary, raising a tiny glinting splash apiece.

"Perhaps," Madame Desnos says, "perhaps."

Suggestions for Discussion

1. To what extent, and to whom, are the following objects symbolic—the loaves of bread, women's hose fallen round their ankles, the man's sock, the woodcut of virgin martyrs, the grave of Colette, Notre Dame, the hotel keys, the city of Troyes?

2. How many things does the title mean?

3. How do the images of women in photographs, woodcut, film, and murals contribute to the meaning of the story?

4. Explain how these metaphors operate in the story: " . . . the shiny white that means clean" and "Her hair is the faded red of a very old dachshund."

5. What effect is achieved by dividing the story into short sections with French titles?

6. A central theme of the story is women's anger against men. Does the author take any authorial distance on this theme, or is her viewpoint identical with the narrator's?

RETROSPECT

Explain how each of the following metaphors or symbols operates in its context:

1. "Cutting Edge," page 19: " 'It fills out his face,' Mr. Zeller said, looking at the wallpaper and surprised he had never noticed what a pattern it had before; it showed the sacrifice of some sort of animal by a youth."

2. "Everything That Rises Must Converge," pages 92-93: "while he, his hands behind him, appeared pinned to the door frame, waiting like Saint Sebastian for the arrows to begin piercing him."

3. Shiloh and the log cabin in "Shiloh."

4. "A time God" in "The Power."

5. "The Masked Marvel's Last Toehold," page 260: "And . . . *I am masked.*"

6. "Battle Royal," page 281: "the eyes hollow and smeared a cool blue, the color of a baboon's butt."

WRITING ASSIGNMENTS

1. Write a passage using at least three cliché metaphors, finding a way to make each fresh and original.

2. Take any dead metaphor and write a comic or serious scene that reinvests the metaphor with its original comparative force. Here are a few sample suggestions (your own will be better):

Sifting the evidence. (The lawyer uses a colander, a tea strainer, two coffee filters, and a garlic press to decide the case.)

Speakeasy. (Chicago, 1916. A young libertine tricks a beautiful but repressed young woman into an illegal basement bar. He thinks drink will loosen her up. What it loosens is not her sensuality but her tongue, and what she says he doesn't want to hear.)

Peck on the cheek.
(Alfred Hitchcock has done this one already, perhaps?)

Bus terminal.	*Don't spoil your lunch.*
Advertising jingle.	*Broken home.*
Soft shoulders.	*Good-bye.*

3. Write two one-page scenes, each containing an extended metaphor or simile. In one, compare an ordinary object to something of great size or significance. In the other, compare a major thing or phenomenon to something smaller and more mundane or less intense.

4. Write a short scene involving a conflict between two people over an object. Let the object take on symbolic significance. It may have the same significance to the two people, or a different significance to each.

5. Let an object smaller than a breadbox symbolize hope, redemption, or love to the central character. Let it symbolize something else entirely to the reader.

6. List all the clichés you can think of to describe a pair of blue eyes. Then write a paragraph in which you find a fresh and new metaphor for blue eyes.

10

I GOTTA USE WORDS
WHEN I TALK TO YOU
Theme

Idea and Morality in Theme
How Fictional Elements Contribute to Theme
Developing Theme as You Write

How does a fiction mean?

Most literature textbooks begin a discussion of theme by warning that theme is not the *message*, not the *moral*, and that the *meaning* of a piece cannot be paraphrased. Theme contains an idea but cannot be stated as an idea. It suggests a morality but offers no moral. Then what is theme, and how as a writer can you pursue that rich resonance?

First of all, theme is what a story is about. But that is not enough, because a story may be "about" a dying Samurai or a quarreling couple or two kids on a trampoline, and those are not the themes of those stories. A story is also "about" an abstraction, and if the story is significant that abstraction may be very large; yet thousands of stories are about love, other thousands about death, several thousands about both love and death, and to say this is to say little about the theme of any of them.

I think it might be useful to borrow an idea from Existentialist philosophy, which asks the question: *What is what is?* That is, what is the nature of that which exists? We might start to understand theme if we ask the question: *What about what it's about?* What does the story have to say about the idea or abstraction that seems to be contained in it? What attitudes or judgments does it imply? Above all, how do the techniques particular to fiction contribute to the presentation of those ideas and attitudes?

Idea and Morality in Theme

Literature is stuck with ideas in a way the other arts are not. Music, paradoxically the most abstract of the arts, creates a logical structure that need make no reference to the world outside itself. It may express a mood, but it needs to draw no conclusions. Shapes in painting and sculpture may suggest forms in the physical world, but they need not represent the world, and they need contain no message. But words mean. The grammatical structure of the simplest sentence contains a concept, whatever else it may contain, so that an author who wishes to treat words solely as sound or shape may be said to make strange music or pictures but not literature.

Yet those who choose to deal in the medium of literature consistently denigrate concepts and insist on the value of the particular instance. Here is Vladimir Nabokov's advice to a reader:

> . . . fondle details. There is nothing wrong about the moonshine of generalization *after* the sunny trifles of the book have been lovingly collected. If one begins with a ready-made generalization, one begins at the wrong end and travels away from the book before one has started to understand it.

Joan Didion parallels the idea from the other side of the typewriter in an essay on "Why I Write:"

> I am not a scholar. I am not in the least an intellectual, which is not to say that when I hear the word "intellectual" I reach for my gun, but only to say that I do not think in abstracts. During the years when I was an undergraduate at Berkeley I tried, with a kind of hopeless late-adolescent energy, to buy some temporary visa into the world of ideas, to forge for myself a mind that could deal with the abstract.
>
> In short I tried to think. I failed. My attention veered inexorably back to the specific, to the tangible, to what was generally considered, by everyone I knew then and for that matter have known since, the peripheral. I would try to

contemplate the Hegelian dialectic and would find myself concentrating instead on the flowering pear tree outside my window and the particular way the petals fell on the floor.

Didion takes a Socratic stance here, ironically pretending to naïveté and modesty as she equates "thinking" with "thinking in the abstract." Certainly her self-deprecation is ironic in light of the fact that she is not only a novelist but one of the finest intellects among our contemporary essayists. But she acknowledges an assumption very general and very seriously taken, that *thought* means *dealing with the abstract*, and that abstract thought is more real, central, and valid than specific concrete thought.

What both these passages suggest is that a writer of fiction approaches concepts, abstractions, generalizations, and truths through their particular embodiments—showing, not telling. "Literature," says John Ciardi, "is never only about ideas, but about the experience of ideas." T.S. Eliot points out that the creation of this experience is of itself an intellectual feat:

> We talk as if thought was precise and emotion was vague. In reality there is precise emotion and there is vague emotion. To express precise emotion requires as great intellectual power as to express precise thought.

The value of the literary experience is that it allows us to judge an idea at two levels of consciousness, the rational and the emotional (or the neocortical and the limbic), simultaneously. The kind of "truth" that can be told through thematic resonance is many-faceted and can acknowledge the competing claims of many truths, exploring paradox and contradiction.

> There is a curious prejudice built into our language that makes us speak of *telling the truth* but *telling a lie*. No one supposes that all conceivable falsehood can be wrapped up in a single statement called "the lie"; lies are manifold, varied, and specific. But truth is supposed to be absolute: the truth, the whole truth, and nothing but the truth. This is, of course, impossible nonsense, and *telling a lie* is a truer phrase than *telling the truth*. Fiction does not have to tell the truth, but a truth.

Anton Chekov wrote that "the writer of fiction should not try to solve such questions as those of God, pessimism and so forth." What is "obligatory for the artist," he said, is not "*solving a problem*," but "*stating a problem correctly*." John Keats went even further in pursuing a definition of "the impersonality of genius." "The only means of strengthening one's intellect is to make up one's mind about nothing—to let the mind be a thoroughfare for all thoughts." And he defined genius itself as *negative capability*: "that is when a man is capable of being in uncertainties, mysteries and doubts, without any irritable reaching after fact and reason."

A story, then, speculates on a possible truth. It is not an answer or a law but a supposition, an exploration. Every story reaches in its climax and resolution an interim solution to a specifically realized dilemma. But it offers neither a final solution nor the Final Solution.

The contrast with the law here is relevant. Abstract reasoning works toward generalization and results in definitions, laws, and absolute judgments. Imaginative reasoning and concrete thought work toward instances and result in emotional experience, revelation, and the ability to contain life's paradoxes in tension—which may explain the notorious opposition of writers to the laws and institutions of their time. Lawmakers struggle to define a moral position in abstract terms such that it will justly account for every instance to which it is applied. (This is why the language of law is so tedious and convoluted.) Poets and novelists continually goad them by producing instances for which the law does not account and referring by implication to the principle behind and beyond the law. (This is why the language of literature is so dense and compact.)

The idea that is proposed, supposed, or speculated on in a fiction may be simple and idealistic, like the notion in "Cinderella" that the good and beautiful will triumph. Or it may be profound and unprovable, like the theme in *Oedipus Rex* that man cannot escape his destiny but may be ennobled in the attempt. Or it may be deliberately paradoxical and offer no guidelines that can be used in life, as in Jane Austen's *Persuasion*, where the heroine, in order to adhere to her principles, must follow advice given on principles less sound than her own.

In any case, while exploring an idea the writer inevitably conveys an attitude toward that idea. Rust Hills puts it this way:

> . . . coherence in the world [an author] creates is constituted of two concepts he holds, which may be in conflict: one is his world view, his sense of the way the world is; and the other is his sense of morality, the way the world ought to be.

Literature is a persuasive art, and we respond to it with the tautology of literary judgment, that a fiction is "good" if it's "good." No writer who fails to convince us of the validity of his or her vision of the world can convince us of his or her greatness. The Victorians used literature to teach piety, and the Aesthetes asserted that Victorian piety was a deadening lie. Albert Camus believed that no serious writer in the twentieth century could avoid political commitment, whereas for Joyce the true artist could be a God but *must not* be a preacher. Each of these stances is a moral one. Those who defend escape literature do so on the grounds that people *need* to escape. Those who defend hardcore pornography argue that we can't prove an uncensored press makes for moral degeneracy, whereas it can be historically demonstrated that a censored press makes for political oppression. Anarchistic, nihilistic, and antisocial literature is always touted as offering a neglected truth. I have yet to hear anyone assert that literature leads to laziness, madness, and brutality and then say that it doesn't matter.

The writer, of course, may be powerfully impelled to impose a limited vision of the world as it ought to be, and even to tie that vision to a social institution, wishing not only to persuade and convince but to propagandize. But because the emotional force of literary persuasion is in the realization of the particular, the writer is doomed to fail. The greater the work, the more it refers us to some permanent human impulse rather than a given institutional embodiment of that impulse. Fine writing expands our scope by continually presenting a new way of seeing, a further possibility of emotional identification; it flatly refuses to become a law. I am not a Roman Catholic like Gerard Manley Hopkins and cannot be persuaded by his poetry to become one; but in a moment near despair I can drive along an Illinois street in a Chevrolet station wagon and take strength from the lines of a Jesuit in the Welsh wasteland. I am not a communist as Bertolt Brecht was and cannot be convinced by his plays to become one; but I can see the hauteur of wealth displayed on the Gulf of Mexico and recognize, from a parable of the German Marxist, the difference between a possession and a belonging.

In the human experience, emotion, judgment, and logic are inextricably mixed, and we make continual cross-reference between and among them. *You've just got the sulks today.* (I pass judgment on your emotion.) *What do you think of this idea?* (How do you judge this logic?) *Why do I feel this way?* (What is the logic of this emotion?) *It makes no sense to be angry about it.* (I pass judgment on the logic of your emotion.) Literature attempts to fuse three areas of experience organically, denying the force of none of them, positing that no one is more real than the others. This is why I have insisted throughout this book on detail and scene (immediate felt experience), the essential abstractions conveyed therein (ideas), and the attitude implied thereby (judgment).

Not all experience reveals, but all revelation comes through experience. Books aspire to become a part of that revelatory experience, and the books that are made in the form of fiction attempt to do so by re-creating the experience of revelation.

How Fictional Elements Contribute to Theme

Whatever the idea and attitudes that underlie the theme of a story, that story will bring them into the realm of experience through its particular and unique pattern. Theme involves emotion, logic, and judgment, all three—but the pattern that forms the particular experience of that theme is made up of every element of fiction this book has discussed: the arrangement, shape, and flow of the action, as performed by the characters, realized in their details, seen in their atmosphere, from a unique point of view, through the imagery and the rhythm of the language.

This book, for example, contains at least five stories that may be said to have "the generation gap" as a major theme: "The Cutting Edge," "Girl," "The Persistence of Memory," "How Far She Went," and "The Gift of the Prodigal." Two of these are written from the point of view of the parent, one of the child, two of a limited omniscient author. In some the conflict is resolved by bridging the gap, in others it is not. The characters are variously poor, middle class, rural, suburban, male, female, adolescent, middle-aged, old, black, white. The imagery variously evokes art, war, nakedness, clothing, animals, food, theft, lies, and sex. It is in the different uses of the elements of fiction that each story makes unique what it has to say about, and what attitude it takes toward, the idea of "the generation gap."

What follows is as short a story as you are likely to encounter in print. It is spare in the extreme—almost, as its title suggests, an outline. Yet the author has contrived in this miniscule compass to direct every fictional element we have discussed toward the exploration of several large themes.

A Man Told Me the Story of His Life

GRACE PALEY

Vicente said: I wanted to be a doctor. I wanted to be a doctor with my whole heart.

I learned every bone, every organ in the body. What is it for? Why does it work?

The school said to me: Vicente, be an engineer. That would be good. You understand mathematics.

I said to the school: I want to be a doctor. I already know how the organs connect. When something goes wrong, I'll understand how to make repairs.

The school said: Vicente, you will really be an excellent engineer. You show on all the tests what a good engineer you will be. It doesn't show whether you'll be a good doctor.

I said: Oh, I long to be a doctor. I nearly cried. I was seventeen. I said: But perhaps you're right. You're the teacher. You're the principal. I know I'm young.

The school said: And besides, you're going into the army.

And then I was made a cook. I prepared food for two thousand men.

Now you see me. I have a good job. I have three children. This is my wife, Consuela. Did you know I saved her life?

Look, she suffered pain. The doctor said: What is this? Are you tired? Have you had too much company? How many children? Rest overnight, then tomorrow we'll make tests.

The next morning I called the doctor. I said: She must be operated immediately. I have looked in the book. I see where her pain is. I understand what the pressure is, where it comes from. I see clearly the organ that is making trouble.

The doctor made a test. He said: She must be operated at once. He said to me: Vicente, how did you know?

I think it would be fair to say that this story is about the waste of Vicente's talent through the bad guidance of authority. I'll start by saying, then, that *waste* and *power* are its central themes. How are the elements of fiction arranged in the story to present them?

The *conflict* is between Vicente and the figures of authority he encounters: teacher, principal, army, doctor. His desire at the beginning of the story is to become a doctor (in itself a figure of authority), and this desire is thwarted by persons of increasing power. In the *crisis action* what is at stake is his wife's life. In this "last battle" he succeeds as a doctor, so that the *resolution* reveals the *irony* of his having been denied in the first place.

The story is told from the *point of view* of a *first person central narrator*, but with an important qualification. The title, "A Man Told Me the Story of His Life," and the first two words, "*Vicente said*," posit a *peripheral narrator* reporting what Vicente said. If the story were titled "My Life" and began, "I wanted to be a doctor," Vicente might be making a public appeal, a boast of how wronged he has been. As it is, he told his story privately to the barely sketched author who now wants it known, and this leaves Vicente's modesty intact.

The modesty is underscored by the simplicity of his *speech*, a *rhythm* and word choice that suggest educational *limitations* (perhaps that English is a second language). At the same time, that simplicity helps us *identify* with Vicente morally. Clearly if he has educational limitations, it is not for want of trying to get an education! His credibility is augmented by *understatement*, both as a youth—"Perhaps you're right. You're the teacher."—and as a man—"I have a good job. I have three children."—This apparent acceptance makes us trust him at the same time as it makes us angry on his behalf.

It's consistent with the spareness of the language that we do not have an accumulation of minute or vivid details, but the degree of *specificity* is nevertheless a clue to where to direct our sympathy. In the title Vicente is just "A Man." As soon as he speaks he becomes an individual with a name.

"The School" speaks to him, collective and impersonal, but when he speaks it is to "the teacher, the principal," and when he speaks of his wife she is "Consuela."

Moreover, the *sense details* are so arranged that they relate to each other in ways that give them *metaphoric* and *symbolic significance*. Notice, for example, how Vicente's desire to become a doctor "with my whole heart" is immediately followed by, "I learned every bone, every organ. . . ." Here the factual anatomical study refers us back to the heart that is one of those organs, suggesting by implication that Vicente is somebody who knows what a heart is. He knows how things "connect."

An engineer, of course, has to know how things connect and how to make repairs. But so does a doctor, and the authority figures of the school haven't the imagination to see that connection. The army, by putting him to work in a way that involves both connections and anatomical parts, takes advantage of his by-now clear ability to order and organize things—he feeds two thousand men—but it is too late to repair the misdirection of such talents. We don't know what his job is now; it doesn't matter, it's the wrong one.

As a young man Vicente asked, "What is it for? Why does it work?" revealing a natural fascination with the sort of question that would, of course, be asked on an anatomy test. But no such test is given, and the tests that are given are irrelevant. His wife's doctor will "make tests," but like the school authorities he knows less than Vicente does, and so impersonally asks insultingly personal questions. In fact you could say that all the authorities of the story fail the test.

This analysis, which is about two and a half times as long as the story, doesn't begin to exhaust the possibilities for interpretation, and you may disagree with any of my suggestions. But it does indicate how the techniques of characterization, plot, detail, point of view, image, and metaphor all reinforce the themes of waste and power. The story is so densely conceived and developed that it might fairly be titled "Connections," "Tests," "Repairs," "What is it For?" or "How Did You Know?"—any one could lead us toward the themes of waste and the misguidance of authority.

Not every story is or needs to be as intensely interwoven in its elements as "A Man Told Me the Story of His Life," but the development of theme always involves such interweaving to a degree. It is a standard to work toward.

Developing Theme as You Write

In an essay, your goal is to say as clearly and directly as possible what you mean. In fiction, your goal is to make people and make them do things, and, ideally, never to "say what you mean" at all. Theoretically, an outline can never harm an essay: this is what I have to say, and I'll say it through points A, B, and C. But if a writer sets out to write a story to illustrate an idea, the fiction will almost inevitably be thin. Even if you begin with an outline, as many writers do, it will be an outline of the action and not of your "points." You may not know the meaning of the story until the characters begin to tell you what it is. You'll begin with an image of a person or a situation that seems vaguely to embody something important, and you'll learn as you go what that something is. Likewise, what you mean will emerge in the reading experience and take place in the reader's mind, "not," as the narrator says of Marlowe's tales in *Heart of Darkness*, "inside like a kernel but outside, enveloping the tale which brought it out."

But at some point in the writing process, you may find yourself impelled by, under pressure of, or interested primarily in your theme more than your plot. It will seem that you must set yourself this lonely, austere, and tortuous task because you do have something to say. At this point you will, and you should, begin to let that sorting-comparing-cataloguing neocortical portion of your triune human brain go to work on the stuff of your story. John Gardner describes the process in *The Art of Fiction*.

> Theme, it should be noticed, is not imposed on the story but evoked from within it—initially an intuitive but finally an intellectual act on the part of the writer. The writer muses on the story idea to determine what it is in it that has attracted him, why it seems to him worth telling. Having determined . . . what interests him—and what chiefly concerns the major character . . . he toys with various ways of telling his story, thinks about what has been said before about (his theme), broods on every image that occurs to him, turning it over and over, puzzling it, hunting for connections, trying to figure out—before he writes, while he writes, and in the process of repeated revisions—what it is he really thinks . . . . Only when he thinks out a story in this way does he achieve not just an alternative reality or, loosely, an imitation of nature, but true, firm art—fiction as serious thought.

This process—worrying a fiction until its theme reveals itself, connections occur, images recur, a pattern emerges—is more conscious than readers know, beginning writers want to accept, or established writers are willing to admit. It has become a popular—a cliché –stance for modern writers to claim that they haven't the faintest idea what they meant in their writing. *Don't ask me; read the book. If I knew what it meant, I wouldn't have written it. It means what it says.* When an author makes such a response, it is well to remember that an author is a professional liar. What he or she means is not that there are no themes, ideas, or meanings in the work but that these are not separable from the pattern of fictional experience in which they are embodied. It also means that, having done the difficult writerly job, the writer is now unwilling also to do the critic's work. But beginning critics also resist. Students irritated by the analysis of literature often ask, "How do you know she did that on purpose? How do you know it didn't just happen to come out that way?" The answer is: you don't. But what is on the page is on the page. An author no less than a reader or critic can see an emerging pattern, and the author has both the possibility and the obligation of manipulating it. When you have put something on the page, you have two possibilities, and only two: you may cut it or you are committed to it. Gail Godwin asks:

> But what about the other truths you lost by telling it that way? . . .
> Ah, my friend, that is my question too. The choice is always a killing one. One option must die so that another may live. I do little murders in my workroom every day.

Often the choice to commit yourself to a phrase, an image, a line of dialogue will reveal, in a minor convulsion of understanding, what you mean. I have written no story or novel in which this did not occur in trivial or dramatic ways. I once sat bolt upright at 4:00 a.m. in a strange town with the realization that my sixty-year-old narrator, in a novel full of images of hands and manipulation, had been lying to me for two hundred pages. Sometimes the realistic objects or actions of a work will begin to take on metaphoric or symbolic associations with your theme, producing a crossing of references or what Richmond Lattimore calls a "symbol complex." In a novel about a woman who traveled around the world, I dealt with images of dangerous water and the danger of her losing her balance, both physically and mentally. At some point I came up with—or, as it felt, was given—the image of a canal, the lock in which water finds its balance. This unforeseen connection gave me the purest moment of pleasure I had in writing that book. Yet I dare say no reader could identify it as a moment of particular intensity; nor, I hope, would any reader be consciously aware that the themes of danger and balance joined there.

Although I can address myself to what Grace Paley ultimately chose to publish as "A Man Told Me the Story of His Life," I cannot recount the theme-worrying *process* of any writer except myself, so I would like to try briefly to outline one such experience.

I quoted earlier from a novel that begins with the burial of a dog. When I began writing I did not know why I wanted this scene in the book, let alone at the powerful position of its opening. I complained in my journal of the time, "It has nothing to do with the plot."

The book was about a theater director, his first wife, who was a costume designer, and his second wife, who did not particularly know herself. The director is directing a play called *The Nuns*, in which three men dressed as nuns murder a young Spanish heiress, bury her, and later dig her up. The director is having trouble communicating with his son. He is also frightened of becoming like his father, who killed himself, while his current wife is frightened of becoming like her mother, who is a prim and colorless bore. The two wives are nervous about meeting each other. The first wife has not quite put the marriage behind her, and is afraid of falling in love with the theater carpenter.

Now, the structure of this book follows the seven-week rehearsal period of the play, and I knew it was to be called *Opening Night* — or, as it turned out, *Opening Nights*. As I wrote I began to discover that all the characters were having trouble "opening up" to each other. I began to notice that there were a lot of windows, doors, keys, and locks in their houses, apartments, motels, offices, and cars. Flowers tended to open here and there. Reading the newspaper one morning before I sat down to the desk I learned that it had been a bad year for earthquakes (a lot of earthquakes went into the book). I thought about how, in an earthquake, the earth can open up and close again — or else not. This was true also of my characters' hearts. Some sexual parallels presented themselves. As the plot developed I realized that a major reason my characters were having trouble opening up was that each had failed to deal with a significant person in the past, either a parent or a spouse. In order to get on with their lives, each had to dig up the past and get it properly buried again. *And of course I had to dig up that dog.*

I have had a good time writing this flippant outline, but it represents a tiny fraction of a process that took seven years, during which I twice decided to give up the novel and once decided to give up writing altogether. And even now, if someone asks me what the book is "about," I answer: *It's about a costume designer in a crummy little town in southern Georgia, whose ex-husband comes to work in the same town.* In other words, I answer with character and plot, which is what my interlocutor wants to know about. But in doing so I feel dishonest and detached. I could answer more truthfully and with more enthusiasm: *It's about digging up graves* (but that would give the false impression that it's a horror novel); or: *It's about dreams coming true* (which would give the equally false impression that it's a romance); or: *It's about professionalism, trash and treasure, getting rid of the past, opening and openings, permission, the occult as a metaphor for the horrors of ordinary life* (none of which, I think, would give much impression at all). Jane Austen once wrote her sister that the theme of her novel *Mansfield Park* was "ordination." In the two hundred years since that letter, critics have written many times the number of words in the novel trying to explain what she meant. And yet the novel is well understood, forcefully experienced, and intelligently appreciated. The difficulty is not in understanding the book but in applying the "kernel" definition to its multiplicity of ideas and richness of theme.

The fusion of elements into a unified pattern is the nature of creativity, a word devalued in latter years to the extent that it has come to mean a random gush of self-expression. God, perhaps, created out of the void; but in the world as we know it, all creativity, from the sprouting of an onion to the painting of *Guernica*, is a matter of selection and arrangement. A child learns to draw one circle on top of another, to add two triangles at the top and a line at the bottom, and in this particular pattern of circles, triangles, and lines has made a creature of an altogether different nature: a cat! The child draws one square on top of another and connects the corners and has made three dimensions where there are only two. And although these are tricks that can be taught and learned, they partake of the essential nature of creativity, in which several elements are joined to produce, not merely a whole that is greater than the sum of its parts, but a whole that is something altogether other. At the conception of a fetus or a short story, there occurs a conjunction of two unlike things, whether cells or ideas, that have never been joined before. Around this conjunction other cells, other ideas accumulate in a deliberate pattern. That pattern is the unique personality of the creature, and if the pattern does not cohere it miscarries or is stillborn.

The organic unity of a work of literature cannot be taught—or, if it can, I have not discovered a way to teach it. I can suggest from time to time that concrete image is not separate from character, which is revealed in dialogue and point of view, which may be illuminated by simile, which may reveal theme, which is contained in plot as water is contained in an apple. But I cannot tell you how to achieve this; nor, if you achieve it, will you be able to explain very clearly how you have done so. Analysis separates in order to focus; it assumes that an understanding of the parts contributes to an understanding of the whole, but it does not produce the whole. Scientists can determine with minute accuracy the elements, in their proportions, contained in a piece of human skin. They can gather these elements, stir and warm them, but they will not be skin. A good critic can show you where a metaphor does or does not illuminate character, where the character does or does not ring true in an action. But the critic cannot tell you how to make a character breathe; the breath is talent and can neither be explained nor produced.

No one can tell you what to mean, and no one can tell you how. I am conscious of having avoided the phrase *creative writing* in these pages, largely because all of us who teach creative writing find the words sticking in our throats. I myself would like to see courses taught in creative algebra, creative business administration, creative nursing, and creative history. I also fully and seriously intend one day to teach an advanced seminar in destructive writing (polemic, invective, libel, actionable obscenity, and character defamation). The mystique and the false glamour of the writing profession grow partly out of a mistaken belief that people who can express profound ideas and emotions have ideas and emotions more profound than the rest of us. It isn't so. The ability to express is a special gift with a special craft to support it and is spread fairly equally among the profound, the shallow, and the mediocre.

All the same, I am abashedly conscious that the creative exists—in algebra and nursing as in words—and that it mysteriously surfaces in the trivia of human existence: numbers, bandages, words. In the unified pattern of a fiction there is even something to which the name of magic may be given, where one empty word is placed upon another and tapped with a third, and a flaming scarf or a long-eared hope is pulled out of the tall black heart. The most magical thing about this magic is that once the trick is explained, it is not explained, and the better you understand how it works, the better it will work again.

Birth, death, work, and love continue to occur. Their meaning changes from time to time and place to place, and new meanings engender new forms, which capture and create new meanings until they tire, while birth, death, work, and love continue to recur. Something to which we give the name of "honor" seems to persist, though in one place and time it is embodied in choosing to die for your country, in another, choosing not to. A notion of "progress" survives, though it is expressed now in technology, now in ecology, now in the survival of the fittest, now in the protection of the weak. There seems to be something corresponding to the human invention of "love," though it takes its form now in tenacious loyalty, now in letting go.

Ideas are not new, but the form in which they are expressed is constantly renewed, and new forms give life to what used to be called (in the old form) the eternal verities. An innovative writer tries to forge, and those who follow try to perfect, forms that so fuse with meaning that form itself expresses.

Mobius the Stripper

A TOPOLOGICAL EXERCISE

GABRIEL JOSIPOVICI

No one ever knew the origins and background of Mobius the stripper. "I'm not English," he would say, "that's for certain." His language was an uneasy mixture of idioms and accents, jostling each other as the words fell from his thick lips. He was always ready to talk. To anyone who would listen. He had to explain. It was a need.

"You see. What I do. My motive. Is not seshual. Is metaphysical. A metaphysical motive, see? I red Jennett. Prust. Nitch. Those boys. All say the same. Is a metaphysical need. To strip. To take off what society has put on me. What my father and my mother have put on me. What my friends have put on me. What I have put on me. And I say to me: What are you

---

I first heard of Mobius the stripper from a girl with big feet called Jenny. She was one of those girls who make a point of always knowing what's going on, and in those days she was constantly coming up with bright and bizarre little items of information in which she tried to interest me. Once she dragged me to Ealing where, in the small and smoke-filled back room of a dingy terrace, a fakir of sorts first turned a snake into a rope, then climbed the rope and sat fanning himself with a mauve silk handkerchief with his greasy hair just touching the flaking ceiling, then redescended and turned the rope back into a snake before finally returning the snake to the little leather bag from which he had taken it. A cheap trick. Another time she took me to Greenwich, where a friend of hers knew a man who kept six seals in his bathtub, but the man was gone or dead or simply unwilling to answer her friend's urgent ring at the doorbell. Most of all, though, Jenny's interest centred on deviant sexuality, and she was forever urging me to go with her to some dreary nightclub or "ned of wice" as she liked to call it, where men, women, children and monsters of every description did their best to plug the gaps in creation which a thoughtful Nature had benevolently provided for just such a purpose. Usually I didn't respond to these invitations of Jenny's, partly because her big feet embarrassed me (though she was a likeable girl with some distinction as a lacrosse player I believe), and partly because this kind of thing did not greatly interest me anyway.

Mobius? a man? A wooman? A vedge table? Are you a stone, Mobius? This fat. You feel here. Here. Like it's folds of fat, see. And it's me. Mobius. This is the mystery. I want to get right down behind this fat to the centre of me. And you can help me. Yes you. Everybody. Everybody can help Mobius. That the mystery. You and you and you and you. You think you just helping yourself but you helping me. And for why? Because in ultimate is not seshual. Is metaphysical. Maybe religious."

When Mobius spoke other people listened. He had presence. Not just size or melancholy but presence. There was something about the man that demanded attention and got it. No one knew where he lived, not even the manager of the club in Notting Hill, behind the tube station, where he stripped in public seven nights a week.

"You want to take Sundays off?" Tony the manager asked when he engaged him.

"Off?" Mobius said.

"We allow you one night a week," the manager said. "We treat our artists proper."

"But it *must* interest you," Jenny would say. "They're all part of our world, aren't they?"

I agreed, but explained that not all parts of the world held out an equal interest for me.

"I don't understand you," she said. "You say you want to be a writer and then you *shut* your mind to experience. You simply *shut* your mind to it. You live in an ivory bower."

I accepted what she said. My mistake was ever to have told her I wanted to be a writer. The rest I deserved.

"Did Shakespeare have your attitude?" Jenny said. "Did Leonardo?"

No, I had to admit. Shakespeare had not had my attitude. Neither had Leonardo.

"Well then," Jenny said.

Sometimes, at this point, I'd be sorry for Jenny, for her big feet and her fresh English face. Mobius. Mobius the stripper. I could just imagine him. His real name was Ted Binks. He had broad shoulders and a waist narrow as a girl's. When he walked he pranced and when he laughed he.

"Well then," Jenny repeated, as if my admission made further discussion unnecessary. I sighed and said:

"All right. I'll come if you want me to. But if we're going to go all the way across London again only to find the door closed in our faces and the—"

"That only happened once," Jenny said. "I don't see why you have to

"I doan understand," Mobius said. "You employ me or you doan employ me. There an end."

"You have rights," the manager said. "We treat our artists proper here. We're not in the business to exploit them."

"You not exploitin," Mobius said. "You doin me a favour. You payin me and givin me pleasure both."

"All right," the manager said. "I'm easy."

"You easy with me, I easy with you," Mobius said. "Okydoke?"

"You're on at six this evening then," the manager said, getting up and opening the door of his little office.

Mobius wanted to kiss him but the manager, a young man with a diamond tiepin, hastily stepped back behind his desk. When the door shut behind Mobius he slumped back in his chair, buried his face in his hands, and burst into tears. Nor was he ever afterwards able to account for this uncharacteristic gesture or forget it, hard as he tried.

Mobius arrived at five that afternoon and every subsequent afternoon as well. "You need concentration," he would say. "A good stripper needs to

---

bring it up like this every time. Anyway, it was you who wanted to see those seals. As soon as I told you about them you wanted to see them."

"All right," I said, resigned. "All right."

"It's yourself you're doing a favour to, not me," Jenny would add at this point. "You can't write without experience, and how the hell are you going to gain experience if you stay shut up in here all day long?"

Indeed, the girl had a point. She wasn't strictly accurate, since my mornings were spent delivering laundry for NU-nap, the new nappy service ("We clean dirt" they modestly informed the world in violet letters on their cream van—I used to wake up whispering that phrase to myself, at times it seemed to be the most beautiful combination of the most beautiful words in the language), and my evenings kicking the leaves in the park as I watched the world go by. But not quite inaccurate either, since I recognized within myself a strong urge towards seclusion, a shutting out of the world and its too urgent claims, Jenny included. And not just the world. The past too I would have liked to banish from my consciousness at times, and with it all the books I had ever read. As I bent over my desk in the afternoons, staring at the virgin paper, I would wish fervently, pray desperately to whatever deity would answer my prayers, that all the print which had ever been conveyed by my eyes to my brain and thence buried deep inside me where it remained to fester could be removed by a sharp painless and efficient knife. Not that I felt history to be a nightmare from which I get in the right mood. Is like Yoga. All matter of concentration."

"Yes," the manager would say. "Yes. Of course. Of course."

"With me," Mobius explained to him, "is not seshual, is metaphysical. A metaphysical motive. Not like the rest of this garbage."

But they didn't mind him saying that. Everybody liked Mobius except Tony the manager. The girls liked him best. "Hi Moby," they shouted. "How's your dick?"

"Is keeping up," he would reply. "How's yours?"

They wanted to know about his private life but he gave nothing away. "We're always telling you about our problems," they complained. "Why don't you ever tell us about yours?"

"I doan have problems," Mobius said.

"Come off it," they said, laughing. "Everyone's got problems."

"You have problems?" he asked them, surprised.

"Would we be in this lousy joint if we didn't?"

"Problems, problems," Mobius said. "Is human invention, problems."

But they felt melancholy in the late afternoons, far from their families,

---

wanted to awake etcetera etcetera, but simply that I felt the little self I once possessed to be dangerously threatened by the size and the *assurance* of all the great men who had come before me. There they were, solid, smiling, melancholy or grim as the case might be, Virgil and Dante and Descartes and Wordsworth and Joyce, lodged inside me, each telling me the truth — and who could doubt it was the truth, their very lives bore witness to the fact — but was it *my* truth, that was the question. And behind that, of course, another question and another: Was I entitled to a truth of my own at all, and if so, was it not precisely by following Jenny out into the cold streets of Richmond or Bermondsey or Highgate that I should find it?

At other times I'd catch myself before I spoke and, furious at the degree of condescension involved in feeling sorry for Jenny — who was I to feel sorry for anyone? — would say to her instead: "Fuck off. I want to work."

"Work later."

"No. I've got to work now."

"It's good for your work. You can't create out of your own entrails."

"There are always excuses. It's always either too early or too late."

"You want to be another of those people who churn out tepid trivia because it's the thing to be a writer? Why not forget that bit and live a little for a change?"

Dear Jenny. Despite her big feet — no, no, because of them — she never let go. She knew I'd give way in the end and if she'd come to me with the news and in the early hours of the morning, when the public had all departed. "Where do you live?" they asked him. "Do you have a man or a woman? Do you have any children, Moby?"

To all these questions he replied with the same kindly smile, but once, when he caught one of them tailing him after a show he came back and hit her across the face with his glove so that none of them ever tried anything like that again.

"I doan ask you you doan ask me," he said to them after the incident. "I have no secrets but my life is my own business." And when Tony came to have a talk with him about the girl's disfigured cheek he just closed his eyes and didn't answer.

"If it happens again you're out," Tony said, but although he would, in his heart of hearts, have been relieved had this in fact occurred, they both of them knew it was just talk. For Mobius was a gold mine. He really drew them in.

Alone in his little room, not many streets away from the club, he sat on the edge of the bed and stuffed himself sick on bananas. "Meat is meat," he

---

in the first place it was only because she hadn't found anyone else to take her anyway. Jenny had a nose for the peculiar, but she was an old-fashioned girl at heart and felt the need of an escort wherever she went.

"Look," I said to her. "I don't want to live. I want to be left in peace to work."

"But this guy," she said. "The rolls of fat on him. It's fantastic. And the serenity. My God. You should see the serenity in his eyes when he strips."

"Serenity?" I said. "What are you talking about?"

"It's like a Buddha or something," Jenny said.

"What are you trying to do to me?" I said.

"Am I one of those people who fall for Zen and Yoga and all the rest of that Eastern crap?" Jenny said.

I had to admit she wasn't.

"I'm telling you," she said. "It's a great experience."

"Another time," I said.

Cheltenham hadn't prepared her for this. Her eyes popped.

"Another time," I said again.

"You mean—you're not going to come?"

"Another time," I said.

"Wow!" Jenny said. "Something must be happening to you. Are you in love or something?"

"I just want to work," I said.

would say. "I'm no cannibal." Bananas he ate by the hundredweight, sitting with bowed shoulders and sagging folds of fat on the narrow unmade bed, staring at the blank wall.

Those were good hours, the hours spent staring at the wall, waiting for four o'clock. Not as good as the hours after four, but good hours all the same. For what harm was he doing? If you don't pick a banana when it's ripe it rots, so again, what harm was he doing? Who was he hurting?

Sometimes the voices started and he sat back and listened to them with pride. "Who's talking of Mobius?" he would say. "I tell you, everybody's talking of Mobius. When I walk I hear them. When I sleep I hear them. When I sit in my room I hear them. Mobius the stripper. The best in the business. I've seen many strippers in my time but there's none to beat Mobius. I first met Mobius. I first saw Mobius. I first heard of Mobius. A friend of mine. A cousin. A duchess, the Duchess of Folkestone. We had been childhood friends. I remember her remarking that Mobius the stripper was the most amazing man she ever knew. I hear them all. But what do I care? That too must be stripped off." Give him the choice and he pre-

---

"You always say that," Jenny said, suddenly deflated.

"I'm sorry," I said, and I was. Desperately. What sort of luck is it to be born with big feet? "Another time," I said. "O.K.?"

"You don't know what you're missing," Jenny said.

True enough, but I could guess. Mobius the stripper, six foot eight and round as a barrel: "That time Primo Carnera was chewing my big toe off. I couldn't get a proper grip on the slimy bastard so I grope around and he's chewing my toe like it'll come off any minute and then I find I've got my finger up his nostril and." Yes. Very good. He was another one I could do without.

After Jenny had gone I stared at the virgin sheet of paper on the table in front of me. When I did that I always wanted to scream. And when I left it there and got out, anywhere, just out, away from it all, then all I ever wanted to do was get back and start writing. Crazy. In those days I had a recurrent nightmare. I was in my shorts, playing rugger in the mud against the giants. Proust, languid and bemonocled, kept guard behind the pack; Joyce, small and fiery, his moustache in perfect trim, darted through their legs, whisking out the ball and sending it flying to the wings; Dostoyevsky, manic and bearded; Swift, ferocious and unstoppable; Chaucer, going like a terrier. And the pack, the pack itself, Tolstoy and Hugo and Homer and Goethe, Lawrence and Pascal and Milton and Descartes. Bearing down on me. Huge. Powerful. Totally confident. The ball kept coming out at me on

ferred the beautiful silence. The peace of stripping. But if they came he accepted them. They did him no harm.

He flicked another skin into the metal waste-paper basket and bit into another banana. When it was gone he would feel in the corners, between the molars, with his tongue, and sigh with contentment. How many doctors, wise men, had told him to pack it in, to have a change of diet and start a new life? But then how many doctors had told him he was too fat, needed to take more exercise, had bad teeth, incipient arthritis, a weak heart, bad circulation, bronchitis, pneumonia, traces of malarial fever, smallpox? He was a man, a mound of flesh, heir to all that flesh is heir to. Mobius sighed and rubbed the folds of his stomach happily. It was a miracle he had survived this long when you thought of all the things that could have happened to him. And if so long then why not longer? "Time," he would say, "she mean nothing to me. You see this? This fat? My body she my clock. When I die she stop." And after all he had no need of clocks, there was a church the other side of the street and it sounded for him, especially for him, a particular peal, at four o'clock. Then he would get up and make

---

the wing. It was a parcel of nappies neatly wrapped in plastic, "We clean dirt" in violet lettering across it. I always seemed to be out there by myself, there was never anyone else on my side, but the ball would keep coming out of the loose at me. It always began like that, with the ball flying through the grey air towards my outstretched arms and then the pack bearing down, boots pounding the turf as in desperation I swung further and further out, knowing all the time that I would never be able to make it into touch or have the nerve to steady and kick ahead. There was just me and this ball that was a parcel of nappies and all of them coming at me. Descartes in particular obsessed me. I would wake up sweating and wondering how it was possible to be so sure and yet so wrong. And why did they all have to keep coming for me like that, with Proust always drifting nonchalantly behind them, hair gleaming, boots polished, never in any hurry but always blocking my path? What harm had I done any of them except read them? And now I wanted to forget them. Couldn't I be allowed to do that in peace? You don't think of it when you look at a tempting spine in a library or bookshop, but once you touch it you've had it. You're involved. It's worse than a woman. It's there in your body till the day you die and the harder you try and forget it the clearer it gets.

I tried aphorisms:

"If a typewriter could read what it had written it would sue God."

"He is another."

the bed ("You got to have order. Disorder in the little thing and that's the beginning of the end"), wash his teeth and get his things together. No one had ever known him to get to the club after five ("You need time to meditate if you do a show like mine. Is like Yoga, all meditation").

When Tony the manager took his annual holiday in the Bermudas he locked up the place and carried the keys away with him. Mobius, a stickler for routine and with a metaphysical need to satisfy, still got up at four, made his bed, emptied the banana skin into the communal dustbin in the back yard, cleaned his teeth, packed his things, and went on down to the club. He rattled on the door and even tried to push it open with his shoulder, but it wouldn't give and he wasn't one to be put off by a thing like that. "I got my rights, same as you," he said to the policeman who took him in. "Nobody going to shut a door in my face and get away with it."

"That's no reason to break it down," the policeman said, staring in wonder at Mobius.

"I got my rights," Mobius said.

"You mean they don't pay you?" the policeman asked.

"The trouble with the biological clock is it has no alarm."

No good. They weren't even good enough to fit end to end and send in as a poem to the *T.L.S.* In the streets Rilke walked beside me and whispered in my ear. He said beautiful things but I preferred whatever nonsense I might have thought up for myself if he hadn't been there. In the mornings I drove my cream van through the suburbs of west London and that kept me sane. I screamed to a halt, leapt out with my neat parcel of clean nappies, swapped it for the dirty ones waiting on the doorstep in the identical plastic wrapper, "We clean dirt" in violet lettering. "Like hell you do," said a note pinned to the wrapper once. "Take it back and try again."

I took it back. They weren't my babies or my nappies and I didn't give a damn but my life was sliding off the rails and I didn't know what in God's good name to do about it.

"Why don't you come and see Mobius the stripper?" Jenny said. "It'll change your ideas. Give it a break and you'll all of a sudden see the light."

"That's fine," I said, "except I've been saying just that for the last fifteen years and I'm still in the dark."

"That's because you don't trust," Jenny said. "You've got no faith."

I had to admit she might be right. Unto those who have etcetera etcetera. But how does one contrive to have in the first place? There was a flaw somewhere but who was I to spot it?

"All right," Jenny said. "Make an effort. Anybody can write *something*. Just

"Sure they pay me," Mobius said.

"I mean in the holidays."

"Sure," Mobius said.

"Well then," the policeman said.

"I got my rights," Mobius said. "He employ me, no?"

"If it's a holiday why not go away somewhere?" the policeman said. "Give yourself a break."

"I doan want a break," Mobius said. "I want my rights."

"I don't know about that," the policeman said. "You've committed an offence against the law. I'm afraid I'll have to book you for it."

"You doan understand," Mobius said to the policeman. "This is my life. Just because he want to go to the fucking Bermudas doan mean I got to have my life ruined, eh?"

"Are you American or something?" the policeman asked, intrigued.

"You want to see my British passport?" Mobius said.

"Stay at home," the policeman advised him. "Take it easy for a few days. We'll look into the matter when the manager returns."

---

put something down and then you'll feel better and you can come out with me."

Something. Mobius the stripper was a genial man when in the bosom of his family. Etcetera. Etcetera etcetera. "Oh, fuck off," I said. "I told you I didn't want to be disturbed."

"It'll do you good," she said, standing her ground. The worse the language I used the more she responded. She had a lot of background to make up for. "Besides," she said, "it's all good experience."

"I don't need experience," I said. "I need peace and quiet. And, if I'm lucky, a bit of inspiration."

"He'd give you that," Jenny said. "Just to look at him is to feel inspired."

"What do you mean just to look at him?" I said. "What else are we expected to do?"

"Go to hell," Jenny said.

"Tomorrow," I said.

"You said that yesterday."

"Nevertheless," I said. "Tomorrow."

Jenny began to sob. It was impressive. I was impressed. "Just because I have big feet," she said, "you think you can push me around like that."

"Jenny," I said. "Please. I like big feet."

"You don't," she sobbed. "You find them ridiculous." When she sobbed she really sobbed. Nothing could stem the tide.

The next time Tony took his holiday he gave Mobius the key of the club, but without the audience it wasn't the same, and after a day or two he just stayed in his room the whole time except for the occasional stroll down to the park and back, heavily protected by his big coat and Russian fur hat. But he wasn't used to the streets, especially in the early evening when the tubes disgorged their contents, and it did him no good, no good at all. Inside the room he felt happier, but the break in the routine stopped him going to sleep and he spent the night with the light switched on. The bulb swung in the breeze and the voices dissolved him into a hundred parts. I first saw Mobius at a club in Buda. In Rio. In Albuquerque. A fine guy, Mobius. Is he? Oh yes, a fine guy. I remember going to see him and. I first heard of Mobius the stripper from a kid down on the front in Marseilles. From a girl in Vienna. She was over there on a scholarship to study the cello and she. I met her in a restaurant. In a bar. She was blond. Dark. A sort of dark skin. Long fingers. A cellist's fingers. There's nobody like Mobius, she said.

Mobius smiled and listened to the voices. They came and went inside his

---

"In men," I said. "I find them ridiculous in men. In women I find them a sign of solidity. Stability."

"You're just laughing at me," she said. "You despise me because of my big feet."

M.E. the foot fetishist. He was a quiet man, scholarly and abstemious. Everyone who ever met him said he was almost a saint. Not quite but almost. Yet deep inside there throbbed etcetera etcetera.

"But I don't," I said. "You've no idea what I feel about feet. I can't have enough of them. That's just what I like about you, Jenny. Your big feet."

She stopped crying. Just like that. "You're despicable," she said. "You're obscene."

"Look Jenny," I said. "I'll come with you. I'd love to see this chap. But tomorrow, O.K.?"

An incredible girl, Jenny. A great tactician. "You promise?" she said before I had time to draw breath.

"You know I'd love to go," I said. "I just don't want to be a drag on you. And if I'm sitting there thinking of my work all the time instead of being convivial and all I—"

"You'll see," Jenny said. "You'll love him. He's a lovely man."

Lovely or not I didn't think I could face them, either Jenny or her stripper, so I locked the door and went out into the park. Walking around there and kicking my feet in the leaves and seeing all those nannies and head and if that's where they liked to be he had no objection. There was room and more. But he missed his sleep and he knew bronzed Tony had a point when he said: "Mobius, you look a sight."

That was the day the club re-opened. "Why don't you take a holiday same as everyone?" Tony said. "You must have a tidy bit stacked away by now."

"A holiday from what?" Mobius asked him.

"I don't know," Tony said. Mobius upset him, he didn't know which way to take him. Maybe one of these days he'd cease to pull them in and then he could get rid of him. "Just a holiday," he said. "From work."

"Look," Mobius said to him. "That the difference between us, Tony. You work and you spit on your work. But for me my work is my life."

"O.K.," Tony said. "I'm not complaining."

"Is there a holiday from life?" Mobius asked him. "Answer me that, Tony."

"For God's sake!" Tony said. "Can't you talk straight ever? You're not on stage now you know."

---

things kept the rest of it at bay. Had Rilke seen this nanny? Or Proust that child? Had Hopkins seen this tree, this leaf? So what did they have to teach me? They were talking about something else altogether. They were just about as much use to me as I was to them. And if it's eternity they wanted, why pick on me? There are plenty of other fools around for them to try their vampire tricks on. I can do without them, thank you very much. And if it's this tree I want to see they only get in the way. And if it isn't what use am I to myself? Their trees they've already seen.

After a while, though, I felt the urge to get back in there and sit down in front of that blasted sheet of white paper. What use is this tree even if I do see it? No use to me or to the world. And even if it is, who says I *can* see it? When I sit down in front of that sheet of paper I have this feeling I want to tear right in and get everything down. Everything. And then what happens? He was a small man with a. I remember once asking Charles and. Gerald looked round. Christopher turned. When Jill saw. When Robert saw. Elizabeth Nutely was. Geraldine Bluett was. Hilary McPherson wasn't exactly the. Everything is the enemy of something, and when my pen touches the paper I go blank. Stories. Stories and stories. Mobius the stripper sat in his penthouse flat and filed his nails. Sat in his bare room and picked his nose. Stories and stories. Anyone can write them. All you need is a hide thick enough to save you from boring yourself sick. Jack turned suddenly and said. Count Frederick Prokovsky, a veteran of the

"You just answer me first," Mobius asked. "Is there a holiday from life, Tony?"

"I don't know what you're talking about," Tony said, and when Mobius began to laugh, his great belly heaving, he added under his breath: "You shit."

At home he said to his wife: "That guy Mobius. He's a nut."

"Is he still drawing them in?" his wife asked as she passed him the toast.

"I don't know what they see in him," Tony said. "A fat bloody foreigner stripping in public. Downright obscene it is. And they roll in to see him. It makes you despair of the British public."

"Try the blackcurrant jam," his wife said. And then: "You hired him. You couldn't go on enough about him at first."

"It makes you sick," Tony said. He pulled the jam towards him. "Bloody perverted they are," he said. "Bloody twisted."

But when Mobius said it wasn't sexual it was metaphysical he had a point. Take off the layers and get down to the basics. One day the flesh would go and then the really basic would come to light. Mobius waited

---

Crimea. Horst Voss, the rowing coach. Peter Bender, overseer of a rubber plantation in. Etcetera etcetera. This one and this one and this one. When all the time it's crying out in me (Henry James was much obsessed by this but there the similarity between us ends, Good-bye, Henry James, good-bye, Virginia Woolf, good-bye, good-bye) crying out in me to say *everything, everything.*

They keep peacocks in the park. I don't know why. But they do. One of them was strutting about in the path in front of me. With big feet like Jenny. Who was to say if big feet are attractive or not? And why ask me anyway? Think of the stripper Mobius with his nightly ritual, slowly getting down to the primal scene and after that what? Why do men do things like that and do they even know themselves etcetera etcetera? All the stories in the world but you've only got one body and who would ever exchange the former for the latter except every single second-rate writer who's ever lived? And they still live. Proliferate. And believe in themselves, what's more. Why then the daily anguish and the certainty that if I could only start the pen moving over that sheet of paper my life would alter, alter, as they say, beyond the bounds of recognition? Because I've read them all? The Van Gogh letters and the life of Rimbaud and the Hopkins Notebooks and the N. of M.L.B. Have they conned me even into this? It was possible. Everything is possible. "Tell me the truth," I said to the peacock with the big feet. "Go on, you bastard. Tell me the truth or just fuck off."

patiently for that day.

"You read Prust," he would say. "Nitch. Jennett. Those boys. See what they say. All the same. They know the truth. Is all a matter of stripping."

"You talk too much Moby," the girls said to him. "You're driving us crazy with all your talk."

"You gotta talk when you strip," Mobius explained to them. "You gotta get the audience involved."

"You can have music," the girls said. "Music's nice. Whoever heard of a stripper talking?"

"O.K.," Mobius admitted. "Perhaps I do like to talk. Like that I talk I feel my essential self emerging. Filling the room."

Outside the club, though, Mobius rarely opened his mouth. Certainly he never spoke to himself, and as for the voices, if they wanted to settle for a while inside his head, who was he to order them away? He sat on the bed and stared at the wall, eating bananas and dozing. I first saw. I first heard. I remember His Excellency telling me about Mobius the stripper. In Prague it was, that wonderful city. I was acting as private secretary to the

---

A woman with an unpleasant little runt of a white poodle backed away down an alley. "Don't you want the truth?" I asked her. She turned and beetled off towards the gates. "Lady!" I shouted after her. "Don't you want the truth?"

It's always the same. That's what gets me down. If I can say *anything* then why say anything? And yet everything's there to be said. Round and round. Mobius sat on his bed and ate one banana after another. But did he? Did he?

The bird had gone and I sat down on a bench and looked up at the sky through the trees. Jenny would have been and gone by now. Or perhaps not been at all. I sometimes wondered if Jenny knew quite as many people as she said she did. Wondered if perhaps there was only me she knew in the whole of London. Otherwise how to explain her persistence? Unless those feet of hers kept perpetually carrying her back over the ground they had once trodden. Myth. Ritual. An idea. More than an idea. A metaphor for life. "It is!" I shouted, suddenly understanding. "It is! It is! A metaphor for life!"

A little group of people were standing under the trees a little way along the path. One or two park wardens. A fat man with one of those Russian fur hats. My friend the poodle woman. I waved to them politely. They seemed to expect it. One of the wardens stepped forward and asked politely why I was chasing the peacocks and using bad language. The man

Duke and had time on my hands. I was down and out in Paris and London. A girl called Bertha Pappenheim first mentioned Mobius to me. Not the famous Bertha Pappenheim, another.

Once or twice he would pull a chair up to the mirror on the dressing-table which stood inevitably in the bay window, and stare and stare into his own grey eyes. Then he would push the chair violently back and go over to the bed again.

"For what is life?" he would say. "Chance. And what is *my* life? The result of a million and one chances. But behind chance is truth. The whole problem is to get behind chance to the TRUTH!" That was when the jock strap came off and it brought the house down. But Mobius hadn't finished with them. Sitting cross-legged on the little wooden stage, staring down at more than his navel, he let them have the facts of life, straight from the chest:

"Beyond a man's chance is his necessity. But how many find? I ask you. You think this is seshual thing, but for why you come to see me? Because I give you the truth. Is a metaphysical something, is the truth. Is the necessi-

-----

was preposterous. Couldn't he see me sitting silent on the bench? I'd chased Pascal down a back alley once, but peacocks? What am I to peacocks or they to me? I said to the man.

"I saw you," the poodle woman said. "Chasin and abusin."

"Don't be more absurd than you can help," I said to her.

"Don't you dare talk to me like that, young man," she said.

What would Descartes have done in my place?

"Chasin peacocks and usin abusin language," she said.

"Are you going to stand there and listen to this woman's grotesque accusations?" I asked them.

"It is an offence under the regulations," the warden said, "to chase the peacocks."

"But I love those birds." I said. "I love their big feet." For some reason I was still sitting there on that bench and they were standing grouped together under the trees staring in my direction. "What would I want to go chasing them for?" I said.

How could they be expected to understand? Or, understanding, to believe? Had I a beard like Tolstoy's? A moustache like Rilke's? "Gentlemen," I said. "I apologize. Good evening."

"He's goin away," the woman said. "You can't let him go away like that. He insulted and abused me."

"In that case, madam," the warden said, "I suggest you consult a lawyer."

ty behind the chance. For each man is only one truth and so many in the world as each man is truths."

Mobius, staring into his own grey eyes in the little room in Notting Hill, occasionally sighed, and his gaze would wander over the expanse of flesh exposed and exposable. Sometimes his right hand would hover over the drawer of his dressing-table, where certain private possessions were kept, but would as quickly move away again. That was too easy. Yet if you talk of necessity how many versions are there? His hand hovered but the drawer remained unopened.

"These girls," he would say, "they excite you seshually. But once you seen me your whole life is change." He had a way of riding the laughter, silencing it. "For why? For you learn from me the difference between on one hand clockwork and on other hand necessity. Clockwork is clockwork. One. Two. In. Out. But Necessity she a goddess. She turn your muscles to water and your bones to oil. One day you meet her and you will see that Mobius is right."

He went home after that session more slowly than usual. If he was giving

---

Bless his silver tongue. The first thing I'm going to do when success comes my way is give a donation to the wardens of the London parks.

I was shaken, though. And who wouldn't be? Examples of prejudice are always upsetting. Upsetting but exhilarating, too. They make you want to fight back. Something had happened down there inside me in those few minutes and now I couldn't wait to get back. This was it. After all those years.

There was no message from Jenny on the door. Not even a single word like "Bastard!" or "Fuck you!" or any of the other affectionate little words we use when we are sufficiently intimate with a person. Well fuck her. I could do without her. Without them all. I was sitting at my desk with this white sheet of paper in front of me and suddenly it was easy. I bent over it, pen poised, wrist relaxed, the classic posture. It was all suddenly so easy I couldn't understand what had kept me back for so long.

I looked at the white page. At the pen. At my wrist. I began to laugh. You have to laugh at moments like that. It's the only thing to do. When I had finished laughing I got up and went to the window. What I couldn't work out was if I had actually believed it or really known all along that today was going to be no different from any other day. That between everything and something would once again fall the shadow. Leaving me with nothing. Nothing.

I turned round and sat down at the desk again. At least if Jenny had them the truth where was his truth? His heart heavy with the weight of years he opened the drawer and took out his little friend. Cupping it in his hand he felt its weight. There was no hesitation in his movements now and why should there be? If his life had a logic then this was it. The weight on his heart pressed him to this point. When you have stripped away everything the answer will be there, but if so, why wait? Easy to say it's too easy but why easier than waiting? As always, he did everything methodically. When he had found the right spot on his temple he straightened a little and waited for the steel to gather a little warmth from his flesh. "So I come to myself at last," Mobius said. "To the centre of myself." And he said: "Is my necessity and my truth. And is example to all." He stared into his own grey eyes and felt the coldness of the metal. His finger tightened on the trigger and the voices were there again. Cocking his head on one side and smiling, Mobius listened to what they had to say. He had time on his hands and to spare. Resting the barrel against his brow and smiling to himself in the mirror as the bulb swung in the breeze over his head, Mobius waited for them to finish.

---

been there it wouldn't have been so bad. We could have talked. I looked at my watch. There was still time. She might still come.

I picked up the pen and wrote my name across the top of the sheet, for no reason that I could fathom. And then, suddenly, out of the blue it started to come. Perhaps it was only one story, arbitrary, incomplete, but suddenly I knew that it would make its own necessity and in the process give me back my lost self. Dear Jenny. Dear Mobius. Dear Peacock. "Gone out. Do not disturb," I scrawled on a sheet of paper, pinned it to the door and locked it. Then I sat down and began to write.

Suggestions for Discussion

1. If you don't know what a Möbius strip is, demonstrate the form to yourself like this: cut an inch-wide strip of newspaper and form it into a single loop. Turn over one end of the strip so that there is a single twist in the loop. Tape or staple the ends together. Now begin drawing a line down the middle of the strip; keep going until you meet the beginning of your line. You will have proved that the strip of paper, which self-evidently has two sides, has only one; and that a line drawn in a single direction makes, in fact, a circle.

How does this concept of the Möbius strip relate to, illuminate, or reflect emotion and judgment in "Mobius the Stripper?" How, in particular, does it illuminate the final clause of Mobius's story, "Mobius waited for them to finish?"

2. Suppose you were told that the theme of this story is commitment to a profession; is the metaphysical need to strip; is the need for others; is self-regard; is self-expression; is truth; is fiction itself. How would you respond? Is it none, one, two, all of these?

3. Mobius can't stop talking. The writer can't start writing. How does this contrast (is it really a contrast?) contribute to the theme?

4. Mobius won't take a holiday; the writer won't leave his desk to go see Mobius. How does this parallel contribute to the theme?

5. On page 353 the writer says that NU-nap's motto, "We clean dirt," seemed to be the most beautiful combination of the most beautiful words in the language." Is this mere whimsy or a clue to the story's meaning? Is it significant that Mobius insists, "You got to have order" (page 358)? How?

6. How do the writer's various mental images of Mobius relate to the story of Mobius as it is written?

7. The writer says that each of the authors in his head is "telling me the truth . . . but was it *my* truth . . ." (page 354). Mobius says, "The whole problem is to get behind chance to the TRUTH!" (page 364). If theme in fiction can be described as a speculation on a truth, is the theme of this story a speculation on speculation?

8. The writer wants to cut out the other authors he has read but that are "in your body till the day you die" (page 357). Mobius hears voices but says, "That too must be stripped off" (page 356). How do these feelings relate to each other and to the theme?

9. Nabokov's "Signs and Symbols" frustrates us at the resolution, but "Mobius the Stripper" frustrates us from the beginning. Did you read it page by page, or across the tops of the pages till you had finished Mobius's story, then across the lower portions until you had read the writer's? Which way should it be read? Would it be more satisfying if it were printed on a Möbius strip? How symbolic, revealing, and essential is the relation between the top and bottom of each page as the story is printed?

10. How is it significant to the total pattern of the story that Mobius's half is written in the third person, the writer's in the first? How much of "Mobius the Stripper" does the writer write?

Cathedral

RAYMOND CARVER

This blind man, an old friend of my wife's, he was on his way to spend the night. His wife had died. So he was visiting the dead wife's relatives in Connecticut. He called my wife from his in-laws'. Arrangements were made. He would come by train, a five-hour trip, and my wife would meet him at the station. She hadn't seen him since she worked for him one summer in Seattle ten years ago. But she and the blind man had kept in touch. They made tapes and mailed them back and forth. I wasn't enthusiastic about his visit. He was no one I knew. And his being blind bothered me. My idea of blindness came from the movies. In the movies, the blind moved slowly and never laughed. Sometimes they were led by seeing-eye dogs. A blind man in my house was not something I looked forward to.

That summer in Seattle she had needed a job. She didn't have any money. The man she was going to marry at the end of the summer was in officers' training school. He didn't have any money, either. But she was in love with the guy, and he was in love with her, etc. She'd seen something in the paper: HELP WANTED—*Reading to Blind Man*, and a telephone number. She phoned and went over, was hired on the spot. She'd worked with this blind man all summer. She read stuff to him, case studies, reports, that sort of thing. She helped him organize his little office in the county social-service department. They'd become good friends, my wife and the blind man. How do I know these things? She told me. And she told me something else. On her last day in the office, the blind man asked if he could touch her face. She agreed to this. She told me he touched his fingers to every part of her face, her nose—even her neck! She never forgot it. She even tried to write a poem about it. She was always trying to write a poem. She wrote a poem or two every year, usually after something really important had happened to her.

When we first started going out together, she showed me the poem. In the poem, she recalled his fingers and the way they had moved around over her face. In the poem, she talked about what she had felt at the time, about what went through her mind when the blind man touched her nose and lips. I can remember I didn't think much of the poem. Of course, I didn't tell her that. Maybe I just don't understand poetry. I admit it's not the first thing I reach for when I pick up something to read.

Anyway, this man who'd first enjoyed her favors, the officer-to-be, he'd been her childhood sweetheart. So okay. I'm saying that at the end of the summer she let the blind man run his hands over her face, said goodbye to him, married her childhood etc., who was now a commissioned officer, and she moved away from Seattle. But they'd kept in touch, she and the blind man. She made the first contact after a year or so. She called him up one night from an Air Force base in Alabama. She wanted to talk. They talked. He asked her to send him a tape and tell him about her life. She did this. She sent the tape. On the tape, she told the blind man about her husband and about their life together in the military. She told the blind man she loved her husband but she didn't like it where they lived and she didn't like it that he was a part of the military-industrial thing. She told the blind man she'd written a poem and he was in it. She told him that she was writing a poem about what it was like to be an Air Force officer's wife. The poem wasn't finished yet. She was still writing it. The blind man made a tape. He sent her the tape. She made a tape. This went on for years. My wife's officer was posted to one base and then another. She sent tapes from Moody AFB, McGuire, McConnell, and finally Travis, near Sacramento, where one night she got to feeling lonely and cut off from people she kept losing in that moving-around life. She got to feeling she couldn't go it another step. She went in and swallowed all the pills and capsules in the medicine chest and washed them down with a bottle of gin. Then she got into a hot bath and passed out.

But instead of dying, she got sick. She threw up. Her officer—why should he have a name? he was the childhood sweetheart, and what more does he want?—came home from somewhere, found her, and called the ambulance. In time, she put it all on a tape and sent the tape to the blind man. Over the years, she put all kinds of stuff on tapes and sent the tapes off lickety-split. Next to writing a poem every year, I think it was her chief means of recreation. On one tape, she told the blind man she'd decided to live away from her officer for a time. On another tape, she told him about her divorce. She and I began going out, and of course she told her blind man about it. She told him everything, or so it seemed to me. Once she asked me if I'd like to hear the latest tape from the blind man. This was a year ago. I was on the tape, she said. So I said okay, I'd listen to it. I got us drinks and we settled down in the living room. We made ready to listen. First she inserted the tape into the player and adjusted a couple of dials. Then she pushed a lever. The tape squeaked and someone began to talk in this loud voice. She lowered the volume. After a few minutes of harmless chitchat, I heard my own name in the mouth of this stranger, this blind man I didn't even know! And then this: "From all you've said about him, I can only conclude—" But we were interrupted, a knock at the door, something, and we didn't ever get back to the tape. Maybe it was just as well. I'd heard all I wanted to.

Now this same blind man was coming to sleep in my house.

"Maybe I could take him bowling," I said to my wife. She was at the draining board doing scalloped potatoes. She put down the knife she was using and turned around.

"If you love me," she said, "you can do this for me. If you don't love me, okay. But if you had a friend, any friend, and the friend came to visit, I'd make him feel comfortable." She wiped her hands with the dish towel.

"I don't have any blind friends," I said.

"You don't have *any* friends," she said. "Period. Besides," she said, "goddamn it, his wife's just died! Don't you understand that? The man's lost his wife!"

I didn't answer. She'd told me a little about the blind man's wife. Her name was Beulah. Beulah! That's a name for a colored woman.

"Was his wife a Negro?" I asked.

"Are you crazy?" my wife said. "Have you just flipped or something?" She picked up a potato. I saw it hit the floor, then roll under the stove. "What's wrong with you?" she said. "Are you drunk?"

"I'm just asking," I said.

Right then my wife filled me in with more detail than I cared to know. I made a drink and sat at the kitchen table to listen. Pieces of the story began to fall into place.

Beulah had gone to work for the blind man the summer after my wife had stopped working for him. Pretty soon Beulah and the blind man had themselves a church wedding. It was a little wedding—who'd want to go to such a wedding in the first place?—just the two of them, plus the minister and the minister's wife. But it was a church wedding just the same. It was what Beulah had wanted, he'd said. But even then Beulah must have been carrying the cancer in her glands. After they had been inseparable for eight years—my wife's word, *inseparable*—Beulah's health went into a rapid decline. She died in a Seattle hospital room, the blind man sitting beside the bed and holding on to her hand. They'd married, lived and worked together, slept together—had sex, sure—and then the blind man had to bury her. All this without his having ever seen what the god-damned woman looked like. It was beyond my understanding. Hearing this, I felt sorry for the blind man for a little bit. And then I found myself thinking what a pitiful life this woman must have led. Imagine a woman who could never see herself as she was seen in the eyes of her loved one. A woman who could go on day after day and never receive the smallest compliment from her beloved. A woman whose husband could never read the expression on her face, be it misery or something better. Someone who could wear makeup or not—what difference to him? She could, if she wanted, wear green eye-shadow around one eye, a straight pin in her nostril, yellow slacks and purple shoes, no matter. And then to slip off into death, the blind man's hand on her hand, his blind eyes streaming tears—I'm imagining now—her last thought maybe this: that he never even knew what she looked like, and she on an express to the grave. Robert was left with a small insurance policy and half of a twenty-peso Mexican coin. The other half of the coin went into the box with her. Pathetic.

So when the time rolled around, my wife went to the depot to pick him up. With nothing to do but wait—sure, I blamed him for that—I was having a drink and watching the TV when I heard the car pull into the drive. I got up from the sofa with my drink and went to the window to have a look.

I saw my wife laughing as she parked the car. I saw her get out of the car and shut the door. She was still wearing a smile. Just amazing. She went around to the other side of the car to where the blind man was already starting to get out. This blind man, feature this, he was wearing a full beard! A beard on a blind man! Too much, I say. The blind man reached into the back seat and dragged out a suitcase. My wife took his arm, shut the car door, and, talking all the way, moved him down the drive and then up the steps to the front porch. I turned off the TV. I finished my drink, rinsed the glass, dried my hands. Then I went to the door.

My wife said, "I want you to meet Robert. Robert, this is my husband. I've told you all about him." She was beaming. She had this blind man by his coat sleeve.

The blind man let go of his suitcase and up came his hand.

I took it. He squeezed hard, held my hand, and then he let it go.

"I feel like we've already met," he boomed.

"Likewise," I said. I didn't know what else to say. Then I said, "Welcome. I've heard a lot about you." We began to move then, a little group, from the porch into the living room, my wife guiding him by the arm. The blind man was carrying his suitcase in his other hand. My wife said things like, "To your left here, Robert. That's right. Now watch it, there's a chair. That's it. Sit down right here. This is the sofa. We just bought this sofa two weeks ago."

I started to say something about the old sofa. I'd liked that old sofa. But I didn't say anything. Then I wanted to say something else, small-talk, about the scenic ride along the Hudson. How going *to* New York, you should sit on the right-hand side of the train, and coming *from* New York, the left-hand side.

"Did you have a good train ride?" I said. "Which side of the train did you sit on, by the way?"

"What a question, which side!" my wife said. "What's it matter which side?" she said.

"I just asked," I said.

"Right side," the blind man said. "I hadn't been on a train in nearly forty years. Not since I was a kid. With my folks. That's been a long time. I'd nearly forgotten the sensation. I have winter in my beard now," he said. "So I've been told, anyway. Do I look distinguished, my dear?" the blind man said to my wife.

"You look distinguished, Robert," she said. "Robert," she said. "Robert, it's just so good to see you."

My wife finally took her eyes off the blind man and looked at me. I had the feeling she didn't like what she saw. I shrugged.

I've never met, or personally known, anyone who was blind. This blind man was late forties, a heavy-set, balding man with stooped shoulders, as if he carried a great weight there. He wore brown slacks, brown shoes, a light-brown shirt, a tie, a sports coat. Spiffy. He also had this full beard. But he didn't use a cane and he didn't wear dark glasses. I'd always thought dark glasses were a must for the blind. Fact was, I wished he had a pair. At first glance, his eyes looked like anyone else's eyes. But if you looked close, there was something different about them. Too much white in the iris, for one thing, and the pupils seemed to move around in the sockets without his knowing it or being able to stop it. Creepy. As I stared at his face, I saw the left pupil turn in toward his nose while the other made an effort to keep in one place. But it was only an effort, for that eye was on the roam without his knowing it or wanting it to be.

I said, "Let me get you a drink. What's your pleasure? We have a little of everything. It's one of our pastimes."

"Bub, I'm a Scotch man myself," he said fast enough in this big voice.

"Right," I said. Bub! "Sure you are. I knew it."

He let his fingers touch his suitcase, which was sitting alongside the sofa. He was taking his bearings. I didn't blame him for that.

"I'll move that up to your room," my wife said.

"No, that's fine," the blind man said loudly. "It can go up when I go up."

"A little water with the Scotch?" I said.

"Very little," he said.

"I knew it," I said.

He said, "Just a tad. The Irish actor, Barry Fitzgerald? I'm like that fellow. When I drink water, Fitzgerald said, I drink water. When I drink whiskey, I drink whiskey." My wife laughed. The blind man brought his hand up under his beard. He lifted his beard slowly and let it drop.

I did the drinks, three big glasses of Scotch with a splash of water in each. Then we made ourselves comfortable and talked about Robert's travels. First the long flight from the West Coast to Connecticut, we covered that. Then from Connecticut up here by train. We had another drink concerning that leg of the trip.

I remembered having read somewhere that the blind didn't smoke because, as speculation had it, they couldn't see the smoke they exhaled. I thought I knew that much and that much only about blind people. But this blind man smoked his cigarette down to the nubbin and then lit another one. This blind man filled his ashtray and my wife emptied it.

When we sat down at the table for dinner, we had another drink. My wife heaped Robert's plate with cube steak, scalloped potatoes, green beans. I buttered him up two slices of bread. I said, "Here's bread and butter for you." I swallowed some of my drink. "Now let us pray," I said, and the blind man lowered his head. My wife looked at me, her mouth agape. "Pray the phone won't ring and the food doesn't get cold," I said.

We dug in. We ate everything there was to eat on the table. We ate like there was no tomorrow. We didn't talk. We ate. We scarfed. We grazed that table. We were into serious eating. The blind man had right away located his foods, he knew just where everything was on his plate. I watched with admiration as he used his knife and fork on the meat. He'd cut two pieces of meat, fork the meat into his mouth, and then go all out for the scalloped potatoes, the beans next, and then he'd tear off a hunk of buttered bread and eat that. He'd follow this up with a big drink of milk. It didn't seem to bother him to use his fingers once in a while, either.

We finished everything, including half a strawberry pie. For a few moments, we sat as if stunned. Sweat beaded on our faces. Finally, we got up from the table and left the dirty plates. We didn't look back. We took ourselves into the living room and sank into our places again. Robert and my wife sat on the sofa. I took the big chair. We had us two or three more drinks while they talked about the major things that had come to pass for them in the past ten years. For the most part, I just listened. Now and then I joined in. I didn't want him to think I'd left the room, and I didn't want her to think I was feeling left out. They talked of things that had happened to them—to them!—these past ten years. I waited in vain to hear my name on my wife's sweet lips: "And then my dear husband came into my life"— something like that. But I heard nothing of the sort. More talk of Robert. Robert had done a little of everything, it seemed, a regular blind jack-of-all-trades. But most recently he and his wife had had an Amway distributorship, from which, I gathered, they'd earned their living, such as it was. The blind man was also a ham radio operator. He talked in his loud voice about conversations he'd had with fellow operators in Guam, in the Philippines, in Alaska, and even in Tahiti. He said he'd have a lot of friends there if he ever wanted to go visit those places. From time to time, he'd turn his blind face toward me, put his hand under his beard, ask me something. How long had I been in my present position? (Three years.) Did I like my work? (I didn't.) Was I going to stay with it? (What were the options?)

Finally, when I thought he was beginning to run down, I got up and turned on the TV.

My wife looked at me with irritation. She was heading toward a boil. Then she looked at the blind man and said, "Robert, do you have a TV?"

The blind man said, "My dear, I have two TVs. I have a color set and a black-and-white thing, an old relic. It's funny, but if I turn the TV on, and I'm always turning it on, I turn on the color set. It's funny, don't you think?"

I didn't know what to say to that. I had absolutely nothing to say to that. No opinion. So I watched the news program and tried to listen to what the announcer was saying.

"This is a color TV," the blind man said. "Don't ask me how, but I can tell."

"We traded up a while ago," I said.

The blind man had another taste of his drink. He lifted his beard, sniffed it, and let it fall. He leaned forward on the sofa. He positioned his ashtray on the coffee table, then put the lighter to his cigarette. He leaned back on the sofa and crossed his legs at the ankles.

My wife covered her mouth, and then she yawned. She stretched. She said, "I think I'll go upstairs and put on my robe. I think I'll change into something else. Robert, you make yourself comfortable," she said.

"I'm comfortable," the blind man said.

"I want you to feel comfortable in this house," she said.

"I am comfortable," the blind man said.

After she'd left the room, he and I listened to the weather report and then to the sports roundup. By that time, she'd been gone so long I didn't know if she was going to come back. I thought she might have gone to bed. I wished she'd come back downstairs. I didn't want to be left alone with a blind man. I asked him if he wanted another drink, and he said sure. Then I asked if he wanted to smoke some dope with me. I said I'd just rolled a number. I hadn't, but I planned to do so in about two shakes.

"I'll try some with you," he said.

"Damn right," I said. "That's the stuff."

I got our drinks and sat down on the sofa with him. Then I rolled us two fat numbers. I lit one and passed it. I brought it to his fingers. He took it and inhaled.

"Hold it as long as you can," I said. I could tell he didn't know the first thing.

My wife came back downstairs wearing her pink robe and her pink slippers.

"What do I smell?" she said.

"We thought we'd have us some cannabis," I said.

My wife gave me a savage look. Then she looked at the blind man and said, "Robert, I didn't know you smoked."

He said, "I do now, my dear. There's a first time for everything. But I don't feel anything yet."

"This stuff is pretty mellow," I said. "This stuff is mild. It's dope you can reason with," I said. "It doesn't mess you up."

"Not much it doesn't, bub," he said, and laughed.

My wife sat on the sofa between the blind man and me. I passed her the number. She took it and toked and then passed it back to me. "Which way is this going?" she said. Then she said, "I shouldn't be smoking this. I can hardly keep my eyes open as it is. That dinner did me in. I shouldn't have eaten so much."

"It was the strawberry pie," the blind man said. "That's what did it," he said, and he laughed his big laugh. Then he shook his head.

"There's more strawberry pie," I said.

"Do you want some more, Robert?" my wife said.

"Maybe in a little while," he said.

We gave our attention to the TV. My wife yawned again. She said, "Your bed is made up when you feel like going to bed, Robert. I know you must have had a long day. When you're ready to go to bed, say so." She pulled his arm. "Robert?"

He came to and said, "I've had a real nice time. This beats tapes, doesn't it?"

I said, "Coming at you," and I put the number between his fingers. He inhaled, held the smoke, and then let it go. It was like he'd been doing it since he was nine years old.

"Thanks, bub," he said. "But I think this is all for me. I think I'm beginning to feel it," he said. He held the burning roach out for my wife.

"Same here," she said. "Ditto. Me, too." She took the roach and passed it to me. "I may just sit here for a while between you two guys with my eyes closed. But don't let me bother you, okay? Either one of you. If it bothers you, say so. Otherwise, I may just sit here with my eyes closed until you're ready to go to bed," she said. "Your bed's made up, Robert, when you're ready. It's right next to our room at the top of the stairs. We'll show you up when you're ready. You wake me up now, you guys, if I fall asleep." She said that and then she closed her eyes and went to sleep.

The news program ended. I got up and changed the channel. I sat back down on the sofa. I wished my wife hadn't pooped out. Her head lay across the back of the sofa, her mouth open. She'd turned so that her robe had slipped away from her legs, exposing a juicy thigh. I reached to draw her robe back over her, and it was then that I glanced at the blind man. What the hell! I flipped the robe open again.

"You say when you want some strawberry pie," I said.

"I will," he said.

I said, "Are you tired? Do you want me to take you up to your bed? Are you ready to hit the hay?"

"Not yet," he said. "No, I'll stay up with you, bub. If that's all right. I'll stay up until you're ready to turn in. We haven't had a chance to talk. Know what I mean? I feel like me and her monopolized the evening." He lifted his beard and he let it fall. He picked up his cigarettes and his lighter.

"That's all right," I said. Then I said, "I'm glad for the company."

And I guess I was. Every night I smoked dope and stayed up as long as I could before I fell asleep. My wife and I hardly ever went to bed at the same time. When I did go to sleep, I had these dreams. Sometimes I'd wake up from one of them, my heart going crazy.

Something about the church and the Middle Ages was on the TV. Not your run-of-the-mill TV fare. I wanted to watch something else. I turned to the other channels. But there was nothing on them, either. So I turned back to the first channel and apologized.

"Bub, it's all right," the blind man said. "It's fine with me. Whatever you want to watch is okay. I'm always learning something. Learning never ends. It won't hurt me to learn something tonight. I got ears," he said.

We didn't say anything for a time. He was leaning forward with his head turned at me, his right ear aimed in the direction of the set. Very disconcerting. Now and then his eyelids drooped and then they snapped open again. Now and then he put his fingers into his beard and tugged, like he was thinking about something he was hearing on the television.

On the screen, a group of men wearing cowls was being set upon and tormented by men dressed in skeleton costumes and men dressed as devils. The men dressed as devils wore devil masks, horns, and long tails. This pageant was part of a procession. The Englishman who was narrating the thing said it took place in Spain once a year. I tried to explain to the blind man what was happening.

"Skeletons," he said. "I know about skeletons," he said, and he nodded.

The TV showed this one cathedral. Then there was a long, slow look at another one. Finally, the picture switched to the famous one in Paris, with its flying buttresses and its spires reaching up to the clouds. The camera pulled away to show the whole of the cathedral rising above the skyline.

There were times when the Englishman who was telling the thing would shut up, would simply let the camera move around over the cathedrals. Or else the camera would tour the countryside, men in fields walking behind oxen. I waited as long as I could. Then I felt I had to say something. I said, "They're showing the outside of this cathedral now. Gargoyles. Little statues carved to look like monsters. Now I guess they're in Italy. Yeah, they're in Italy. There's paintings on the walls of this one church."

"Are those fresco paintings, bub?" he asked, and he sipped from his drink.

I reached for my glass. But it was empty. I tried to remember what I could remember. "You're asking me are those frescoes?" I said. "That's a good question. I don't know."

The camera moved to a cathedral outside Lisbon. The differences in the Portuguese cathedral compared with the French and Italian were not that great. But they were there. Mostly the interior stuff. Then something occurred to me, and I said, "Something has occurred to me. Do you have any idea what a cathedral is? What they look like, that is? Do you follow me? If somebody says cathedral to you, do you have any notion what they're talking about? Do you know the difference between that and a Baptist church, say?"

He let the smoke dribble from his mouth. "I know they took hundreds of workers fifty or a hundred years to build," he said. "I just heard the man say that, of course. I know generations of the same families worked on a cathedral. I heard him say that, too. The men who began their life's work on them, they never lived to see the completion of their work. In that wise, bub, they're no different from the rest of us, right?" He laughed. Then his eyelids drooped again. His head nodded. He seemed to be snoozing. Maybe he was imagining himself in Portugal. The TV was showing another cathedral now. This one was in Germany. The Englishman's voice droned on. "Cathedrals," the blind man said. He sat up and rolled his head back and forth. "If you want the truth, bub, that's about all I know. What I just said. What I heard him say. But maybe you could describe one to me? I wish you'd do it. I'd like that. If you want to know, I really don't have a good idea."

I stared hard at the shot of the cathedral on the TV. How could I even begin to describe it? But say my life depended on it. Say my life was being threatened by an insane guy who said I had to do it or else.

I stared some more at the cathedral before the picture flipped off into the countryside. There was no use. I turned to the blind man and said, "To begin with, they're very tall." I was looking around the room for clues. "They reach way up. Up and up. Toward the sky. They're so big, some of them, they have to have these supports. To help hold them up, so to speak. These supports are called buttresses. They remind me of viaducts, for some reason. But maybe you don't know viaducts, either? Sometimes the cathedrals have devils and such carved into the front. Sometimes lords and ladies. Don't ask me why this is," I said.

He was nodding. The whole upper part of his body seemed to be moving back and forth.

"I'm not doing so good, am I?" I said.

He stopped nodding and leaned forward on the edge of the sofa. As he listened to me, he was running his fingers through his beard. I wasn't getting through to him, I could see that. But he waited for me to go on just the same. He nodded, like he was trying to encourage me. I tried to think what else to say. "They're really big," I said. "They're massive. They're built of stone. Marble, too, sometimes. In those olden days, when they built cathedrals, men wanted to be close to God. In those olden days, God was an important part of everyone's life. You could tell this from their cathedral-building. I'm sorry," I said, "but it looks like that's the best I can do for you. I'm just no good at it."

"That's all right, bub," the blind man said. "Hey, listen. I hope you don't mind my asking you. Can I ask you something? Let me ask you a simple question, yes or no. I'm just curious and there's no offense. You're my host. But let me ask if you are in any way religious? You don't mind my asking?"

I shook my head. He couldn't see that, though. A wink is the same as a nod to a blind man. "I guess I don't believe in it. In anything. Sometimes it's hard. You know what I'm saying?"

"Sure, I do," he said.

"Right," I said.

The Englishman was still holding forth. My wife sighed in her sleep. She drew a long breath and went on with her sleeping.

"You'll have to forgive me," I said. "But I can't tell you what a cathedral looks like. It just isn't in me to do it. I can't do any more than I've done."

The blind man sat very still, his head down, as he listened to me.

I said, "The truth is, cathedrals don't mean anything special to me. Nothing. Cathedrals. They're something to look at on late-night TV. That's all they are."

It was then that the blind man cleared his throat. He brought something up. He took a handkerchief from his back pocket. Then he said, "I get it, bub. It's okay. It happens. Don't worry about it," he said. "Hey, listen to me. Will you do me a favor? I got an idea. Why don't you find us some heavy paper? And a pen. We'll do something. We'll draw one together. Get us a pen and some heavy paper. Go on, bub, get the stuff," he said.

So I went upstairs. My legs felt like they didn't have any strength in them. They felt like they did after I'd done some running. In my wife's room, I looked around. I found some ballpoints in a little basket on her table. And then I tried to think where to look for the kind of paper he was talking about.

Downstairs, in the kitchen, I found a shopping bag with onion skins in the bottom of the bag. I emptied the bag and shook it. I brought it into the living room and sat down with it near his legs. I moved some things, smoothed the wrinkles from the bag, spread it out on the coffee table.

The blind man got down from the sofa and sat next to me on the carpet.

He ran his fingers over the paper. He went up and down the sides of the paper. The edges, even the edges. He fingered the corners.

"All right," he said. "All right, let's do her."

He found my hand, the hand with the pen. He closed his hand over my hand. "Go ahead, bub, draw," he said. "Draw. You'll see. I'll follow along with you. It'll be okay. Just begin now like I'm telling you. You'll see. Draw," the blind man said.

So I began. First I drew a box that looked like a house. It could have been the house I lived in. Then I put a roof on it. At either end of the roof, I drew spires. Crazy.

"Swell," he said. "Terrific. You're doing fine," he said. "Never thought anything like this could happen in your lifetime, did you, bub? Well, it's a strange life, we all know that. Go on now. Keep it up."

I put in windows with arches. I drew flying buttresses. I hung great doors. I couldn't stop. The TV station went off the air. I put down the pen and closed and opened my fingers. The blind man felt around over the paper. He moved the tips of his fingers over the paper, all over what I had drawn, and he nodded.

"Doing fine," the blind man said.

I took up the pen again, and he found my hand. I kept at it. I'm no artist. But I kept drawing just the same.

My wife opened up her eyes and gazed at us. She sat up on the sofa, her robe hanging open. She said, "What are you doing? Tell me, I want to know."

I didn't answer her.

The blind man said, "We're drawing a cathedral. Me and him are working on it. Press hard," he said to me. "That's right. That's good," he said. "Sure. You got it, bub. I can tell. You didn't think you could. But you can, can't you? You're cooking with gas now. You know what I'm saying? We're going to really have us something here in a minute. How's the old arm?" he said. "Put some people in there now. What's a cathedral without people?"

My wife said, "What's going on? Robert, what are you doing? What's going on?"

"It's all right," he said to her. "Close your eyes now," the blind man said to me.

I did it. I closed them just like he said.

"Are they closed?" he said. "Don't fudge."

"They're closed," I said.

"Keep them that way," he said. He said, "Don't stop now. Draw."

So we kept on with it. His fingers rode my fingers as my hand went over the paper. It was like nothing else in my life up to now.

Then he said, "I think that's it. I think you got it," he said. "Take a look. What do you think?"

But I had my eyes closed. I thought I'd keep them that way for a little longer. I thought it was something I ought to do.

"Well?" he said. "Are you looking?"

My eyes were still closed. I was in my house. I knew that. But I didn't feel like I was inside anything.

"It's really something," I said.

Suggestions for Discussion

1. How do the structure and tone of the narrator's sentences help to characterize him?

2. The narrator uses sloppy generalizations (*she read stuff, that sort of thing, etc., more detail than I cared to know*) and clichés (*enjoyed her favors, jack-of-all-trades, pooped out, hit the hay*). How do these tricks of speech contribute to the theme?

3. By contrast, on page 370 the narrator imagines the blind man's wife in grotesque details. Immediately thereafter he refers to the blind man for the first time by his name, Robert. Why?

4. The story is called "Cathedral." It is about a blind man's visit. How do the ideas of *cathedral* and *blindness* relate to each other as themes?

5. Do you consider "jealousy" a theme of the story? Why or why not?

6. The story contains realistic details having to do with the inability to hear, to remember, to describe, to understand, and also with the drugging effects of food, nicotine, alcohol, and cannabis. How do these contribute to the idea that the blind man can see more vividly or exactly than the narrator?

7. On page 376 Robert makes a little speech about learning. How does it relate to the narrator's experience in the story?

8. What discoveries does the narrator make in the course of the evening that prepare us for the discovery he makes at the end?

RETROSPECT

1. "Girl," "Shiloh," and "Underground Women" all offer speculations on male-female relations and women's liberation. How do differences in structure, detail, setting, characterization, and point of view differentiate their themes?

2. Consider the themes of home, homesickness, foreignness, and patriotism in "The Bella Lingua." What speculative conclusions does the story suggest?

3. Which of the stories in this volume offer an inversion of a "truth" that you ordinarily accept—about, for instance, the nature of reality, sanity, time, goodness? How successfully does each offer its alternative truth?

4. In which of the stories in this volume can a central character be said to "find" himself or herself in the crisis and resolution? How do emotion, judgment, and logic fuse in these epiphanies to suggest theme?

WRITING ASSIGNMENTS

These final five exercises are arranged in order of ascending difficulty. The first is the easiest, and it is likely to produce a bad story. If it produces a bad story, it will be invaluably instructive to you, and you will be relieved of the onus of ever doing it again. If it produces a good story, then you have done something else, something more, and something more original than the assignment asks for. If you prefer to do exercise 4 or 5, then you may already have doomed yourself to the writing craft, and should prepare to be very poor for a few years while you discover what place writing will have in your life.

1. Take a simple but specific political, religious, scientific, or moral idea. It may be one already available to us in a formula of words, or it may be one of your own, but it should be possible to state it in less than ten words. Write a short story that illustrates the idea. Do not state the idea at all. Your goals are two: that the idea should be perfectly clear to us, so that it could be extracted as a moral or message, and that we should feel we have experienced it.

2. Take as your title a common proverb or maxim, such as *power corrupts, honesty is the best policy, walk softly and carry a big stick, haste makes waste.* Let the story make the title ironic. That is, explore a situation in which the advice or statement does not apply.

3. Taking as a starting point some incident or situation from your own life, write a story with one of the following themes: nakedness, blindness, thirst, noise, borders, chains, clean wounds, washing, the color green, dawn. The

events themselves may be minor (a story about a slipping bicycle chain may ultimately be more effective than one about a chain gang). Once you have decided on the structure of the story, explore everything you think, know, or believe about your chosen theme and try to incorporate that theme in imagery, dailogue, event, character, and so forth.

4. Identify the belief you hold most passionately and profoundly. Write a short story that explores an instance in which this belief is untrue.

5. Write the short story that you have wanted to write all term and have not written because you knew it was too big for you and you would fail. You may fail. Write it anyway.

APPENDIX A

NARRATIVE TECHNIQUES
Workshop Symbol Code

Format

Manuscripts should be typed, double-spaced, with generous margins, on one side of 8½ x 11-inch white paper. Use a new black ribbon and well-cleaned keys. Title and author's name and address (or class identification) should appear on a cover page. Some editors (and teachers) will not accept Corrasable bond or Xerox copies. Always keep a copy of your work.

The symbols listed here are a suggested shorthand for identifying common errors in usage and style. A few of the marks are standard copy-editing and proofreading symbols.

Usage

sp.   Misspelling.

gram.   Grammar at fault. Consult Strunk's *Elements of Style*, Fowler's *Modern English Usage*, or any good grammar text.

¢   Paragraph. Begin a new one here.

ς   No new paragraph needed.

↗   Comma needed. Insert one here.

ⱥ   No comma needed.

p/c   You have used a possessive for a contraction or vice versa. *Its, their,* and *your* are possessives. *It's, they're,* and *you're* are contractions of *it is, they are,* and *you are. They're going to take their toll if you're not sure of your usage.*

p/p   *Participial phrase at the beginning of a sentence must refer to the grammatical subject. "Failing to understand this, your prose will read awkardly," means that your prose fails to understand.*

s/i   *Split infinitives tend to always read awkardly. Try to immediately correct it and to never do it again.*

T   *A pointless change of tense. It leaves the reader not knowing when he is.*

n/s   Not a sentence. Technique okay if effective, otherwise not. Here, not.

tr.   Transpose. This can refer to letters, words, phrases, sentences, whole paragraphs.

Insert a space here (between words, paragraphs, etc.).

Style

V

This is definitely vague. Or, you have used a generalization or an abstraction where you need a concrete detail. Specify.

A/

Use the active voice. If "she was happy" or "she felt happy," she was not nearly as happy as if she laughed, grinned, jumped, or threw her arms around a tree.

un.

Unnecessary. Delete.

↓↑

Compress this passage to half the words for twice the strength. You're writing *long*.

?

Either you are confusing or the reader is confused or both. What do you *really* mean?

awk.

Awkward. This sentence is related to the auk, a thickbodied, short-necked bird without grace. Restyle.

R

Repetition to unintended or undesirable effect.

∝

Cliché.

m/m

Mixed metaphor.

o/w
o/s
o/i

Overwritten, overstated, overinsistent. You're straining. Lower the key to raise the effect.

conv.

In the exceedingly likely and, one might say, almost inevitable event, in view of your enrollment in this class, that you are not Henry James, the use of convoluted language is considerably less than certain to contribute to the augmenting of your intended effect. Simplify.

coy
pomp. }
prec.
pret. }

Coy, pompous, precious, pretentious — all meaning that you are enjoying yourself more than the reader is. No reader will forgive you.

chron.

Chronology unnecessarily violated. "She sat down after having crossed to the couch." Except for very special effects, let the reader's mind follow events in their order.

d/t

Unnecessary dialogue tag. " 'Shut your stupid mouth!' he said angrily." We do not need to be told that he said this angrily. If he said it sweetly, then we would probably need to be told.

dial.

Dialect is overwritten. You are probably misspelling too much, so that your character sounds stupid rather than regional. Let the syntax do the work; keep misspellings and grammatical mistakes to a minimum.

int.

Author intrusion. You are explaining, judging, or interpreting too much. Show us, and let us understand and judge.

APPENDIX B

SUGGESTIONS
FOR FURTHER READING

This is a short list of books of various sorts that can be useful to the practicing writer.

Books on Technique

Authors of the books in this first group address themselves more or less directly to techniques of writing and the problems writers face; all contain useful insights and advice.

Aristotle, *The Poetics*. The first extant work of literary criticism, and the essay from which all later criticism derives. There are numerous good translations, of which one of the best (particulary for its full and helpful comments by O.B. Hardison, Jr.), is that by Leon Golden, *Aristotle's Poetics*, Prentice-Hall, 1968.

Booth, Wayne C., *The Rhetoric of Fiction*. University of Chicago Press, 1961. This is a thorough, brilliant, and difficult discussion of point of view, which well repays the effort of its reading.

Brande, Dorothea, *Becoming a Writer*. J.P. Tarcher, 1981. For those who are over-meticulous, or who have a hard time getting to the typewriter, Brande's mind-freeing exercises may be enormously helpful.

Braine, John, *Writing a Novel*. McGraw-Hill, 1975. Braine gives writerly advice very much from the perspective of his own experience, which will not be useful to everyone. But *Writing a Novel* is anecdotal, interesting, and readable.

Forster, E.M., *Aspects of the Novel*. Harcourt, Brace, Jovanovich, 1956. Forster delivered these Clark Lectures at Trinity College, Cambridge, England, in 1927. They are talkative, informal, and informative; still the best analysis of literature from a writer's point of view. A must.

Gardner, John, *The Art of Fiction: Notes on Craft for Young Writers*. Alfred A. Knopf, 1984. A new classic among books on writing. Gardner's advice is based on his experience as a teacher of creative writing and addressed to "the serious beginning writer." The book is clear, practical, and a delight to read. Also recommended is Gardner's *Becoming a Novelist*, Harper and Row, 1983.

Gibson, Walker, *Seeing and Writing*. David McKay, 1974. This is a book of exercises in perception, aimed primarily at the writer of essays rather than fiction. But it is nonetheless provocative, fresh, even startling, in its suggestions for observing and capturing sense detail — and therefore useful to the fiction writer as well.

Hills, Rust, *Writing in General and the Short Story in Particular*. Bantam, 1979. A former literary editor of *Esquire Magazine*, Hills has written a breezy, enjoyable guide to fictional technique with good advice on every page.

Knott, William C., *The Craft of Fiction*. Reston (Prentice-Hall), 1973. An excellent practical text with useful exercises.

Minot, Stephen, *Three Genres*, 3rd ed. Prentice-Hall, 1982. This text covers the writing of poetry, fiction, and drama, so that each is necessarily treated briefly. Nevertheless Minot is direct and insightful, well worth reading.

Strunk, William C., and White, E.B. *The Elements of Style*, 3rd ed. Macmillan, 1979. Strunk provides the rules for correct usage and vigorous writing in this briefest and most useful of handbooks.

Sloane, William, *The Craft of Writing*, edited by Julia Sloane. W.W. Norton, 1979. This book was culled posthumously from the notes of one of the great teachers of fiction writing. The advice he gives is solid and memorable, and the reader's only regret is that there isn't more.

Surmelian, Leon, *Techniques of Fiction Writing: Measure and Madness.* Anchor Books (Doubleday), 1969. Surmelian occasionally falls into some strange observations ("The exclamation point has all but vanished from rugged masculine prose like Hemingway's, but women still use it."), but the author's discussion of narrative elements, especially characterization, is insightful.

Ziegler, Alan, *The Writing Workshop, Volumes One and Two.* Teachers and Writers Collaborative, 1981 and 1984. The author calls these useful books a "survey course" in writing. They are mainly intended for teachers of writing, but can be adapted to use as a self-teaching tool, and are full of interesting practical advice.

Anthologies

Short-story anthologies abound, and you will find your own favorites. Here are a few I've particularly liked for their selection or their comments or both:

Cassill, R.V., *The Norton Anthology of Short Fiction.* Norton, 1978.

Hogins, James Burl, *Literature: Fiction.* Science Research Associates, 1973, 1974.

Howard, Daniel F., *The Modern Tradition.* Little, Brown, 1979.

Gasarch, Pearl, and Paul Gasarch, *Fiction: The Universal Elements.* Van Nostrand Reinhold, 1972.

Madden, David, and Virgil Scott, *Studies in the Short Story.* Holt Rinehart & Winston, 6th ed. 1984.

Mizener, Arthur, *Modern Short Stories.* Norton, 1979.

Pickering, James H., *Fiction 100.* Macmillan, 1974.

Pushcart Prize: The Best of the Small Presses. Pushcart Press and Avon, 1976—the present. An annual collection of the best fiction, poetry, and essays from the hundreds of literary magazines published in America and Great Britain.

Personal Statements

These diaries, interviews, and essays are of particular interest because they give a candid view of the personal problems, predilections, and writing methods of practicing authors.

Dillard, Annie, *Living By Fiction*. Harper and Row, 1982. One of the brilliant essayists of our time speculates on the question, "Why read fiction to think about the world?" The results is full of insights for writers as well as the reader.

Plimpton, George, ed., *Writers at Work. The Paris Review Interviews*. There are now many volumes of this valuable collection of interviews, all originally published in *The Paris Review*. The collections are published by Viking Press and Penguin.

Porter, Katherine Anne, *The Days Before*. Harcourt, Brace, 1952.

Sternburg, Janet, ed., *The Writer on Her Work*. Norton, 1980.

Woolf, Virginia, *A Writer's Diary*. Harcourt, Brace, 1954.

Critical Works

These are works of literary criticism aimed at the reader rather than the writer of fiction. But each is a classic in its way and each provides a valuable perspective for the writer.

Daiches, David, *The Novel and the Modern World*. University of Chicago Press, 1960.

Fiedler, Leslie, *Love and Death in the American Novel*. Stein & Day, 1966.

James, Henry, *The Art of Fiction and Other Essays*, ed. Morris Roberts. Oxford University Press, 1948.

Josipovici, Gabriel, *The World and the Book: A Study of Modern Fiction*. Paladin (London), 1973.

Leavis, F.R., *The Great Tradition*. Chatto & Windus, 1948.

Robbe-Grillet, Alain, *For a New Novel: Essays on Fiction*, trans. Richard Howard. Grove Press, 1965.

Sarraute, Nathalie, *The Age of Suspicion: Essays on the Novel*, trans. Maria Jolas. Grove Press, 1963.

Marketing

Of the guides and services offered to writers, three of the most helpful follow.

Associated Writing Programs (Old Dominion University, Norfolk, VA 23508). Those enrolled in the creative writing program of a college or university that is a member of AWP are automatically members. Others can join at a reasonable fee. AWP's services include a newsletter, a catalogue of writing programs, a placement service, an annual meeting, and a number of awards and publications. The organization is probably the nearest thing to a "network" of writers in the nation, and can provide contact with other writers, as well as valuable information on prizes, programs, presses, and the ideas current in the teaching of writing.

Poets & Writers, Inc. (201 W. 54th St., New York, NY 10019). Poets & Writers issues a bimonthly newsletter, *Coda* that has articles of high quality and interest, and provides information on contests and magazines and publishers soliciting manuscripts. The organization also has a number of useful publications that are periodically revised: a *Directory of American Poets and Fiction Writers*, a *Sponsors List*, an *Awards List*, guides to agents and bookstores, and a trade publishing survey. It's well worth subscribing to *Coda*, thereby gaining access to the other services and publications.

Writer's Market, edited by Paula Deimling assisted by Kathleen Vonderhaar, Writer's Digest Books (Cincinnati). A new edition comes out each year with practical advice on how to sell manuscripts as well as lists of book and magazine publishers, agents, foreign markets, and other services for writers.

(Acknowledgments continued from page vi.)

Quotations

Margaret Atwood. Excerpts from *Lady Oracle* by Margaret Atwood. Copyright ©1976 by Margaret Atwood. Reprinted by permission of Simon & Schuster, Inc., McClelland & Stewart, Ltd., and John Farquharson Ltd.

Robert Coover. Excerpts from *Pricksongs and Descants* by Robert Coover. Copyright © 1969 by Robert Coover. Reprinted by permission of E.P. Dutton and the author.

Joan Didion. Excerpt from *A Book of Common Prayer* by Joan Didion. Copyright ©1977 by Joan Didion. Reprinted by permission of Simon & Schuster, Inc. and Wallace and Sheil Agency, Inc.

Laurence Gonzales. Excerpt from *The New York Times Book Review*, Vol. LXXXV, No. 6, p. 13. Copyright © 1980 by the New York Times Company. Reprinted by permission.

Maxine Hong Kingston. Excerpts from *China Men*, by Maxine Hong Kingston. Copyright ©1977, 1978, 1979, 1980 by Maxine Hong Kingston. Reprinted by permission of Alfred A. Knopf, Inc.

Flannery O'Connor. Excerpts from "The Life You Save May Be Your Own" from *A Good Man Is Hard to Find and Other Stories* by Flannery O'Connor. Copyright 1953 by Flannery O'Connor. Reprinted by permission of the publisher, Harcourt Brace Jovanovich, Inc., and Harold Matson Company, Inc.

Tom Robbins. Excerpts from *Even Cowgirls Get the Blues* by Tom Robbins. Copyright ©1976 by Thomas Robbins. Reprinted by permission of Bantam Books. All rights reserved.

Diane Roberts. Excerpt from "Lamia" by Diane Roberts. Copyright ©1982 by Diane Roberts. Reprinted by permission of the author.

Paul Simon. Excerpt from "Still Crazy After All These Years" by Paul Simon, ©1974, 1975 by Paul Simon. Reprinted by permission.

INDEX